THE LIONESS NEVER CRIES

With Compliments
Prabir + Kalpana

Kamal Malaker

Copyright © 2022 by Kamal Malaker
All rights reserved.

About the book: Messages and commentaries

ABOUT THE BOOK

The author was suddenly catapulted in an African equatorial forest from Elite London to work as a medical doctor. This memoir is a saga of a very young man, green in life and profession. The heartbeat is his daring sense of adventure. He faced, accepting and adopting, cultural, social, professional challenges. Surmounting geographical, environmental, and perceived gaps in the provision of Medical care empowered him to take ever-increasing risks and tackle all impediments. His tale of embracing the social, cultural, and varied, yet unified concept of human values and its misconstrued division melded in his mind. An adventure story of uncertainty, understanding, acceptance, and learning from challenges makes it worth presenting, which will excite and exhilarate readers.

***Message from*:**
Mr. Andrew Dutfield
President and Chairman of the Board of Directors: Manitoba Writers Guild (MWG), Winnipeg. Canada.

Kamal Malaker has written a fascinating memoir that magically captures the time and place.

I was taken back to a different time when society was more structured, and the influence of the British was still strong in that part of the world.

His recollections are at the center about the people encountered and with whom he experienced many of life's ups and downs, along his difficult and so rewarding professional and personal journey as a District Medical Officer.

His recall and detail are amazing considering the span of time, and it is clear that his time in West Africa left a lasting and grounding impact on his life.

He packed more life experiences in his short time in Africa than many of us do in a lifetime. As a result, a host of life lessons can be drawn from the pages in this Book, and I feel privileged to have been asked to review the manuscript.

Anybody with an interest in postwar African history and the sense of what life was like, day to day in the early 1960s, will enjoy this readable Book.

Message from:
Dr. Danie Botha MD. *
Southern Africa & Canada

It was with growing pleasure that I read *The Lioness Never Cries*. From the moment Kamal Malaker sets foot on the train to reach Liverpool, before sailing to Freetown in Sierra Leone, I was struck by his uncanny ability not to paint apt word pictures of man, beast, the and machines but also how he succeeded in depicting the stark contrast between the 1960s British Colonialist and subject, the grandeur and opulence while doing so with refreshing insight and understanding. Having been born and raised in Africa myself, having lived there for four decades, before immigrating to Canada 23 years ago, reading *The Lioness Never Cries immediately* transported me to the continent of my birth. It was impossible not to relive and sense the heartbeat of Africa, experience its intimidating beauty, Its (at times) unforgiving fauna and flora, what with 20-feet man-eating crocodiles, and again meet its melting pot of people and cultures.

Early during his two-year stay in Sierra Leone did Kamal discover one of the driving philosophies of the continent: " There was no rush in Freetown. There is always tomorrow ." And little further, he states, " Africa is Africa, there has never been a shortage of surprises." Indeed!

Having worked and worked as a physician myself in several countries of Southern Africa during the 1980s and 1990s in state-run, missionary, military, and private medical facilities, I can only salute Kamal Malaker's rich tale of how he as a 23-year-old newly trained MD from Calcutta, not only survived the tropical forests of West Africa but learned how to thrive and impact the people of Sierra Leone, shedding a few tears of his own when he had to say goodbye in the end. A must-read.

In concluding my remarks, I would like to say " The Lioness Never Cries but a Lion May Shed few tears ." I give him 5 stars for everything relating to this Book.

Dr. Danie Botha is a specialist physician, an accomplished writer, a Littérateur, a mentor, and a motivator for aspiring young writers.

Message from:
Prof(Dr) Sisir Kumar Dutta MD. MRCOG, FRCS(C) **
The United Kingdom, Kolkata (India), Dhaka (Bangladesh)

What a fascinating and breathtaking story of Kamal Malaker's real-life sensation in his book " The Lioness never cries." The setting is early 1960s post-Colonial Sierra Leone in West Africa. What a remarkable memoir is coming out of a 23-year-old Indian Doctor inexperienced in every corner of life skills, on his humble admission, who embraced the challenges of stepping into the unknown. Inspired by David Livingstone, Albert Switzer, and others with visions of discovering and understanding Africa and Africans and facing all challenges to encounter.

He confesses his fear and prejudice, confusion, and mystification of being in Africa that overwhelmed his rational thinking. Yet envisaging exciting possibilities akin to other pioneers, he describes his feelings in a seductive hypnotizing tone. Any reader will feel the sensation of the narration. I was awe-struck.

Challenges of living and working in Africa, at every step, every breath, every day, everywhere, and in every climb and every fall, he narrates in a picturesque visual form. It kept me stuck from page to page, from chapter to chapter, starting on the train from London to Liverpool and then by boat from Liverpool to Freetown. First, he was surprised by the opulent and sophisticated lifestyle of colonials and the creoles (the mixed-race); which put him off the track of his beliefs. Then the life of practicing medicine, trekking and traveling, dealing with unknown diseases, criminals, dangerous animals, tribes, and cannibals is one side of his story he details meticulously. This is captivating, inspiring, and just as petrifying and blood-curdling it can be.

On the other hand, his faithful, honest, and caring coworkers, government officials, local Serra Leoneans, The Chiefs', expatriate Europeans, Lebanese and Indians, their support, affection, friendship, and amity kept his lonely life in the dark equatorial jungles, on a moral course lest slipping into being an alcoholic and resorting to debauchery and life of afallen man.

Apart from being a page-turner, teeth- clencher, the hypnotizing memoir written by Kamal Malaker; to me, the impact is hugely persuasive and profound. Kamal Malaker's book is more like an "*Epic*" than a memoir. I believe all readers, for whom this book is "a must-read", will have the same exhilarating experience and profound impact as I have had.

*** Prof Sisir Kumar Dutta is the President of the Indo-American Association of Retired Physicians, an acclaimed Gynaecologist, and an avid globe trotter.*

With a heavy heart and sadness, we wish to announce that Prof Dutta passed away in October 2021 in Kolkata. He made these comments just before his death. He provided his comments to the author. As a mark of respect and for his lasting memories, the author expresses his gratitude for Prof Dutta's introspection by reserving his space posthumously.

Africa

In the restless tides of that primordial dawn

When the creator himself despaired of crafting you

And struck angrily at the fresh clay again and again,

In that hour of impatience and rage

The arms of the brave seas

Plucked you from the clasp of the lands of the East,

Removing you far from them all, Africa…….

Alas, shadowed beauty,

How well you hid yourself under the veil of night,…

The naked hunger of the civilized

Stripping them down to their inner shameless brutality…..

Come forth, Oh poet of change

Stand by the last ray of this evening's sun

Where this unfortunate woman waits,

And say, 'Forgive me!'

In the midst of fierce delirium,

Let that be the final reparation made by your civilization"

Rabindranath Tagore, 1937

"I was totally ignorant of the interior, and it was difficult at first to know what I needed, in order to take an expedition into Central Africa"

Henry Morton Stanley

"Doctor Livingstone, I presume"

Henry Morton Stanley

DEDICATION

This book is dedicated to my deceased parents, Dr. Manasa Charan Malaker and Mrs. Soroshi Malaker. I would like to dedicate it also to the people and Government of Sierra Leone during the immediate post-colonial independence period.

ACKNOWLEDGEMENT

It would not have been possible for me to have written this book without enthusiastic encouragement and blessings from the late Dr. Amiya Kumar Sen, Director of Chittaranjan Cancer Hospital and Chittaranjan National Cancer research center (CCH&CNCRC) of Kolkata. Professor Sen was also my eternal mentor and Guru, which has shaped my life today, including writing as a tool for self-discovery, expression, and sharing and guiding me to publish the first Cancer journal in India. Likewise, in later life, Dr. Lionel Israel of the Cancer Care Manitoba and Dr. Norman Coleman of Harvard Medical School, whose personal influence, guidance, friendship, encouragements, and above all, mentorship, not only for my professional life but in my personal life, kept me right on course. Never will I forget their kindness, sense of humility, and humanity that empowered me to accept all challenges in life.

I must acknowledge sincere help from Mr. Bamforth, the then Permanent Secretary of the Government of Sierra Leone. Dr. Boardman, Chief medical officer, Ministry of Health, Government of Sierra Leone, the Late Dr. Bidyut Guha Thakurta, Senior Consultant Physician, Connaught Hospital, Freetown, mentored me on life, working, and living in West Africa, particularly in Sierra Leone. Unfortunately, his untimely death at 52 years of age left a deep scar in my heart.

My wife, Baljit, my daughter, Sharmeela, our two grand daughters, Anaya and Ariya, and Jagjeet, my son-in-law, for their unabated encouragement, interest, patience, and witty remarks, while I was writing this book.

My siblings, Kalyani Chakraborty (Mejdi), Nirmal and his wife, Krishna, Sajal(Buro), and his late wife Purabi, Utpal(Bachhu), and his wife, Namita, Parimal (Bablu) and his wife, Sumita, for their encouragement, everlasting inquisitive demeanor, seeking, "What next?" kept my enthusiasm buzzing.

My first cousin, the late Bimal, a bureaucrat turned author, whom I encouraged and mentored. Aside from the family connection, one of my closest friends, who had been with me during my good days and bad days, my school days and college days, my "sporty days," and in sick days. His sharp and analytical mind made me think twice before I leaped. Unfortunately, his passing away left a big vacuum in my heart.

Dr. Danie Botha meticulously reviewed the manuscript and suggested several important changes, which are most helpful in highlighting and emphasizing some emotions embedded in the narration. Dr. Botha's contribution is gratefully appreciated.

All the Staff of Kailahun General Hospital and senior government officers of the district, their welcoming, friendly spirit, and sincere help made my stay not just enjoyable but exhilarating as well. Memories are still bright and shining, decades after I had left Kailahun and Sierra Leone.

Thanks to my Secretary, Amina Toussaint, for meticulously editing the text and Ranveer Brar for technical and editorial assistance.

I cannot express enough gratitude to my two doctors, Dr. Bharat Shah, my family physician, and Dr. Sachidananda Sinha, my cardiologist. Together they have kept me kicking and ticking with vigor. I have come so far with their support, wishing for even further.

PREFACE

It was just a matter of a fortuitous, unplanned event in London at 4 Mill Bank, the office of the Crown agent. I arrived in London to be working as a research scholar. Unfortunately, some unexpected logistic problem was poised to delay my research program by six to nine months. I was disappointed and disheartened, thinking of a way to return home. However, a chance meeting with a senior official of the crown colonies at the Crown Agent's office lifted me out of despair and uncertainty, and enticed me to the excitement of the exploration of wild, unknown, and treacherous lives of pioneering explorers of the Dark Continent. I was offered the position as a medical officer to work in forested equatorial Africa. I did not give it a second thought. I had no idea of the country, where it was, its people, what they look like, how they live, what they wear, or what they eat. Nothing.

The adventures of David Livingstone, Henry Morton Stanley, Mungo park, Richard Burton, Ibn Battuta, Lawrence of Arabia, the savages, Zulu kings, head hunters, the pigmies, Victoria Falls, the river Nile Trans Saharan Camel Caravans, the plunderers and pirates, elephants, zebras, giraffes, and lions, all crowded my mind, my imagination, my fear and insatiable anticipation for the unknown. There was no quarrel between "Yes," I go or "No, let me think." It was resoundingly," Yes, I go!" being my response to take the offer.

Within two weeks, I was enticed from the world's most prosperous, most powerful and most vibrant, sophisticated city of culture and innovation, London, the capital of aristocracy and demeanor, to the darkest and most dangerous part of the Earth, the Gold Coast, or more appropriately, the Golden Coast and White Man's grave. The country is Sierra Leone, in West Africa.

A memorable ocean voyage from Liverpool to Freetown; scary, built the courage to face the most dangerous moments, survive and learn to live with and learn from the unknown.

Immediate post-Colonial independent Sierra Leone, still thriving from colonial heritage. A clear unrivaled distinction between the colonist's disciples, proud native multi-tribal, multi-linguistic, multi-religious, multi-cultural societies, lived side by side, without infringement into one another's domain.

Cultural uniqueness made me understand the difference; friendly gestures appeared to be terrorizing hostility yet grew with a strong bond of friendship.

In my mind, the uniqueness of Sierra Leone's immediate post-Colonialism exposed me to everything I had dreamt of Africa; welcoming Stanly Morton-like handshake, Burton-like trekking through equatorial forests, crossing rough fearful rivers with dangerous dwellers, ferocious animals, and tribes.

Meeting well-to-do, successful expatriate businessmen and professional communities, their agility for adjustment, their success stories, loneliness, social isolation, and depression made the expatriate communities uniquely welcoming to strangers yet sticking to each other, a culturally different but uniquely friendly, supportive environment.

Dreaming of Dr. Albert Schweitzer denouncing a comfortable life of luxury in France and starting a life of a doctor in equatorial Gabon, by Ogooue River, was my source of strength, impetus, and dream to work as a dedicated doctor in the tropical jungles of Sierra Leone. Dr. Schweitzer started his African Odyssey when he was thirty years old. At twenty-three years of age, working in the equatorial jungle as a doctor had been a life-changing experience, which impacted my entire professional life, dealing with patients, students, and fellow human beings for the next fifty years. However, what I learned was no matter how big and enlightened the factories for career-building operations or academic centers were, they could never have been able to give me, or for that matter, anyone else, what I learned here in Africa.

Life in Freetown had been no less illuminating than the life in the Jungles of Kailahun, in the extreme eastern border of the country. I got a taste of the savvy touch of the lives of European colonists' relatively luxurious living onboard MV APAPA on my way from Liverpool to Freetown. The Brits tried to give the best personal lifestyle to their officers in the provinces, but amid muddy roads, mosquitos, loneliness, cultural vacuum, and social isolation, these little comforts were meaningless. Slipping away from the norm was more "normal" than living a moral life. Debauchery, alcoholism, and suicide were likely to be more normal. That was a choice I took, endured, and successfully avoided any of these and returned to London, much wiser and with much broader shoulders.

Despite the fact that racial, cultural, and lifestyle divides, the coherence of human social behavior, empathy, cordiality, personal safety, and comfort had been constantly monitored through the eagle's eye of officers and particularly that of a black African Sierra Leonean Nurse, Sister Thomas (not real name), who never took her eyes off my safety and comfort from the time I embarked on MV Apapa in Liverpool until I boarded on Sierra Leone Airlines flight bound for Europe.

Even after lapse of several decades' impact of the Dark Continent on me as a human being, as a physician, as an academic, and as a mentor had been so profound, I felt compelled from the bottom of my heart to share my experience, my African Odyssey with the rest of humanity. The memory of which I held dearly, close to my heart, for nearly half a century.

I sincerely hope its impact and profundity will bestow on my fellow human beings, especially the younger generation, as it did me, change and shape in thoughts, life, and what it means to be human.

CONTENTS

1. Suddenly, Sierra Leone 1
2. The Memorable Voyage to Africa 9
3. Crossing the Bay of Biscay 19
4. Devil's Nightmare – Fantasy Ride 25
5. Sunrise in Hell 39
6. Tranquil Market in Gambia 47
7. Cruising on River Gambia 55
8. The Introduction in Freetown 71
9. At the Government Guesthouse 77
10. At the Ministry of Health 85
11. My First Day at Connaught Hospital 93
12. Walking the Wards 99
13. Night on Call on a Broken Ladder 105
14. District Medical Officer gets Pushed Back 109
15. Dr. Thakuta (Bidyut Guha Thakurta) 115
16. Fun in Freetown 123

17. Sunday in Freetown 135

18. District Medical Officer (DMO) in Kailahun 141

19. Road Trip to Kailahun from Freetown 147

20. Kailahun, a World Apart 177

21. Learning from an Unexpected Source 193

22. Nightmare at Midnight 205

23. The Spears, Drums, and War Dances 211

24. Scary Guest in Darkness 219

25. At the High Court in Freetown 227

26. The Exhumation: Science or Sorcery 233

27. The Deadly Return to Kailahun 239

28. My Turn to Accept Help 251

29. Recovering to a New Life 257

30. Visit the Site of Accident 261

31. Convalescing: Ayesha, my Friend 267

32. Mr. Jesudasan, the Principal 275

33. The Saads: Lebanese in Sierra Leone 289

34. The Phoenician Fantasy and the Krio Crush 309

35. A Guest at Camp Vianini 323

36. The Volunteers: American Peace Corps and British VSOs. 333

37. Theater at Market Place: A Court House *Drama******* 347

38. Meeting a Diamond Runner 357

39. On the Road to Monrovia 373

40. Waking up from Monrovia Ecstasy 391

41. Back on the Saddle in Kailahun 409

42. Scouting Kailahun 419

43. Visit Pendembu 425

44. Last Call – Going to Daru and
    Other Untrodden Terrain 431

45. Visit Segbwema and Nixon Memorial Hospital 447

46. Revisit Koindu and Eastern Projection 459

47. Wake Up and Pack Up, the Dream Is Over 467

48. A Side Trip to Koidu and
    Yengema – The Diamond Capital 479

49. Preparing to Check Out 491

50. Unprepared and Unwilling to Let Leave 503

51. Last Days in Freetown 519

52. The Lioness Never Cries 533

Chapter 1

SUDDENLY, SIERRA LEONE

"I can't think of anything that excites a sense of childlike wonder than to be in a country where you are ignorant of almost everything"

Bill Bryson

Sierra Leone had never been on my schedule, nor in my itinerary. Not even in my plan, but now I can say, by a stroke of luck, that the door to Sierra Leone got opened suddenly for me, promising an exciting social, cultural, and professional adventure. I could not resist the lure; I jumped at it from my heart, not my head.

It was London in the early sixties of the twentieth century.

On a grim New Year's Eve, in a dark, gloomy, sleety, and slushy morning, which is very usual for London this time of the year, I arrived in Euston station to catch the "Mailboat train" to Liverpool. This special train takes passengers to travel by "Mail boat' to West Africa. I was well attired, befitting the British expectation from one of their colonial subjects. The controller at the platform entrance asked my name, looked at

my ticket for the Mailboat, and said, "Hmm.... Doctor? ....."
The porter had all my baggage on his trolley. The controller at the entrance asked, "Sir! If you want any luggage to carry with you, please show it to me, and I will tag those. The rest will be booked directly for Freetown and stored in the baggage hold until you arrive in Freetown. Until you disembark in Freetown, you will not be able to access your checked luggage unless it is a dire emergency.

Now, if you will kindly follow this gentleman," he said, indicating one of the attendants, "he will usher you to your compartment and find your seat. We will bring the baggage to your compartment shortly so that you may settle in."

As we walked the platform, I could only see scores and scores of Africans, smartly dressed, well-mannered, and courteous. For a minute, I was bewildered, uncertain of where I was and where I was going. Where are the Londoners? Of course, these people are primarily Africans returning to Africa, their home, since this was an Africa-bound journey, first by train and then by the "Mailboat."

I never had such an experience anywhere, being in a crowd of people who I had not expected to be there. Aside from being African, they behaved no different from the country's people, who were just about to leave. The cultural impact of Brits on my fellow African travelers was phenomenal. Within such a short period, just as I was walking the platform, watching the crowd speaking to each other, interacting with each other, the courteous gesture and the making way for me to walk past them impressed me. I still could not stop thinking about where I was.

Eventually, the attendant brought me to my coach, clearly and boldly written "First class Sleeper." The young man brought me to my compartment where another person was waiting at the door. He opened the door and let me in. Fortunately, my suitcase had already been delivered into my compartment. I realized I was the only occupant as the usher took a courteous bow and departed. The attendant took over and asked if I needed any help or drinks. As it was nearly English teatime, I said that a cup of tea would be fine.

Within minutes he reappeared with a tray carrying a pot of tea, biscuits, cakes, small cut sandwiches, and a small bowl of fruits. There was also a small bottle of Perrier. This was a traveling luxury at its peak in the early '60s.

It was more than one hour before the train would leave for Liverpool. So, first, I had an excellent tea and a short rest, and then I went out to walk the platform. I wanted to have a better look to ensure that I was at the right place, on the right train, and going to the right destination to connect us to the "Mail Boat" bound for West Africa.

By this time, the platform was almost empty. All those Africans who crowded the platform had vanished, except a few who were still searching for their seats and compartments, and others taking longer to say goodbye to their friends and relatives who came to see them off.

Just as my walk took me to the end of the platform, a railway officer approached me and asked if he could help me with anything. Then, courteously, he asked me to present my ticket. Suddenly he became a little stiff and returned my ticket politely and said, "Sorry for the trouble, Sir!"

I asked why the platform was so empty when we still had a couple of hours before leaving. "Yes, sir! Everybody is in their compartment. The dinner will be served at 6.30 pm, must finish by 8 pm and we leave at 8.30 pm for Liverpool. May I show you to your compartment?" He walked with me to my compartment and wished me an enjoyable dinner.

As I returned to my cabin, the attendant appeared from somewhere and asked if I would like to have my dinner in the cabin, or would like to have it in the restaurant car. I thought this would be a good opportunity to meet some of my traveling companions. The attendant showed me the restaurant car, and we entered. A well uniformed, polite, and polished gentleman took over and asked my cabin number.

"Oh! We have a table already reserved for you. If you would kindly follow me, sir." And I did.

This did not look like any restaurant car I had ever been in a train, and I have been on many. This is a "fine dining suite, of a five-star hotel" with waiters fully dressed in white gloves, both men and women. It was beautifully furnished and decorated; not just the dining compartment, but the dining tables were just as sophisticated as can be.

Inside the dining car was an entirely different scene. Almost all the tables had been taken. Nearly all the diners were white, fully dressed for dinner, bow-tied with white, or black jackets. Ladies were in their gorgeous dresses. Several men had impressive mustaches, which gave me the notion that they were most likely military generals or brigadiers. Only one black couple sat far away by the end of the compartment. They did not look any different from the rest of the crowd except for their complexion.

I was impressed yet perplexed at the reception and grandeur of the dining car, even though I knew I was traveling in first class, all the way to Freetown, along with many others. There must have been close to one thousand people traveling on that train.

What happened to the others? Maybe they had decided to dine in their compartment in their privacy and solitude.

But later, I gathered that this dining car and the entire compartment were reserved only for white (strictly not necessarily) "The Crown" appointed high-ranking civil and military officers traveling to West Africa, including doctors. I happened to be a "crown appointed" medical officer bound for Freetown in Sierra Leone. So this was my first exposure and encounter with the British aristocracy.

All the guests only whispered. The only sound I could hear frequently was "thank you," and "thank you," and "thank you again." Almost everyone smoked cigarettes, but quite a few of the men smoked cigars and their pre-dinner drinks or cocktail. The smell from the cigar smoke was romantic but choking. Some ladies also smoked with their long cigarette holder pipes.

Many people were coughing, but most could hide their discomfort with little difficulty. However, it was hard for me to hide since I had no training in sneezing or coughing among high society.

Several waiters entered the car just before dinner was to be served. They went to each table and helped extinguish the burning entertainment by dipping the burning end of the cigarettes or cigars in the water poured in the bottom of the fume trays. Almost in five minutes, the compartment became smoke-free.

The entrées followed the appetizers, salads, soups with varieties of bread, and on the menu the sweets, the cakes, puddings, and fruit bowl and a hot drink of my choice; I enjoyed all eight courses as promised. I wanted Black tea to wash and clean my throat and help me stay awake for the rest of the evening to absorb all the planned and unplanned entertainment for guests in the first-class compartment of the mail-boat train.

A gentle request on the overhead speaker announced to all passengers to return to their respective cabins or seats in preparation for the train to leave at 8.30 pm, bound for Liverpool Quay station.

Calmly, the dining hall was emptied. I deliberately decided to be the last man to have the opportunity to experience the theatrical performance of exiting the dining car, couple by couple, diner by diner, passenger by passenger, until my call came to leave. I was then escorted to my cabin. I found that my sleeping suits were stretched and the bed made as I entered. The attendant knocked, asked if I needed anything, and reminded me that the nightcap would be at 10.30. I did not understand what he meant. He left. I started to wind down in luxury beyond my comprehension.

Tired but not exhausted enough to drop to sleep, I carried Forester's *Passage to India*. I should have been reading Livingstone's *African Expedition* instead. By 8.30 pm, the train slowly rolled out of Euston station and headed north, splicing through various London Burroughs. For the last time, I could see the lights of St Paul's cathedral. The remaining London landmarks were drowned in neon signs, making it challenging to identify one from the other. There was fog that was more prominent in London's outskirts. 8.30 pm in London winter is deep in the nightfall, which did not help. I stopped looking outside from my window as disappointment and desperation forced me to bed.

I got absorbed in Forester's India that existed centuries before my existence on this earth. Still, I found that the book took me back to Forester's time. I imagined his era as existing, dreaming of his time and events, with regular rhythmic cranking of the iron wheels on rails. I dozed off for how long, I do not know, but woke up on hearing a knock at the door. I opened the door and found the attendant with a tray full of cut fruits, typical British Sandwiches, or, as the Americans would say, "bite-size" assorted sandwiches, and a pot of hot water. He placed the tray on the pullout table and asked, "Do you need hot or cold drinks? Would you like any 'shots?'?"

By this time, I knew what a shot meant and politely declined. Any hot drink? I thought that would be nice in the cold, even though the cabin was well heated.

"Tea? Coffee? Hot Chocolate?" He asked.

"Yes, hot chocolate if you have."

"Of course, we have all varieties. Hot Chocolate is the favorite drink for ladies on this train." So, he prepared a long cup for me with milk and sugar. I had the first sip; "Heavenly!" I said and gave him a half-crown coin. He was delighted.

Before leaving the cabin, he reminded me that tomorrow's breakfast would be at 6.30 am. And that we would board the boat at 8 am. The ship was due to sail at 11 am for West Africa. He said he would serve the breakfast in my cabin at 6.30 am, but would give a wake-up knock at 6 am.

"Excellent!" I said. He departed. The train continued to chug along, powered by a coal-fired steam engine. Railway electrification in the UK was happening, but at its speed, in the mind of the British people, it was still a dream which might happen one day.

The musical, rhythmically repetitive cranking of the wheels put me to sleep almost immediately, only to be woken up by the attendant at 6 am, as he promised. He was wearing his freshly laundered and pressed uniform, and asked quietly how I would like my eggs.

"Eggs?" I said, "Oh! Eggs for my breakfast? 2 eggs fried on both sides." He left as quietly as he had entered.

As Bengali Indians, we were not privy to learning the 'lingo,' or the 'mannerism' of Brit educated class, although their education system educated us. My nineteen-day trip from Bombay to London, on P&O Ocean Liner, Oriana, traveling on first class with my cabin and personal steward, oriented me nicely to the English way of life. From my steward, I learned to have bed tea with two biscuits and how to dunk biscuits without losing them in the teacup. Fifty years since I got the first lesson, that habit is still with me. I learned many things about British mannerisms from my Irish steward on board Oriana, including how to tie a British Tie knot. Then several weeks in Hotel Bonington in Russell square, which was an important transit location for "officers" appointed by the crown agent for British Colonial Services worldwide.

When my cabin attendant returned, I had shaved and brushed my teeth. He entered with a tray full of breakfast, placed the tray on the table, and asked if I wanted tea with milk, sugar, or lemon.

"Just English tea," I said. He understood. He prepared the cup of tea and opened the cover of my breakfast plate, and quietly left.

At 7.45 am, he returned to collect the tray and reminded me again that I must be on board no later than 8.30 am. After that, another attendant would help me to my cabin onboard MV Apapa.

Chapter 2

THE MEMORABLE VOYAGE TO AFRICA

"It is better to travel well than to arrive"

Buddha.

What a difference. Liverpool was sunny, bright, and completely dry. No snow or sleet anywhere. The mail boat train brought us to the platform, across the mooring site of several ocean-going ships. As I stepped out of the train onto the platform, I could see my boat berthed just across. There can't be any better connection. A new porter took my luggage as I said goodbye to my cabin attendant.

He reciprocated, saying, "Goodbye, sir!" He also wished me a safe and enjoyable voyage. We crossed the berth from the platform and approached the bridge to the gangway. An officer from Elder & Dempster Ocean Liner checked my ticket, passport, and appointment letter, saying I was a Crown Agent appointee for the Government of Sierra Leone as a medical officer. He checked the passenger list while apologizing for the process and let me in with my porter, who took me to my cabin on the third level. I still remember the cabin number, C 33. The porter explained that I was on the third level, and my cabin was No. 3 in section 3. There were five sections on each level, and each section had its service facility and steward. It was a very well-organized arrangement with no chance of getting lost or confused.

This is what I did learn; the sense of discipline, courtesy, organization, and being respectful to each other. This was a cabin for one person, smaller than I had in the P&0, Oriana, from Bombay to London. But it had everything else; the bed, the lighting, and the fans despite the cabins being air-conditioned. It also included a small collection of books and a working table. The attached bathroom could only allow showers but was beautifully appointed and maintained. The interior was a wooden finish, and the floors were covered with artificial marble. My room was on the port side, and I had my deck chair on the opposite deck side of the boat. It was not my personal, assigned to the cabin, but anyone could use it if the occupant was not using it. However, they had to vacate whenever the occupant wanted to use it. There had never been an issue over the right. There were more than enough deck chairs for every person on this ship.

Slowly, I started to settle down. Finally, I could see the sister ship 'Accra' moored not very far from us.

MV. Accra was a giant ship that I could see from my porthole. MV Accra was not going to Freetown this time; it would go to Monrovia, Liberia's capital and major port. However, in those early colonial days, Freetown still had the largest capacity for exporting and importing varieties of goods through the ports and others in the Freetown estuary.

Anyway, as passengers started to settle down, the bars, the shops, and restaurants also started to get busy. A message came from the captain by noon, welcoming everyone on board. He then wished everyone a pleasant voyage and reminded them that lunch would be served at 12.30 noon. Passengers were requested to be seated at their assigned table for ease of service. Any change of table was not permitted.

Passengers who traveled in C and D floors were to go to the dining hall on the main floor, and those of A, B, and the Deck where to go to the dining room on floor '0'.

I had no difficulty understanding the reason for the discriminatory allocation of dining halls. The main floor was mostly for Europeans or highly Anglicized non-Europeans, and floor "0" for the rest of the world. These introspections were my afterthoughts. At the time, I never thought about this, but later I began to understand the dynamics. I was so excited and scared at the same time of the prospect of my adventure to Sierra Leone.

I spent a few days in the British Library in London to research Sierra Leone. Google had not yet been conceived. Therefore, not a great deal of information was available. Perhaps I was an amateur library explorer at that time, but I got more practical information from the office of the Crown agent about the present political, social, and economic environment. I was convinced that it would not be like the meeting of David Livingstone and Henry Morton Stanly extending his hand to shake and pronounce the famous phrase 'Dr. Livingstone, I presume.' After all, Sierra Leone was a newly independent British Crown Colony.

Moreover, I had some idea of the legacy of the British administration for their 'Let go' colonies. After all, I am from one of them anyway. Grim anticipation, to the vitality of excitement of discovery, I was directed to the dining hall on our floor, and then from the entrance to my assigned table.

As I sat down, one waiter appeared. He helped me to the seat at my assigned table, and asked me if I would like any drinks before lunch.

"A cup of green tea will do nicely in this weather," I responded.

Lunch was an elaborate affair, with décor and courteous presentation by the waiters with arrangements fit for a princely reception. The drinks, the aperitifs, were served one after the other to be followed by several courses. Some I took, others I gratefully returned. Yet, I was well fed and ready for a siesta at the end of the course. I thought most of my fellow voyagers would feel the same. But it was far from my expectation.

The smoke room was packed. A mixture of smokes from cigarettes, cigars, and pipes was blended to make a concoction of aroma that I had never experienced before, a dreamy narcotic smell enhanced by the strong scent of brewing Arabic coffee. Waiters were serving the coffee in trays to the guests who desired some. The waiters in their bright attire were in attendance to serve at any time.

That was not the end. As I passed by the smoking lounge, I saw the Billiard rooms with four tables, all engaged in satisfying its users. Next door was the table tennis room that was busy with gamers. Adjacent, but on the opposite side, a luxurious lounge fitted with tables for card games of various sorts, Carom boards, Bagatelle, and many other board games, most of which I could not comprehend. The entertainments and joys of all the board games were provided to enjoy the ship's guests. Through a complete glass enclosure, I could see racks of books and newspaper hangers just ahead. There were also working desks, easy chairs, and side tables for those who loved to think, read, dream and write and wished to keep up with world affairs. No TV, no radio; only newspapers, magazines, and bulletins were provided. That was supposed to be a quiet room.

I passed the dining and entertainment area and entered my section of living quarters. It was not difficult to find my cabin, C33, which meant that I was on the C deck, cabin No. 3, in the third section of the division, as the butler taught me. There were five sections on my deck. Others had six to eight sections.

As I entered my cabin, there was a message on the overhead system informing all passengers to assemble on their respective decks at 3 pm for a short training in emergency drills. So today, all I had to do was to be present there.

It was already 2 pm, and I had just finished a formidable lunch. Now I was ready for a siesta. The environment, the decor, the services all directed me to go for a nap. As I closed the door, a soft knock sounded.

"Come in," I said.

A young man opened the door and identified himself as Albert. He informed me that he was the butler for this section of our boat, the five cabins in section 3. He asked me if I needed anything, and then came in and rearranged my luggage. He hung some of my clothes in the cupboard, took the sleeping suit and sleepers out, and put them more or less in the places where I would have placed them anyway. Before leaving, he reminded me about 3 p.m.'s emergency drill training. He informed me that he would knock at the door at around 2.45 pm. Then he showed me a red button just above my headboard to press at any time I needed him for anything. Finally, he departed with a courteous bow.

The emergency drill was to give us some information about emergencies. First, they showed us the rescue package with the life jacket, what else it contained, and what the items were used for, as well as when and how to use it. The actual emergency drill would be tomorrow. Next, we were to pick up our emergency packs from our cabin, which were to be stored in the cupboard for easy access. They also requested us to check all the materials and equipment; to ensure that everything supplied was intact and usable. A list of materials in the bag was kept inside, with a copy posted behind the door, where various other information was also posted. We were to read them carefully.

The boat was scheduled to set sail at 6 pm. That was a night of the new moon. The Irish Sea was expected to be rough. They hoped to get out of the Irish Sea by midnight before it started to get rough due to a high tide. Dinner would be served at 7 pm, just after we set sail.

There were about twenty people in our group; other groups were yet to come. We tried to socialize a bit and introduced ourselves to each other as much we could. I gathered that the majority were seasoned travelers on Elder Dempster Liners. As I mentioned to some of them, this was my maiden voyage to West Africa by ship, and I did not hide my feeling of excitement.

The Irish Sea could be rough, but the Bay of Biscay is generally challenging even with many experienced sailors. Unfortunately, I had no idea what they were talking about.

Continent of Africa

"The dark continent is not so dark after all"

The author.

Post-colonial Sierra Leone

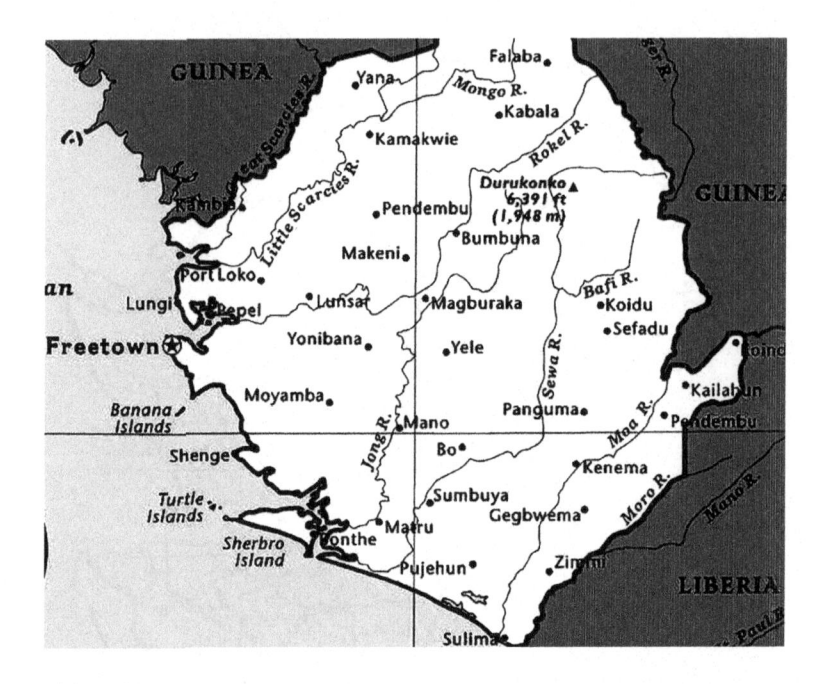

The country of Lion Mountain is the home of Kindest Lioness.

The author 2020

District of Kailahun in Eastern Province of Sierra Leone

"*Diamond runner's paradise*

"*Adventurers arena to fight, win or lose.*"

The author.

Chapter 3
CROSSING THE BAY OF BISCAY

"Life's roughest proves the strength of our anchors"

Anonymous

The voyage from Bombay to Tilbury was so smooth and pleasant; I wondered why we did not live on board. No dust, no traffic, no noise, just a peaceful way forward to the destination, with the splashing noise of the ship's hull shearing through the ocean water. P&O Oriana was massive. As the Boat had just been commissioned, everything was new and novel. Oriana had the capacity for two thousand passengers and several hundred crew members. The difference with MV APAPA was that it had a capacity maximum of 500 people, including the crew. But it carried lots of goods and mail to West Africa from the rest of the world. These liners were the lifeline of most British or English-speaking colonies and others. The contribution of these liners to the development and modernization of West Africa was formidable. There was no question about that. So, the arrival of the 'Mail boat' in any country's port was a matter of relief, hope, and celebration.

The interior décor and management style benefitted only the rich, famous, and influential.

I had no idea where I fit in, with this lifestyle's sense of opulence and luxury. I was just a newly qualified doctor from India who happened to be an outcast thrown in by accident. But thinking back, I did steer myself well in this uncharted, unknown, and mysterious waters, pretending to be another actor. I was not even aware that I was a pretender. Now I know, I did not know then that merely being a doctor commanded very high respect and cordiality in the communities of both the white colonists and the black 'colonized.'

The African west coast was known as the 'Gold Coast' because of its riches. But it was also known as "White man's grave." The news of white men dying of yellow fever, malaria, a whole host of parasitic diseases went round the world faster than it was happening. But blacks were not immune to any of these illnesses. They were dying more in numbers because of their living conditions, quality, and dietary imbalance. That was 'no news.' However, doctors saved lives irrespective of skin color, whether in huts, bungalows, or palaces. Doctors earned their position, respect, and affection in society because of their passion, selflessness and hard work.

In almost all West African countries, elected presidents or prime ministers were qualified physicians during the early sixties, starting from Senegal to Cameroon. Even simultaneously, all the British East African Independent Colony's elected heads of government were also qualified physicians.

I did not know then. I do know now the difference. But, I must still admit, at that time of my life, my career, the level of respect, the standard of reception, and cordiality baffled me.

I returned to my room and tried to rest a little. Then, I checked my emergency kit for the next day's exercise.

Around 4:30 pm, Albert knocked at the door and asked me what I would like for my tea. Of course, afternoon tea was an integral part of British life—what an excellent thought. My one month's stay in Hotel Bonington on Southampton Row in Holborn gave me an intensive crash course in the British way of life and also that of a colonist's standards and expectations.

He returned with a tray that had a potful of hot water, a plateful of biscuits, cakes, and the famous cucumber and sardine sandwiches. He poured water into the cup and strained the tea of my choice as tea bags were not yet widespread. Finally, he stirred with milk and one spoon of sugar, as I instructed. "Anything else I can do for you, Sir?"

"Thank you, that'll be all," I said.

"Please ring the bell should you need me."

It was the first time I was being addressed as 'Sir.' Until now, I addressed everyone else as sir. The change was too sudden and profound for me to absorb.

A moment later, there was a knock at the door again. "Please come in," I said. The cabin door opened; I could only see part of the person because of the height.

"Dr. Malaki!" A black lady who introduced herself as Sister Thomas called out to me. The lady was almost twice my height and three times my weight. She did not look obese, but smart and well-built, like an athlete.

She was also traveling on the same boat to Freetown. I invited her in. There was a chair for a guest, but I quickly offered to sit on the bed, used as a settee, until I went to bed. She was a little hesitant.

She kept staring at me for a few seconds with a completely vacant look. I was a little embarrassed; I thanked her for searching me out and taking the trouble of tracking me to my cabin. Then, "Dr.!" She said, "Mr. Bamforth, the Permanent Secretary of the government of Sierra Leone, requested to make sure that everything was all right on your trip to Freetown on this ship." I had no idea who Mr. Bamforth was, but then I realized he was the most important and powerful government bureaucrat.

She said she came to the UK for a course in nursing administration, which lasted for six weeks in Edinburgh. She was happy to have found me and contacted me on board. She would inform Mr. Bamforth to that effect. The purser of this boat would send the Telex to him.

After the boat set sail, it would have been difficult for her to visit me, so she took this chance before the action. She would return and be in touch. She also told me to ask Albert to contact her if I needed any help.

"Good night," she said, "and enjoy the dinner, Sir!"

I also thanked her for the support and the sense of confidence she gave me, and the trouble of tracking me to my cabin.

Right at 6 pm, the ship's warning signal went off. The boat was about to leave.

I came out to the deck to bid farewell to England, for a short while anyway. The boat slowly moved away from the jetty, untied all the ropes, and raised anchor. We could see the imposing buildings of the Liverpool City Port Authority, just as impressive as the Elder –Dempster's ocean liner's office. It was early winter. Sunset had been almost two hours ago. The city lights were dazzling, welcoming the new boats, new traders, and the New Year. The sky was pitch black, and stars were twinkling in the millions, without a shred of cloud in the sky.

By 7 pm, the dining room was abuzz with people, and slowly, all the chairs were taken. Then the parade of waiters and waitresses started. Course after course came one after the other. There was live music played from one corner of the dining hall.

We had already been warned of the rough sailing in the Irish Sea, so most of us had a very light dinner to deter the sickness from the rocking boat in the mid-Irish Sea.

The sky was dark, teemed with millions of twinkling stars and soft baroque music piping, just right for a dreamy night. I

fell asleep.

Chapter 4

DEVIL'S NIGHTMARE – FANTASY RIDE

"Courage consists not in hazarding without fear but being resolutely minded in a just cause "

- Plutarch

The night went well. I slept like a baby. The anticipated rough sea, new moon, its horror, all spared us. Instead, we had smooth and calm sailing through the night of the new moon into a restful morning, leaving the unruly, unpredictable Irish Sea behind. Little mercy, but a big help.

The following day, routine bed tea, walking on the deck, and 11 am mid-morning coffee. I could relax either on the deck or in the smoky lounge, which was not as smoky as before. The games, reading, and library were busy, filled with happy, carefree, and fun-seeking people. As you walked along, you could hear passengers talking about the calm Irish Sea and what the Bay of Biscay might hold. The climate, the price of commodities, the fast-changing political environment, the economy, transportation, and many other issues affected their lives upon arrival at their destination countries.

As I approached my cabin, I saw Sister Thomas waiting outside the door. "Good morning, Sister Thomas," I greeted her. She looked happy and well-rested. She asked how my night was, and the events that kept me occupied in the morning. She was delighted that the Irish Sea was kind and calm, yet it was the night of a new moon, despite rough weather and the prediction of the rough sea. The mythical new moon was a new beginning, drowning all evils that came and went or stayed longer than they should with the ebbing and waning of the moon goddess. The shadow of the darkness of the new moon bathed us to purity in a new beginning. That is the blessing we have from the sky. But in reality, missing the moon's light on the earth, which is shrouded by the darkness of the new moon, many scary and evil things happen; thieves, bandits (thugs), terrorists, rapists find it is easy to attack their prey under the darkness of the new moon. Many battles were fought, won, or lost due to the blessing or curse of the darkness of the new moon. On the earth, the new beginning means someone should lose or sacrifice for the opponent to win in order to have a new beginning. That is a fascinating way to think of the new moon's influence on human beings and society.

Again, one can't stop thinking that a calm Irish sea on a new moon's night points to a harsher and rocky passage through the Bay of Biscay. Who knows? For the time being, let us count our blessings anyway for the little mercy.

"On this voyage, I am happy that you are well and all in one piece; let us pray the rest of the journey is safe and calm. I will look in another time," she departed with a smile of satisfaction.

It seemed that most of the passengers were keenly interested in the weather forecast and condition of the sea. I guessed many were seasoned voyagers who experienced various situations that may have affected them either in a very pleasant or not so pleasant way. I had no history in the West African Ocean voyage, hence had no anticipation, only excitement of the experience of exploration. Every minute was a vision for the future.

The day went by lazily. We had our fire and emergency drill at 4 pm. By 7 pm, we were ready for dinner. This was the third night on board. This night, a live musician played piano and sang a Doris Day song. The waiters were busy when a man came to me asking if my meal and courses were to my satisfaction. With a nine-course meal, how can it not be satisfactory? He told me that if I needed any particular dish, diet, or drink, I would let my butler know the previous night, and they would do their best to accommodate my request. I read on his name tag Jos Gomez. I was confident he was a Goan culinary person. At one time, Goan's represented a very high proportion of staff in almost all major Ocean liners, whether passenger or carrying goods or both: mainly in the culinary activities. They also had a significant stake in hotels and cruise ships as musicians and instrument players, some of whom had an international reputation. The mixture of Indian and Portuguese culture and lifestyle made them especially suitable for these professions, which needed an international touch. In later life, I have heard them playing in London Hilton, in Park Lane, Hilton on Manhattan, Rafael's in Singapore, and of course, The Taj in Bombay. Never have they disappointed my expectations, anywhere ever.

The third night went safely without any incidence. By the fourth day, we were already in the middle of the Bay of Biscay, sailing along the side of the west coast of southern France. Clear sunny morning, calm and tranquil ocean passage to Bathurst, our first port of call in the Gambia, en route to Freetown, in Sierra Leone. Then the Boat would stop at Accra in Ghana, and from there to Port Harcourt in Nigeria.

We expected to moor in Bathurst, Gambia, on the night of the 12th day of our voyage, and on the fifteenth day, expected to be mooring at the Freetown Harbor on M.V. Apapa. Currently, we were floating along the western coastline of Portugal, steadily and in the calm sea. We couldn't see the coastline, but the captain said we were twenty to fifty kilometers from the shoreline.

We were sailing along the northwest coast of North Africa, most likely Morocco but couldn't see any coastline. Casablanca was not far but unreachable. We were getting closer and closer to Africa, by the day, by the hour, by the minute. We were on our fourth day on board.

It was a calm and lazy day, a lazy afternoon, when the purser announced teatime. If you were lounging on the deck, your tea would be served; there was no need to go to the dining room. But teatime was also time for socializing, exchanging news from home and each other's destination. So generally the time was utilized to do just that—nothing exciting or unusual from either direction. The sea was calm, and the boat was sailing as if over a piece of silk. Yet, we were still in the bottom end of the Bay of Biscay, soon to be leaving and entering the expanse of the Atlantic Ocean. The rough Biscay behaved tamely. We started to feel relieved.

By 5 pm, a message over the pipe came from the captain, informing us that there may be a bit of bad weather with thundershowers ahead. The wind speed would not exceed more than 30 km/h, with rain associated with the moderate blowing wind.

It is a delightful sailing, at least for now. I was hoping the captain would be wrong about his weather forecast. However, I could not convince myself to prepare for predicted impending danger.

So instead, I sank into "now," one of life's beautiful moments, onboard Apapa, sailing along the West African Coast.

At 5.30 pm, a further overhead message from the captain came through, requesting all passengers to be at dinner at six instead of 7 pm, in the anticipation of possible bad weather. However, the captain again reassured that it was just a preemptive measure in case the weather turned rough, which might disrupt the enjoyment of dining onboard MV Apapa.

Like drilled school children, the entire crowd of passengers, leaving all their relaxing activities, slowly in a casual but orderly pace, chatting, laughing, some even whistling gentle romantic songs, made their way to their respective dining area and dining table. I found the table and seat assigned to me, being directed by a waiter, and courteously helped to take the chair. My dining partners joined me just a few seconds later.

As we all settled into our respective seats, the pianist started to play soft, sweet, and romantic-sounding music in the far right-hand corner. Beside him stood a very pretty tall and slim lady with a giant Gallic Harp, ready for action. Soft sweet music, the pianist continued to play with support from the Harpist. The musical ambiance created by the duo made all of us forget why we were here at the dining table earlier, not to be entertained an hour longer, but to finish the dining business, before the anticipated storm arrived.

Surprisingly, the atmosphere was not fearful anticipation, but joyful enjoyment of the moment.

I did not know how to prepare or react if the "spoiler" storm arrived. But I must say, I was not ready for an early dinner but simply floated along with the mood. Most of my co-passengers were veteran seafarers and well-adjusted, both physically and mentally, to these uninvited, undesirable spoiler moments; otherwise, a serene and beautiful time onboard, on the ocean. They did not let a single moment of happiness slip away from them.

At that moment, that was my company, my mood, and my joy, despite repeated cautious warnings from the Captain. Each dining act onboard MV Apapa was a performance, not just a service. I liked and enjoyed the dramatic part.

The music continued. Waiters and waitresses lined up with the first course to serve. Then, suddenly, they all proceeded to their assigned table, and it felt as if this drill was being conducted by an invisible Maestro, with clicking sounds of china, tinkling sound of silver, and whispers from each waiting team, asking your permission to serve.

Course after course was served, in strict discipline. While we were slowly but surely enjoying the service and the dinner, we could feel slightly more rolling of the boat. Mostly from front to back and just about perceiving rocking from side to side. We could also hear the sounds of the wind.

It is still pleasant; it is still slightly more romantic with the live music from the dining room corner. The boat is rocking, yet no one is alarmed.

The service continued as rhythmically as it started. We continued to enjoy the hospitality of MV Apapa.

The rocking and rolling started to increase. Wind force and rain became more and more apparent. Yet, the service continued.

Captain continued his reassurances. He was not at his table to dine with some selected guests picked up from the guests onboard. At every dining event, he would have either his first officer or the chief engineer or his purser as his dining company, and another chosen six members from the passengers.

Apparently, it was a great honor to be invited by the Captain to join him for dinner or lunch. This way, I thought he could get to know as many passengers as he could personally entertain and know. Besides, it was excellent PR for business for the shipping company. Unfortunately, I was not one of the lucky ones to dine with the Captain to this day. However, I still believe I would find my day to share the dining pleasure at the Captain's round table extravaganza. Indeed, I looked forward to hearing from the captain to be his dining companion before I left the boat; I looked forward to the commanding experience.

The boat continued to sail in the storm, tossing and turning. The curtains were all drawn so that what was happening outside the ocean couldn't disturb our dining pleasure. Unfortunately, the rocking and rolling began to worsen to the extent that the dining table with its servicing elements began to rock. We had to keep the dishes and cutleries, glasses, and serving gears in place, stopping them from running away from the table. Not an easy task to do when trying to dine, eat or gobble, whatever has been on the plates to finish "the duty" fast and return to our cabins. Some people had already started to walk away before all nine courses were served. Some were crouching forward with their hands and shutting their mouth, perhaps trying to stop throwing up because of the rocky boat. A sense of unease, fear, and restlessness prevailed.

The piano and the harp continued to play to calm people's fear and anxiety. The boat-hardy voyagers continued with their dining adventure even on the rocky boat. We could hear the howling wind and pounding waves against the hull of the ship; scary but not scared.

By this time, half of the guests had left. All the waiters stood steady on their spots. They assisted anyone who needed help to return to their cabins. They directed to the washrooms, those who were ready to throw up. The restrooms were nearly packed.

Suddenly, a tremendous jolt rolled the boat on its side at least thirty degrees, if not more. The ship swung to the opposite side. In the meantime, all the dining wares were thrown from the table onto the floor. There were bone cracking sounds of smashing china and other tableware, becoming scarier. Gangs of cleaning crew appeared to clean the floors of all broken china and other elements. The boat sailed forward, swinging from side to side, creating havoc in the dining rooms and throwing most diners off balance. One time, I felt that the boat was about to swing sideways so much as to capsize on one side.

Now there was total chaos on the decks and the rest of the open spaces where people gathered, some ready to jump overboard, fitted fully with emergency gear. The Captain repeatedly announced for all passengers to return to their respective cabins where help was waiting, in case of any emergency.

I kept sitting steady at my table until I was virtually thrown out of the chair onto the floor by a heavy jolt from powerful waves hitting the sides of the boat. I was giddy; I felt nauseated but did not throw up. My stomach was churning as if I would throw up any time. Just at this point, I was thrown aside due to the rocking of the boat. I saw another lady on the floor. My vision was unclear, and I heard buzzing noises, slowly worsening. But no mistake, the pianist and the lady harpist continued with their music. Erratic at times, yet unmistakable baroque, uplifting and melodic.

Several people rushed to help me get up. I had some bruises on my left chin, and my vision was blurry, but I had no difficulty cooperating with the people trying to help me up and back to my cabin. The dining hall was virtually empty, and floors were covered with pieces of shattered china and glass, water, and food.

The attendants were prompt in clearing the floor and cleaning the tables and chairs, yet after every jolt, fresh bouts of breakables shattering, splashing of liquids, and scattering of food on the floor, made walking very risky in the dining hall. Attendants, the waiters, waitresses, and other passenger-volunteers also pitched in for the safety of co-passengers and all staff on board.

Nobody was screaming nor had made any sound of distress, except the howling of the storm and high thrashing waves.

As I stood up, I was about to fall on the floor. Two strong waiters came to my rescue. Both of them grabbed hold of me. I pretended that I was well enough to walk back to my cabin, but far from it. Unfortunately, I had no strength to walk. I certainly needed their help.

As we walked towards my cabin, I was very nauseous. I did my best not to throw up. Slowly we got back to my cabin. Constant rocking and rolling were most unpleasant. As we entered my cabin, I almost threw myself on the toilet bowl and threw up everything I had in my stomach for the last several days. Before going for dinner, we were warned not to drink much fluid.

I retched and retched and retched until the last drop of water and food were thrown up. Finally, I had nothing left in my stomach. Still, I did not stop retching. That was a harrowing experience. My stomach muscles almost gave way. There was not much strength left in my body. I slipped on the floor. Two waiters were still standing behind me. They picked me up and put me on my bed. They reassured me that as I fell asleep, all the discomfort would go away and that when I woke up, I would feel fresh, like a new person.

I believed them. The boat was still rocking and rolling. Sometimes more than other times. With the ship, my cabin, and my bed rocked and rolled in concert. There was no way I could fall asleep. Lying in bed made me feel more uncomfortable. There was a constant feeling of nausea and giddiness.

I sat on my bed. I could stop my body rocking with the boat but felt slightly better. I thought if I stood up, perhaps, I would feel even better. I slowly got up from the bed holding the side rails. That was a mistake. As I stood up, I had no control of my legs, shaking and rocking with the boat. My giddiness and nausea got worse. My vision blurred. I inadvertently fell on the bed. Fortunately, I did not have any injuries. Being on the bed gave me small relief. Unfortunately, the rocking bed did not help me with my symptoms. I sat up again. This way, I was in control of my body, but the symptoms persisted. A couple of times, I staggered to the washroom to throw up. But still, I retched and retched, squeezing the last ounce of the strength of my stomach, my chest, and muscles of the throat. I had no strength to even scream for help. But the panic buttons and emergency buttons were all there. Everyone was in my shoes. I helped myself back onto my bed.

Outside, the howling of the wind and storm, with the thrashing sounds of vigorous wild unruly waves continued. I sat on my bed, holding the poles so that I did not fall. I cannot remember how long I sat. The stress, exhaustion, dehydration all overtook my body. Finally, I must have slid into my bed and fallen asleep, for how long I do not know.

I woke up by someone tapping on my chest and stroking my cheek. I opened my eyes. I had no idea where I was, what I was doing here, or what was happening. I could see an African woman standing beside me as I woke up. She said, "Sorry, Sir! I could not come early to check on you, but the waiters informed me that they helped you back to your room unhurt and safe. How are you feeling, Sir?" I realized the lady was Sister Thomas, traveling with me to Freetown, in Sierra Leone.

I tried to sit up but could not. Finally, sister helped me to and gave me two white tablets.

"Please take these. I will get you some water."

She went to the washroom. She brought a glass of water and suggested just sipping the water, swallowing the tablets, and not drinking too much. I did exactly what she asked me to do. Then I gathered my strength and courage to ask, "Sister, what are these tablets?"

"They are 'Avomin' tablets, what we use for seasickness," she said. "I am sure you will feel better, and these will make you sleep. When you wake up, you will be a different person altogether. If you feel there is a need for more, I will leave this bottle. It has another six tablets; you can take another two tablets in eight hours. But I will be checking on you."

I almost forgot to ask her how she was, overwhelmed with all my problems. Then, as she closed the door, I shouted, "Sister! How are you managing?" She turned back.

"I am managing. I have gone through quite a few of these on my several trips between the UK and Sierra Leone. I think this is one of the worst we are experiencing. But it will clear by tomorrow. We keep our fingers crossed. Captain and the Chief engineer just stopped short of calling "Mayday." The crew and the officers were highly efficient, and I trusted their judgment."

"You should return to your cabin and rest." She smiled and said that she was lucky to have another senior nurse from Ghana traveling with us. I could not understand what she meant.

"There have been several injuries. The doctor is busy, but unable to do much for the injuries which needed suturing, because of the unstable boat. He has a nurse and a nice operating room. We all are trying to stop bleeding and help them with their pain. The seasickness of those injured is not helping either. But we are managing. You try to catch up with your sleep. I will check on you again. But do not hesitate to press the emergency button if you need to do so."

She left.

The boat continued to rock. I sat on the bed and felt drowsy. Finally, I must have dropped onto the bed and gone to sleep.

This time my steward woke me up. He asked what I would like for breakfast. He said, "We are serving breakfast in the cabins. Captain feels that the sea is not calm enough to serve meals in the dining room. However, if you would like to try, I can help you walk to the dining room."

I neither had the energy, nor appetite to go to the dining room to have my breakfast. However, the steward knew precisely what I needed. After a few minutes, he returned with a tray with some cut fruits, toasts, hard-fried eggs, and a couple of grilled sausages. No fruit juices, only green tea. I guess that is what the chef prescribed.

My nausea was better, but giddiness and tiredness were insurmountable. I was afraid to eat or drink anything, especially since drinking has been an awful feeling. But, slowly, I started to eat.

A knock at the door, then Sister Thomas entered. "Good morning Sir!" Said she. I did the same. She said she looked in once at night, but I was fast asleep. Now she was happy to see me trying to eat my breakfast. "Still do not drink much, just sip to keep your mouth and throat moist, eat only dry stuff." Almost a motherly instruction.

She looked happy! She said she would check in again. They were still busy with several injuries from last night. But none serious enough, she said to me before she left the room.

Chapter 5

SUNRISE IN HELL

"Live as if you are to die tomorrow, learn as if you were to live forever "

Mahatma Gandhi

By the time I managed to have some breakfast, it was 11 am. Not sure what would be the local time where we were at present. It could not have been much different since we almost sailed vertically southward within the same meridian.

I was fragile but in better spirits. I thought if I could walk about the deck or go to the game room, a diversion might boost my soul and body. The decks were virtually empty except the cleaning and other service people around, trying to bring back the normal look of the boat.

It had been showering heavily. The wind was not as heavy as last night, but still more than what was needed to upset the composure of the boat. The boat was sailing fast forward, rocking enough to make me feel giddy again. The ever-growling powerful engines continued to shake the floors, making one unsteady on their feet. I had the feeling of nausea but was not strong enough to throw up. I did not feel like taking another dose of "Avomin," which would invariably put me to sleep and deprive me of the unwelcome excitement and chaos that was the experience of a lifetime.

As I got out of my cabin, my steward appeared as if he was ever ready and 24/7 on call. "Good morning, Sir," he said, "Hope you managed to catch up with some of your sleep, and perhaps feel a little better to venture on the deck on your own.

The captain said we are not yet out of the woods, but the jungle is getting thinner and hopefully will continue that way. We expect to have a clear sky and outside the stormy patch."

Last night's forecast was slightly out of step. It came several hours early. Despite being forewarned by the captain, people had little time to prepare.

The boat was pushed closer to the African coast. That was the reason why the rocking and rolling got worse. Had we been away from the coast, the impact on the boat and the passengers would have been much less. However, the force of the gale was too strong for a small boat to stay on course against the storm coming from the west. It was part of El-Niño gushing towards the western coast of Africa. Due to the strong western trade wind, the boat was drifted closer to the northwest African coast, more like the southern part of Mauritania and the northwest Atlantic coast of Spanish Sahara. Usually, we would not have been sailing within 200 km of the coast. But the storm drifted the boat as close as 50 km from the northwest African coast. As the ship came closer to the coast, the impact of the storm got worse and worse. However, the Crew could keep the boat further than 50 km, and gradually by daybreak, the ship was at a much safer distance from the coast. The impact of the burgeoning storm also got less and less. But the boat was not totally out of its grip of gusting AL-Nino.

As I started to walk along the gangway towards the game room, I felt that my head was still reeling, and the nauseous feeling started to come back. I saw several people playing cards and various other board games in the games room. I wondered if I should join them to take my mind off the constant rocking that made me feel very uneasy.

I tried but could not concentrate on any kind of game. Then I walked to the table tennis. There I found a young man waiting for a partner. I asked him if we could try. I took the first service. Just to return his strike, as I tried to shift to the left, I rolled to my right side and fell on the floor. The jolt was not hard, but I was more embarrassed than distressed. I tried to get up, which I could not do without the help of my partner. I apologized. That was the end of my trial for a game of table tennis.

Still, I did not want to give up. I thought perhaps a game of snooker would help keep my mind off the ailments. I was alone. I got the table ready and the balls in place. I hit the balls without any problem. Much to my satisfaction, the first hit was good to disperse the balls on the table, all within strategic distance in winning – like distances from the corner pockets of the table.

I could not concentrate on the most likely ball that I could score. Not only was my vision hazy, but I kept seeing double. Initially, I thought those were two separate balls, but I missed both as I attempted to strike. My striker not only missed my target, but kept going in a different direction.

The boat was still rocking, and the growling noise of the engines was still shaking the gaming room floor. I was feeling better but still giddy, and I felt like going round and round.

Not sure if I was still seeing double, all my sinuses were stuffy and blocked. My mouth was parched. I thought it would be a misadventure if I continued to find a distraction to keep my mind otherwise occupied away from my severe seasickness. This was my very first experience of "seasickness." I did feel bad about other sufferers. However, it was no one's fault—our choice to venture on this voyage.

I held the wall as I dragged myself from the snooker table, hoping to walk back to my cabin. Using the wall for support, I took my first step. As I was preparing to stride forward, I felt all my energy had been drained. I had no strength nor muscle power to walk with the support of the wall. I dropped to the floor. From nowhere, Sister Thomas appeared.

"Good that you took the challenge of coming out of the cabin, relatively calm weather and less rocking and humming engines. It does take time to get adjusted or get over the seasickness. Let me help you back to your cabin."

It was past midday, and the staff prepared the dining rooms for lunch. I had no appetite for anything. I asked Sister Thomas how she was. "No problem, Sir," She said, "except that we were busy all night, I did not have a good night's sleep. Four of us, a nurse from Ghana, the nurse of the boat, and two other female volunteers were helping the doctor with whatever assistance he needed. We checked all passengers and crew, how they were doing during the stormy weather. There were quite a few of our fellow voyagers who needed help." I kept my poise and steady stride as the sister helped me back to my cabin.

As we were entering, a warning from the overhead announcement alerted everyone that "We are expecting a helicopter from the Spanish Air force coming from Las Palmas to pick up a sick patient. Therefore, all guests are requested to remain in their cabin during the lift-up unless otherwise stated.

This is to prevent chaos on board and stop the possibility of the boat being capsized due to imbalance."

Within ten minutes, a red helicopter began to rove above us. The Helicopter roved around the ship a few times, going up and down, I guessed, trying to find a spot to land. I knew there was a helipad in the front part of the ship, but that was not fit for this military-heavy ambulance machine. They tried to come as close as possible to the vessel. The wind was still strong, and the boat was rocking to all sides. There was no chance they would lower the hammock to lift the patient.

The helicopter was moving and unsteady. Although the crew managed to stop the boat, the boat was rocking, not moving forward. But the wind and the mischievous waves would not allow the vessel to stay reasonably still so that the helicopter crew could lower the hammock.

They attempted to lower the hammock. It was swinging so much that the ground staff had difficulty arresting the hammock. The Helicopter team continued to try. Lifted, put some weight, and lowered again. This time, the swinging was even faster and more challenging. The hammock was swinging in all directions. The helicopter was also unsteady. Because of the wind, it had to change its position and could not stay in one position. That made the hammock grabbing by the people on the deck that much more difficult. The helicopter crew almost gave up and called the coast guard to send one of their tugs to transport the patient. They thought they would give it one last try.

They brought the helicopter closer, and one of the men from the helicopter came on board the hammock. The swinging was terrible, but the ground staff could grasp the hammock with an extended hook used for the big heavy curtains in various rooms for entertainment. Four people held the pole to hook the hammock. As they caught the pole, it was pulled off their hands and was almost thrown into the deep sea. The attendant in the hammock was able to grab the pole, preventing it from being thrown into the sea.

The pole and the man in the hammock all started to swing in concert, avoiding the people on the deck to stop the swinging. Finally, after several trials and errors, the helpers on deck were able to grab the hook and prevent the swinging of the hammock.

The man in the hammock, a crew member from the helicopter, was also safely helped to get off the hammock onto the deck.

They quickly put the patient in the hammock. The man who came down happened to be a nurse. He grabbed all support systems and organized the patient in the hammock in a couple of minutes.

Off they went up. The nurse had to stay back for the next trip. Since the weather was so erratic, they were concerned about the lift with two persons in it. The patient and the hammock went in. Within a few seconds, it was lowered again. With some trick, the hammock was hooked, and the nurse was up into it. Hurriedly, the hammock was then rolled up. The nurse was inside the Helicopter, and the door closed instantly. The helicopter rushed back to Las Palmas Military Hospital.

Later, the helicopter pilot was instructed to abort the exercise since the weather worsened. Finally, they were ready to send a heavy tug to ferry the patient. By that time, the proud crew of the helicopter had already landed in the hospital premises.

Later, Sister Thomas told me there was not much damage to our ship, but human suffering was worse than initially thought. Many had cuts and bruises, while some had several deep wounds and fractures. The Doctor, his nurse, Sister Thomas, and the other nurse treated them all. Most of them could wait until the boat arrived in their next port of call, Bathurst, in the Gambia. The only sad exception was one person, who was a hefty individual; he was close to six feet and four inches tall, and about two-hundred and seventy-five pounds in weight with a severe head injury. He was a military general from one of the ship's destination countries. His port of disembarkation was still three weeks away. He slipped and hit his head, becoming unconscious, and soon after, had difficulty with his speech and was paralyzed in the entire right side. He was also incontinent of both urine and bowel. He had hemiplegia due to internal brain hemorrhage. The doctor on board, and his nurse, kept him alive for the first several hours. After that, they got instructions from the patient's government, via Elder Dempster Corporate office, to transfer him to his country by air ambulance as soon as this could be arranged. As the helicopter arrived in Las Palmas, he was transferred to the waiting air ambulance for another five-hour flight instead of twenty-one days of a boat ride.

I hoped he made it through.

I went inside my cabin without any thought, popped in two Avomin tablets, and dropped onto my bed, straight into a deep sleep. I woke up almost twenty-four hours later, the following day at noon, still feeling groggy, tired, very thirsty, hungry, and confused. Where was I? What was I doing here? How did I come to be here? Were we going somewhere? This room and the bed did not look like anywhere I had lived before.

Slowly the veil of confusion started to lift. Sister Thomas stood in front of me and said, "Hello, Sir! Hope you slept well?" I was embarrassed to admit that, indeed, I did not sleep. I was almost semi-comatose.

"I guess you missed the breakfast time," said Sister Thomas. "But let us call your steward to serve your breakfast, if you wish, and whatever else you wish."

She pressed the red button to call the steward. In less than a minute, he was at the door. Sister Thomas spoke to the steward and requested that he serve my breakfast, and she excused herself and promised to look in again later.

Chapter 6

TRANQUIL MARKET IN GAMBIA

"If I have ever seen magic, it has been in Africa "

John Hemingway

We were on our tenth day on board. Today was the fourth day after we were hit by a nasty, heavy tropical storm, short of being caught in a tropical cyclone. It was nasty indeed, but it left many exciting and memorable moments behind. I feel sorry for all the injured and the military general, who had to be airlifted, back to his own country. Otherwise, the memory was thrilling, dangerous, frightening, and full of multiple personal, tragic, and profound eventful moments still haunting me and many others.

The crew, the Captain, the Chief Engineer, and the doctor all admitted that this was one of the worst weather conditions they had to struggle through in decades, because all the helping hands had a rough time with so many injuries and at least one "near death."

This was the tenth day of our fifteen days of sailing to Freetown in Sierra Leone.

The weather was undoubtedly calmer, with minor rocking and rolling. I should have said "pleasant slight rocking. But the memory of the last three days of experience with the tropical storm in the Atlantic, which turned and twisted our ship, scarred our hearts and minds so severely that even the slightest repetition was repulsive. None of us would like to dream of going through the exercise again!

Yet the truth was, rocking was to be a part of our voyage, so we had to get used to it. But I couldn't understand why the engines' growling could be felt, as a constant shivering of the floor. It was not pleasant at all, and this added to the discomfort from the steady rocking of the boat, however minor it may have been.

We were told that there was nothing wrong with the engines. It was very noisy from time to time, but not harmful. We just needed to tame the fear. Yet, some of us needed to be awake and alive too! I felt rather sad at the response from the officers. Maybe it seemed rather insensitive!

On the other hand, this was my first real sea voyage, and it had turned into a nightmare. The officers and other crew members made these trips day in and day out for their living. They have faced all kinds of risks and adventures, emergencies, May Day calls, and point of abandoning the boat during their work. They would know when to panic and when to relax. I gave them the advantage of experience and the ability to read reality.

I tried to play table tennis, snooker, and varieties of board games provided by the management on board. Unfortunately, my range of interest for any of these games was from a few seconds to a few minutes. Unable to keep my mind on the games, it was entirely out of control, with runaway thoughts. My run-away mind could have been put better to positive thinking and productive imagination.

Fortunately, the quiet room also had a library. It had several magazines and teleprinter editions of a few English and American newspapers. In addition, there were small but well-stocked popular books with reasonable collections of African exploration. As a result, I had more time to read and virtually explore Africa more profoundly. Of course, I read and re-read some, but none excited me more than the one on David Livingston's Journey into Deep Africa and the historic meeting between Mr. Henry Morton and Dr. David Livingstone in present-day South Africa. The famous sentence from Mr. Morton to Dr. Livingstone is "Dr. Livingstone, I presume." which has been immortalized since the same voice and vision of shaking hands in the deepest African forest came haunting again and again.

Several books on deep Africa, ancient and newer maps kept me excited and engaged for the entire day. Finally, I was relieved of my giddiness, nauseous feeling, and aching stomach, to some extent. I learned something about Sierra Leone in the British Library, but nothing else. I had no idea what to look for.

Over the overhead tannoy, we were told that we were closing down to our next port of call, Bathurst, the capital of Gambia. I had no idea about the Gambia or where the Gambia was. Why had we stopped? Where is Bathurst, the capital of Gambia? Looking through the collections on the Gambia on board, I learned more about Sierra Leone, Gambia, Bathurst, the rediscovering of Mongo Park, and other courageous explorers. Some dared into impenetrable Africa, on boats, canoes, hammocks, horseback, and even on foot, walking miles and mile through the deep jungle where the sun never shone, all the while dodging ferocious man-eaters, venomous serpents, poisonous insects, toxic trees, and of course, unfriendly and killer tribes.

The Gambia River estuary, where it meets the Atlantic Ocean, was the entry point of many who dared to explore deeper and inner Africa. Aside from Mongo Park, earlier Carthaginian, Hanno the Navigator, Arab intellectual, Ibn Battuta, later, Portuguese captain, Nuno Tristao (1446), Venetian, Luiz de Cadamosto (1455), Genoese, Antoniotto Usodimare (1455), an Englishman, Richard Jobson, all have contributed to discovering the Gambia, the Gambia river and deeper into West Africa. I picked up this information from several books on African Exploration, which I found in the ship's library.

We kept counting the hours to anchor in Bathurst. Finally, the Captain informed us that we would be docking in the Gambia at 6am the following day. There were still fourteen hours to go, but nobody was complaining.

The boat continued to roll with grumbling and gnawing noises. Standing anywhere, you were constantly reminded you were cruising on MV Apapa.

Sister Thomas checked in on me to see if I was well. I couldn't stop admiring the brave, challenging, and dedicated professional services the medical staff provided during the entire hazardous journey, through the angry tropical storm-ravaged boat, carrying six hundred souls to their safety and comfort. I felt that while the ship's doctor and nurse were attending to individual patients, Sister Thomas, aside from assisting the team, scouted the boat for any person who might need medical help. Despite her busy engaging time, she never failed to drop in and make sure I was safe and if I needed any help.

The evening and the night were safe and uneventful. The dining room was full again; the pianist and the harpists were trying to entertain and cheer the passengers up to get out of the previous few days of gloom.

At 5am, the butler knocked at my door. He apologized and said our boat was anchoring in Bathurst, Gambia, our first stop, and if I would like to have some bed tea at this time or sleep it through.

I was interested in observing the process. "Yes!" I said, "May I have some tea and biscuits (a must untold formality that goes with the service of bed tea)." I woke up, washed my face, and changed my pajamas as I got ready for the service. Moments later, the butler appeared with fully-serviced bed tea, not only with biscuits, but varieties of bite-size pastries.

"Enjoy your tea, Sir! Generally, the anchoring process is very smooth but can get a little rough. That should not bother you, I hope." He departed, reminding me to press the red button if I needed anything else.

I came out of my cabin on the gangway. So many activities on the port; cars, trucks, and cranes were all busy on the jetty. People were running around in what appeared to be a business-like and purposeful manner. Noises, as if coming from far away. Remember, this was their fortnightly 'Mailboat,' lifeline of the coastal West African countries. Aside from delivering mail, they provided almost everything the country needed from food, clothes, livestock, and household equipment to vehicles of all sorts, building materials, and most importantly, people, the primary resource of recently independent colonies.

The ship was slowly easing towards the mooring bay and aligning with the anchoring jetty. We could hear the anchors being dropped. Strong and heavy-built workers threw the towing ropes towards the workers in the jetty. At least six thick towing ropes were tied to the poles on the jetty. As soon as the ship was stabilized, one stair was dropped onto the jetty and tied to poles from the gangway. Unfortunately, the gangways were too high for bridging the level of the gangway, and the mooring jetty.

People started to rush out of the ship. They were the passengers disembarking in Bathurst. While the unloading of people and the merchandise was happening, the tower announced that the ship's departure would be delayed by about twelve hours due to some maintenance work. As a result, the ship was expected to set sail the following morning at around 6-7am instead of 6 pm that evening.

Disappointed in the delay, but reassured of our safety for the remaining voyage. Not surprising that it needed serious maintenance work, considering the non-stop battering it went through for almost two days. Concern was raised for the safety of the ship and the rest of the voyage. But the captain, senior officers, and the Chief Engineer all reassured us the boat was in good condition for the rest of the voyage. This maintenance was a precautionary measure and fixed some minor damages caused by the storm. It was better to do it now rather than later.

That was more of an instruction than gathering the pulse of passengers' desire. In this case, we needed to listen and rely on the experts. I felt blessed that we had one extra day of rest.

When all the Gambian passengers were off the ship, the remaining passengers were permitted to go on shore for a walk around or organized trips. We needed to leave our passports with the purser, who would issue an official identity card, which we had to carry with us all the time, for official inspection by any government agency, but never to hand over to anyone. If anyone demanded, we would report to the nearest police station or escort them to the ship's officers.

Busy dockyards, people disembarking, and goods being offloaded. So many other people were poised to embark. I found Sister Thomas standing a few feet away, watching the activities. Suddenly, she turned towards me and said, "This is a long way to climb down on a rope ladder from your level. But I guess you did manage. I was watching you, thought you might need some help to get yourself acquainted with the port and its facilities."

The first thing I could say was, "You know, Sister, for a few blissful moments, I could not believe that I was back on solid ground. But then, I stood steady and fast with no rolling, rocking, grinding noise, and no shaking of the floor. That was the ground surface of the real dockyard. No gnawing sound, except the noise of human activities."

I was back on solid ground, a curious feeling. So calm! No sickness, no vertigo, no sense of being off-balance; I could walk straight, no double vision, and even tango. Such was the difference.

I felt like I was missing the sensation of the floor that was rocking and rolling with monotonous vibrating sound "grrr-rd-rd-rd-rd," possibly coming from the overworked engines. It felt like a different planet altogether as we stood on the ground. At times, I asked myself, why did I accept the job? I could have worked in England or gone back to Calcutta under the umbrella of protection and prosperity provided by Dr. Sen. There was no need to suffer so much. I could have gone back home and had told my mother that I would return in two years. Look what a good boy I was, returning in only two months after I left home for England!

The last ten days on board, especially the last three days of sailing through the notorious tropical storm, just short of being a hurricane, was a memory that would linger for a long time. But, for the time being, we were happy and safe, feeling adventurous and secure again. Visions of Livingstone, Stanley, and Mongo Park all returned with fresh vitality and fiercer imagination.

As we walked along the shops, we observed hawkers, including a very tall turbaned African. Most of them spoke perverted English, which we could follow with difficulty and imagination. Nevertheless, it was possible to converse with the vendors through speech and gestures. For example, I asked Sister Thomas if she spoke Gambian English. She laughed and said, "Sir! We in English-speaking West Africa speak our own English, known as 'Creole,' 'Patua,' or pidgin English, which is a mix of English with local vernaculars, of which there are many.

Chapter 7

CRUISING ON RIVER GAMBIA

"Travelling: it leaves you speechless, then turns you into a story teller"

Ibn Battuta

While we were walking, we passed a small office that belongs to Elder & Dempster Shipping Corporation. On the jetty was moored few 'launches,' which are part of the mail and ferry services for the interior of Gambia, carrying goods, produce, and passengers as well. I went inside the office and befriended one of the officers. He told me all about these boats. Most of them traveled up the river, sometimes for days, stopping at various settlements along the river. I was told Elder-Dempster had trading posts along the riverbank. These boats were also the lifeline of company staff for their provisions and travel along the river to Bathurst, for returning home in Europe or returning from home to start their tour of duties in Bathurst or any other settlements along the riverbanks or the districts or provinces. There were settlements even larger than Bathurst, which were trading, administrative and educational centers for the provincial region.

The first boat would sail to the Brikama area about sixty kilometers away. Brikama city was larger than Bathurst or post-independent Banjul, in both size and population. Sister Thomas was knowledgeable and familiar with the territory, geography, people, and culture. I was pleased to hear from her as we walked along the riverbank, which appeared to be very wide, maybe ten to twenty miles close to its meeting point with the Atlantic. Despite the various boats going up and downstream, the river was very calm. It was still early in the morning, and people had just started to go about their business. It was very different from the noise, activities, people rushing about, and occasional heavy security checking of passersby by the Police, and arresting one or two, pushing them into a police van. The Police van was behind us, going at a snail's pace, watching people and their activities. Hawkers hawking, musing passersby and off the boat visitors. A feeling of 'go-quick-run fast–catch the bird,' otherwise the tell-tale prophecy 'you will miss the boat' and lose the game. I have seen similar activities in the ports of Bombay, Aden, Port Said, Naples, Marseilles, and Gibraltar, on my sea voyage from India to London.

I construed a different imaginary vision of Bathurst. Despite hawkers, hustlers, traders, people running or pushing carts helter-skelter, it was relatively slow-moving. Unloading and loading on and off the ship, people who just disembarked, some still waiting for their luggage, others were waiting for their transport on the road or the river. They all had to go through the immigration, customs, police checks, health checks, etc. That was what Sister Thomas told me.

She suggested that I take a tour of the city or take a boat ride up the river. "If I have the choice, I will take the boat ride up the river, providing we return on time, not to miss the boat, M V Apapa." After about ten minutes, she walked to the E&D office and returned with a big smile. I guessed she would tell me I could take the boat ride.

But she had a triumphant look, "Yes, Sir!" she said. "You can do both the city tour and the river cruise, because the maintenance of MV Apapa will be at least twelve hours, maybe more. So you have plenty of time."

"Well, sister," said I, "Would you like to take the trips with me? After all, I am new to everything." She kept silent. I asked what the prices were. The shipping company would provide their bus and driver for the City of Bathurst tour, courtesy of E&D Company. It was to leave at 10 am and return at 1 pm, just before lunch. The boat trip would cost five pounds and the return from Bathurst to Birkama about thirty-five miles from Bathurst on the southern shore of the River Gambia. It would take about four hours for the return trip.

I was excited to take both. But Sister Thomas looked worried. Then, finally, she said that it was okay for the trip to the town, but not sure if the Ministry of Health in Sierra Leone would approve it. So she went back to the office of Elder Dempster on the port.

She returned in fifteen minutes, happy and smiling. I felt she did win the war. Having discussed with the resident officers and the Captain of the boat, I got permission to go on the river trip, particularly as MV Apapa was disabled and ran twelve hours late. It would cost five pounds. That was a large sum in those days. I did request Sister Thomas to join me on the trip. Sister was hesitant, but I reassured her that the officials at the Crown agent at 4 Mill Bank Street London had paid me enough money for out-of-pocket expenses to cover the journey.

She was embarrassed but relieved and said, "Mr. Bamforth, the Chief Secretary of Sierra Leone will be pleased to learn that someone is keeping an eye out and taking care of you."

"What do you mean, Sister?" I asked.

"Mr. Bamforth, whom you met at the Crown Agent's in London, has special instructions to help and generally be watchful on your voyage. I am sure he would approve of me tagging along with you in the Gambia."

I asked who Mr. Bamforth was.

"He is the Chief Secretary for Sierra Leone Government."

I could clearly remember meeting him twice in London; once at the Crown agent and the second time, at the Bonington Hotel on Southampton Row, in Holborn in London, when he personally came to inform me about my job in Sierra Leone.

Mr. Bamforth is a polite soft-spoken, tall, highly myopic scholarly looking English gentleman. Very respectful, exact, direct, and precise in his expression. He did tell me that he was retired from the Indian Civil Service (ICS) and spent most of the time in the Madras presidency. He was the Chief Secretary of the Madras Presidency before being transferred to Viceroy's office in New Delhi.

I realized he had fond memories of his life in India as a top civil servant. After retirement from the Indian Civil Services, he was posted to Sierra Leone as the Chief Secretary of the Colony and then of the Government of Sierra Leone, as the top bureaucrat. He transitioned the country from being a British Colony to an independent sovereign nation in 1961.

I also realized that his opinion mattered and was of extreme importance. So, again, Sister Thomas was my eye-opener and de-facto tutor, for me to face all adversaries and enjoy many happy moments, even before landing in Sierra Leone.

The bus drove us through the city streets. The City was clean and not heavily trafficked. There were no high rises. Four-story was a high rise, one can see. Along all main roads, there were various types of stores. Many had Indian owners, many owned by Lebanese and Syrians. But, of course, most of the roadside trading was carried out by Africans. Finally, we stopped at Albert Street Market, the main business center in the city, in the country, and perhaps even in this whole region of West Africa.

All the Government houses were painted white, primarily three floors high—impressive entrance with Corinthian pillars to support the entrance and portray the Government's strength. A personalized statement from every brick positioned in the prominent institute's corner. This display of power was not much different in a small country from a much larger one.

We walked through the famous Albert Market, busy with traders on roadsides, pushcarts, and small and big shops. The vegetable market was packed with fresh vegetables, fruits, and mangoes. The fish market was an exhibition to see. Just think or even imagine any seafood, and they had it on display, courtesy of River Gambia and the whole expanse of the eastern Atlantic Ocean. We noticed many fishing trailers and small boats at Bathurst port, away from the liners' berthing area.

Colorful as you can imagine women's clothes to be, and all the women covered their hair with a turban; few covered themselves from head to toe in black clothes. Men were tall and muscular, and mostly wore long white robes with white turbans. Some men had colorful, locally printed clothes. I found that very few men or women in the marketplace were wandering in European clothing or, more suited, in American garments. The climate perhaps did not favor it, or the Gambian culture remained uncontaminated. Mostly British-made cars were on the street. Volkswagen beetles were in abundance. We drove to the eastern edge of the town, where I saw authentic African thatched, conical roofed huts for the first time. Some of the huts were made from palm tree trunks and bark.

It was a fascinating, short, but revealing tour as the first introduction to Africa. Finally, we returned to the Port to start our river cruise. We were disappointed at not being able to taste Mongo Park's Africa, Livingstone's harrowing trek through the deep jungles or the Kalahari, contact with real African natives, his native caretakers, and slaves. Instead, we started our two-hour Gambia River cruise to Birkama and returned with great excitement and exhilaration.

I was overwhelmed with excitement, anticipating Mongo Park's adventures in this river, Prince Rupert's struggle and settlers from Holland in various islands in the river, as well as riverbank trading outposts. But, unfortunately, greed for Gold and ivory masked the documentation of the colonist's actual number of deaths and the extent of the suffering of these pioneers. That was more than three hundred years ago. But Africa is Africa; there has never been a shortage of surprises. Including unanticipated encounters with men or beasts, big or small, illnesses unknown to human beings, unbearable weather, tropical showers, cyclonic storms, scorching sun, insects, fleas, serpents, and amphibians. Aside from forests where the sun never rises and the expanse of arid desert where the sun never sets. Crawling centipedes, fierce quadrupeds, like lions and cheetahs, gentle bipeds, gorillas, people, and many more.

There was no shortage of surprises in Kenya's highlands, where human beings first learned to walk, in the banks of the Nile and the Nile Delta, where the earliest human civilization took root. With all these thoughts in my mind, we boarded the launch, which could take at least fifty people. Although it was just about twenty, most of them were E&D company employees, going about their daily job, or some were returning to their posts in Brikama, at the E&D Office.

Being on hard and stable ground for several hours, I had forgotten the horror of the rocking ship in the Atlantic, which we all endured for three long days. The memories were still fresh. I was concerned about the riverboat trip in a small boat; how would it behave if the weather was unfriendly? We discussed it with the captain, and we were assured of the fine weather and almost absolutely calm and unperturbed flow of the river, even in bad weather.

I was happy realizing that we would be traveling on a river, not on the Ocean. Rough weather in the ocean has a much worse impact than on a river; that is what expert mariners told us. Reassured but not content, I was left with a feeling of wait and see for events to occur. We had to undergo a short training in river safety and self-protection if any unexpected event occurred.

The jetty was close to where MV Apapa was moored. It was in the estuary of the Gambia River. The terminal branches of the river formed a conglomeration of small islands, cutting through the coastal land. River Gambia finally terminates in the northeast Atlantic Ocean after traversing one thousand one hundred and twenty kilometers from the plateau of Fouta Djallon in northern Guinea. Three major rivers of West Africa start from the same plateau; the river Senegal, the River Niger, and of course, the River Gambia.

We were moored at the port of the city of Bathurst, the capital of the Gambia, which was still a British colony. Bathurst conveniently grew at the mouth of River Gambia, in the island of St Mary's, controlling all traffic in and out of Gambia, off the ocean, on the river, or by land. The river was as much as two to three miles wide, slowly, quietly, and peacefully joining the Atlantic. No ferocity, no wildness, no cataracts, no monstrous river beasts. The genteel manner of the river, despite its vast expanse, shattered my vision and imagination of an African river. Busy with traffic on the water or traveling the riverside roads, could not tamper with its tranquility.

Here, I felt the tranquility and immense expanse of the river could engage human beings more than strolling in the Piccadilly, Manhattan, or Champs de Élyseés. The mind races toward giving, not taking.

These were the little chats I had with the veteran Captain who piloted many African riverboats. We chatted with Sister Thomas and the Engineer, Mr. Bodinoch, a French man from Senegal. Everyone had some unique experience to share. Without any question, our little chats enlightened me at the same time. I was a hungry listener, a novice voyageur, a poor narrator, but an engaging company.

Before the boat started to roll, we had some snacks, one of which was fried banana instead of potato chips. There was no shortage of varieties of bananas in India, but this was my debut in tasting fried banana chips. I did not fancy the taste, but later in life, I did get the real taste of these fried banana chips and fell for it. After that, we had a quick and light lunch. My memory of the stormy days onboard the MV Apapa was still vivid and raw. I dreaded having similar feelings again on this river trip, so an empty stomach or light lunch was reassuring.

The boat set sail slowly, eastward. The calm, cool breeze was the company of flowing water in the river. The monotonous sound of the engine was almost hypnotic, but the enormity of the river kept us awake, expecting the unexpected. Noisy streets, people's activity, busy marketplaces, and colonial buildings, with their elegance, slowly began to fade away. We were close to the south side of the river. The north shore was almost invisible because of the width of the river.

We started to see huts with conical roofs, made of straw or leaves of various descriptions. We could see people on the shore with their native attire going about their daily business. Not many were distracted by the noise of the boat. They had gotten used to it, I guess. Moreover, this ship neither stopped nor brought anything for them and their village. So far, we had not seen any strange water dweller nor fish of any kind. Various tropical birds, whose pictures I have seen in the picture books, were sitting on the branches of the riverside trees. The trees were not giant, what we imagined to be of the tropical jungle. The Captain said we were in the western part of the Sahara, known as the Sahel, where vegetation was unlike tropical or equatorial forests, with shorter bushy trees, not as densely grown as tropical Africa. The region was an amalgamation of desert and tropical forests. It was easy to see the movements of birds and small animals roaming around.

We saw the Captain coming towards the coach. What he said was contrary to our experience. He did mention that there were too many crocodiles that day, close to the riverside, which may cause damage to the boat and harm the passengers. We were surprised. None of us could vouch for seeing a single crocodile around the boat. The captain said, "Believe me, I can feel them in every turn of the engine. So, we will sail through the middle of the river away from the crocs."

So, he did. Soon, we saw the floating backs of some ten to twenty feet long, black crocodiles swimming close to the boat. From time to time, we saw them swimming above the water level, just the snout showing. Huge and vicious-looking, some swimming too close to the boat and sometimes trying to grip anything they could on the hull. We were worried that these monsters could tip the boat on its side, along with all the passengers and goods.

There were thousands of crocodiles in that river. They mostly made the banks of the river their resting place. They did follow big or small boats from time to time, fishermen from small boats known to have been attacked and killed by the crocodiles of the Gambia River. Generally, the crocs were the victims at the race with larger boats or ships. We were a mid-sized boat. A race between groups of huge, fierce Gambia River crocodiles with our boat, we hated to imagine the fate of the looser.

For another fifteen minutes, the race went on. Captain kept reassuring us that this was not uncommon in the Gambia River. They would go away. But what kept him wondering was why so many crocs were swimming with the boat. Their movements were not quite rhythmical, but more like a war dance. Captain had seen it all. He went back to the pilot room. We felt that the boat was slowing down and almost came to a stop.

Then we heard the engine revving at double or triple its speed and suddenly reversed back at high speed. We were alarmed minutes before the maneuver and ordered to strap ourselves securely. The boat sped in reverse for about a minute, slowed down, and began to move forward. We saw the river water behind us turn red, very red indeed. Finally, we realized what had happened.

The boat sped forward in super high speed and a 'Boom". We were all stunned at what had happened. However, we did not see any crocodiles floating with us for the rest of our one-and-a-half-hour sailing to the coastal outpost.

Captain sat down with us for afternoon tea. All was quiet and normal. He said we were not allowed to kill the crocodiles, but it was not a crime if we could not save them from accidents. But he indeed saved the boat and all the passengers with his quick-witted maneuver. He did tell us later what a great catastrophe we managed to avoid. More than a dozen of the enormous African river crocodiles were trying to attack the boat with their organized military precision. He had never seen this kind of behavior before, beyond his wits and experience. So many years in African rivers, he saw smaller fishing boats capsized by powerful aquatic animals, mostly crocodiles and rarely hippopotamus up the river. He admitted that Gambian river creatures were generally docile, unlike their counterparts in the river Congo.

That was one hell of an encounter for the experienced Gambia River Captain and sailor.

We stopped at the mouth of a tributary, Kibuni. Our ship moored at the river port of Kibuni. We all got off to take a short bus trip to the city of Brikama.

The road to Brikama, the largest city in Gambia, was paved, tree-lined, but with more bushes than big trees as I envisioned. It was more significant in population, area, human activities, and business houses. Coffee houses of both colonial types and natives lined the side of the leading market area. Several British Banks were seen. Roads were generally wider, cleaner, yet busy with more activities. Some upper-end hotels like Hotel Marlborough etc., were there, although it was an inland town, not far from the Atlantic coast and the banks of the great Gambia River. For trading, the river was the most important avenue of transportation. Much cheaper, cleaner, and without any traffic jam or race to beat the competition. They got you there as promised, but our experience told us a different story. So, they did not promise complete safety against the river monsters of Gambia. There was certainly much less "traffic death," of whatever cause, in the river than on the road.

Roads were well connected from Brikama to other parts of the country. Road travel was fairly competitive because the number of buses was more than needed. Buses were, generally, rapid and comfortable. It was close to one hundred and thirty-seven miles by road to Bathurst, but only thirty-seven miles by boat or other motorized water transportation.

The company coach was comfortable and relaxed, perhaps even air-conditioned.

Brikama was considered the country's intellectual center, as the guide in the coach told us, also considered the birthplace of Gambian politics. The town looked prosperous. Main roads were paved with tar, but side roads were unpaved or "marram" roads.

The city gave me the feeling of a district headquarters in India, which it indeed was. Busy with people going about their daily business, women mainly carrying a basket, a pitcher, or a reasonably sized packing on their head and at the same time, a baby in a baby hammock on their back. Many cyclists, several mopeds, some made in England, some in America, several Volkswagen Beetles, all driven by men alongside the lorries carrying goods. Buses were quickly overtaken to get to their destination. The faster they returned, the faster they could get on with the next trip filled with passengers. Buses also transported goods, materials, poultry, and small animals like goats, pigs, etc., although these were mainly transported on waterways.

That was the pulse of the city center.

It was time to return to the port, assuming our way back to the ship would be pleasant, without any chase, rocking, or stalling, and we would be on time, before dinner.

Our return boat was different from that on which we came. Smaller, but could carry comfortably ten to twelve passengers. Sleek and faster. But we still remembered the crocodile chase on our way to bira from Bathurst. The memory was more frightening than the actual chase. None of us knew of the pursuit nor had the foggiest idea of its danger. We realized we could have fallen into a death trap. The reason the river turned red behind the boat was a riddle until Captain explained what had happened and how he got us out of the nightmare.

The Captain and all of us wondered why so many crocodiles decided to follow our boat as a group. Was it that they just wanted to compete with another speedy monster in a racing game or dance with our craft or anticipated a communal grand feast soon?

We had four crew on this boat; the captain, his mate, and two other helpers. This was a new boat. The officers from the ship, who came with us, stayed behind in Brikama to start their tour of duty in the Gambia. They did speak to us and said their life was in The Gambia. After all, they were British colonist officers; their lifestyle was envied by many in the Gambia throughout the Empire, of all colonial employees. I did not know then, but I do know now.

I am not envious, but I regret that I missed all the fun and wealth they had. Although, I did try hard to imagine the lavish lifestyle they were enjoying.

A company bus drove us to the site of the boat. It took exactly twenty minutes. The boat was ready and we jumped into it. We were welcomed by the Captain, with a reasonable choice of hot and cold drinks and some snacks to go with it.

I did speak to the Captain about our Crocodile chase. He said his friend had already told him about the excitement. But we were not expecting any such thing since, by that time, they were all back to their resting caves by the riverside. He reassured us again and wished us a pleasant and memorable one-and-half hour ride back to Bathurst.

Indeed, it was a delightful late afternoon. The boat was steady, no rocking or swinging. It was still and calm daytime. We could see flocks of birds flying back to their nests with hypnotizing calls of various pitches, monotony, and repetitive performance.

As we disembarked, Sister Thomas just could not help but loudly pray, "Thank you, God, for bringing us back to the ship, happy and unharmed, so that I can let Mr. Bamforth know that we are all safely back on the boat and on our way to Freetown."

She indeed looked relieved. I had no idea how concerned she was for this short boat trip in the River Gambia, an unknown territory, even to her, being a native West African, and for the new doctor, who was yet to join the government.

When I left Bombay, I had not heard of Sierra Leone. It was a chance meeting with Mr. Bamforth, the Chief Secretary of the Government of Sierra Leone, at the Crown Agent's office in No 4, Mill Bank, and London, which brought me to Sierra Leone. But the most impressive bureaucratic gesture was that the Government of Sierra Leone started my tour of duty as a medical officer from the day I left Bombay, just about six weeks before I began my work in Freetown. That was the beauty of being a colonial officer under British rule. I was a serving colonial officer on paper, which may have prompted Sister Thomas to be extra cautious. But that was just a tiny part of the puzzle, which was not even known to her.

We boarded MV Apapa, remembering the exciting day. We returned to our respective cabins, got ready, and attired for dinner. Knowing that the ship was not leaving for another six to eight hours, we had a leisurely dinner. The pianist and the harpist were back in their place. They started with soft, pleasant music to entertain the diners. I saw several new faces, who must have been new passengers sailing with us to other parts of West Africa.

The Captain arrived with his dining companions. He looked happy and in a pleasant mood. As we were all about to take our seats, he announced, "Guests, I have excellent news, after the three days of mortal dance with the weather, we all deserve something to cheer us up. I am glad to announce that the ship's maintenance work was significant, which involved setting up a new engine and multiple other small but important repair works that needed to be done; all have been satisfactorily completed. Our Chief Engineer and his staff have worked nonstop for the last forty-eight hours to see it through. The Company has flown in one of their senior superintending Engineers for his assistants to assess the complete seaworthiness of the ship. And we have passed with flying colors," he said, "so we will be able to sail before dawn, much ahead of our previous estimate."

Most of us had no idea how battered the ship was, and at one point, the question to call "Mayday" was also considered. We had been repeatedly warned, advised, and commanded to stick to all safety rules and watch our surroundings including any fellow passengers in trouble.

In reality, most passengers were so sick, except for Sister Thomas and her two companions, who were confined to their beds and likely safe. Sister Thomas and some staff from the ship visited each passenger during the rough times. We all wondered how she and her companions were unaffected, walking straight and continuing to help others.

The following two days were a smooth ride, which rarely happened on Atlantic voyages. The ocean was calm, with no wind, except a pleasant sea breeze, clear sunny skies, beautiful moonlit nights, and the occasional passing of fishing boats. The boat was so smooth; it felt like gliding on a silky ocean, no rocking, no tilting, no vibrating and thudding noises. The vibration was so uncomfortable that it was painful to stand in one spot for any time, with or without one's shoes.

This uncomfortable vibration and noise were from the damaged engine, which had been replaced. No wonder the noise and vibration we felt had gone. Now, it appeared peaceful, 'Heaven.' Unfortunately or fortunately, we were led to believe that the noise and vibration were normal but exacerbated by the storm and wind. Maybe the ship's engineer and crew were just as in the dark as we were.

The last three days' memory of the horror slowly began to leave us, fading away to tranquility and a peaceful voyage.

We were now on our way to the next stop, Freetown, Sierra Leone, my destination, for which I had been eagerly and anxiously waiting with a strange mixture of fear and, at the same time, joy of curiosity and anticipation.

Chapter 8

THE INTRODUCTION IN FREETOWN

"Out of suffering have emerged the strongest soul. The most massive characters are seared with scars"

Gibran Khalil Gibran

After three nights and two days of peaceful and tranquil voyage from Bathurst along the western coast of West Africa, passing by the shores of Senegal, Guinea Bissau, Guinea (French), we arrived before dawn in the darkness of early morning at Queen Elizabeth II Quay in Freetown, otherwise known as the port in Cline Town. I was fast asleep. At 4am my butler knocked at my cabin door to wake me up. I was half-awake anyway. Although the berthing process did cause some noise and jolting, it started and was over before I woke up.

As usual, the Butler returned quickly with bed tea and British biscuits to give me a push to wake up and get up. It reminded me that I had arrived in Freetown, the Capital city of Sierra Leone, after almost seventeen days of, mildly said, fretful voyage, fighting with the Atlantic Cyclone.

I looked through the portholes; it was dark even on the port side, with little movement or activity.

"We just arrived," reminded my butler, "You may take your time to get yourself ready for disembarking. The breakfast will be at 7am. You are expected to disembark by 10am. The ship will leave again for its next destination, Accra in Ghana, at around six in the evening."

After so many anxious days filled with physical and mental stress, excitement, and anticipation for the unknown, the bed tea put me to sleep again with a feeling of relief and relaxation.

I fell asleep until another gentle knock at my cabin door woke me up again.

I thought it was the butler again, returning with some more pleasantries and another pot of fresh tea to see me up and about.

I said, "Come in, please, come in."

I was still in my pajamas and was not expecting any visitor at that unearthly hour. We were trying to catch a few extra hours of sleep, which we lost during the voyage. It was still very dark outside when the door opened. I could hear a deep human voice saying, "Good morning; Dr. Malaker, I presume?" (Maybe he did say, maybe he did not, I just heard it loud and clear, perhaps it was the personification of my imagination).

Africa – Dark Continent – explorers – dangerous life and living- frightful, yet full of the courage, strength, and, most importantly, Stanly Morton's famous sentence of greeting, "Dr. Livingstone, I presume."

It was just not the short phrase of greetings of the first meeting of two remarkable personalities, the circumstances they met, the events that led them to the greeting, the inhospitable dense forests where the sun never rises, the dangerous environment, the man-eaters, the head hunters, mauling Lions, gouging and huge "tusked- (Elephants)," the land crocs, crushing Pythons and not least, the killer mosquitos. Those who brought Malaria, which killed millions. All came with it once you imagine the famous phrase of the first greeting and meeting of two great African explorers.

The picture has been in my imagination from the time I was first asked by Mr. Bamforth, at the exquisite and opulent office of the Crown Agents in the heart of the seat of power of the British Crown, if I would like to come to Sierra Leone, in West Africa. I did shake hands with Mr. Bamforth. My mind immediately raced to the jungle of Botswana, where the famous handshake took place and the famous phrase– "I presume…." was born.

I was sure in my imagination that the voice at the door indeed said, "Good morning, I presume it is Dr. Malaker?"

The door opened. It was the voice again. I could not see anyone; maybe it was a dream. But suddenly, when the voice at the door said again, "Welcome to Sierra Leone," with a big smile, I could clearly see his set of white dazzling teeth. There was no person yet but the deep, soft voice in a pure English accent again. The room was dark, but the outside was even darker. I felt a little out of step, not clearly knowing whether I was awake or dreaming of the famous encounter, which played in my imagination in Crown Agent's palace. Again and again since.

Again, the voice said, "It is dark here; let us get some light." Someone switched on the cabin lights, most likely the voice. Standing in front of me inside the cabin was a gentleman who had to bend his head to stand inside the cabin. He was probably six feet three to four inches tall. A well-dressed, smart African gentleman introduced himself as Dr. Boardman, the country's Chief Medical Officer. He just dropped by to check if I needed any assistance with paperwork and whether I arrived well and intact. He had, of course, heard of our rough ride in the Atlantic on our way to Sierra Leone from Liverpool.

His complexion was so well balanced with the absolute darkness, in and outside the cabin, only his shining teeth and the glittering eyeballs brought some contrast to identify his presence in the dark.

I was amazed but highly pleased to see Dr. Boardman, the CMO, coming to check on my wellbeing right onboard and in my cabin. Soon after, Sister Thomas appeared. They both exchanged greetings and spoke in local vernacular; later, I gathered that Creole was a broken English spiced by regional, Mende, Temne, and some other languages.

They spoke and plotted for a few minutes. While Dr. Boardman was speaking to Sister Thomas, one phrase stuck in my mind, but looking at me said 'e-na-Pekin' the word 'Pekin' came a few times, while sister Thomas was smiling, looking at me. I realized; they were saying something about me. I thought, if it was essential, they would relate to me. There was no language barrier since they spoke excellent English without any accent.

Dr. Boardman appeared to be happy seeing me arrive. "The boat will be in the port till the evening; you can take your time to disembark. The ministry transport will come to the port to pick you up between 10 and 11 am. They will inform you when they arrive to take you to the Government Guesthouse. Sister Thomas has volunteered to stick around to see you disembark and transfer to the Government Guesthouse in Freetown, where most of the crown officers are lodged on their arrival or in transit. I will meet you on Monday around 10 am at the Ministry of Health, when we can discuss your plans and program," Dr. Boardman said.

He departed. I had difficulty shaking hands. I could grab only three fingers, and the rest were out of my reach.

Chapter 9

AT THE GOVERNMENT GUESTHOUSE

"Falling down is not failure. Failure comes when you stay where you have fallen"

Socrates

After Dr. Boardman left, I lazed on my bed for a while, dreaming the impossible, thinking of the unthinkable yet with great expectation of exciting work as a doctor and the life that came with it in a completely unfamiliar environment.

I had just been qualified as a physician in Calcutta and used to live in a dormitory for junior doctors or a shared room or, if lucky, got a separate cubicle for privacy and personal activities and expected to study for postgraduate works. Fortunately, I was one of the lucky ones to have a private cubicle. I guess it was a favor, being close to the Director, Prof Amiya Sen, my dad's med school buddy. But, more importantly, my engagement in various academic activities, including initiating the first Cancer journal in the country, under Prof Sen's editorship played a significant part. It had been a hard uphill battle, with regulatory bodies financing the project, but jealousy and silent non-cooperation from senior colleagues could not deter the project. However, the tremendous support from Prof Sen and my stubborn energy and desire withered all oppositions.

There was no match from the dorm to the Donjon (Fort with Moat), a quantum x (quantum) leap; -if an expression exists to express the change in my lifestyle, from being a "just promoted Registrar" to a senior crown colonial official. Astounding at every corner and every step, up or down.

By 10.30am, I was packed and ready to leave the boat. Sister Thomas came with two gentlemen, one in uniform.

Happily, the sister said, "If you are ready to leave, these two gentlemen will help you with your heavy luggage." Mostly books, papers, my "pink portable typewriter," clothes, and personal utilities.

Slowly and carefully, we came down the gangway. The exit gate was bridged with the berthing jetty. It was easy disembarkation than the flexible rope ladders, which I had to use to embark on P&O's MV Ariana in Bombay. There were lots of activities. Remember, this is a mail boat, the country's lifeline, not only for fetching mails, but food, livestock, cars, trucks, buses, bikes, mopeds, small and heavy pieces of machinery, trading commodities, and most importantly, its passengers from laborers to lords and ladies. Some were coming in, and others were going out.

Freetown seaport was the most significant natural harbor in the entire West Africa at that time. I believe it still is, serviced not only Sierra Leone, its hinterland, but also neighboring countries as their life support.

As we walked past the quay, offices, and shops, Sister Thomas was greeted and welcomed by scores of men and women, which appeared to be a hero's homecoming jubilation. I was interested in watching her popularity and reception by many people who happened to be there. If not powerful, a popular lady indeed. I was not surprised, watching her tireless leadership and helping all passengers and overworked medical staff on board during the severe tropical storm. Her exceptional attention to my safety, comfort, and easy transition from Liverpool to the Government Guesthouse in Freetown in Sierra Leone, was also memorable.

I was expecting a minivan or a taxi or one of the Ministry of Health's official transporter to drive me to the guest house. Instead, the uniformed gentleman stopped near a luxury large sedan car of cream silvery color. He opened the back seat door for me. I asked Sister Thomas if she wished to come with me. She looked slightly perplexed. I understood from the escort that none of the Health Department's courtesy vehicles were available to pick me up, so CMO sent his car with his official driver to pick me up and drop me at the Government guesthouse. Sister Thomas also decided to accompany us. I asked her to sit with me in the back seat. She excused herself and sat in front, beside the driver in the passenger's seat.

As we settled down in the car, I could only admire the vehicle's luxurious interior.

I asked the driver, "What make is the car?"

It was not a Rolls Royce but a Bentley, the most cherished car of British medical consultants. Expensive and highly prestigious, only second to Rolls Royce on the scale of prestige and measurement of social standing.

Aside from my first introduction to a chauffeur-driven Bentley, a vehicle suited only for the royalty, I was humiliated by the respect and level of genuine intimate reception I received from the CMO and Sister Thomas, which remains with me even for half a century after I left Sierra Leone.

The car rolled out of the protected quay VIP parking area. CMO's car was well known to the officers, and we indeed received a royal exit. Slowly with elegance, the car started to roll forward. We took a hillside road connecting Cline Town to Queen Elizabeth II Quay to the city center of Freetown. We drove along the hillside, well-maintained tar road. The rising hill, covered by dense tropical jungle to our left, was my first impression of Freetown. However, we saw several Orange, Star fruit, and Mango trees along the side of the road, merging with other bushes on the slope of the hill. On the other side of the road, same vegetation, but looking through the bushes and over the trees on the downward incline of the hillside, the large stretch of the Port and almost endless white sandy beaches, several of them appeared to be in the estuary of a river, draining into the sea. Again, a beautiful hillside road, going to the city center.

After a forty-five minute drive, we arrived at the main entrance to the Government rest house. Next, we drove to the reception and club area.

I was checked into a single suite, A303. It was a classy "bedsitter." The building had five accommodations like mine, best suited to a single person.

Sister Thomas and the two people from the Bentley helped me with my luggage into my room. The driver said that either he or another colleague from the ministry would report at the reception at 9.45 am to be at the Ministry by 10 am for my appointment with the CMO.

A nicely decorated, elegantly furnished, and equipped, studio-type accommodation made the guest comfortable and happy. I could see the stretches of empty beach beyond the foothills of the guesthouse compound. A barrier of dense forest with bright red flowers in big trees separated the beach and the lower outer boundary of the Government guest house campus. The entire campus was built on the slope of the hill, midway between the peak and the foothills. There were ten to twelve buildings, each containing four to five apartments. A few detached individual cottages were also there. The reception and the clubhouse were built at the center of the campus so that distances from the single and attached cottages were all likely to be more or less equal. Tennis courts, Badminton courts, and squash courts were also built around the central facilities. Aside from these outdoor games, there was plenty of indoor entertainment. A small library or smoking room, table tennis, billiards, and several other board games were also offered. An attendant was posted for any assistance or felicitation. A covered semi-indoor swimming pool was also made available outside the clubhouse for the guest and their family.

After arriving in my room, I was so tired. I fell asleep before I knew it. At around 7.30 in the evening, a waiter from the reception woke me up to remind me that the dinner started at 8.30 pm if I wished to dine at the guesthouse tonight. He also checked if my telephone was correctly placed. He told me they could not get me from the reception on my extension, so he was dispatched to check up on me. I thanked the waiter and said I would be at the restaurant by 8.30 pm.

The telephone was off the hook; maybe I did it accidentally. That had been corrected. That was not difficult to fix. Even I could do it.

I had to dress up for dinner. In fact, any time I wished to use the restaurant, there was a dress code for each occasion. I did not mind. I did for the discipline and formalities as required. Fortunately, or regrettably, I have maintained the same level of practice till today, if it is practical.

Maintaining the dress code for any occasion had been routine for my stay at the Government Guesthouse in Freetown.

The bar remained busy from lunchtime onwards. It was a lunch break meeting place for residents, their guests, and visitors as well. It was a place to meet socially, and a meeting place for business. I met high-level Government Officials, Foreign Embassy staff, Business leaders, Academicians, Politicians, and people from various walks of life, those who assembled at the reception court and loved the services and environment.

There was a mini ballroom, which was regularly used on Friday and Saturday nights. Frequently, that was a venue for meetings and conferences. The staff were quite proficient in converting a ballroom to a conference center and vice versa.

There was piped music, creating a very romantic atmosphere. In the evenings, there was live music, playing frequently, romantic, classical, popular film music from Hollywood, country music, Jazz, etc. Those were the early 60s; no rock-and-roll, reggae, hip-hop, or disco was on the entertainment menu.

During my first three months stay at the Government Guesthouse, I met people from different countries, different professions, different life outlooks, and from different walks of life. Sierra Leone and nationals of other countries of different races, religions, cultures, languages, and varied personalities were sometimes easy to get along with, and sometimes an impossible exercise or an impossible dream.

But I kept dreaming of individuals, groups, cultures, nations, foods they eat, clothes they wore, the air they breathed, and families they reared; how that would affect me, I wondered. This was a very new environment, new socio-cultural impact, education, and confusion just as intriguing.

Chapter 10
AT THE MINISTRY OF HEALTH

"I speak and speak [...], but the listener retains only the words he is expecting {....}. It is not the voice that commands the story: It is the ears.

Marco Polo.

The following morning, I got a phone call from a lady from the Sierra Leone Government Ministry of Health, reminding me of my appointment with the Chief Medical Officer at 10.30 am. A ministry transport would pick me up from the Guesthouse reception lobby.

I was ready for the transport waiting in the lobby. A uniformed chauffeur approached me, introduced himself, and directed me to the car. There was another passenger, a young black lady. We exchanged greetings. She was a nurse from the USA who came to help reduce infant mortality during labor. That was her specific assignment, and she was expected to spend one year in Sierra Leone. This was her second visit. I admitted that this was my very first job outside India.

During my voyage and contacts with Black African people from Africa, she had no resemblance to black Africans except her color, which was also not as black as Africans. Whatever I had seen so far of her, she was not Black African. She was Black American. I did learn much more with time spent in West Africa about the difference between the two.

Ministry of Health did look like a bureaucratic mansion, a double-story wooden building. We walked the corridor into departmental divisions, passing a few rows of cubicles, and came to a reasonably sized waiting room, moderately furnished. A lady walked towards me from her desk. She introduced herself as Miss Croaker, CMO's receptionist. I made sure that I had indeed come to see Dr. Boardman, the Chief Medical Officer.

She said yes, the CMO would see me soon, and she proceeded to offer me a seat on one of the chairs. Finally, the driver left, wishing me a good day and good luck.

After five minutes, CMO came out of his office, the same, close to seven feet tall, dark, athletic, smart, and very polite, polished gentleman. He greeted me and invited me into his office.

I was wondering about the reception and his office that was of a high-ranking colonial professional bureaucrat. The country just got its independence. The colonial vibe left by Brit rulers and the ambiance were everywhere. Except that the tables had been turned. The ones being ruled were the rulers now, sitting on the Northside (semantic) of the table.

We entered a large room with a high ceiling. Strange, I could see an old-fashioned "Pankha (a manual overhead fan pulled back and forth by a person called Pankha -puller" hanging close to the ceiling. The Pankha puller's rope extended to the back wall attached to the fan and a pulley in a small opening high up in the back wall of the 'manual fan.'

Interestingly, there were a few ceiling fans and a few others on the floor. They were all working to keep the room cool.

On the sizeable leather-topped mahogany table, stacks of manila files in several rows along one edge of the enormous table, and on the other side, three trays labeled as "Urgent," "In," and "Out." Although I could see a few files in the "Urgent tray," the "In tray" had the highest stack of files, appearing almost ten times higher than the 'Out' files.

On the right-hand side, there were three phones, one red and the other two black. The table was large. The phones were quite a distance from his chair. I would have to climb up the desk to reach any of the phones. But Dr. Boardman, a tall person with long arms, had no difficulty reaching the furthest. The "red phone" was used only for emergencies and to speak to the Minister of Health, Prime Minister, governor-general, national emergencies, etc.

There were several bookcases against the walls.

The books inside the highly ornate wooden bookcases against one side wall and part of the wall behind CMO's desk were his personal collection and other official reports and documents. One set did not escape my curiosity; *the complete works of William Shakespeare*, a leather-bound copy of *Gray's Anatomy*, and the other was William Osler's *Textbook of Medicine*. At least five hundred or more books were in his office collection, he confided to me in one of his nostalgic moments.

Several beautiful African wood-crafted statues, figurines, animals, birds, and flower vases were placed in strategically selected offices for his visitors to appreciate the beauty of art and African craftsmanship. But, to my utter surprise, I noticed a bronze statue of a sitting Buddha at one corner on a pedestal, about one and a half feet tall. He later told me that this was a gift from one surgeon from India, being seconded by the Indian Government. The Surgeon discussed Buddha and Buddhism from time to time, which was how he became familiar with Buddha and eventually fell in love with Buddha and Buddhism, yet stayed a devout Roman Catholic for the rest of his life.

He offered me a chair on the opposite side of the table across from him.

He asked me quietly how I would like my tea. It was a very English Colonial gesture of sophistication, be it office or home.

I was overwhelmed by the gesture. It was impressed with the British colonial legacy and the degree of social sophistication it infused in certain sections of its colonial subjects.

Dr. Boardman officially welcomed me as an officer of the "Crown" and said to rest after a long, somewhat arduous, and frightening sea voyage from Liverpool to Freetown.

He said, "Try to get to know the country, the system, people, and colleagues you will be working with. Then, you will stay in Freetown for professional orientation and acclimatization to the social and working environment."

He mentioned Dr. Boyel-Hebron, the Deputy CMO, Dr. Abouko Cole, the Medical Director of Connaught Hospital, the main National Tertiary Care Hospital, particularly requested one of my countrymen, Dr. Dhakutta, to help me settle.

As he was leaving, he said he would personally inform Mr. Bamforth, the Chief Secretary, about my safe arrival and his plan for my engagement.

I realized then that Mr. Bamforth, whom I met by accident at 4 Mill Bank, Office of the Crown agent, Ex Indian Civil Service Officer, initiated my appointment with the Ministry of Health, Government of Sierra Leone. Mr. Bamforth was the Permanent Secretary of Sierra Leone at that time. The top civil servant.

No wonder the reason for the extra welcoming gesture. But most of the people I came across later were all gentlemen; polished, humble, and helpful.

After about a half-hour, the CMO had to leave and asked his personal secretary to arrange my return to the "Government Guesthouse."

As I was waiting in the waiting room, someone suddenly tapped on my shoulder. I was not expecting to be so close. I looked back. An Indian gentleman introduced himself as Dr. Guhathakurta, the senior Medical Specialist at the Ministry of Health, who worked out of the Connaught Hospital. CMO informed him about my arrival and wanted him to help me.

He said he would take me back to the Guesthouse if I had finished with the Ministry's business.

I said, "Let us make sure with the CMO's secretary that I have completed all I am needed to do."

Dr. Thakuta knocked at her office door and went in. In a few minutes, both returned. Secretary, Mrs. Wilson, had a form for my signature.

"Doctor!" She said, "There are few formalities to go through. Those can wait for a few days, but this is to confirm your arrival in Sierra Leone and at the Ministry of Health. After that, we can ask the finance department to start processing your salary and other dues, or if you require any funds in advance. We are making arrangements to complete your contract, India as your country of origin for recruitment purposes."

So, I signed on the dotted line and thanked her.

Dr. Thakuta (Bidyut Guha Thakurta) asked me to follow him to his parked car outside the Ministry building.

His white Fiat 1100 remained a permanent fixture in my daily life, integral for the first month in Freetown.

As we sat down in the car, we exchanged information about our medical education, aspirations, and my decision to come to Sierra Leone, as well as our families, and our professional circle.

As we talked about our common friends, we discovered that one of my cousins was his classmate at the Calcutta Medical College in Calcutta, and was the brightest star in the class with aiming for the sky. So, they both decided to explore Africa after their specialist examination. So, Dr. Guha Thakurta came to Sierra Leone and my cousin to Ghana. They had been in close contact since and checking up on each other.

That was also the beginning of a lifelong friendship until Dr. Thakuta succumbed to an untimely death at the tender age of only fifty years, leaving behind his only daughter and his widow.

He asked if I had any important business at the Government Guesthouse; if not, he would take me to his home to have lunch with his family.

I had none, so we headed to his house. Mrs. Guha Thakurta was expecting us. She was friendly, and happy, with a bubbly personality. Within ten minutes of my arrival, with glasses of fruit punch, I had given her all my life's story and why I was in Sierra Leone.

They had a beautiful well-furnished two-story apartment overlooking the Atlantic Ocean, far beyond the low hills, separating the housing community and the beach. Since the house was built just slightly above the rising foothills on the opposite side across the main thoroughfare, the view of the sea was unhindered by the parting vegetation.

From his house, one could see both sunrise and sunset in the Atlantic Ocean.

After almost two months, for the first time, I had home-cooked Bengali dishes, which I devoured hungrily.

After lunch, he dropped me at the guest house and rushed back to start his afternoon clinic at Connaught hospital, promising that his driver would pick me up the following morning to get introduced to the administration of Connaught Hospital. But, instead, Dr. Thakuta was advised by the Chief Medical officer to usher me around.

Chapter 11

MY FIRST DAY AT CONNAUGHT HOSPITAL

"For those who exalts themselves will be humbled, and those who humble themselves will be exalted"

Mathew 23:12

As arranged, the following day, Dr. Thakuta's (as he was known in Sierra Leone) driver came to pick me up at 9.15 am. We then returned to his house to pick him up to go to the hospital together.

It was about half an hour's drive. The road was winding along the foothills of the mountain. Most of the time, the entire city of Freetown was visible from the high road to the city.

While driving, he asked me how I knew Mr. Bamforth, the country's Chief Secretary, the top bureaucrat. I was surprised and caught off guard. But, I did say, I did not know Mr. Bamforth, until a chance meeting at the Crown Agent's office, on 4 Mill Bank in London. I told him; it was Mr. Bamforth who secured my job in Sierra Leone.

I was supposed to meet him at the Health Ministry building after I had finished with the CMO, but he had to attend a special meeting with members of the Cabinet.

We passed several fenced or walled houses. For example, he pointed out the Embassies, Consulates, Housing for senior government officials, and several fenced houses. Most of them had large, covered carports in front of large colonial-style colonnaded verandas, and large ornate main entrance gates to the buildings.

We turned to the main city center, past the famous "hundreds of-years-old Cotton tree." As the story goes, this was the tree under which the black slaves from Britain and North America were liberated from their bondage of slavery and let to settle and live like any free individual of the entire British Empire. Thus, the settlement's name became "Freetown," eventually the capital of the recently independent nation of "Sierra Leone."

We will speak more about Freetown and Sierra Leone in the hump of West Africa along its Atlantic coastline; soon, in the chapters to follow.

We entered Wilberforce Street, passed the city's only four-five-star hotel, the Paramount hotel. Soon after, we arrived at the entrance of Connaught Hospital. The guard gave an attentive salute to Dr. Thakuta (in the rest of the text, for the sake of brevity, I will refer him as "Dr. Thakuta," as the locals' preference instead of Dr. GuhaThakurta) and let the driver inside the hospital premises, close to his office.

The driver dropped us and returned to Dr. Thakuta's house to drive Mrs. Thakuta around the city to attend to some of her chores.

His nurse quickly briefed him of the day's scheduled activities as he entered.

She was introduced to me and walked me to the office of the Hospital Medical Director, Dr. Abouco Cole. A slightly overweight gentleman got up from his chair, greeted me near the door, and steered me to his desk. He requested that both of us take a seat. Next, a uniformed bearer appeared with water and cups of tea in trays for both of us.

Dr. Abouko-Cole said he expected us, having had a call from CMO. Dr. Thakuta left with the understanding that when Dr. Cole finished with me, he would come to pick me up for my next appointment at the Ministry.

Dr. Cole took me to various sections of the Hospital, including the administration, pathology, radiology, operating rooms, the Intensive Care facility, and the Accident and Emergency department. I guess the staff was all smartly attired, mostly in white and some with different colors because of their job descriptions. However, everyone was polite and expected to work with me in the future. They wished me well and welcomed me in Connaught Hospital as a "Doctor."

I was overwhelmed with the friendly, welcoming gesture.

Then we walked back to Dr. Thakuta's office. They said I would be working with Dr. Thakuta as a Medical Officer in the Department of Medicine for the next two weeks.

This would be part of my orientation and gentle introduction to the African practice of medicine. The plan was to rotate with various consultants for six to eight weeks, and then I would be posted as a District Medical Officer, as the system required, somewhere in the country.

I was ignorant about the system, yet looking for adventure and challenge in the so-called "Dark Continent," as our geography teachers taught us in school. We grew up with the same notion, until luck and circumstances allowed me see how dark it was on the scale of darkness, if there was even one.

Dr. Thakuta picked me up from my residence daily at 9 am for the next two weeks and drove me back to his house for lunch and back by 2.30 pm; apparently, that was my entire workday. Except when I was on call, I had to be available to attend all emergencies and admissions in the medical unit.

What a different workday compared to my hometown. Housemen and registrars come at 7.30 in the morning and see all the ward patients with ward sister in preparation for the Consultant's ward round. Then the consultant's round starts around 9.30 am and could continue till 1 in the afternoon.

After a short lunch break, we returned to the ward to update instructions from the consultant's round, arrange tests, cross consultations, and discuss with the doctors about the cross-referrals. By then, it was already 5 pm. Or, if the consultant had an outpatient clinic, join him to help and learn. That took us to 5 pm for the afternoon tea break.

We return to the ward again by 7 pm for the evening rounds, which sometimes went on till midnight if there were many new cases for admission.

That was the life of a house man or registrar in Calcutta National Cancer Center at that time.

No mandatory weekend off. We were told that this rigorous routine was an essential part of post-qualification training.

That was the way it had been. Nobody complained or expressed any dissatisfaction. Hospitals, wards, patients, consultants, and the nursing staff were our world, where we worked, slept, lived, ate, sometimes fell in love or spent our rare break in the library or catching up with lost sleep or calling family and friends.

Chapter 12
WALKING THE WARDS

"And so I tell you, keep on asking, and you will receive what you ask for; keep on seeking, and you will find, keep on knocking and the door will be opened to you. For every one who asks receives. Everyone who seeks, finds. And to everyone who knocks, the door will be opened.

Jesus Christ, Luke 11:9-10

As a junior doctor at Connaught Hospital, Freetown, my day started at 9 am and finished by 2 pm, unless I was on-call once every two weeks or every month for the weekend coverage.

I must admit, my serious attention to taking down details of patients' history and documenting them in an orderly fashion frequently with added sketches and diagrams (my particular interest) had certainly matured, enhanced, and became one of my clinical passions. This grew while I was working as a medical officer at Connaught hospital in the medical wards, under the guidance and mentorship of Dr. Thakuta and the Head of Internal Medicine division, Dr. Metzger. Dr. Metzger was an elderly, sharp-tongued, uncompromising perfectionist. Despite being an excellent clinician, disciplinarian, and caring physician, colleagues and medical officers preferred spending as little time as possible with him. As for myself, I was focused on fixing my mistakes, omissions, and undue commissions roughed on me by Dr. Metzger. I accepted the perceived abuse grudgingly, with a smile. I knew that by the end of all the abuses, my clinical documentation of the patient's history and physical examinations would be envied by my co-medical officers. However, he did not forget to complain to Dr. Thakuta about my inadequacy in documenting clinical notes and that of the patient's Clinical History, as well as detailed physical examination. He thought that Dr. Thakuta was my older brother because we were both brown Indians. He thought it would be quite to get a "spanking" from him for not performing well in the medical ward, where Dr. Thakurta was a senior specialist!

On the other hand, working with Dr. Thakurta had always been a pleasure. He had a kind and smiling face, yet serious enough not to forget that he was the Senior Specialist consultant. He was popular amongst other specialists, medical officers, and nursing staff. He was an excellent and competent physician of a very high caliber. Professionally, he established his reputation amongst the higher authorities in the country. He was an attending Physician of the Governor-General, the Prime minister, other powerful politicians, ambassadors, and company Directors. Sierra Leone had several diamond mines, gold mines, large European construction companies, and several international treading companies. They all depended on him during their sickness. He was a permanent guest of these "powers" during their happiness, throwing parties and important state receptions. Doing ward rounds with him had been a pleasure. He would sit down, discuss the cases, their management plan, and ensure my history and physical examination were adequately documented. He appreciated my competence in detecting clinical findings, which he admitted, at times he missed which did not escape the drum of my stethoscope or, for that matter, the "mallet of my hammer."

He would spend hours in the afternoon clinic seeing patients with me and making me write patients' histories and physical examinations findings, discuss with me, in a collegial manner, the importance of accurate documentation of patients' medical history and clinical findings.

One day, as we finished our clinic and had our afternoon tea, he was as if talking to himself, "I do not see anything that is a "problem." On the contrary, your clinical examination findings are impressive. The only problem is now you need to write what you see, ask, and hear and feel as you examine your patients."

The "Old man" wanted everything written down in an orderly fashion, in a way he was taught in his undergraduate medical school in New Castle. Dr. Thakuta said it was a good habit and a good practice.

Then I realized "The Old man" must be talking to him. The Old man was obviously Dr. Metzgar.

I should be upset. But, in fact, I was not. So, instead, I started to pay more attention to writing and documenting along with sketches, where I found it suitable to give a more descriptive understanding of the illness.

I was grateful. That "kick" was an excellent incentive for writing not only the "history and physical "of patients, but writing in general, which I felt passionate about; writing what I see, what I feel, what I imagine, and what I dream and more.

History and Geography were my favorite subjects. I used to get excited about kings, princesses, wars, rivers, oceans, mountains, jungles, expeditions, and all those, in school. My history and geography teachers made me stand in front of the entire class and talk. I felt good that I was asked to do that. I did well in the tests and for the pleasure of my teachers.

One day, unknown to any of us, our history teacher was not in the class. So our Headmaster decided to take the class. He was a perfect Anglicized aristocratic, highly educated, soft-spoken gentleman.

No one was expecting him. Instead, we saw him just passing by for his periodical inspection of classes from time to time. He was highly respected in the country as a pioneer educationist.

We were all numb. He asked if all was well and asked me what the subject of the last class was. I knew and told him. That was the first and the last time I could answer any question he asked me. I was numb, and so was the entire class. The boys were expecting me to answer all his questions. Generally, my hand used to be up on a typical day, even before the teacher completed his questions.

That day, I fumbled, stayed numb, with a vacant look and somewhat surprising reaction from the headmaster, known as "Rai Bahadoor," a title bestowed by the British, close enough to British "Sir." He would usually smile, answer clearly, and discuss history with us as friends. Then, he quietly left as the bell rang, announcing that the period was over to alleviate everyone's anxiety.

We all breathed a sigh of relief.

The next day, our history teacher came. He did not look at me, nor for that matter, anyone in the class. He started talking about the Battle of Plassey, where the East India Company was firmly established in India. He spoke for almost the entire period. Just before the bell rang, he asked me what happened to me and the rest in the class when the headmaster took over his class in his absence. Nobody spoke; if I tried to say, I choked. The headmaster understood. But he had promised to come another day with our history teacher to teach and learn more about the class. He understood our class was far ahead of other classes in the school. That was the most distressing feeling, being unable to live up to his expectations. This class produced an internationally respected Astrophysicist nominated for the Nobel Prize in Physics; this class created the chairman of the public services commission for the Government of India and many more successful professionals in life. Rai Bahadoor Mishra, the Headmaster, had a good reason to be disappointed and vision to focus harder.

However, my interest in history and geography was rooted in my early days in school. That may be the reason for my keenness in writing a patient's medical history and clinical findings. Moreover, that may be the foundation of my passion for writing in general.

After my orientation with Dr. Thakuta and Metzger, I had to work with Surgeons, Mr. Roxy Harris, a big, superbly energetic man, who never lost his temper, even when the assisting theater nurse was clumsy, slow, or inattentive. He somehow got to like me and gave me lots of attention, direction, and independent scope of surgery. He held my hand and took me step by step into the complexity of doing a "Hernia" operation, which would be the bulk of surgical work I would have to deal with as a District Medical Officer, aside from some others. "Some others" was an understatement.

Mr. Olu Williams was the chief of surgery. A tall thin, athletic-looking, quiet man. Astute observer. He took me as his 1st assistant during the surgery and would discuss various surgical procedures often unrelated to the case, yet never veered away from what he was focused on doing. Known amongst his peers as highly intelligent, academic, very hard working and devoted to his work, I was expected to be with him from the time he arrived until he left; that could be, at times, 8 or 10 pm.

Generally, if I were not in the hospital and had done all I needed to do to complete the day's assignments, my workday would finish by 2 pm. Again, a very different working routine compared to my previous experience in the medical department.

After one month of intensive orientation, I was told I needed to spend a few weeks in Gynecology and Pediatrics units.

In medical school, I was good at Gynecology. The chairman of the Gynecology department enticed me to take up gynecology as my specialty. I had not made up my mind. Even early in my career, my focus was to become a cancer specialist. Prof Amiya Sen was my idol.

Chapter 13

NIGHT ON CALL ON A BROKEN LADDER

"You are not required to set yourself to fire to keep other people warm"

Shrimad Bhagabad Gita.

Two days into my third rotation, I was called in for some emergency one night. As I reached the hospital, the charge nurse from the ward was waiting for me just at the entrance. She told me there was a problem with using the staircase to the first floor, going to the Gynecology-ward. There were no other stairs. They had temporarily erected a ladder to connect to the gynecology ward. She said they had been using the ladder since that morning. She just wanted to caution me as I went up the ladder.

I did not think this was a problem. Sister helped me to get on. I was going up carefully. But as I was close to the last couple of rungs, my foot slipped, and I slipped from the first-floor level to the ground level. I was grazing my groin on each rung as I was slipping down. One doctor from the Emergency department rushed in and took me to the emergency department on a stretcher as I fell. I was partly saved because the supporting ladder checked the speed of the fall.

I did not break any bones; there were minor bruises, except for my groin on both sides. Painful, but no bruises or ulceration. The ER doctor gave me some painkillers and an appointment to see the surgeon the following morning.

Back in my guesthouse room, I was very uncomfortable with the pain getting worse and worse. I had difficulty passing urine. So many guest house staff were around. The Guesthouse had an "On-Call" doctor. He noticed bruises in the groin area with generalized tender swelling in both testicles. The pain was getting worse as the swelling started to throb.

The Doctor called the ambulance to take me back to the ER. He was mainly concerned about my inability to pass urine. He did not understand the reason. Then, it started to become very painful.

In the hospital, I was heavily sedated.

The next morning, I woke up with pain, nausea, headache, and giddiness. The swelling in my groin had gotten worse. My bladder was full.

I was still unable to stand up.

In the morning, Dr. Thakuta came to see me. He examined me thoroughly. His main concern was that of internal injury. Then, Dr. Roxy Harris, the surgeon, arrived. This time he examined me internally. That was very uncomfortable, embarrassing and I felt very sick after his examination.

He reassured us that there was most likely no internal injury or fracture.

He ordered to drain my bladder with a catheter and several x-rays of soft tissues of the pelvis. At that time, there was no concept of CAT or MRI scans. I trusted the five senses, talent, and wisdom of my two doctors, Dr. Thakuta and Mr. Harris.

I was transferred to the Hill Station Hospital for Officers, VIPs, and Politicians.

As I was stretchered into my room, I was surprised to see Sister Thomas waiting in my room. She helped to move me onto the bed.

Finally, I was settled and comfortable.

Chapter 14

DISTRICT MEDICAL OFFICER GETS PUSHED BACK

"If your actions inspires others to dream more, learn more, do more and become more, you are a leader"

John Quincy Adams

My planned orientation was supposed to be completed in the next two to three weeks in preparation for my posting to a District Hospital. However, I needed to complete my mandatory orientation before my posting.

The following day, Dr. Harris came to see me. Now I was under him. In a cheerful mood, he announced that there was no fracture on X-rays, and no soft tissue issues either. Urine examination was also clear. There was no trace of blood. He thought the sudden stoppage of urine was most likely a reflex response to the trauma to the groin; hopefully, this would not recur.

I had severe bruising of the back of my right leg from the buttock till the mid-calf. There was no open skin laceration, since I was wearing a relatively tough trouser and on top of that I had the white lab coat on. That protected me from the skin laceration in the leg, but I had few on my right arm. I did have severe painful scrotal swelling. Initially they thought of acute torsion of right testicle and edema of the scrotum due to soft tissue crushing. The pain was unimaginable, only controlled with a morphine injection. Dr Thakuta and Mr Harris both resisted any surgical procedure suggested by other colleagues. I salute both of them for their precious determined opposition to any surgical intervention that was advised by senior colleagues.

Unfortunately, the swelling in my groin got worse, and it began to throb. The pain was unbearable at times. I developed a high fever. At one point, I thought I was developing abscesses in my groin swelling, which would need draining. I discussed this with Mr. Harris and Dr. Guha. They did not disagree entirely, but wanted to follow conservative treatment, assess daily, and carry out surgical drainage if it became essential.

Conservative treatment, antibiotics, painkillers, and some other medication with controlled physiotherapy were prescribed. Gradually my fever and symptoms started to show signs of improvement.

Sister Thomas reminded Dr. Harris that I was supposed to be starting my posting in a district in three weeks. She suggested that it had to be delayed. Mr. Harris agreed.

Both of them left and promised to return soon. In about ten minutes, they returned and told me that Mr. Harris had informed them that my District posting should be delayed and would be assessed in four weeks when I might be able to start my District Medical Officer's position. I was excited and looked forward to jumping into another unknown.

For the next two weeks, Sister Thomas's care, the Nursing and Medical officer's team of the Hill station Hospital, Mr. Harris's regular visit, and a friendly visit by Dr. and Mrs. Thakuta made me feel at home. In addition, Mrs. Thakuta insisted that she send my lunch daily from home, and their driver delivered it on time without missing any day.

Hospital food was quite good, and I could have lived with it. They also gave me options of varieties of menus. There were many snacks in between; drinks, hot or cold, could be requested any time.

The following day, I was surprised to see Dr. Boardman, the Chief Medical Officer, and the Chief Nursing Officer come to visit me. Dr. Boardman asked me about the circumstances of my accident and to let them know if something else was needed from a medical point of view.

He also reassured me that my transfer to the district would be reassessed in a month, providing my recovery was satisfactory.

He also confirmed that the problem of the staircase leading to the second floor in Connaught hospital for the gynecology ward had been fixed. The temporary ladder had been removed. So when I resumed, I need never use the ladder again. He laughed.

Despite the suffering, the extent of love, care, and concern for me was overwhelming. I was unsure if I would have any better treatment, both medically and humanly, anywhere else.

They were ready to depart. Ms. Wilson, the Chief Nursing Officer, turned around and said, "We will keep Sister Thomas at the Hill station Hospital as Sister–in-charge for the next couple of weeks, before she is transferred to her preferred position."

"Thank you, ma'am," I said. "She has been kind, helpful, caring, and compassionate beyond my expectation."

Sister Thomas informed me that Mr. Bamforth, the Chief Secretary, had been regularly informed of my progress.

I did get better, although any activity involving my hip was trying at times. I returned to my Government Rest House suite two weeks after being admitted for the accident.

Another week at home, rested well and ready to tango. Unfortunately, however, I had a somewhat problematic gait.

I returned to my job at the hospital, but I did not know who or where I was to be working. So I started with Dr. Williams, a recently returned UK gynecology consultant. After that, I went to the Gynecology Hospital to resume my duty.

She was happy to see me back. But, unfortunately, they had to place someone to carry on my work during my absence. Gynecology was a hectic department. So medical officers were the main force to provide services.

But as per the MOH arrangement, I needed to have Gynecology orientation and clinical re-training.

She went away for a few minutes. Then, she said that she spoke to the Medical Director and Dr. Boardman, the CMO and both agreed that I would, for the time being, work with Dr. Thakuta for the next two weeks and then return to Gynae and pediatrics until I was ready for the district.

The Gynae Hospital was not within the main campus of Connaught Hospital, so transport was sent to drive me to Connaught Hospital. We reached Dr. Thakuta's office in about fifteen minutes. He was aware of this arrangement from the CMO a few days before I was discharged from the Hill Station Hospital.

While I was sitting there, I began discussing my ordeal and praising Dr. Harris' wise decision not to operate but to treat me conservatively, which got me where I am today. Everyone liked Dr. Thakuta. So, by association, Dr. Thakuta's friends and close colleagues, also by default, got special attention as I did.

It was 11 am, time for a break (a very English habit). One of the nurses brought a tray with a pot of tea, biscuits, and fruits for the two of us. Very civil indeed.

He did inquire about my health and ability to perform everyday activities. "With occasional restriction, I am OK," I said. In that case, I was allowed to go to the ward, be with the senior medical officer, another Dr. Wilson, and just observe him and help him if needed.

A nurse escorted me to the medical ward. We stopped on our way at the office of Dr. Abouco Cole, the Hospital Medical Director, just to say hello and let him know that I had resumed my duties that day. After inquiring about my state of health, he said, "I guess you are on your way to the medical ward. Dr. Wilson is waiting for you. He has had several admissions and will appreciate your help, whatever you can do."

Without wasting much time, we headed for the medical ward. I remember meeting Dr. Wilson before. I asked him how I could help him.

He was happy to see me and said, "We have three new admissions. I would like to finish these patients' history and physical examinations before Dr. Thakuta comes to the ward for his round, after he finishes his outpatient clinic, at around 12.30 noon."

"Fine," I said, "In that case, let us get on with it."

Chapter 15
DR. THAKUTA (BIDYUT GUHA THAKURTA)

"Efforts and courage are not enough without purpose and direction"

-JFK

I am now in a new country, new environment, entirely different culture, language, much to contend with, and much to learn, absorb, retain and practice. I was not expecting to meet Dr. Thakuta under these unfamiliar circumstances. All professionals spoke excellent English since most of them were educated in the UK. But ordinary people, patients, their relatives spoke in "Creole," a mixture of English and local native languages. I got used to speaking to people in Creole. After listening to creole for a few days, I understood and managed to speak it just about enough to communicate with patients.

The Ministry of Health did circulate a document of useful phrases and words in Creole and Mende (another frequently spoken language) for doctors and nurses, which indeed came in very handy.

Dr. Thakuta was a unique personality. We met for the first time at the Ministry of Health building. Since then, he was made to believe that I was his brother; so was I. All the Doctors, nurses, and staff got used to Dr. Thakuta's brother and treated me as his younger brother.

He was an excellent academic mentor. I must admit, lots of my houseman-ship etiquettes and detailed relevant clinical documentation I learned from him. While working with surgeons and surgical wards, we did not have much time to write detailed medical histories aside from presenting surgical condition. Yet, he never failed to appreciate my accurate clinical findings and my obsession with sketching clinical findings, and making those a part of the dynamics of the patient's progress in the their case notes. So, there was two-way learning, a sense of give and take. The relationship was never a boss or professor, but rather an empathetic watchman and a rookie, a vulnerable private (soldier).

I inherited this mutual respect for my staff, residents, and students from him. His impact had forever been a vital part of my personality and professionalism.

He was highly respected as a physician, well respected by his colleagues in power, politicians in offices, and wealthy businessmen. During my stay, his services were requested by neighboring French Guinea and other countries to treat powerful and socially important individuals.

As I was known as his brother, I was invited to many exclusive meetings, parties, professional, social-political, business development forums, which allowed me to come to know many intellectuals, politicians, and wealthy people in business, ambassadors, high commissioners, and sometimes foreign dignitaries. One of them was Papa Doc, President of Haiti, during his state visit to Sierra Leone. He was a grand older man with very thick glasses, yet impressive with his assertive personality.

Amongst many I met as a privileged "brother of Dr. Thakuta" was Prof Arthur Porter, the Vice-Chancellor of Fourah Bay College, the first English medium university in British West Africa. He was a short person, medium built, unassuming, but the heat of his wisdom, intellect, and vision penetrated one after he started speaking softly, slowly, and kindly. Indeed, he was intellectually brilliant without being assertive or any air of superiority.

Now when I recall our first meeting, I did not know who he was, but after a few minutes of speaking, it appeared that he created the environment, which led me to take over the conversation, responding to his short and pointed questions. Nothing out of my mark; my early student days in school and generally in India, my family, brothers, and sisters, my choice to become a doctor, my intention in coming to Africa, and particularly that in Sierra Leone. I had many stories to tell. At some point, he slid into more academic topics, like Ancient Indian glory, its history, etc. I lit up as he discussed the subject of history. I had very little knowledge of African history, even during colonialism and practically nothing pre-colonial Africa, except Egypt. Then, he began to speak on ancient Indian culture, Mohenjo-Daro, Harappa, Alexander the Great's retreat, Mahabharata, Ramayana. Indian Ayurveda system, Science, Philosophy, Mathematics, nothing was out of bounds over the subsequent few chance encounters I had with him in different circumstances.

I did not know who he was, and then I realized he was not only a strong man of the country's academic bureaucracy, but also one of the most respected and revered historians of entire English-speaking Africa (since the real knowledge of non- English colonial and non-colonial Africa was hard to get and understand). Prof Porter's contribution excelled, illuminating the history of pre-colonial and ancient Africa, notwithstanding the modern political developments in the post-colonial period. A man, not just a showcase of facts and knowledge, but a visionary with a keen analytical mind and sense of prediction.

I believe knowledge and wisdom nurture humility, humanity, and greatness. That was what Prof Arthur Porter Senior was.

Over the years, I thanked Dr. Thakuta for giving me access and exposure to the social, intellectual, and sanctuary of opulence, which I would not have otherwise experienced.

That was the taste of the world I was to face in my future life. Either glide along or fight ferociously for existence. A microcosm of the world around which we float, swim forward or sink. The experience could not have come from dozens of "Fellowships" from Royal colleges or "Certifications" from certification granting Boards, PhDs from elite academies, or hours of Pastoral sermons.

Wisdom and enlightenment can be bestowed upon one from anywhere. Just think, Isaac Newton changed the concept of the physical world, sitting under an apple tree. This impact reverberates, leading to a man walking on the moon and penetrating deep space. So likewise, Buddha meditating under a Peepal or Aswattha tree envisioned the world of peace and love that impacted universal, social, and moral growth, which is still at work and dearly needed in this restless and vengeful world.

Thousands of pilgrimages may not have given me what I needed. But, just keeping all my senses open, learning with respect, all that was happening around me, all that was spoken to me, and seeing a silver lining in every dark cloud, may have the power to make me think deeper, move forward, and look at humanity differently.

It is not Dr. Thakuta; his wife also looked after me and treated me as a family member. Perhaps we all missed our family, friends, and culture thousands of miles away. Sporadic contact with them on long-distance telephone phone calls just held the thread. Hearing them from time to time assured our existence, yet the emptiness of disconnection may be overwhelming. So, the little spot of the green oasis of affection amid nowhere (as it may be) in a vast, desolate desert or a speck of a desert island in the middle of a vast ocean, that was all we may have had to cling on.

Over time, I became a family member, and they were mine.

In the meantime, I had to purchase my car. Not only that, but I also needed to learn to drive and obtain a license to drive. With Dr. Thakuta's help, I got a government loan to purchase a car. My first ever owned car was a Morris Mini Minor, popularly known as the "Mini." I had to hire a driver to drive me to work and back. Also, one of Dr. Thakuta's patients took the responsibility to give me driving lessons. After two weeks of intensive practice, I was awarded a Learner's License, which meant, while driving, I must be accompanied by a licensed driver. So, I had to keep the driver driving me around and my driving practices as time permitted.

After three weeks of working with Dr. Thakuta, I returned to my scheduled rotation with the Gynecologist. She was young, energetic, and just returned from the UK after obtaining her medical degree from the Royal Free Medical College, the only medical college reserved for female students. Then she worked in several midland hospitals, training for Gynecology and Obstetrics specialty, which she finished with flying colors.

Finally, after spending about 11 years in England, she returned home, absolutely Anglicized. A perfect Creole lady.

She did say I had to be conversant with Cesarean Sections (CS) and must be able to manage some minor complicated labor. After observing my first CS, she said, "Do not waste any more time; you better be prepared for your posting in the district."

Yet, I had to spend another week in the Pediatric department. Pediatrics was not my forté. So, I spent long hours with the consultants, in the Pediatric emergency, with another Medical Officer and house officer colleague.

The same week, I was surprised to see Dr. Boardman visiting the Pediatric hospital. He met me at the office of the sister-in-charge. He asked me about recovery and improvement in my health, as well as progress with the orientation program. He did not forget to ask me about my family at home in India. He also reminded me to see Mr. Harris and Dr. Thakurta soon, early the following week. If they were happy and I had no other issues, then the ministry would soon arrange my posting as district Medical Officer (DMO).

I was so happy I could skip and run! I was already told by Dr. Thakuta, that as DMO, my salary would increase, and I would be receiving several other perks. For example, help with a gardener, housekeeping, and transportation for all government duties, including my daily visit to the Hospital, shopping trek to Freetown once every month, if needed, etc. I was not interested in the details but keen to go where the adventure took me.

Sierra Leone had two major divisions: Freetown, the colony or Western region, and the rest as the territory or the provinces. Local administration of the province was entrusted to the Paramount Chiefs for their traditional Chiefdom. The territory was divided into three provinces, and each province was divided into several districts. Provincial commissioners were responsible for provincial administration, District Officers as chief of administration of the district, DMO or the District Medical officer was also the District Health Officer and inspector of Prisons (as necessary). As the proverb goes, "With power and wealth comes responsibility."

In the Freetown region, also known as the colony, lived the Colonists and Anglicized creoles; they were generally black African or mixed-race, locally known as mulattos. In addition, in the territory lived natives, for example, Mende, Temne, Mandingo, Susa, and many other tribes.

Of course, I had no idea where I would be posted. It would be in one of the districts in the territory. So I was apprehensive, yet excited about my posting and the new life to kick off.

Chapter 16

FUN IN FREETOWN

"The leader is one who, out of the clutter, brings simplicity......out of discord, harmony....and out of difficult, opportunity"

Albert Einstein.

Despite the introduction to West African life, the three months I stayed in Freetown had many amusing and fun-filled times. Generally, the *Freetowners*, both expatriates and "locals," lived an excellent, relaxed, essentially stress-free, and healthy life. The majority were Christians. So, church activities were an integral part of the lifestyle. Yet dancing with the rhythm of wild music, late-night partying in moonshine or darkness, and fun in the sun were essential social activities.

Freetown's Lumley beach was one of the longest, cleanest, safest beaches in entire West Africa. Natural palm trees lined it, and rows of thatched huts were some of the beach's mesmerizing attractions. Yet, the stretches of mile-long beach with its white powdery clean, free-flowing sandy beach were hauntingly empty, aside from scattered roadside vendors.

As we drove close to the south end of the beach, one could see a few clusters of large, tall, and wide bushes. In addition, one could also hear old music coming from that direction.

Inside the bushes, two of Freetown's most popular nightclubs were very busy from Thursday night till Sunday late at night. The outside look had no resemblance to what was inside. A well-decorated bar and restaurant, dancing floor, and performing stage assured a five-star entertainment spot. It was expensive. I presumed that the Palm and The Beach Club were popular with local rich and famous tourists, and the nouveau-riche with deep and burning pockets in diamond and gold business. They provided high-class entertainment and excitement in a club-like environment and, at times, local or foreign invited artists performing on stage. Weekend nights were noisy, and unruly drunk guests would get into a "brawl," with authorities. The management controlled and handled such issues respectfully and amicably for their clients. They also provided rides home after the party was over if they had come in a self-driven car. Many aristocracies had chauffeurs to drive them around or hired one, especially for the weekend nightclub expedition.

Piped or live music of Elvis Presley, Chuck Berry, Harry Belafonte, Frank Sinatra, Diana Ross, Ella Fitzgerald, Billie Holiday, Maurice Chevalier, Edith Piaf, and many others, I heard. However, the atmospheric ambiance was highly mystical and romantic, smelled of expensive cigars, and the tinkling of wine and glasses of scotch and Cognac had a different charm.

I was told that clients from neighboring Liberia not infrequently sailed from their rubber or Coffee plantations and diamond mining lodges to burn their desires in Freetown's Nightspot hideouts.

In the city, several Bars and restaurants were catering for local people entertained by local talents of various levels of amusement and trickery. It kept people happy and entertained. Unfortunately, those places could become violent at times. However, both the owners and clients were well attuned to these situations. As the noise and physical abuse exceeded the tolerance of the clients and spectators, they were contained by the clients, management, and, not infrequently, by the police. Though it happens, dangerous crime was not a common spectacle.

These were places where people did not smoke cigars but handmade "chuttas." Some drink, not Bourbon, scotch, Bordeaux, Cabernet, Remy Martin or Courvoisier, but mostly Guinness, stouts for women, all varieties of Sandie, pale ales, or for high rankers, Heineken's famous pint from the tap, Spitfire, Bishop's finger, and on and on.

One day, a young Sierra Leonean doctor colleague invited me to visit one of the famous pubs in Sackville Street in the market district of Freetown. Of course, that was a busy market street. But, having heard my exciting impression after several visits to the nightclubs in Lumley beach, he insisted that I experience the *real* world and meet *real* people.

I told Dr. Thakuta about my evening out. He was shocked, but having seen Dr. Jones, he was reassured, and we drove to our destination in Sackville Street. The pub and amusement center were on the second floor. We had to climb through a narrow staircase, had two guards, one at the bottom and the other at the top of the stairs.

That was a Friday evening. The pub was noisy, smoky, packed with men and women of all ages, some dressed elegantly, fit for a Friday outing, and others with traditional Sierra Leonean attire. Printed Sarong, short, flared dresses, no longer than to cover upper thigh, with matching head gears for women and men with trouser and shirt inside with locally woven striped baggy overall with loose, full arms. There were many tribal, traditional, and cultural variations.

It was quite a collection of a traditional parade of costumes for a Friday night pubbing and partying, and possible eyeing for a partner.

One usher escorted us to a quiet part of the floor with a table for four in anticipation. I was not yet used to alcoholic beverages, but I was most excited to absorb as much as I could from one of the social norms of the West African lifestyle. Dr. Jones ordered a bottle of chilled Heineken and a glass of Coke with ice for me.

Although this was in the middle of a local marketplace, it appeared on the higher end of its scale, looking at the ambiance, people's attitude, and reasonably well-uniformed staff. They all spoke English. Dr. Jones informed me that this was one of the places for students of Forah Bay College who tended to congregate for their Friday outing, dates, or amusement. A live singer and a local artist started with the local band and musical instruments, singing Sinatra, Perry Como and the likes. He also sang one of his own compositions in Krio. I could not understand the words but appreciated the rhythm and music.

The real rocking and rolling started with faster beats, noisier music, and faster movements a little later. Almost everybody got up on the floor, with their partners, and the ones who did not have one, procured one. Lady waitresses came to our table again and again asking if we needed another drink. Some of them knew Dr. Jones and asked him why he was not dancing. They realized I might be the one preventing it, so they were willing to be happy to be my dancing partner if I wanted. I thanked them and respectfully bowed out of their offer.

I asked Dr. Jones, "Is it a rude or uncivilized gesture to refuse a lady?"

He laughed and said, "Unless you are free for the rest of the evening." I understood what he implied.

I asked him if this was supposed to be the students' haunt. Well, generally, they knew what their red line was. So, as the general clientele, people came here for amusement and entertainment, but after a few bottles of Guinness or glasses of rum, the level of self-control withered away. The owners and staff generally were keen to keep this place clean.

He was interested to know my reasons for coming to Sierra Leone. I did explain that the reason was a chance and an accident. But now that I was here, I had no regret that I did not fight the accident, but embraced it with curiosity and anticipation. After the initial shock and amazement, I started to like the place, hoping to learn more. We discussed the hospitals, consultants, and the life of a junior doctor or a medical officer. He gave me a hint of how life would be in the provinces. We were indeed in the depth of our discussion.

Suddenly a tall man came and stood by me, asking me if I could spare him a couple of quids (slang for English pounds). Dr. Jones asked him, "Sir! What can we do for you?"

The man suddenly got angry and shouted at him and said, "I am speaking to my friend, Masta Shotram."

I did not know the man. He was, frankly, drunk and kept shouting at Dr. Jones; "I am speaking to Masta Shotram, my friend, let me speak to the Masta." Dr. Jones stood up and gently tried to steer him away.

The place was packed with people, drinking and dancing to the beats of music. The man's scream faded in the noise. He pushed away Dr. Jones and attempted to come closer to me, shouting, "Masta! Masta Shotram, you know me! I am Abdulla. I need a couple of quids. I am your manager in your Liverpool Street office."

I was dumbfounded. Dr. Jones was distraught and furious as the man came close to me and tried to twist my arm; he grabbed his neck and collar and pushed him on the floor. By this time, the happy dancers were ready to see different dancing. Some started to run away, thinking there was an attempted robbery in the pub.

Management and staff all surrounded the man and restrained him. He still kept saying, "Masta. Masta, help me." I thought, should I pay him a couple of quid?

Apparently, the man was well known to the pub and a regular client. However, he usually got drunk, and they watched him carefully so that he did not misbehave.

Abdulla was an employee of a large regional trading company owned by an Indian Businessman, Mr. Choitram Advani. They suspected that under the influence, he mistook me as Mr. Choitram, the millionaire businessman, who on rare occasions, visited this pub.

I felt sorry for Abdulla. Dr. Jones kept apologizing, so also the pub's management and staff. By this time, a couple of police officers came in. This was not an unusual event in this type of business. Police couldn't get involved in minor skirmishes in pubs and shops, but they told Dr. Jones that District Police Superintendent instructed them to be close by in case of any trouble. Apparently, they had been watching the pub for the last three hours. Dr. Jones was surprised to hear that, but later we learned that the request came from Dr. Thakuta to the Police Superintendent to be extra vigilant since I was new and unfamiliar with the city.

It all ended without anyone being struck down, handcuffed, or jailed. Instead, Dr. Jones drove me back to my suite in the government guesthouse. It was 11 pm by then. As I entered, my phone rang; it was Dr. Thakuta asking me about my pub outing with Dr. Jones. The reality was, he wanted to make sure that I had returned home safely.

Dr. Thakuta had only one daughter. She was at school in Calcutta, staying in the dormitory, but was looked after by family members of both parents, those who lived in Calcutta. Dr. Thakuta was born in Malaysia, grew up there. He had his medical education at Calcutta Medical College. He was a well-accomplished scholar all through.

It was the time of spring break. His daughter was scheduled to join them in Freetown, traveling by air from Calcutta to London, then to Freetown. He would pick her up and ask me if I would like to join them for the ride.

"Of course," I said. Freetown had a new airport opened six months before, which I had not seen because I had come by boat.

We set out to meet our treasured princess, as he said. After a half-hour drive, the car was parked by the bank of a river; apparently, that was the estuary of the Sierra Leone River, which separated the airport from Freetown. Lungi International Airport was on the other side of the river in the coastal region. So, we had to take a ferry to cross the river. Several short-distance cars were available for rental, drives to the airport. We could have ferried the vehicle, but it would have been costly and risky at times, especially during the rainy or wet season. In addition, bad weather could delay, or stormy winds may steer the ferry off its course, sometimes miles away from the point of disembarkation.

Anyway, we took the ferry. The flight from London was delayed, so we wandered around the airport and checked the facilities. It was just like any international airport, designed and built by an Israeli construction company. They did an excellent job. Well ahead of the capital's township development.

The young lady arrived, escorted by a Sierra Leone Air Lines air hostess, overwhelmed and joyful for the reunion and surprised to see me. Dr. Thakuta introduced me as a new "Uncle." She was a little disappointed not to see Mrs. Thakuta. He said "Mom" was busy fixing her room and cooking her favorite dishes. We set out to return to our car on the other side of the river. Generally, it would take twenty to thirty minutes to cross the river. We got on as all the passengers, cars, goods, and animals were on board, ready for the crossing and a pleasant ride.

The boat started to roll with bone-shaking vibration and hard rattling noise, signs of life and progress. We were happy and anxious to return home. Suddenly, a few minutes after we started, the noise got weaker; the vibration softer and softer. Eventually, both stopped as well as the ferry. We wondered what happened; we expected the ferry to start rolling soon. Then, an announcement from the captain, apologizing for the stoppage due to some mechanical failure, which the engineering team was working hard to fix, and expected to be a rapid fix, and that we would be on our way soon.

As the ferry lost its power, it had no control over its movement. Nevertheless, it started to float, slowly gliding with the power and flow of the river water. There were small powerboats on both embarking points. It could have sailed ten miles along the river in an hour.

We were waiting for the good news of the resumption of our return journey to the other bank. The young lady looked very tired and almost fell asleep as we were waiting amid a windy river, and the boat was slowly floating along with the current of the river.

We were getting more and more exasperated; we must have floated a mile along the river by this time. Then, I guess, suddenly, the engineer woke up and lowered the anchor to stop further drifting downstream. Yet no word from the captain on progress.

We noticed two lifeboats leaving the ferry with two big oil drums. We did not know what was happening. They returned fifteen minutes later with the barrels.

Then an announcement from the captain confirmed our worst nightmare that the ferry ran out of fuel. He had now obtained enough oil to restart again. That was reassuring, but quite disturbing that failure to check the logbook for maintenance was scary.

The Captain announced that the two generators on board were not powerful enough to propel the ferry. It could only maintain the electric supply and ventilation, etc.

We noticed that at least seven or eight fishing boats had surrounded the ferry with plans to stop its downward drift towards the sea and pull it towards its mooring berth. Both the ship's anchor and help from the fishing boats helped stop further drifting downstream.

We heard the chugging of another boat heading towards us from the port, which was further south. That was a tugboat. Within minutes the tug boat came close to the ferry, attaching itself to the ferry.

By then, we could hear the rolling back sound of the anchor.

All the small fishing boats steered themselves clear of the ferry. The tugboat started to push the ferry upwards towards its mooring birth.

The two sailors on a lifeboat had already returned with two barrels of diesel, which was missing from the ferry's inventory.

Dr. Thakuta's daughter was completely dazed and could not understand what was happening. Twenty minutes return ferry ride took two and a half hours to moor. Most of the passengers were calm, though a sense of anxiety could not be wiped away. We got off the ferry unhurt but with some confusion. The driver had the information. He had already informed Mrs. Thakuta about the delay, trying not to be specific. We called her again and said we would be home in half an hour.

We were supposed to return at 11 am; instead, it was 2 pm and time for lunch. Dr. Thakuta downplayed the incident, but the daughter gave a detailed real-time narration of the horror in her excitement. It was interesting to hear how the incident impacted the young mind just arriving from England for her first welcoming encounter in Freetown and Sierra Leone.

She traveled to West Africa, mostly accompanied by her parents, while Dr. Thakuta worked in Ghana. This was her first trip to Sierra Leone and Freetown, which was exciting as well, as she said afterward. She was not scared or afraid in the least. But, I wondered, would she have appreciated the consequences of this disaster had we not had the helps we desperately needed?

Later we were told, during the wet season, due to heavy rain and gale-force winds, that ferries did veer downstream at times. But it never happened in the dry season; it did just happen because the ferry ran out of fuel.

It was headline news on the next day's nation's leading daily newspaper and radio. We learned more from the public media about incidents like these that happened in the past and all efforts made by the authority to stop them from happening.

This unexpected runaway of the ferry was a minor issue compared to my four days of hell in the MV Apapa en route from Liverpool to Freetown as we were caught in a torrential tropical storm. But the runaway ferry with a few hundred human beings and its cargo could have turned into an absolute nightmare.

The next few weeks of my stay in Freetown were spent busy socializing. Getting to know several Freetown heavyweight businessmen, professionals, academicians, and political powers, all courtesy of Dr. Thakuta, with some of whom I had a long-term friendship and some others I was happy to meet.

My neighbor was a German deputy consul from the German Embassy at the guest house. A pleasant soft-spoken lady in her late forties or early fifties. Before coming to Freetown, she was an advisor at the Max Muller House in Calcutta for about three years. She had many fond memories of her time in India. She could speak Bengali, the language of Calcutta, and Hindi, the lingua franca of India. She preferred to speak to me in Bengali, my mother tongue, and English. Never pretended to indict me into learning German. We did get along well. She had considerable knowledge of India and South East Asia in general. She was my breakfast–table partner. We could spend extra time since the German Embassy was not far from the Guesthouse. I enjoyed her company. I used to accompany her to Lumley beach some days after work. She owned a Volkswagen, which was fully loaded with stuff for the beach experience.

She was highly energetic, enthusiastic, and with a likable personality. During our time, she did most of the talking with me as a patient listener.

The Guesthouse had several indoor and outdoor gaming facilities, well maintained and supervised.

Dr. Thakuta's daughter came to play table tennis, which she was good at. Mrs. Muller, the German neighbor, was an occasional badminton partner. I am, by nature, not a competitive athletic person, but I did like to play both table tennis and badminton, from time to time, but not passionate about either one.

The guest house had a large swimming pool for residents and a well-maintained outdoor turfed field for football and cricket.

Chapter 17
SUNDAY IN FREETOWN

"Nothing in life is to be feared, it is only to be understood, now is the time to understand more, so that we may fear less"

Marie Curie

There was no rush in Freetown. There was always a tomorrow. The population generally was content, and occasional evening brawls in the pubs were usually free from violence or serious crime.

The Brits anglicized the creole community very well. They were the ones who got their post-secondary education, and they were the ones who got professional, technical, and administrative training in England. Upon return, they were given important public positions and a salary to match, which was generally higher than those in Sierra Leone, born and bred. Therefore, Creoles had a better social status and standard of living. That was what I felt as my initial impression.

When Brits left, they gave independence to Sierra Leone. Many colonists stayed behind to help run the country, but most of the positions were taken up by Creoles. Unlike the French in the neighboring colony, French Guinea, they were educated, efficient, and patriotic. As the French gave them independence, after ruling the country for nearly a century, they completely deserted the country almost overnight, without leaving a single technocrat to continue to run the country during the transition. It was in absolute chaos and pandemonium. No Guinean had any experience running the country, maintaining the bureaucracy, hospitals, schools and healthcare services, public transport, and other necessary logistics. After a couple of days, the newly appointed president requested that the French Government help him run the country. Over the subsequent several months, with the help of French specialists, they got the country back on track and regained its standard of life and living as it was under French rule.

But in Sierra Leone, the scenario was very different. An orderly transition from Colonial rule to independence took place on the 27th of April, 1961. It took over a year and a half before I disembarked in Freetown. The city was clean, orderly, well-controlled traffic flow, well-managed government bureaucracy, health care, educational institutes, police, law and order, and well-maintained infrastructure. Government buildings and public houses were well maintained. The postal and telecommunication services were satisfactory and reasonably efficient. It gave a sense of security, order, and prosperity. In the private sector, business was booming, shops were well stocked, and the markets were well supplied with local produce and catch from the rivers and the sea.

Very different from what I envisioned before leaving London for Freetown.

Most senior government positions were filled by well-educated, British-trained Sierra Leonean technocrats and professionals as the British left. However, it was impossible to replace the majority of ex-pats with Sierra Leoneans without much disruption, but the transition was unlike what happened in Guinea.

Many colonial and ex-pat officers stayed on for running the country with locals and experts. The arrangement did work well. The "rulers" became "ruled," and "ruled" ones became "rulers." The table turned around one hundred and eighty degrees, but there was amicable symbiosis, in my opinion.

Sir Maurice Henry Dorman was the first Governor-General of Sierra Leone, appointed by the Queen. Sir Milton Margai, a Physician from the provinces, became the first elected Prime Minister of Sierra Leone. Thus, executive, bureaucracy, and political systems were all in place at the time of independence.

I could feel the orderliness, security, and good governance during my stay.

Sierra Leone is predominantly a country of Christian faith. Churches of various denominations dotted the city and were spread over the provinces. The next common religion is Islam, which was brought by Arab traders from North Africa, mostly scattered in the country's northern part or Sahel region. I do not remember seeing any mosques in the city, but the roads were dotted with churches. There was one Synagogue. Several visionary Maroons, the rebel and freed slaves of the West Indies later settled in Freetown and built their ornate churches; others were simple boxes crowned by a cross. But they all were active and regularly attended by the faithful congregation. Sunday was a day almost every person in Freetown would go to follow their mass.

One Sunday, I tried to explore the town's religiosity. We drove along many main streets with several churches, including the cathedral.

We set out from the guest house at 9.30 am to feel the pulse of the churchgoers. We noticed rows of men, ladies, and children walking towards the church as we drove. Men in their best suits, some in tailcoats with their top hats. Women in floral and colorful dresses, some ankle length and some just below the knee with elbow-length white gloves. All the ladies were wearing different designs of full floral hats. Some ladies carried tiny umbrellas of exquisite color and pattern. It was a beautiful sunny, cool breezy morning, without a trace of cloud anywhere in the sky or any corner of the horizon, for that matter. Some men wore highly polished oxford shoes. Children were also dressed fully as adults, walking gently with their parents.

I could see the slowly advancing faithful believers, moving towards the church's main entrance, only from the back, unable to see their faces, not even from any other direction.

I remember similar congregations walking to the church, just like possessed people walking towards the church entrance.

We generally were unable to see from the front their anatomy, their emotions, and the level of devotion in submitting to the Lord.

It felt like a dream, as if I was standing in front of the English countryside in front of the village church on a Sunday morning, just before the beginning of Sunday holy mass. I missed their faces but looked at the rest of their bodies from the back, stunningly like what I am experiencing in Freetown today.

I spent the morning on Lumley beach, then to the seaside sheds, which was pretending to be a Bar and a Café. Lots of varieties of tropical fruit juices and punches were on the list. So many ex-pats, men, women, and children to keep each other company congregate in these places from time to time. Several miles of open expanse, clean white sandy beach lined by coconut trees, would one day be the delight of beach lovers. I guess it was yet to be discovered. At present, a few upturned, abandoned, shattered fishing boats along the beach, only a painful sight, a blemish to its beauty; I felt these did not belong there.

Early afternoon, returning to the Guesthouse on our way back from the beach, we took the same road and passed by a few churches. By then, the services were over, and congregations were returning home. But, this time, I could see their faces. These were all devout, God-loving, black African Sierra Leoneans, with a few exceptions of white men and women.

The transformation was absolute, and the feeling that God created all men equally is unequivocal and unconditional. I personally felt a little more divine now than this morning on our way to Lumley Beach.

Chapter 18

DISTRICT MEDICAL OFFICER (DMO) IN KAILAHUN

"Now a days, people know the price of everything and the value of nothing"

Oscar Wilde

It was a Saturday evening; I was sitting at the lounge of the Guesthouse. I saw Dr. Boardman, the Chief Medical officer, walk in. He greeted me and shook hands. As usual, it was difficult to reach his hand. He said, "You look well! I hope you're feeling that way too."

We talked about my days in Freetown, my working experience, and how I was adjusting to my new life, being alone. I mentioned that Dr. GuhaThakurta had been an enormous help aside from other colleagues at Connaught Hospital, introducing how medicine was practiced -though not much different from my training in India- and introducing me to local professionals and academics, as well as business communities.

Then, he asked me if I felt well enough to take over the position in Kailahun as the District Medical Officer. The DMO in Kailahun would be going on his annual leave, and they were planning to send me there as the next DMO. I was impressed, in a gentlemanly way he gave his order, so humane and sympathetic and more or less casual, not to make me feel his subordinate.

"I am fit and ready, Sir!" I said.

He slowly walked to the bar to join some of his friends to spend the evening.

The next day, I went to see Dr. Thakuta and mentioned my meeting with Dr. Boardman and their decision to send me to Kailahun. He was not enthusiastic, somewhat surprised, and asked why Kailahun? I did say about the DMO going on leave, where they needed a replacement soon. But, again, he did not give me an enthusiastic vibe.

Two weeks went by. I had not heard from MOH. Then, one morning, Dr. Cole called me to ask if I could be ready in half an hour to see Dr. Boyel-Hebron, the Deputy Chief Medical Officer. A driver from the Ministry would come to pick me up.

I was right on time at Dr. Boyel-Hebron's office. He was also a big but bulky man, not as athletic looking as Dr. Boardman. I met Dr. Cummings, a Sierra Leonean, who Dr. Hebron introduced to me as the principal Medical Officer for the Eastern Province. Kailahun was one of the three districts of the eastern province. Dr. Hebron asked me some personal questions and said that he had instructions from Dr. Boardman to arrange my posting and travel arrangement as soon as possible.

I said, "I'm ready. Just let me know when you want me to pack up and go."

Dr. Cummings asked me about my understanding of life in West Africa and how much I knew about Kailahun.

"This is my first trip to Africa. In the last three months, I learned a lot about Africa and the sea voyage from Liverpool to Freetown. I do not know Kailahun; all I know is it is 411 km from Freetown, on the opposite side, in the east of the country bordering Liberia. And I love your *Jollof rice*," both Dr. Hebron and Dr. Cummings roared in laughter.

"OK! Dr. Malaker," Dr. Hebron said, "We will start the process for you to assume the DMO's position in Kailahun. Dr. Cummings will be glad to see you in Kailahun sooner than later."

"I am ready, Sir! I need only twenty-four hours' notice," I said.

"Mrs. Winston will coordinate and arrange for your relocation."

Entered a lady in her early fifties or late forties, of mixed race. I had met her before. She was delightful, polite, and energetic.

She said the driver would take me back to Connaught Hospital. She would keep in touch about the relocation to Kailhun soon.

I said bye to everyone and returned to Connaught Hospital to continue my Pathology Department work.

Mentally I was getting ready for my new job, full of anticipation, uncertainty, and excitement.

I was not only ready but eager to face the mysteries, marvels, and challenges of my four hundred-plus miles of road journey to Kailahun right across the country and the prospect of doctoring in the deep equatorial forested cluster of human habitation. My imagination ran amok as I waited for "D" day to begin. After my last meeting at the Ministry, I felt there was an urgency to be in Kailahun since the place would have no doctor to support the remote community.

It was exactly two weeks after my meeting that I got a call from Mrs. Winston that I should get ready to travel on the coming Friday, just over a week. She said the transport from Kailahun would pick me up just after breakfast from the guest house. So naturally, I was thrilled to end the wait and anticipation.

I spoke to Dr. Thakuta, and he invited me to have dinner with him at his house in the evening. I spent the next few days and most evenings with his family. I felt that they were a little concerned about my posting. Jokingly I told him, "You're my mentor here, but it is David Livingstone who is the instigator for my adventure in the poisonous insect-infested dense forest, filled with deadly prowling animals, ferocious head hunters and man-eaters looking for their prey, and treacherous slippery- large potholed-like "quicksand's" may be the norm in my journey to Kailahun. But if I could have traveled half the world away from home, another four hundred odds miles of a relatively dangerous road trip may be just the icing on the cake, which is what I was trying to convince myself of. I tried to convince them that I was ready to face and accept the challenge. But inside me, the excitement of facing the unknown somehow overshadowed my real feeling of fear and anxiety of the "unknown."

On Thursday night, the ambulance driver from Kailahun met me at the guesthouse and said we needed to leave by eight in the morning to arrive in Kailahun by early evening, since we had no plan to overnight anywhere on our way. The driver introduced himself as Mommahdu and his helper as "Boukhari."

In the morning, I met my German friend in the breakfast room. I was happy to see her. She had been a wealth of information about life in West Africa, which did help me a lot in the future. We had breakfast together, and we finished just before 8 am. She would also have to be at the Embassy by 8 am. She wished me well and to have a very safe journey. She asked for an address where I could be reached. I gave her my Calcutta address. Someone from there could tell her where I could be found. We exchanged our contact addresses and shook hands to say goodbye for that day.

As I was leaving, I saw that Dr. Thakuta and Mrs. Thakuta had just parked their car in the portico. Both of them got out and said they just had come to say goodbye, and Mrs. Thakuta gave me a package with a couple of bottles of water and a thermos flask of hot coffee.

The supply was for my road trip; enough for two meals for two people. I was pleasantly surprised. I could not express enough gratitude for their feelings and kindness.

As it was getting late, we shook hands and said goodbye for that day, expecting to meet soon.

We set off for our twelve to fourteen-hour journey into the unknown, at least for me, with high anticipation.

Chapter 19

ROAD TRIP TO KAILAHUN FROM FREETOWN

"If I have ever seen magic it has been in Africa."

John Hemingway

Mr. Mommahdu, the driver, told me they had to bring a patient from Kailahun to Connaught Hospital, which was why they were delayed; otherwise, the plan was to come four days early. Anyway, he said, the road was good, and we could make it to Kailahun before the sunset. "We will be in Bo just after noontime," he said.

As we left, we had to drive through the city center, and then we came to the outskirt of the city. Shacks lined the road with corrugated roofs and mud-brick walls. There were shops with varieties of merchandise, tea shops, bus stands, parked cars, motorcycles, heaps of garbage here and there. People were busy walking, women carrying loads on their heads and some carrying a baby in a hammock on their front and loads on their head, not an uncommon sight. Several repair shops, be it cycle, motorcycle, old cars, furniture, electrical equipment, you name it, they could fix in these areas.

As we drove further, we noticed the traffic was different. There were more domestic animals, i.e., goats, cows, chickens loose on the street or in cordoned-off areas; I guess for sale. There were a few butcher shops we noticed on the roadside. One had to be very cautious, driving to avoid animals strolling on the street.

Gradually we were outside the city boundary, and soon we entered the next village, with houses on both sides of the highway. There were small chalet-type stores by the roadside. The houses and buildings were mostly built from mud bricks with corrugated tin roofs.

The road to Bo was supposed to be paved. It was indeed paved, but there had been erosions in places with potholes and mud from recent rains. But generally, drivable and safe.

Every few miles, we had to pass through villages along the way. Some were just a collection of a few cottages and others with clusters of dwellings and huts. Small roadside shops with electricity were not uncommon. Most of these villages grew after the British built the road, making traveling easier. Access to bigger cities and availability of public transportation to bigger cities and towns made local people move their houses and shops closer to the main road, from the interior deeper jungle which was secluded and less accessible. Some of them became chiefdom. I understood that all villages have a chief, and a cluster of several villages was ruled by a paramount chief, appointed by the colonial government or elected by the local people, then sanctioned by the Government. They were the local governments, with some independence, but answerable to the Colonial government in Freetown.

We passed Waterloo, the second largest town and district headquarter of the Southern District of the Western Region. It maintained its colonial sophistication to some extent. We had to drive through the town center, clean, paved roads. They were well-maintained three to four-story dwellings by the main street. The broad road may have been built as an afterthought of building Freetown. Waterloo was also on the railway line that connected Freetown to Daru on the eastern border.

We skipped stopping in Waterloo, thinking of the long and perhaps challenging drive ahead.

As we passed Waterloo, we entered the protectorate or the province of Sierra Leone, where they call the country "Sa'lone," which was a tribal colloquial name for the country. The road may have been paved or partly paved, but as we drove, most of it was a dirt road but wide enough for two heavy, wide-bodied lorries to pass each other.

We were entering the forested road. The road was cut through dense tropical forest. The hills of Sierra Leone were on the north side, gradually becoming higher and higher, stepwise. Deep thick jungle appeared to be impenetrable, but one could see trails of human activities going inside the jungle, disappearing progressively into the dark, dense, and mysterious part of the forest.

The forest was less dense on the roadside but tightly packed with bushes and shrubs on the south side of the road. We noticed some small and large patches of forest cleared for agricultural produce. Cut and burnt for forest clearance was the primary way of reclaiming land from the forest for agriculture, even for setting up villages and small towns by the side of the road. We came across several of those transplanted communities on our way.

As we went further, the mud-brick houses had been replaced by circular mud houses, covered by thick husk-roofs. The villages were peaceful yet lively, with varieties of human activities, primarily by women, which was inescapably noticeable. We were told that the men folks had either gone deep into the forest to hunt and gather other edibles, or were working in the cities or nearby towns or the fields for agricultural produce.

Mommahdu, the driver, was concentrating on driving, minding the pot-holes, mud-heaps, water cesspools, and gravels, and small boulders, those washed onto the road from the hills during heavy tropical showers. That was not all; cars, lorries carrying goods, sometimes heaped up to two stories with their goods and an extra foot or two widened both sides to maintain the center of gravity. Buses overloaded with passengers and their baggage. The overburdened loaded buses appeared frighteningly off-center, threatening to tip on its side any time. Speeding and honking seemed to be the birthright of all vehicular traffic, no matter what its contents were or the destination it was. Road traffic accidents were prevalent on these highways and roads. Even on the forest tracks and walking lanes, two-wheelers tried to speed and overtake each other in that unpredictable terrain, especially inside the forest under the darkness day or night in these dense tropical forests.

Momodu's cautious driving at manageable speed was admirable. However, humps and bumps and occasional slip-sliding on the road couldn't be avoided, just as aches and pains from this captivating adventure. But, who cared what the kind of feeling was as we drove on.

We arrived at our first planned stop, at Masiaka, a trading junction town, a meeting point of two highways, the Masiaka-yonibana highway that connects Freetown to the east and Kailahun. The Masiaka-Lunsar Highway continued as Lunsar-Makena Highway, further north to Makeni. This highway starts at Masiaka Junction and connects to the north of the country. Hence the town of Masiaka commands a critical place in both trade and governance of the country.

We stopped at the city center near a Mosque and shared the food package from the Government Guesthouse. Mommahdu was happy with water, and I had my rationed half cup of black coffee, the remaining to last the rest of the journey.

The people in Masiaka were mostly Temne-Muslim. The town had about two thousand people, but gave the impression of a much bigger and busier place. Several Lorries, trucks, buses, cars, and dozens of two-wheelers waiting by the roadside, ready to take off for their destinations. Busy shops and shop keepers, so also their clients. Unlike Freetown, people on the street, in the shops, driving cars, spoke in much louder voices, exuding the town's energy. Incredible!

Except for a few office goers and school kids, both men and women wore typical Sierra Leonean native garments like most of the people we saw in the street. I just started to feel the real spirit of Africa for the first time since I landed in Freetown.

It was late morning. We had yet to travel a long way on this road. So we set off for our journey, aiming for our next stop at Bo. As we progressed towards Bo, the second largest city of Sierra Leone, the road was comparatively better, but the jungles were getting thicker and denser.

En route, we came across several small villages. We traveled along the foothills of the range of hills stacked one after the other and slowly fading away at a great distance. This range of hills extended from the southeast of Guinea into the eastern and central parts of Sierra Leone. We had been traveling along the southern foothill of this mountain range. For the first time, we noticed extensive plantation of Date-

Palm or Palm oil trees, occupying acres and acres, sometimes in medium and others very large parcels. On the other side, we saw tropical evergreen bushes and tall trees. Sometimes a long stretch of the road was entirely covered by tall trees, like Red Ironwood, Mahogany, Cedar, and even bamboo shrubs several meters tall, and other such trees and creepers covered the entire road, giving a stable canopy over it. There were no sun rays, pitch dark at places even in the middle of "high noon." We chugged along.

There were some herds of African monkeys, and families of baboons could be seen on the wayside. We met a small herd of water hogs leisurely crossing the road further away. Water pools or a shallow river must have been close by. Suddenly, as we entered a cleared part of the road, it was sunny, dry, and maintained reasonably well, with relatively thin bushy trees and vegetation lining the roadside. There, unexpectedly, we noticed a rather elegant-looking couple of Bongo, Brown-furred Bongo, with zebra-like stripes, standing majestically in the middle of the road.

Sierra Leone has varieties of antelope species, i.e., waterbuck, duikers, etc. These generally live in the central Sahel area or Northern sub-Saharan dry land. They are rarely seen in the Southern equatorial rain forest or muddy shrub and grassy land surrounding a waterlogged cesspool. However, it is not uncommon to see water buffalo, pygmy hippos, and warthogs enjoying the tropical sun and the cool in the muddy water of these shifting lakes.

Through the deep and dense forested road, with large areas of palm oil plantations, we passed by a few small villages, mostly made up of round mud houses with thatched roofs, some of them as little as five houses to make up the village, and others a few more. People were mostly sitting idle, smoking long, thick local cigars.

Some villagers seemed to be herding cattle, goats, and poultry. It was more of a common practice in the northern part of the country, which was part of the savanna grassland of the sub-Saharan region. We also noticed the villages' agricultural lands of paddy, pulses, and vegetables. Generally, we found women doing household chores, looking after children, cooking, and men mostly sitting around. They always greeted us. As we slowed down, older people walked close to our car. Some villagers gestured us to sit and rest with them. Mommahdu could understand their invitation.

Then I asked Mommahdu, "What do men folk do in these small isolated villages?"

He said, "They are all hunters and gatherers."

"What do they hunt? And how do they hunt?" I asked.

He said, "I will show you."

He stopped the car and asked if we could look at the traps for large animals they had set in the forest. There were traps for small animals also in another part of the forest. As I got used to looking for the traps, I could see several by the roadside. Women and children also helped in trapping small animals. Men were engaged in tribal warfare for the chieftaincy. They mostly used spears, bows, and arrows, which could be very dangerous due to the poisoned tips. They also went fishing in the river, lakes, or ponds, of which there was no shortage in Sierra Leone. Fish is one of the main dietary proteins for the natives, aristocrats, and Sierra Leoneans of all ranks and colors. Sweet water fish are abundant, aside from the harvested from the sea. Men also find work as day laborers in the bigger towns and cities.

We passed by Yonibana, a town close to the Date Palm plantation. Like most of these towns, a Mosque or two are dominant features of the town. This is the Headquarter of Yoni Paramount Chiefdom, one of the powerful ones in Northern Province. It fought long with its colonial rulers to retain its independence before merging into the Colonial territory. It is a junction town, connecting with further north and North West. The local population is of the Temne tribe. Most of the houses are mud houses with some mud-brick structures. We passed the town center and sped along.

The plants and vegetation are sparer by the side of the road. So we get the air of being close to the Savana. But, Mommadu said, frequently at night, one can come across Leopards, which can be dangerous to people and the dairy farmers. Fortunately, it was still mid-day; I expect they are resting for their night excursions.

Then we passed by the village of Taima. We crossed the Tai river to approach the town. The river was full and rough. It seemed to be due to heavy rain up in the hills. The bridge was not complete, so we had to take the ferry to cross the river. There was already a lineup of five to six vehicles. Mohmmadu parked the car behind the last one. Mohmmadu walked to the ferry gate and spoke to the gatekeeper. The Gatekeeper walked back with Mohmmadu, gave me a sharp military-style salute, looked at the car, and made sure it was the Ambulance of Kailahun District General Hospital. He spoke to each driver waiting ahead of us and made space for us in the front.

The returning ferry had one small car. As it got off the ferry, we were first to board. It could take another small car, but the next was a heavy lorry full of merchandise. The ferry master thought it might be risky, mainly as the river was full and rough. It usually took only seven to eight minutes to cross the river. But mid-way during the crossing, the ferry stopped. We realized something was wrong with the pulley system, which pulled the ferry both ways by power but was controlled manually. We were stranded in the middle of the river. The Ferry Master said that it would be fixed soon. If the worst happened, it could be pulled manually by people power. That was not encouraging. After ten minutes of waiting, in the rather powerful current of the river, knowing this river was full of crocodiles, giant snakes, and hippos, I started to get worried. I saw three to four people coming from the other side on a boat. The captain said there was a problem with the mechanical pulley. So the people were going to hook the ferry with ropes and pull them manually. That was not very reassuring. The people on the boat were fast enough to attach the ferry and returned to the opposite terminal with three ropes tied to the ferry. On the other side, the ropes were fed into a manual pulley, and two people started cranking the pulley, and two people held two different strings to keep the ferry on course. This was an extra precaution they had to take due to the high current of the river.

I can't swim. I have an eternal fear of drowning, although we were all wearing floating devices. Still, I started to count my blessings. The operation went smoothly, and we disembarked without getting wet or being mauled by the river animals. I broke into a cold sweat but kept my calm. Mohmmadu told me that they were pulling the ferry manually before the power pulley was installed, so they were well experienced. I thanked Mohmmadu for reassuring me, but I knew that my confidence level was at the ground level, if not in the pits. First, I had not seen many rivers full of dangerous animals and never had to cross any river on a ferry, mechanical or manual. Being a non-swimmer did not help. But I reassured myself that this was Africa, and I expected worse challenging situations. I tried to imagine the life of David Livingstone and Stanly Morton and all those who dared to explore the continent. They were the inspiration as to why I was here, I guess.

We could see the tower of the Mosque of the town. We had no plan to stop and beat the sunset; we continued our journey towards Bo.

The road surfaces were getting better. But the traffic was getting worse, drivers rushing, sometimes with heavy loads and wide-bodies, not suitable for these roads. But I must credit tactful drivers for not causing as many as accidents one would anticipate. Nevertheless, any accident or breakdown was likely to cause a traffic jam or shutdown for hours.

On our way to Bo, we came across several small villages. People were different. They were scantily dressed. Most of the women and young girls were bare-breasted. Mohmmadu said we were in a territory of some native tribes, who still lived their lives as they lived for centuries. But lights of civilization were dimly shining. The colonial rulers had not done anything to educate or expose them to modern life. They were hostile to the Europeans and the other tribes. Frequent wars, fighting, and killing were still the norm amongst these tribes. However, they were ordinarily respectful to others and did not harm unless any harm was done.

Mohmmadu said that a child from one of the tribes was abducted and sacrificed for ritual purposes a few days earlier. It was not uncommon, but we found out more about these incidences because they were more exposed to laws, government, and news media. For example, the killing of this girl was reported in the Freetown newspaper, like a banner on the front page, "Human stew," with a quarter-page photograph of some meat cooked in earthenware. That was scary. To make it worse, Mohmmadu said, we had to drive through both the tribal villages before going to Bo.

We passed by the next big village, Baima, but had no intention of stopping, so we carried on.

We could hear the beating of drums and rhythmic music. I asked Mohmmadu if any kind of festivities were happening. It sounded like war drums, reminding me of the Film "Shaka

Zulu." Mohmmadu said this kind of drumming and music meant some ritual events were taking place. As we progressed, the drum beating got louder and songs clearer.

Mohmmadu said we had to go through the villages where the girl was kidnapped and ritually killed last week. The emotions were still high. I hoped we would be safe passing through the highly charged environment.

As we were driving, Mommahdu flagged down an oncoming car. Then, he asked about the situation in that area.

He said one village's people are singing and dancing in the street. It was not violent, but most likely, they were expressing their ritual grief through humming, dancing, and singing. Men were in their war attire carrying sticks and hammers, but no spears or bows and arrows. There were police guarding both villages to stop the eruption of further violence.

"Is it safe to go through the barrier?" Mohammadu asked the driver.

He said, "Police are stopping all cars both ways and making sure there is no problem."

Slowly we arrived at the first village from where the girl was abducted. The officer greeted me with a salute. He said there was no problem. People had calmed down. But the emotions were still high. As we were ready to drive away, five people from the village arrived and told the police officer that they wanted to speak to the doctor from Kailahun; they expected that he was likely to be traveling in the ambulance. I got out and greeted them with shaking hands. I asked how I could help. Of course, I did not understand. One of the police officers acted as an interpreter.

The local chief, the older man, said there was a very sick person in his house. He would like me to see the patient.

The police officer asked, "Why did you not take the patient to Bo hospital?" He replied they were afraid that the patient's life was at risk. They would like the doctor from Kailahun to see her. If the doctor was here, then they would follow his advice.

In my mind, I said, I am just traveling in the government vehicle and have not yet commissioned myself as DMO of Kailahun.

The police officer asked if I was happy to see the patient and walk to the Chief's house."

"Of course, I would," said I.

I left the car with Bukhari, the driver's helper, who could speak their tribal language, along with two police officers escorting me with the Chief and his entourage.

As I arrived, I saw a young girl in her early teens or even less severely disfigured with multiple congenital disabilities on her face and lips. In addition, her speech was distorted due to her complete cleft palate. Otherwise, she appeared healthy and robust, scared and shy. Like all other women, she had only loin cover with bare breasts.

The chief told me that the girl's mother fled her village two days ago and took refuge with this Chief's family. The Mother said she overheard the village elders discussing many problems in their village and community. They think the girl brought ill omens and bad luck. So they decided to sacrifice the girl to appease the demon and pray to the god.

Being frightened, unknown to the rest of the villagers, she fled with the girl and took refuge with the chief.

I knew it would require a multi-stage plastic and reconstructive procedure, which was the only way to help her. But that kind of expertise was not available in the country. I did not say much. All I told them was, yes! She can be treated, despite being a complex clinical condition. It would be best to take her to Dr. Patel, the surgical chief at Bo General Hospital.

I met Dr. Patel at the Government Guesthouse in Freetown on several occasions and got to know him.

"They can come with me if they are ready, and I will take her to BO general hospital," I said.

In that case, the Constable–in–charge said, "I suggest you also take one of my constables with you."

"My people told me that many young and elderly men from the next village, with sticks and spears, were blocking traffic as they passed through. They are looking for the girl to try to escape from their village. They are stopping each car and looking for her. We have placed four armed police officers there if there is any violence. So far, they are only looking in the cars, not making anyone get off and search inside. Police are discouraging them from opening any vehicle without their permission. The policemen have been instructed to do a physical search if the villagers want them to. But you never know. Just to take extra safety measures. I will send a police escort with you till Bo."

The drummers and several young ladies danced around my vehicle as we got to the car. Mommahdu was sitting inside. All the ladies were only dressed in their loincloths. They cleared my way as we started the car, young girls still singing and dancing. They kept singing and following my car, flinging their arms in the air.

Bokhari told me that they were saying that they all want to come with me, at least take one of them. So I asked Boukhari why they wanted to come. He said, most likely they liked you, and they know I am the doctor who can save them from any danger.

I asked again, "Boukhari, is what they are singing, or do you think that maybe they have another motive for singing and dancing while following the car?"

"Sir! That is actually what they are saying in their song," said Boukhari.

I was dumbfounded. My reaction was beyond surprise.

Mommahdu gradually increased the speed, and the music and dancing ladies were left behind and disappeared into the greeneries of Sierra Leone.

We passed through the crowd in the next village. The Constable introduced me to the police on guard, and the tribal folk who were loitering around greeted me and cleared my way to proceed to Bo. I guess it was the government ambulance that deserved all the credit.

It was early afternoon when we entered BO general hospital. We went straight to the Emergency Department. I introduced myself and wanted to see Dr. Patel, the Senior Surgeon. A nurse came back with a message that he was in the Operating Theater and would be free in a half-hour if I would like to wait in his office.

I said, "I'll be back in a half-hour," and asked the girl and her mother to wait at the emergency room."

With an anticipated delay in completing his procedure, we thought we would use this time for our lunch. So we went back to the ambulance, and all shared the package Dr. Thakuta brought for our subsistence for the course of our journey. Mrs. Thakuta was an excellent cook. She prepared several Indian snacks. Mr. Mommahdu and Bochari happily shared. They seemed to have enjoyed it. I had my rationed black coffee, and they were happy with bottles of water.

We returned to the Emergency Department. After ten years of British life, Dr. Patel, who qualified as a physician in India and trained as a Surgical Specialist in England, joined the Colonial Service and came to Sierra Leone as a surgical specialist. He had acquired all British manners and became a well-adjusted Colonial Officer in the last five years of his stay in Sierra Leone. He was athletic, played tennis and golf with his white colleagues. He was, apparently, a regular customer at the European club, a signature of British colonial life.

As he came out to see us, he was delighted to see me, and immediately asked me if I would like to spend the night with him and his family. I thanked him and then told him my real reason was to come to get his help and advice. Finally, he agreed to take the girl away from the region. Otherwise, this could have been a cause for starting a tribal war.

We took the girl to an examination room and both examined her. Even being a surgeon, he was startled initially, looking at the extent of her face with an extensive congenital disability. He examined her carefully and told me that we needed a maxillofacial and a plastic surgeon. He could handle the maxillofacial part, but more challenging the plastic reconstructive part required to be done by an experienced plastic surgeon.

We could refer the patient to Freetown or wait for the visiting plastic surgeon to come from England to the Nixon Memorial Hospital in Segbwema. He had worked with them on various occasions. Yet this would be a major technical challenge.

The mother decided to stay in Bo. However, I did warn him that the village folks might chase her to Bo and carry out the sacrificial act as per their priest's advice.

Dr. Patel said, "That is a real possibility. But I feel that, as the devil is out of their community, they may be happy to think that the community is safe and that the devil is gone."

The patient was admitted under Dr. Patel. The mother was allowed to stay with the patient since she was still a minor, physically compromised, and her head was on the line.

Dr. Patel wanted me to visit his home, but I had to excuse myself from a genuine invitation since we still had to go a long way to Kailahun, and we were hoping to get there before dark. So we left the patient in the excellent care of Dr. Patel and drove away to Kenema.

Bo was the second-largest city in Sierra Leone. It had around 10,000 people. It was the Headquarter for the Southern province and also for the district of Bo. The roads were wide and clean. Most of the main roads were paved, but the majority were unpaved. The main roads had electric lights and well-maintained piped water. Some residents claimed that life in Bo was better than that of Freetown. Because its location was high in the mountain, it was cooler, and issues with the mosquito-borne disease were fewer. In addition, it was connected with the rest of the country by road, mostly mud roads. As a result, the traffic was heavy in and out of the city.

We did not have much time to drive around in Bo. So I would leave it for my next visit and entertain Dr. Patel's invitation.

We were on our way to Kenema. It was a wide dirt road. Traffic was not as busy as we noticed on our way to Bo. However, many heavy trucks with massive loads, primarily produce, were coming and going both ways. We were entering a dense forest area. In some places, it was completely covered with an overhead canopy. Mommahdu said this was a dense forest, and many leopards lived in these forests aside from chimpanzees, and baboons, which find a home in these giant trees. The leopards were just as clever and expert climbers of trees as monkeys.

The new road would be finished soon, which would cut short a one-hour trip to Kenema from Bo. The distance was ninety kilometers on the present road, but it would be just about seventy kilometers on the new route.

"God willing, we can make it in less than three hours," Mommahdu said. He went on to say the leopards were swift runners. "There are many poisonous snakes around. We will not come across many villages until we come close to Kenema."

Suddenly Mommahdu slowed down the car and told me to look at the left side of the forest. I could not see anything. Then he said, "Yes, we can only see the shining eyes of leopards' pride, maybe four of them."

Again, I could see several of them, about ten to twenty feet inside the jungle with a brutal look. I had never seen these animals freewheeling anywhere. From local wisdom, Mohmmadu said, they must be hungry. That was why they were so close to the road. This was not a safe time to venture outside to photograph the beasts. We carried on. We were driving just above the foothills of a range of mountains that ran from west to east in the central part of the country.

As we drove, we saw groups of chimpanzees clinging to the branches of trees. Some of the chimpanzees were carrying babies. I hoped these did not become dinner to the pride of leopards we just left.

Mommahdu said, "It is quite possible; we must leave this area." On the left side, we found several cesspools. If we waited long enough, we would certainly be able to see bush pigs and hogs coming for their mud bath. These were traps for both predators and human beings for hunting.

The vegetation was getting thinner and thinner as we came closer to Kenema. We noticed a few large Date palm oil and banana plantations. This area was the beginning of native coffee, either growing wild or by planned plantation. We were high in the hills as we approached Kenema. The town was on the mountain. Kenema city was the administrative headquarter for Eastern province and the district of Kenema.

It was at a higher altitude, and, they claim, the weather was relatively better, cooler than the rest of the southern province and the western region. I did feel the air was dryer and slightly cooler. I did not sweat as usual, as I had in the rest of the places I had lived in Sierra Leone.

I thought I would give a courtesy call to Dr. Cummings, the Provincial Medical Officer (PMO) of Eastern province. I know he struggled to manage Kailahun District Hospital, rotating his staff from Kenema and Koidu in Kano district, two days per week.

We called at the MOH office in Kenema. It was nearly 4 pm, and he generally stopped work at 2 pm. Someone called his residence from the office to let him know that I stopped by on my way to Kailahun. He wanted to speak to me and asked if I were not rushed, he would be happy to see me in his residence for tea. It was the perfect time for the Colonials for their afternoon tea.

Mommahdu knew the road to his bungalow. It is about a ten-minute drive from the MOH office, located on top of a hill. One could easily see most of the town and beyond from the veranda of his residence. It was built with some kind of red stone beautifully planned for their colonial officer, with a private tennis court, a large, well-designed garden, and separate staff quarters within the compound. Indeed a nice place to live.

I had met Dr. Cummings before. He was in his early forties. His training was in Public Health from the Liverpool School of Tropical Medicine, as he told me at one time. Despite being a Krio Sierra Leonean, he was almost of my height, maybe an inch or two taller, soft-spoken, perfectly mannered, with high myopic glasses. He gave me the impression of a scholar, a college Professor, rather than a colonial Health Care bureaucrat. Very different from that of my first introduction to Dr. Boardman, the Chief Medical Officer on Board MV Apapa in Freetown. Very different indeed.

I sat down in his well-furnished reception room. Soon a lady entered with a tray and another person following her.

"Well! Dr. Malaker, please meet my wife Helen," I stood up and bowed to greet her. She appeared to be of mixed race, well-spoken and asked me to have something with tea. She understood that I had to rush to reach Kailhun before dark. So

I enjoyed the old-fashioned tea with a spot of milk and a dash of sugar with some sandwiches and pastries to go along with it.

Dr. Cummings welcomed me to Kenema, Eastern province, and Kailahun. He said I would be delighted to work there; people were amicable, and he would be available whenever I needed help.

He did admit to serious shortcomings for not having a telephone in the office of DMO in Kailahun. To correct this, he was arranging an extension from the office of the Superintendent of Police, who was just across the road, a two-minutes' walk from the Office of the DMO. But the extension would be in the office of the DMO so that you did not have to run to the police station to receive or make a telephone call. But soon, there would be a direct telephone line in the hospital.

He, himself, felt uncomfortable about the "Telephone status-quo." He was surprised why this had not been corrected years before.

Mrs. Cummings was a nursing administrator and also taught at the Nursing School in Freetown. However, she was more interested in knowing about my family and feeling confident living alone in a new and unknown environment.

I quickly said that was the advantage. I could spend all my time looking after the people of Kailahun and carrying on the plans and programs as assigned by the MOH.

She was quiet, wished me good luck, and said to drop by their residence whenever I was passing through Kenema, time permitting.

Later, I gathered that her father was a British doctor working in Sierra Leone, married to a Sierra-Leonean nurse. Her father died in Sierra Leone when she was only six years old, and her brother was two years old. Her mother was from a wealthy farming family. The Colonial government looked after her. As per the expatriate contract, her mother got the widow's pension, which was much higher than the local appointees. The government paid for her education in the UK. Also, for her brother's education, who became an engineer. He decided to live in the UK after his qualification because the job opportunity for a mechanical engineer was not great at that time. He lived in the UK with his Sierra Leonean wife.

Dr. Cummings was my immediate boss, but we stayed as good friends in Sierra Leone many years after leaving the country.

After a delightful reception and a wonderful break in this tiring journey, I felt refreshed and ready to hit the road for the last leg of my journey to Kailahun.

It would take at least three hours to reach Kailahun. We were in the early "wet season." It was a dirt road, but very wide. The area was densely forested and a habitat for many wild and ferocious animals, especially the leopards, forest buffalos, aggressive baboons, whole varieties of monkeys, bush pigs, and warthogs. Many poisonous snakes called this part home.

As we left Kenema, the road appeared dry but dusty. Further down, it was getting wet and muddier, with potholes that seemed to have been recently filled up by dirt and stone chips. These fillers were OK for a few days or until the next heavy rain or flooding caused by heavy rain up in the mountain.

We could hear drumming and people's voices, but no sign of any village or human being. Mohmmadu said the villages were away from the road. People were afraid of killer animals, poisonous snakes, and more; from the savages and head hunters, the people still lived in the Stone Age lifestyle.

Mohmmadu was an expert driver on these roads, yet, getting anxious at times, trying to negotiate the dirt-filled large potholes, not knowing how deep or strong these might be to withstand the heavyweight of the ambulance.

We did notice one big lorry half sank in one of the deep potholes, tilted to its side. It just had half sunk on one of the "Quick mud holes." There was no way it would rescue itself or wiggle its way out from the trap.

It was fortunate that it had no load.

The driver said he had sent his helper to Daru to round up help and that he would be back soon. The sun would be there for another three to four hours. Not very safe to be stranded here. We assured the driver we would approach the nearest help, either the police or the military base in Daru. We left the driver behind alone in his truck stuck in the mud. We started to drive fast; luckily, we met the police rescue truck coming from Daru with the driver's assistant of the ill-fated lorry. They had several young men with them. I stopped the police vehicle and mentioned that we witnessed the truck stuck in the mud and needed help to be rescued. One man was identified as the driver's assistant. I asked them to hurry, as the driver was alone. The police rescue driver said they would arrive at the accident site in the next ten minutes,

I was relieved, and we proceeded towards the next town of Segbwema.

Segbwema is one of the large towns in the region, and it grew up at the tributary of one of the main rivers, river Moa. It is a grain, produce, and poultry distribution center. The population at that time was ten to twelve thousand. Diamond traders were also quite active. Segbwema is best known in the country and the region for its highly reputable Nixon Memorial Hospital.

It is a national referral center for tertiary specialist care in the region. It does attract patients from neighboring Guinea and Liberia as well.

The road to Segbwema from Kenema was just as challenging, lined by deep tropical forest and thick impenetrable bush and shrubs. Some kind of tall grass, like bamboo, also made the jungle challenging to enter. Perfect hideout for all types of predators, and most dangerous were tribal hunters. The road was shrouded by darkness even in the mid-afternoon because of the dense jungle. It took about two hours to drive forty kilometers from Kenema to Segbwema.

It was a clean city, with wide roads, primarily paved in the city center. The unpaved roads were also well maintained, dusty, but not many dangerous "mud holes."

We had to drive by the city center. I asked Mohmmadu to check the car, pressure, gas, oil, and especially windscreen wiper fluid. We went to the closest gas station, and it was checked as best as they could do. This Vehicle was built for rough African roads, for that matter, any challenging roads anywhere in the world, as the manufacturers claimed it to be. However, we had been reasonably confident in its agility and sturdiness.

Without waiting much longer, we headed for the next town of Daru, which was just about fifteen kilometers away from Segbwema. It could take anything between half to one hour. The road was just as muddy with a risky cesspool to negotiate with. However, we did not come across any dangerous mud holes or waterlogging. As we proceeded in a partly deforested part of the road, we noticed a pond, maybe forty to fifty yards. We found several bush pigs and warthogs, enjoying their muddy bath.

Mommahdu said that the tribal hunters built this pond to trap animals for hunting. But, unfortunately, it was also full of poisonous snakes. A little earlier during the day, one could see different species of monkeys and birds in the trees. As soon as the tribal hunters find out they had trapped an animal or two, they would quickly gather around and float in a canoe to attack the prey.

If they fell in the water accidentally, the chance of coming out was not great. But, on the other hand, the risk of being bitten by poisonous snakes or eaten by a short crocodile was very high indeed.

I knew I would be visiting Segbwema soon after I joined to get acquainted with the medical staff of Nixon Memorial Hospital. So without waiting, we headed for Daru.

It took close to one hour to reach Daru. We had to take a ferry to cross the Moa River before entering Daru city. The ferry crossing was fair and went without any incident. However, the bridge across the river was closed to the public. A new bridge was being built. Next time we would be lucky, we hoped.

An Italian construction company built a new road from Kenema to Kailahun and planned to extend it to the border. I was told the road had been completed. It was now in the process of being commissioned. We were to expect it opened to the public in a month or two. The ninety-kilometer broad highway would reduce the traveling time from four hours to one and a half or two hours.

Daru is an important city in the eastern part of the country. It is the Sierra Leone railway terminal that connects the east to Freetown. It is also the home of Sierra Leone Armed forces' eastern command. Daru is also a major center for the production of Palm Oil, known as yellow gold because of its pale yellow golden color. It is highly profitable to produce; the name is entirely appropriate. We passed through the town.

It seemed to be well designed, with a paved road in the city center. One could not miss noticing several well-stocked and well-lit stores in the city center, owned mainly by Lebanese or Indians. Daru was also an important transit point for legal and illegal diamonds and gold transactions.

We left Daru for the next major town of Pendembu. It was only 17-18 kilometers from Daru. The forest was less dense. We saw acres and acres of cultivated Palm oil trees replacing the natural equatorial evergreen vegetation. Also, for the first time, I noticed planted Coffee and Mango trees. The forests were getting lighter and lighter. The road to Pendembu followed the river valley for several miles. Then, we changed our course traveling on the hilly road. Palm oil plantations and coffee fields were on both sides of the road. Interestingly, instead of wild animals, we noticed herds of cattle and goats were ranged for pasturing; by cattlemen, women, and children walking along the main road.

We felt some sense of settlement and purposeful living, as opposed to villages consisting of a cluster of thatched houses, built not necessarily in any organized fashion, although the basic living pattern was the same. Subsistence agriculture meant they slash and burn the forest for cultivation, hunting wild animals for food. I am not sure if there was a differing concept of family as we know it in the west or older communities in the East. I would find out later.

It was about 30 kilometers distance from Daru to Pendembu. This part of the road was hilly. Pendembu is a town built on top of the hill stretching from central Sierra Leone to the eastern border. It took us just over an hour to reach Pendembu from Daru. Aside from being hilly, the road was safe and broad, lacking mud heaps and mud holes. There were several coffee plantations and cotton trees on the roadside. Deep and dense rainforests still line sections of the road. Pendembu was essentially a one-road town. Substantial habitations, government offices, post office, the health center, shops, schools were all by the side of one main street. There were few side roads, for people's houses. The paramount chief's compound was on one of the side roads leading to the hilltop. We noticed many purpose-built mud-brick houses with corrugated tin roofs. Pendembu was also an important transit point for all kinds of smugglers. Violent clashes between rival groups were known to happen from time to time. The chief was well educated. I was told he had progressive ideas.

Since we had some daylight left, I thought I would stop over at the office of the paramount chief for a courtesy call. But, unfortunately, the chief was away in Freetown. But the first lady of the chief, who helped him in many of his businesses, was kind to meet us and expressed her regret. She spoke excellent English, and her manners gave away her lengthy association with Brits, either in the colony or back at home in England.

We did not have much time, so we left after the introduction and promised to stop by next time I happened to be in Pendembu.

We were on our way to Kailahun, our last leg of the journey.

We thought this might be a good time to have our last picnic before arriving in Kailahun. So, outside the town center, we stopped and shared the snacks and sandwiches from Freetown. My final cup of coffee was still warm, an excellent combination with the remaining snacks. The driver and his assistant were happy with the water as usual.

It was already six in the evening. Kailahun is thirty kilometers from Pendembu. It was a dirt road, but the surface was better maintained or retained its shape due to less heavy traffic. As we started to drive along the Kailahun highway, the density of the forest was just as much like the road from Kenema. Bushes and shrubs mixed with the trees made the woods generally more impregnable and covered the road's side. However, after clearing the natural forests and faunas, we noticed large areas of palm oil plantations. The same we noticed on our way out of Daru to Pendembu. It was good for the country's economy, but what it was doing to the environment? The people and the animals called it their home. Only time would tell.

This area was relatively dry. But that relative dryness or lack of rainfall made little impact on the area's wetness. The ground got dry faster with the equatorial sun, but only the open spaces. As a result, this region had more chimpanzees, baboons, and varieties of monkey populations compared to the rest of Sierra Leonean equatorial forests. These can be a nuisance to the driving vehicles, people traveling in two-wheelers, and pedestrians as well. One striking thing I noticed was the increasing invasion of two-wheelers, of various makes and innovative designs, fit for the need and usage. The number of two-wheelers increased as we went further away from Freetown, which we observed. These were a significant addition to transportation needed for trade and commerce, not just for the riders of two-wheelers.

The journey would end shortly. Not sure who would be there when we arrived at my Bungalow in Kailahun. But it couldn't be that bad as the previous DMO stayed there with his wife.

We arrived at the entrance of the City of Kailahun. In a high arched concrete built gate, it was written: "Welcome to Kailahun."

It was a reasonable-sized district headquarter town. The town center was not far from the entrance. We noticed several two to three-story concrete buildings on our way in. There was a built-up covered market at the town center. There were several shops around the marketplace. The town was well electrified. Roads, shops, and several dwellings were supplied with electricity.

That was a big relief. Roads were not paved in the town but were well-kept and reasonably maintained.

It was already 8 pm; still, the town was awake, with lots of traffic and pedestrians. Most of the shops were open. We had to take a turn to go to my bungalow at the town center. First, we passed by the hospital and the District Police Headquarters. Then we entered into the somewhat secluded residential area for senior government officers.

It was not quite dark as we entered into the compound of my bungalow. I saw a car following us and stopping behind us as we entered. I was surprised to see Sister Thomas getting of the vehicle.

"Welcome to Kailahun, Doctor," she said. "My quarters are not very far. I asked one of the watchmen to call me as soon you arrived. I have the key to your house."

"Let us get in," she said. "You must be exhausted after twelve hours of travel on the road. Dr. Cummings, the PMO from Kenema, sent me a message as you left Kenema. I was expecting you about an hour ago, but here you need to give an extra two to three hours if you are lucky."

She opened the house, went into all the rooms, and switched the lights on. She showed me the washroom. There was some food on the table. The fridge had some supplies.

Sister said, "You can take a shower, then have your dinner and go to bed. Take a good night's sleep and rest well. I will send you a proper English breakfast tomorrow morning."

I could not be any more surprised and curious seeing her here. I asked, "Sister! What are you doing here?"

"Thanks for asking," she said. "It is a short story. Tomorrow is Saturday, and we have plenty of time to talk and discuss. The night watchman is around the compound. He will be close by most of the time. Should you need anything, just let him know."

"Thanks, Sister!" I said good night to her as she left. I was getting ready for a long stretch and deep sleep.

I kept wondering, where am I? What am I? What am I doing here? Many more questions; I had no answers, at least not for tonight, nor will it ever be? After a wash and a quick dinner, I went off to bed.

Chapter 20

KAILAHUN, A WORLD APART

"Nothing but breathing the air of Africa and actually walking through it, can communicate the indescribable sensation"

William Burchell

In the morning, I got up fresh but stiff. Every muscle in my body was either screaming with pain or groaning with aches. I forced myself to get up, not keeping track of the day, date, or the place where I got up from bed. I staggered out of my bed, quickly washed my face, brushed my teeth, changed from my overnight clothes, and put on something more practical. I walked to the dining room. I found Sister Thomas, sitting, waiting for me to wake up. I was a little surprised. I remembered that she mentioned last night before leaving, something about breakfast.

She said, "As promised, your English breakfast is ready."

She would make coffee, but I said, "Not to worry, I will give it a try."

I did enjoy an excellent breakfast and made coffee for myself and tea for Sister. Then, we started discussing life and how to adjust. I had been so used to her being around, and I forgot to ask her how she ended up here. "Let us fix you first, then I will tell you how I got here," Sister said. "You will do fine, not to worry. But you will need someone to cook, clean, do your laundry and keep the place tidy and livable."

She said, "Let us go to the lounge." I followed her. She went outside and brought two people with her. She accompanied an elderly man in his mid-forties or early fifties and a lady in her late thirties or early forties. They looked poor but gave their best shot with clean white clothing to look presentable and smart.

Sister introduced the man as Mommoh. She said Mommoh was the cook for three years for the previous doctor from Bangladesh. He learned to cook Indian dishes. He was also experienced in British cooking as well as our local dishes. The lady was "Jollo," the cleaning, washing, and laundry lady. She also looked after the previous doctor's household. Then she said that I might like to try both of them on a trial basis and then make them permanent if I was happy. Sister said there were living quarters for both the "Cook" and the "Maid" at the back of the house. Mommoh would be cook-in-residence, but Jollo needed to go back to her home every day to look after her kids and other family members.

There was a government-employed gardener, who maintained the lawn, landscaping, cleaning the yard, and generally looking after the safety of the house from predators, cats, ants, rats, mice, snakes, and scorpions; all those threatening your life. She laughed. There was also a resting room for the Gardener behind the house. We would check later.

I asked Sister about the salaries of the cook and maid. She said, "Start with what they were getting from the other doctor.

Although your work will be much less, you may decide after a month."

"Ok, Sister! Thanks very much for your help. I would not have any clue how to find these people. They can start from today if they are ready." Then we called both of them into the lounge.

Sister told them that they should start from that day.

"Although the doctor's work will be much less than the previous doctors, he will pay you the same salary for the first month and see your work, and then decide how much you will be paid."

"OK! Mommoh and Jollo, you know the house, you need not have a tour, and you can go and start now."

Both of them were happy, saluted me, and left.

Sister said, "One time, we will go around the house and the compound with the gardener. Should you have any questions or notice something unusual, let me know." Then, she said, "I must go now; I will see you later for more talks. Perhaps you would like to visit the hospital during the weekend so that you can start well informed on Monday?"

"An excellent idea," I said. I thanked Sister Thomas from the bottom of my heart as she left my house.

I returned to the lounge and organized my wardrobe and the library. I brought several books; I got them in preparation for postgraduate studies.

Now I had the chance to look at the accommodation. My residence was a large bungalow with four bedrooms and a lounge extension to the dining area. Then, on the other side, a separate room which was supposed to be study and office and had two large windows in front and on one side. So it was possible to look out the front and one side of the house sitting in this room. I knew this would be my favorite room. There were two full and one-half bathrooms, one attached to the master bedroom, and the other two tucked in easy access to the rest of the house.

In the old days, before the days of electricity, there were large fans hung from the ceiling, pulled manually back and forth on a pulley by a person known as "Punkha Puller." Their job was to pull the fan back and forth to keep the occupant cool. There were two hanging *Punkha*, one in the lounge and the other in the master bedroom. They were still hanging, but the "Punkha Pullers" were long gone, replaced by an electric fan. There were ceiling fans in every room, also one table fan in reserve. All the rooms were well furnished, made with teak or cedar wood furniture. The dining table and the chairs matched the house's sentiment, so did the large table in the office.

The kitchen and the pantry were separate from the main house but connected by a covered walkway. On the back, there was a paved courtyard with a concrete boundary. The cook's and servants' quarters were outside this enclosure but attached to the building. They had their separate living arrangement. It looked like; quite an elaborate living arrangement. The Brits built these, the colonial rulers, to make their officers' lives as comfortable as possible during their tour of duty.

Mommoh asked me what he should prepare for lunch and dinner. I told him to cook anything that he cooked for Dr. Ahmed. I gave him some money and told him to buy anything he needed to prepare today's dishes. I told him to buy some good quality English biscuits. I always like biscuits with my tea and coffee.

While I was organizing and inspecting the interior of the house, Sister Thomas came to take a tour of the outside of the house and check the compound. She confessed that she had never done so.

"But let us give it a try. Let us inspect the building." We climbed down the front staircase.

It was a large wooden bungalow built on piles. A covered walkway attached the kitchen and other utility facilities to the main bungalow. The wooden houses were cooler and less likely to be struck by lightning, which was not uncommon during the rainy season. Aside from being cool, wood was plentiful and durable to protect the houses from termites and runaway gushing water during heavy tropical rains. It also discouraged creepers, particularly the snakes, which were abundant here, rats, moles, and other larger rodents from digging under the house to make it their home and make the life of the residents fearful. There was a river behind this residential enclosure, about half a kilometer away. There was plenty of fish and snakes that could creep into the compound. The boundary wall was made of solid wooden planks hidden inside the creeper vegetation covering them, a solid barrier for any intruder, man, or beast. But anything could happen.

I have a pathological fear of snakes. I had no qualms in admitting it. Friends and some of my teachers said I might have a condition called "*Ophidiophobia*," or abnormal fear of snakes. I urged them; please do not treat me for my psychopathic condition or fear of snakes. I would rather live with my phobia, not let any snake escape with its life on my watch. I suggested making sure they check for snake invasion daily and plant raw Phenyl (Phenol) soaked fabric placed at the fence every four to five yards apart. Phenyl was in plentiful supply for preventive and safety in Hospitals and public health facilities.

This would be another added precaution. At home in India, this was a well-tried effective "snake-repellent."

Replenishing phenol would be an added and essential work of the gardener. So, with the help of Sister Thomas and the district health inspector, the Phenyl-soaked fabrics in various containers were placed all along the boundary wall. At least it eased my anxiety to some extent. The gardener poured a little bit of Phenyl every week into the container to keep their potency alive against the creepers.

The compound had extensive, well-kept gardens and walkways. There was a tennis court on one side of the compound. There were seven to eight houses for senior officers in this protected area; mine was the last, where civilization ended, and the reign of the jungle began. My house was also closest to the river. Others were protected by distance from the river and intruders of all shapes and forms. But none of the houses were visible from outside as one walked or drove along the access road from the hospital.

We did an extensive inspection of the house and the compound. Then, sister asked me if I would like to visit the hospital on a Sunday. I said, "If you are agreeable and available, I will be happy to do that so that we can get on with our real work, taking care of the patients from Monday."

"Alright! In that case, I will request Mr. Amara, the Administrator, and Mr. Joseph, the senior nurse/anesthetist responsible for the operating room, and do all liaison with the pharmacist in Kenema for our medication needs."

Before Sister Thomas left, she took out mail for me, which arrived at the ministry the previous week. There was a letter from my father. The letter was first addressed to Prof Wellborn of Hammersmith Hospital, in London, the UK, who very kindly redirected this letter to the Ministry of Health in Sierra Leone Government, then to me. This journey took seven weeks to deliver the mail to me, most likely how it had to traverse the world to track me down. Thank goodness I did receive the letter from my father, instead of it floating in the Mediterranean Sea or across the beaches of West Africa.

She said she would pick me up at 10 am to go to the hospital. I thanked her and promised to meet the following day again.

I could not wait to read my dad's outdated letter. It was still new to me. I could not wait to read it. I opened the envelope with a small kitchen knife and read it with so much expectation: two letters, one from my father and one from my mother.

The following day which was Sunday morning, I was ready to be picked up by Sister Thomas. I had breakfast, the first time prepared by Mommoh, the cook. He prepared the breakfast exactly what Sister Thomas brought for me the day before. I asked him if the food came from Sister Thomas. Mommoh was shy and generally very polite. He said he had prepared what Sister Thomas had brought. I was impressed with his sense of responsibility and observation. Then, he asked what he should prepare for lunch. I could not think of anything.

"Well!" I said, "Make what you would do for the other doctor." I had no idea what it might be. But knowing that the previous doctor was from Bangladesh, my palate is not much different, so whatever he would serve would be acceptable.

I said, "Thank you, Mommoh, it is great." I hoped he was pleased.

Together with Sister Thomas, we left for the hospital.

It was called Kailahun District General Hospital. We entered the compound. The hospital was fenced by barbed wire fencing. I met Mr. Amara, the hospital manager, Mr. Joseph, the nurse anesthetist, Mohmmadu and Boukhari, the ambulance driver, and Mr. Boukhari, the ambulance assistance. An Italian NGO recently donated the ambulance. The previous ambulance was a Jeep, converted to carry patients and doctors as needed, but had many problems and downtime. This new ambulance was a Range Rover, redesigned to carry patients and stretchers. It could be converted back to carry passengers as needed. Mr. Amara said the previous one was removed about a couple of months ago, having been idle for nearly eight months.

A concrete wall surrounded the large compound of the hospital. I could see five chalet-like buildings. The first building we entered was the Outpatient clinic; the surgical operating theater at the end of the building, the storeroom, the nurses' restroom, and DMO's office were tucked in between. Across the field, the first chalet, which had the central storage for the hospital, office of the Head Nurse, District Nurse and the midwife, office of the Hospital Manager and his store were all well-spaced and well-kept rooms.

Next, the longest chalet was the hospital inpatient facility for twelve hospital beds. A unisex hospital ward, where both male and female patients were admitted in the same ward. A social arrangement far advanced in social equality at that time. All beds had their screens. A locally made wooden screen separated the male and female sections on both sides of the ward. The division changed depending on the needs of male or female patients.

The nursing station was at the end of the ward, connected by a door to a small room with two beds.

I asked Sister, "What happens in this room?"

She told me that these beds were for post-operative patients or patients who were too sick and needed frequent attention from the medical staff or patients who were too noisy to be kept in the main ward. However, there was one patient in one of the beds. I asked her what was wrong with this patient.

"We do not know what is wrong with the patient. He is delirious and speaks to himself almost all the time. The doctor put him on a sedative, so he remains sedated except for feeding or being nursed for personal care. The doctor from Kenema visits Kailahun every Friday. He saw the patient. We were following his instruction. He was expected to come back next Friday and would decide on the next step.

When the patient was brought to the hospital last week, he was physically violent and abusive before his admission. He was tough to control. Finally, his relatives got him from the deep jungle of the southeast, told us the demon had possessed him; they were afraid of his rumblings, and he wanted to set fire to the entire village. They were petrified, but with the help of their chief, they got him to the hospital. Apart from medical supervision, he remains under police surveillance."

That was a fascinating case. I would go through the notes the next day.

The ward was connected to an annex by a covered walkway. It was the kitchen. Usually, patients' relatives bring all food from home. But some do not have the support, and then the hospital would supply all their meals.

"That is a fair arrangement," I said.

There were two isolated chalets, a bit far from the ward. One of the buildings was used to keep patients who died in the hospital until relatives took them for final rituals. The other nearby chalet was the morgue for autopsies. To remove the bodies from the hospital had not been a real problem. Kailahun was dominated by the Mende-speaking tribe, who were of the Muslim faith. According to the religious mandate, all dead bodies had to be buried within twenty-four hours of death unless a strong case could be made to delay through a law officer. So there was never a backlog in either room that dealt with dead bodies, waiting for the eternal farewell.

Another small chalet across the field was the storehouse for housekeeping and garden equipment. Every chalet has its covered veranda; there were wooden benches for the visitors to rest while waiting for their sick family or friend or to see the doctor or any other staff. So many floral and bush plants were well distributed through the compound; a uniformed guard and two gardeners kept the hospital premises clean and pretty. Then we went to check the nitty-gritty of the outpatient clinic: the operating room, instruments, all the storage facilities, and the manager's office. I also checked the kitchen, water supply, power station, and control room.

The hospital did have its own small generator for emergencies in case of a breakdown of the main power supply.

It was already 2.30 pm. I thanked everyone for spending their Sunday morning, skipping the "church time" and away from their family. Sister Thomas volunteered to drop me at my bungalow. Mohmmadu, the driver, said he would pick me up just before 8 am the following day. Sister said that the hospital ambulance would be available for official or personal transportation until I had a car. But Sister would be available to drive me anywhere I needed to go.

I thought this transportation arrangement needed to be resolved sooner than later. I pondered how to purchase a car for my personal use. However, I do not know the town or any town's people. What to do?

Monday morning, I was ready for work with my briefcase and diagnostic set. The ambulance arrived just in time. It was a five to seven-minute drive from my residence. I went to my office. Sister Thomas was waiting for me. I greeted her with my best sincerity. Then Mr. Amara arrived with several young ladies. I could distinguish the three nurses. I greeted them. Another uniformed young lady was a nurse, but her job was to be my interpreter and assist me in the outpatients. She was also responsible for the Outpatients attendance registry and appointments. The concept of the "appointment" system was yet to be understood and acceptable to the community we were expected to serve. It needed some basic education and understanding of a process that needed discipline.

I established the pattern, most notably to follow up on the seriously ill patients using government health care facilities or offices of local chieftaincy. Much more education and health consciousness were needed. But more importantly, a sense of purpose, perseverance, and an attitude of being a solid team player were essential components of the initiative. But also needed was compassion, empathy, and a deep understanding of local culture, belief, faith, and respect. It was impossible to bring these changes overnight or during my first term contract for eighteen months. I believe in sowing the seed and waiting for the tree to grow while nurturing the growing plants.

I met Mr. Joseph officially, my main support in the operating room. I also made a special issue of meeting the head cook, the mortuary technician, and the pharmacist, who was based in Kenema. The pharmacist visited once a week, and the mortuary technician on an as-needed basis. In addition, Mr. Harding, the District Health Inspector, and some of the midwives came later at the request of Sister Thomas.

As I was getting ready to start the clinic, I had two important guests. Both arrived together. Mr. Williams, an athletic-looking man well attired in a well-pressed three-piece suit, spoke in "Queen's English." A dark Sierra Leonean introduced himself as the District officer (DO) while the other was thin, spritely, uniformed, giving away his identity. He introduced himself as the District Police Superintendent. His office, the police headquarters, was just across the street. The Police Super said himself and the rest of the regiment were at my disposal whenever I needed any help or assistance.

I found them easy-going, humorous, and friendly. The District Officer asked if I found the accommodation satisfactory since he got it checked by the Public Works and Electricity Department. He also said I could call him directly or his office with any housing concerns.

He said we came together to share the time of our introduction so that you could carry on with your actual business of looking after patients. He promised to meet again soon in a relaxed environment with more time to discuss issues and get to know each other better.

As they were leaving, the Police Super said, Sister Thomas told him that I would be looking for a car if he could help. He said he would scout around and get back to me soon.

I could not have been any more delighted, meeting these two fine and friendly officers, with whom I would be working closely for the next eighteen months.

The clinic was a little crowded. There had been no regular doctor for the last six weeks, and the process was a little unfamiliar to me. I had to depend heavily on my interpreter that day. I guessed this would get better with time. Only a few patients were waiting for surgery. After assessing and deciding on the type of surgery needed, Mr. Joseph took care of them and gave them the instructions and the date of admission for the surgical procedure. The midwives asked several young pregnant ladies to be seen by me. After seeing the patients, I made my clinical notes while the nurse prepared the next patient for examination.

As the clinic finished, Mr. Amara, the Hospital Manager, entered and asked if I would like to look at the work schedule and my full responsibility as DMO.

He said, "We can look at the details of the inventory when we have enough time on our hands."

I said, "Maybe you can tell me about my responsibilities today so that I can be prepared mentally to work out a plan."

"Well!" he began, "As the DMO for the district of Kailahun, you will be responsible for running the District General Hospital. There are four health centers in the District, which you are expected to visit at least once every two to three months. Several villages have midwifery services supervised by the District Nurse under your guidance. You are also the District Health Officer, administrator of the jail, and overseer of the school health program run by District Nurses. Another important responsibility is to perform the duty of a Coroner for the district. As the DMO, you must also submit an annual budget by January each year. As Mr. Amara explained, it is broadly what you need to cover and work with Dr. Cummings, the Provincial Medical Officer, who works out of Kenema."

"It sounds a lot, but I am sure you will have a good time tackling all these, Sir! Others have done the best way they could do."

I felt I had a good, cool-headed experienced, responsible and conscientious individual as an office manager. I could do business with him. We indeed got along well throughout my stay in Kailahun.

Then Sister Thomas entered. "Oh! You are still here?" I asked.

She said she had to deliver a baby, who came around 11 am.

"She had no problem. This is her third pregnancy. I did not want to bother you after a busy clinic day, and you have been meeting with Mr. Amara." She said she could not offer me any hot or cold drink after a hard day, but they would get organized tomorrow.

"That was exactly, what I was going to ask you, to set up an arrangement for making tea and coffee, cold drinks when we need. First, I will prepare a short shopping list to determine what we can get here."

Then I asked Sister, "It was a delightful surprise to see you here in Kailahun. What made you come here?"

"Yes!" She said, "I had no idea that I would be working furthest from Freetown, where my family lives. As a part of my scholarship to go to England for postgraduate training for two years, I must serve in the provinces at least for two years before I am posted in Freetown or Bo. I had agreed to this arrangement. The position of Kailahun District Hospital was vacant for some time. The government could not find someone suitable who would be willing to work in Kailahun. So the Ministry said they would post me to Kailahun for twenty months instead of twenty-four months as per the contract. They also agreed to extra home leave and a few other incentives. I was happy to accept the assignment."

"When you were admitted at the Hill station Hospital, I heard, after your recovery, that Dr. Boardman is expecting you to go to Kailahun as DMO. So, I thought I would be working with you. At least I know that you are a gentleman. So, I have been in Kailahun for the last one month. I do like the place and the community. I had no idea how cosmopolitan this area is, especially because of the diamond and gold mining and other rare minerals. But for shopping, I have to go to Freetown when I become "shopping starved.""

"That is great!" I said, "At least you will be here until the end of my contract. So I am happy and reassured."

It was nearly 4 pm. We all left to return home. Mohmmadu dropped me at my residence.

Mommoh, the cook, fell asleep, not knowing when I would be back. He woke up quickly at the sound of the vehicle. He asked if he should warm up my lunch.

I said, "Yes, please."

I was more than surprised to see the dishes on the dining table. I felt as if I was back home. There was boiled rice. There were lentils cooked in Bangladeshi style, semi-fried Okra-curry, fish curry, and small fried fishes. I could not have dreamt even in my wildest dreams, that I would be eating home-cooked dishes in this "God-forsaken place." Thousands of miles across the ocean, deserts, dense jungles of equatorial forest, a place mainly outside the domain of civilization, and rarely close to it.

I thanked him for the most delicious dishes and said I would write home about my food here. He looked pleased. We still have a bit of a language barrier.

I went to the lounge, took one of my books on African history, and dozed off in the settee.

I woke up at around six pm; it was still daytime. Mr. Amara's list of my responsibilities kept buzzing in my head. I was trying to figure out how to cope with the enormous responsibilities. I started to think that with the prestige of a District Medical Officer comes risks, responsibilities, adaptation of skills, managing skills of people for which we had no training, being a coroner, or being an administrator for the prisons. But I kept reassuring myself that if others had done the job, then I would try to do it even better. For example, my knowledge of a coroner's work came right out of a hundred-page medical jurisprudence book in medical school, and I had no idea how to manage a prison, nor was it in my undergraduate medical education curriculum. But the powers of the Government thought it appropriate to make a senior physician the administrator of prisons because the physical, mental, and behavioral health of prisoners, which the prison officers had to deal with daily, needed lots of coordinated planning for its execution.

As far as I knew, the British government established the role of DMOs or Civil Surgeons in the colonial empire. I was familiar with the system because my father was a civil Surgeon for several years in Districts with several millions of people, dozens of sub-divisional hospitals, aside from the District General Hospital. Several scores of Doctors and other medical staff worked under his watch, including the central jail and the Public Health Department. I never thought I would be given a similar responsibility after medical school. Nevertheless, I would take the risk, even if I had a choice.

Chapter 21
LEARNING FROM AN UNEXPECTED SOURCE

"The true wisdom comes to each of us when we realize how little we understand about our life, ourselves and the world around us"

Socrates

In West Africa, one expects any sickness, situation, social order, social disorder, climatic or environmental surprises. However, the perception may be relative to the unknown and unexpected challenges through the eyes of a curious and adventure-seeking, aspiring young doctor, whose present world was more than he learned from the books. This is because, even more than the wisdom given to him by his learned professors, whom he revered with the highest esteem, the insight from daily challenges and encounters in living in the equatorial forest in Africa was very different indeed.

I could recite every step of performing a hernia operation, explain each step clearly from the start of the incision to closure. The first hernia that was slated for me was a 55 year-old healthy but "wiry" individual who had been nursing his illness for the last eight to ten years; a retired prison officer. He told me that he got used to the disease, which generally did not bother him except the inconvenience and fear of getting stuck. In fact, for the last two years, it was slowly getting challenging to push the swelling back. He was worried that it might get stuck and may not be able to move it back into his abdomen.

That was a perfect reason for seeking advice for surgical treatment. He was a well-motivated and understanding patient. The ground for my success had already been laid down. We discussed the surgery, and the consequences of not doing the surgery sooner rather than later were grim. The patient understood the risks very well. After that, we were all set to go.

Mr. Joseph put the patient under anesthesia; Sister Thomas put the patient on the operating table and got him cleaned, disinfected, and draped. Now it was my turn to start the surgery. I gave the incision a book-perfect opening. I incised through the first layer, then I could not see the second layer, as we were taught how it should look. Although I have performed and assisted in the past, I was confident of seeing what I expected to see, a layer of a part, silvery looking with striations, firm and tough tissue to the touch, but not to be seen anywhere. I started to dabble in and out of the field of operation. After about fifteen minutes into the exploration, Sister Thomas quietly told me that the patient's hernia was old. Maybe he had an extra false layer on top of the layer I was looking for. Perhaps I should splay it away and go underneath.

I understood what Sister Thomas was saying. But this had not been described in any textbook, nor had I seen it before in a similar situation. Sister may have seen many surgeries, some with similar conditions. I took the bait of her suggestion and started to splay the layer with the handle of two scalpels gripped in two hands. I had to make a small nick to access the full thickness of this extra layer. As I opened up the gap, I could clearly see the shining silvery layer underneath.

Mission accomplished. As the visualization was good, with a blind dissection, I exposed the next silvery layer, then the next, then the next, and finally the hernia "sac," cleared of unexpected and unwanted materials and fixed the Hernia. Closed the incision layer by layer and woke him up, and he was ready to return to the ward. He was well awake and asked for water but, regrettably, could only offer small chunks of ice cubes. He looked good; his vitals were as expected as in a post-operative recovery period.

"Small problem, big palaver!" As they say in "Sa-lone."

The staff I had in my team never ceased to surprise me with their tribal belief and knowledge, at the same token, time-honored social and cultural wisdom, particularly that of their elderly folks.

One day a 14-year-old boy was brought to the clinic by his father from a further interior in the forest, saying the boy "Plenty, plenty sick." He looked concerned. The child looked dehydrated and uncomfortable, wearing his normal village garb. He was slightly hot. Otherwise, his vital signs were normal. He looked pale. I asked the nurse to take him to the examining room to have a good look.

On the couch, I asked him to remove his clothes. His entire abdomen and chest wall were covered with multiple vesicles with a blackhead, to my utter surprise. Maybe fifty of them scattered throughout the front of his torso, but none on the skin of his pelvis. There were a few similar vesicles in his arm, but not as big as those on his trunk. I looked carefully.

To me, those looked like the typical textbook picture of Smallpox. I must admit, never had I seen any case of smallpox in my life. If this was the case, then it was a serious public health hazard. I asked if anyone in the village had a similar condition. The father denied it, and the patient also denied seeing any of his friends having a similar situation. He did not know anyone he knew who had so many vesicles. Maybe one or two, but those got better. I had to alert the Ministry of Health if it was so. Why was it only confined to one part of his body if it were smallpox? That went against how smallpox presented itself. I wondered if it was not smallpox, what it might be. How contagious it may be. I did not want to take any risk but to deal with it as if it were smallpox or a similar highly contagious viral condition. I wondered who I could speak with for advice.

I needed to speak to Dr. Thakuta in Freetown about his experience of the incidence of smallpox in Sierra Leone. I had to ask the District Officer's office to connect me with Connaught Hospital in Freetown and, specifically, with Dr. Thakuta. The District Officer had a "RED" emergency phone line. His office was kind enough to get Dr. Thakuta.

I described the picture to Dr. Thakuta. What I told, he agreed, was the possibility of smallpox, but as far as he knew, smallpox had been eradicated from Sierra Leone, or there had been no cases in the last five to six years. He suggested that it could be chickenpox or some other similar viral infection. I said the vesicles were rather large for chickenpox.

Sister Thomas had returned from her other nursing activities, waiting in the outpatients' to check the patient with a possible smallpox infection. I showed her the patient and said, it looks like smallpox, I said. She was also surprised to see so many concentrated in the front of his body and the front of both arms, but none at the back. The child had no fever; he was alert and coherent and responded to Sister's questions and whatever my interpreter asked him.

He did not look toxic, but complained of considerable pain and muscle ache. These symptoms did not fit precisely with my diagnosis of smallpox or, for that matter, chickenpox, either.

I had no idea what it was. Still, we admitted him to an isolated room to protect anyone else from getting infected. Then, with the help of the police superintendent in one of his vehicles, I dispatched the District Health Inspector to the area where the patient came from to gather more information from the community and the region. Then, as the patient settled in his room and all possible arrangements for isolation nursing were made, the patient's father agreed to travel back to his village with the Health Inspector.

Later in the afternoon, I went to see the patient again. He was comfortable, having painkillers and intravenous infusion. Looking back at all his vesicles, we discovered that all those had a small blackish white head, not ulcerated. Either small or chickenpox would form crust or vesicles. Sister agreed. Reluctantly, she said these could be mosquito bites. I stared at her. He was asked what kind of mosquito bite this could be. In the meantime, Mr. Joseph, the nurse, and the anesthetist came in to give a helping hand. He had not seen smallpox either, but agreed with Sister that these might be mosquito bites, but so many of them cover only his body's front part? That was unlikely to be any form of pox and did not make sense having so many; indeed, it looked like an infection.

I asked them what kind of mosquito bite could give this nodular vesicle with a blackhead. Most mosquito bites looked like a small red papule, disappearing within a couple of days. But this had been going on for more than a week without any sign of resolving. Sister and Mr. Joseph looked at each other.

Sister suggested these could indeed be by mosquito larvae, known as "Tumbu" fly. However, they appeared white by carefully examining the heads, and the blackish pigments surrounded the whitehead.

Anyway, Sister suggested that if these were due to Tumbu maggots, then let us cover these with Vaseline, and they would come out, unable to breathe. This was one simple way of removing them from the human skin. So, to give fair credit to Sister's suggestion, we covered the entire chest wall with a thick layer of Vaseline and waited for a couple of hours.

I returned to my bungalow, planning to recheck the patient in the early evening.

Around 5 pm, I saw Sister's car pulling into my driveway. So I came outside to invite her in. Her face was full of joy and smiles. Then, without having me ask her about the patient, she said, "Sir, I have not seen these before. You need to come and see the patient. You will find it very interesting. I will wait for you in the hospital; please come now."

I got dressed. Within ten minutes, I was with the patient. I could not believe what I saw, which I had never seen before, nor read in any of my textbooks, nor any of my revered professors spoke or taught about what I saw.

Scores of small maggots came out of some of the lesions, some half out, and a few of those remained intact. I had no words to thank Sister and Mr. Joseph. We agreed these were from Tumbu mosquito bites, whose larvae grew in human skin before becoming pupa and adult flies and leaving the host with a painful, sometimes infected, suppurating vesicular ulceration.

The ones that were half out, Sister and Mr. Joseph, squeezed out, and the few that did not heed Vaseline application, perhaps were dead or too weak to force through the crater. Sister and another nurse cleaned the area with an antiseptic solution.

These were certainly not due to Smallpox or any pox, for that matter. Instead, these were most likely from Tumbu mosquito bites leaving their eggs to grow into larvae at the site of the bite.

We covered the rest of the body and all lesions with Vaseline.

The following day we noticed again almost all remaining vesicles discharged the larvae. The ones that did not come out, Sister squeezed them out with the help of another nurse. The ones that still did not come out, I felt, needed to be surgically removed; otherwise, they would develop into infected ulcerations, leading to complications or even toxemia.

We kept him for the next few days on intravenous hydration, pain killers, and antibiotics. The total damage to his entire skin could be compared to a major surgical operation.

The following day, as I arrived back in my office, the District Officer paid a visit, just to say hello, as he said. "Sir!" He asked me, "Did I hear that you have a patient with smallpox?" Before I told him anything, he said it was right to take the preventative action I'd taken. "I know that you sent the Health Inspector to the village to look at the region for any other cases. Please let me know when he returns. In the meantime, please let me know if I can help you in any way with my resources,"

I smiled and took him into my office. We both sat. My good Sister sent tea and some biscuits for the two of us. "You are right," I said, "I thought the boy had smallpox. It is a serious health care issue to tackle. But before I pressed the panic button, we did lots of thinking, and with the help of Sister Thomas and Mr. Joseph, we found out that this was an extreme case of larvae infestation from the Tumbu Mosquito bite. It could have killed him if left untreated, but like smallpox, it would not infect nor would have caused an epidemic.

He stood up for a minute and said, "You mean to say there is no smallpox in Kailahun?" "Exactly, there is none at present," I said. "What a relief, Sir! I can't express how grateful we are for so efficiently handling of the situation," the District officer responded. Finally, I said we must thank our staff, Sister Thomas and Mr. Joseph, the nurse - anesthetist.

Later in the afternoon, our health inspector returned with a smile all over his face. He could not find any case of smallpox in the village or the region, but did see a couple of people with rashes, which looked like mosquito or insect bites. He immediately conveyed the findings to the district officer; he was eagerly waiting for the report.

Next week, the remaining lesions were cleared of their embedded larvae surgically. The child recovered. We diagnosed his illness. Sister explained to the boy and family how to take care of himself in the future from such attacks.

A few days later, I called Dr. Thakuta and gave him the detail of the case. What I thought looked like a "textbook" type of smallpox was an extensive Tumbu Mosquito Larvae infestation. Unfortunately, the lesions looked anything but what I had ever read of in any medical textbooks or was taught in medical school. Fortunately, the patient recovered.

He said, "I know."

"How did you know?" I asked, "We are so isolated from everybody; the message traveled so fast before I could tell you."

"You did not have to tell me, Dr. Boardman; the CMO called me to relay the incidence. But, you know, everywhere the "bush telegraph" travels faster than any media."

A month later, the DO came to tell me that the Ministry would install a "hotline" phone in my hospital office, like to the District Officer and the Police Superintendent.

I was glad, indeed, and delighted to convey this to all my staff.

I hoped that was the end of this story. Months after this shocking encounter, I was in Freetown for government business. I was back as a guest at the Government rest house while visiting Freetown on a government assignment. In the afternoon, I was not feeling energetic after attending the high court as the coroner for a case I dealt with in Kailahun. I ordered the set of afternoon tea. I saw my old friend, the lady from the German Embassy, walk in as I was waiting. I greeted her and invited her to join me. She was pleasant and happy to be my guest. After exchanging some pleasantries, she asked me about my work and life in Kailahun, which to the locals was known as a "God-forsaken place" in Sierra Leone. She had visited Kailahun on a few occasions. But as far as an interior equatorial rural community, the town had its own charm. She thought it was perfect for meditation, yoga, and other higher metaphysical activities.

I agreed.

I had much muscle ache, swelling of my right arm, and fever. It could be due to a small vesicle and much redness in the entire outer aspect of my right arm. A small pimple was just above my right elbow, just below my deltoid muscle. I thought that was an insect or a mosquito bite. Not unlikely these innocuous bites could become an abscess. I thought it was getting infected. I just happened to mention my mosquito bite and some discomfort associated with it to her. She felt sorry, and asked if I had consulted any doctor in Freetown. I replied with a no.

As curious as this German globe trotter was, she asked me to show her the sore area. First, she carefully looked at it. Then, she adjusted her reading glasses a couple of times, asking how long I had been in Sierra Leone. I said about nine months; four months were in Kailahun.

"You need not go to see a doctor. I will fix it, and you will be better by tomorrow." I did not understand what she meant. Then, she reassured me that she trained as a nurse in Freiburg. She worked at the university hospital for two years, then joined trainee support services with the German Foreign Services department and started her work in Sri Lanka; that was just over twenty-two years ago. From being a trainee secretary to becoming the Deputy Consul for the German Embassy in Sierra Leone, it took lots of walking and climbing from a nurse to be a Diplomat, an exciting career befitting her energy and enthusiasm. She said she still had the touch of her nursing hands. She knew what I had. She said, "I can cure it, but I would like to invite you to my suite for privacy." "Really?"

Without asking many questions, I followed her to her suite. She had some first aid materials, cleaning the area with spirit. She started to squeeze the ulcer from side to side as if she expected to drain the pus from inside. After a few seconds of squeezing, she extracted a white clotted blob from the lesion. But it was a maggot she expressed out of my skin lesion at a close look. She said it was a maggot from a bite of the Tumbu mosquito, which was common in the West African sub–Saharan region. She had these several times and expressed those out every time, herself. That was another surprising German fit of action.

By this time, I knew something more about Tumbu. I was grateful yet utterly devastated. The picture of the 14-year-old boy completely took over my thoughts. I was wondering how many more maggots were eating my flesh. I felt sick. I could not get over the nightmares of hundreds of Tumbu maggots crawling under my skin or burrowing through some other parts of my body. That was a terrifying feeling. The biological name of these mosquitoes is *Cordilobia Anthropophagi*. The name *Anthropophagi* came from the Greek word *Anthropologos*, which meant human eater.

It was not the head hunters or the man-eater tribes of this country who were after my flesh, but the flesh-eating mosquitos had already started to eat my flesh, bit by bit. Disgust was a better emotional reaction than fear. I was extremely disgusted.

I kept examining myself to find any mosquito bites or suspicious pimples. I spoke to Sister Thomas and checked as much I could with civility. She did that from time to time for the rest of my stay. I covered myself with Vaseline every five days for the next two months, expecting the larvae to be asphyxiated and expelled. But none showed up again.

I instructed Mommoh, my Cook, to spray the house with all kinds of mosquito repellents, regularly, every night, making sure that my mosquito net was tucked in well after I got into my bed. The ceiling fan ran at full speed. The Health Inspector instructed the gardener to ensure no mosquito breeding place was in or near the compound. The Health Inspector regularly checked the compound for any potential mosquito breeding spots. The feeling lingered with me for a long time, even after leaving Sierra Leone and returning to London.

Hundreds of Maggots were crawling all under my skin, eating my flesh bit by bit, a nightmare, and a fearful disgust I had to live with for a very long time. Unreasonable fear, even in a medical professional. Only I can explain my first encounter with the 14-year-old boy. His entire body was infested by maggots, an otherwise healthy teenager; looking through my ignorant mind, the darkness of knowledge and inherent belief that Africa was full of savages was the reason for my unreasonable fear.

Chapter 22
NIGHTMARE AT MIDNIGHT

"I am not afraid of an army of lions led by a sheep; I am afraid of an army of sheep led by a Lion"

Alexander the great

Not long after I arrived in Kailahun, I got used to the work, working environment, colleagues, staff, and living comfortably in a relatively luxurious bungalow in the middle of an equatorial forest. Notwithstanding mysterious people of different colors, cultures, beliefs, and faith, I slowly but surely adapted to my new life and unique lifestyle.

It was a day when I had a hectic clinic, a few minor surgeries, and a very long meeting with the office manager, Mr. Amara, about budget and budgeting. I was utterly ignorant and a novice, but I was a keen learner and astute observer. I had no qualms asking him about the process, procedure, and things I could not comprehend. He was an experienced government health care manager, and was very aware of my ignorance and deficiencies in hospital financial management. He took maximum care to give me the information and tactical tips without hurting my pride. He was, indeed, a polite, honest, and conscientious officer.

I returned to my nest by 5 pm. Mommoh was ready with my afternoon tea and snacks. I listened to some of my favorite music. I brought with me several old-fashioned records and a record player. Then I went back to studying Anatomy and Physiology, dreaming of taking the basic science test for surgical specialization.

By eight O'clock, Mommoh was ready with my dinner. I had my shower. I made it a habit to shower in the evening before supper or before I went to bed. Because, as a medical student, I did not have the luxury of time for taking a shower in the morning while preparing for 8 am lecture classes or ward rounds. So after dinner, I picked up one African Jungle book of adventure and started reading it.

I fell asleep. I can not recall at what time. Around midnight, I heard knocking at my front door. The whole house was dark. I was not willing to respond. There was no sign of Mommoh anywhere. I switched on the reception room light and the light on the porch. Again, I did not respond to the knock. Then I heard:

"Sir! It is Sister Thomas. May I come in? A young girl just arrived with complicated labor."

"Come in, Sister," I said.

She looked anxious and worried. I asked if the patient was already in labor. Yes, she said, but it was a case of obstructed labor. I did not want to harass her by asking any more questions. So I said, "You go, set up the intravenous drip. I will follow you in five minutes."

It took just a few minutes to get to the hospital. A 19-year-old girl was brought from Pendembu, about a half-hour drive from the hospital, with complicated labor. In full-term, and this was her first pregnancy, Sister told me.

She looked well, not in agony but confused. As I examined her, I found she was in full-term pregnancy and presented with prolapse of the baby's hand. This was one of the saddest obstetric situations.

I examined the baby. Both the baby and mother were in good condition. However, the accompanying midwife said she had the hand prolapse for about an hour and a half. The midwife knew best not to try anything in such a case. Instead, refer to the nearest hospital as soon as possible. That was what she had done.

I examined the baby's hand, which was cold, but could not feel the pulse. Baby's heartbeats were fast but felt normal. I told Sister to cover the baby's hand with a warm towel. The prolapsed arm was slightly swollen, but there was no sign of gangrene setting in due to the blood supply being cut off, but that was inevitable.

I thought of using my obstetric skills to deliver the baby normally. But in this situation, time was crucial to saving the mother's life. By this time, I started to lose the baby's heartbeat. I knew it was just a matter of minutes, and the baby would stop breathing and die. This was what happened in patients presenting with "hand prolapse." The dead fetus was removed in pieces to save the mother's life. Because of prolonged impaction of the shoulder in the vagina, gangrene of the arm would develop. The development of gangrene leads to septic infection, affecting the mother, causing blood infection, and eventually leading to death.

Under these circumstances, the textbook says, the main focus should be to save the mother at any cost, even sacrificing the baby. That was standard teaching.

I kept looking at and examining the prolapsed arm and the mother. Finally, I had no time to lose. I knew that I would not save the baby, so I sacrificed the baby and delivered it in pieces to save the mother. She was only nineteen years old. I couldn't let her die while attempting to save the baby's life. Time was running out. The baby's heart sounds were absent by then, and the arm remained cool, more swollen.

From my heart, I could not convince myself to remove the baby in pieces. My gut churned; I felt sick just because of the thought of killing the baby. Although the baby may be dead by now, the mother's vital signs worsened, giving me cause for concern.

I couldn't wait any longer. I had to act now.

I asked Sister to prepare the patient for Cesarean Section. I would bring the baby out intact, maybe dead, but I would not feel guilty of severing the unborn baby's body parts into pieces to deliver. However, I knew it might be challenging to bring the prolapsed arm back into the uterus because hours of compression and impaction may have caused enough swelling of the arm, and I may not be able to push the arm back into the womb again. In that case, I may have to surgically amputate the arm to deliver the fetus through the C-section. I explained this to Sister Thomas and Mr. Joseph, the anesthetist.

The patient was prepared for a Cesarean section. I asked another nurse to lubricate the arm and keep it warm, and gently try to push it back into the womb. She tried, but I asked not to try harder but to keep the pressure on it.

Within minutes, I was in the womb, dislodging the impacted head of the fetus. In the operation site blood and amniotic fluid all over. Sister could not get it sucked up fast enough. In the meantime, Mr. Joseph tried to maintain the patient's vitals, controlling the fluid and oxygen. The operating field looked like a war zone.

As the pressure from inside the womb was eased off slowly, sliding the prolapsed arm back into the womb was possible.

I was able to deliver the baby intact through the C section. I handed the baby over to Sister and let her take total care of the baby, if still alive. Sister Thomas was a very experienced and devoted nurse.

In the meantime, I had to deliver the placenta, clear the abdomen of amniotic fluid, and pack the womb with towels to stop the bleeding. It was still a war zone. Finally, I asked the nurse to aspirate all blood, filter the collection through gauze a couple of times, and put them in a transfusion bottle. She collected about three hundred milliliters of blood.

The plan was to re-transfuse the blood back to the patient. I had seen this process by surgeons at Connaught hospital in Freetown. The country's blood transfusion services were there, but there were very few donors. So this was how the surgeons started auto transfusion of patients to counter surgical blood loss.

Somehow my good senses kicked in and reminded me that this blood was mixed with amniotic fluid, and I was well aware of the severe consequences of amniotic fluid when it entered the bloodstream. Very serious symptoms, including death, could occur. So I had to dampen my over-enthusiastic idea of auto-transfusing blood in cases of a C-section. I thanked God for giving me the little wisdom. However, once I trained the staff on the principle of auto-transfusion, I motivated my staff to do it in appropriate cases only, which we had done during my tour of duty in Kailahun.

As the bleeding stopped, the uterine cavity was curated and cleaned, residual oozing was mopped out, and the bleeding had stopped. I closed the patient in a stable condition.

I was afraid to speak to Sister to ask her about the baby. I was not expecting the baby to survive. I walked to the ward, and I found Sister Thomas and another nurse changing the baby's wrapping towel. She said the baby was breathing but had not cried yet. I checked the arm, and it was warmer. The baby's heart sounds were galloping but audible. It did not look cyanosed, barely alive. I felt a little more confident. At least I did not have to amputate the baby's arm in a hurry. We would watch which direction it took.

It was 3 am. Sister said I needed to go to sleep. They would watch the patients and let me know of any changes to either of them. As I got into the transport, I saw many more men and women waiting outside. I was told they were relatives and friends from the same village. I waved at them and left.

It took just a few seconds before I fell into a deep sleep. Mommoh was awake and waiting. Asked me if I needed tea, coffee, or any drink. It was almost four hours since leaving for the hospital.

Fortunately, that was a Friday night, and I did not have to get up early in the morning to dress up and go to work. I gave an uncomfortable sigh of relief as I left the hospital as both the mother and the baby were breathing. The rest was in someone else's hands.

Chapter 23

THE SPEARS, DRUMS, AND WAR DANCES

"Don't be afraid of being outnumbered. The Lion walks alone while the sheep flock together"

Anonymous

I thought I was dreaming. I woke up with the sound of war drums coming from somewhere. It reminded me of the Hollywood film "Shaka-Zulu" marching with his fighters, beating drums rhythmically as they danced forward. It must be a bad dream. I went back to bed on a chilly morning with no intention of getting up soon.

The drums kept beating, and I felt I was dreaming of inspiring war drums from the comfort of my bed.

So I thought, and I dozed off. The drum beating did not stop in my head. The sounds could be pleasant at times, rhythmical and monotonous, and annoying when you want to shut your mind. But it did not put me to sleep. I looked at the clock; it was 6.30 in the morning. It was dark outside. It should have been sunny and bright by this time. I got disoriented, not sure if it was 6.30 in the morning or 6.30 in the evening. Was it possible that I slept for eighteen hours after last night's hugely challenging and fearful struggle?

I set one of the heavy curtains aside and peeped outside. It was a cloudy but clear day. What I saw outside, I thought, was still dreaming. However, it was not a dream. The sounds of drums were real for sure. At least one hundred to one hundred and fifty men and women surrounded my bungalow just inside the compound, quite a bit away from the building, with their drums and sticks, some thumping on the ground, some jumping up down, with women making some noise. I thought it was the type of noise you heard during harvest time or the start of a war game. I was totally disoriented, away from reality, unable to rationalize what was real and what was nightmare or fantasy.

Suddenly, I woke up. I woke up in real fear! The events of last night flashed through my imagination again and again. The baby's prolapsed hand, young mother's agony, bloody war zone at the operation site, pulling the baby out, and all these frightening events, and the uneasiness I noticed in the face of the anesthetist, Sister Thomas's calm and confident face, and scores of anxious relatives and friends outside which I had to handle. I was not aware of my patient nor did the baby and what happen to them seven hours after I finished the surgery.

I tried to convince myself against the odds; as responsible as Sister Thomas was, she would have informed me if anything had happened to the baby or the mother. The baby perhaps had the first breath of air from Heaven, and the nineteen-year-old mother's innocent face kept appearing in front of me. At times the images were so authentic, I had difficulty in shaking them off.

What was inevitable, that the baby might have died, but with hope against all hope, I was expecting the mother to make it. Then, suddenly, an electric shock-like sensation went up to my spine, and I felt my legs were going numb, and I was about to fall.

The drum beating continued, frightening sounds of war-like singing and dancing just outside my house still happening. I thought that most likely the baby and the mother were dead, and now it was the turn of her relatives to take my head off to their village as a token of revenge for killing both the mother and the child. This paranoia was not unrealistic in the Jungles of equatorial Africa, where I am now.

Then I went back to see what Mommoh was doing. He also had a very long night like me. His room reeked with the smell of alcohol. He was in deep inebriated sleep. Drumming, singing, and dancing did not wake him up. I woke him up. He was startled to see me in his room. I stood up and apologized for being late for breakfast. I told him to wash his face and come to the sitting room straightaway.

I was waiting for him. I asked him if he could hear the drums and noises. He stared at me and said, "Yes, Masta! " Then pulled one of the curtains aside; I thought he had seen a ghost and was flabbergasted. He said, "Plenty, plenty people."

"Why?" I said. I thought he also looked slightly scared. I asked him if he could understand what they were saying and what they were here for. I asked him to go outside and speak to them and find out what they wanted? Money? Food? Clothes? Anything, they would get it. These were your people, and you could speak to them and find out what they want.

Initially, he was hesitant and scared. But I convinced him to go out and find the reason why they were here and what they wanted. Then, I asked him to put on his uniform, to appear more official, with authority.

He went outside with a big smile, perhaps a smile of confusion and ignorance. He went straight to someone who looked like the head man and shook hands with him with a big smile. They chatted for a couple of minutes, then he went around and shook hands with some of them and bowed in front of some elderly ones. After that, all the ladies shook hands with him. I was watching every move. I thought of calling the Police Super or the District Officer to send help to rescue us. Finally, after about half an hour of intermingling, he turned around with a big smile, a huge smile indeed, and quickly came in.

In the meantime, the drums got louder, and singing went at a higher pitch.

I asked him what had happened. He was happy to tell me that the chief sent them to thank me for the safe delivery of the chief's youngest daughter's first child, a granddaughter. So! Both of them were alive then, but I did not know what might follow later. The people wanted to see me personally and thank me on behalf of the chief. At least at this time, my head was spared, and I expected to live a little longer or forever!

I quickly changed and met with the crowd, one at a time, and extended my thanks to the chief and all his people. By this time, the drums were getting louder, the singing more penetrating. As I was about to return, a group of six or seven young ladies encircled me and started to dance and sing. Soon they were joined by the rest in circle after circle. I had to dance with them to add to their happiness. Finally, in about ten minutes, the episode ended, the troupe slowly dispersed, to my great relief.

But my fear and sense of uncertainty lingered; I was still worried about the patients and their fate. I was wondering why Sister had not contacted me yet. I walked to the hospital, about a ten-minute walk from my residence. I went straight to see the patient. I was hugely relieved to see both the mother and the baby in a deep sleep. Sister Thomas was also half-asleep beside the patients. She woke up and said she had been watching them all through the night, and Mr. Joseph also came in from time to time to check on her. I saw the entire staff were anxious but energized. I checked the mother and the baby. The baby's vitals were OK. The right arm was much warmer, and I could feel the pulses. Yet, I remained concerned about the baby's viability. I pondered if I should send the patients to the Nixon Memorial Hospital, where a pediatrician did lots of neonatology work. I had to send both of them.

The journey may be too risky for the baby. I was not worried about the mother now, except she was still at risk of developing infection and septicemia. Her operation site was dry. There was no vaginal discharge. Her urine was clear, and her vitals were back to normal. She had a slight fever, which needed no interference at this point.

With the help of the Police Superintendent, I was able to get connected by phone with the Pediatrician and described the case in detail. He advised against travel unless the child developed fever or any sign of gangrene of her right hand. But he promised he would check back with me again the next day or contact him if I became worried.

We continued to take care of both of them the best we could. I returned home around three in the afternoon. I had my light dinner and dosed off. Around Five pm, I woke up again with war drumming and singing nightmarish sounds. I thought these were a recall of the sensation from this morning. I tried to convince myself that the sounds were a hallucinatory reaction to my anxiety. But as I dared to look outside, it was the same scene again. This time there were fewer people, but the drummers were more enthusiastic. The anxiety, the fear of losing the patients, one or both, was still sitting on my chest like a ton of weight. I dared not to think what might have happened to my patients, for me to deserve the second visit by the cheering or maybe warring crew.

I sent Mommoh again. He went and mingled with the crowd and turned around with a broad smile, holding something in both arms. As he came closer, I realized those were two baby goats. He said the chief sent this as gifts for saving his beloved daughter and the first granddaughter. I went out to meet everyone, greeted, shook hands, and asked them to convey my sincere thanks to the chief for his gifts and understanding.

Secretly, in the deepest corner of my heart, I wished the chief would wait a bit longer to see them fully recovered. The scare and fear of something going wrong with either mother or the baby were still very much in my mind.

I went back in the evening, found the Sister still there, and both the patients were resting. There was no fever for either of them. The baby's arm was warm, not showing any sign of gangrene anywhere. So I felt a little more hopeful and had a fairly restful night.

Monday morning, around 8 am, I entered the Hospital. The place was buzzing with activity. I went straight to the ward, and to my most pleasant surprise, I could hear the baby crying, which was long-awaited music to my ears. Sister was not there, but one of our midwives, standing in for her, never leaving the patients alone. The baby's right arm moved stronger, responding to me tickling the palm.

I went back to my clinic, where several patients were waiting. They were ready to start the day. As I was about to get into action, I got the message from Police Super's office for a telephone call from Nixon Memorial Hospital. I ran; as promised, the pediatrician was on the line to get an update on my patients. I gave him a detailed rundown of the baby's condition. With a sense of relief, he said we were perhaps out of the woods. He had discussed with the surgeon the need for possible amputation. They were mentally prepared if it was essential.

Days passed, and both the baby and the mother continued to improve. Never before had a baby's cry been such wonderful music to my ears until now, as I heard this baby cry. Finally, on the fifteenth day, I was confident to discharge them home, with arrangements of home visits by the District Nurse and the Midwife.

Chapter 24

SCARY GUEST IN DARKNESS

"Darkness can't drive out darkness: only light can do that, Hate cannot drive out hate only love can do that "

Martin Luther King Jr.

Once or twice every month, I traveled to Freetown as an expert Forensic witness, anywhere from the High court to the lowest government legal offices. There was one of those mandatory subpoenas from the High Court in Freetown. I was legally bound to attend the court; non-attendance without any emergency, or physically being unfit to participate in or out of the country, led to serious consequences, and might end up losing the job. Moreover, I loved these court attendances for telling some high profile, fierce British "Temple(er)" educated and trained Barristers what to do. Generally, they had been nice to me but never missed any chance to jab me as a young, green, perhaps "inexperienced" medical expert. They did it legally or out of the point of order.

I had no reason not to attend, but with a glitch. I was out on a planned regular inspection of a couple of other medical centers in the district. The message from the high court came a day before; by that time, I had already left town on my trek. I could not have returned to Kailahun before 8 pm. I would have missed the last flight from Kenema to Freetown by that time. My ambulance driver suggested that if we leave Kailahun by 10 pm, we would reach Freetown by 6-7 am the following morning. I might have enough time to get dressed for my court duty. We traveled through the night to make it for the next day's court appearance. I asked the driver how he felt and if he could handle it, even after the full day of driving, to return to Kailahun from the district. He seemed to be unperturbed.

Unfortunately, the subpoena came from the court after leaving for the district. So I had no idea what it was all about.

We returned to Kailahun Hospital just before 8 pm. The Office Manager, Mr. Amara, and Sister Thomas waited for me. Tea and snacks were ready. I shared it with the driver. Mr. Amara handed me the thick envelope from the court. I asked him if he knew what the issue was. He had not opened the envelope and did not know the content and message. But it was hand-delivered, and the messenger informed Mr. Amara that I had been directed by High Court to be present as an expert witness the next day at 9 am. That was an official, verbal instruction.

I opened the envelope. There was the instruction from Justice Tucker of Sierra Leone High Court to attend the High Court as an expert witness, to see if giving my opinion on an "exhumation" of a 68 year-old gentleman could be helpful. A man brought to the hospital by his relatives was very sick. He was admitted nine months ago. He died in the hospital the following day, after admission. A mandatory autopsy was carried out. My predecessor did that. The cause of death was due to "natural causes," no foul play was evident. However, now the relatives were asked to re-examine his body "by exhumation" to detect any foul play by poisoning. They had gathered evidence that may be the case.

I had no choice but to give my opinion. I read all the information over and over again. I was trying to visualize as if I was the person who did the first autopsy. But, unfortunately, there was nothing much to go on. Death due to natural causes, no bodily injury or evidence of foul play was recorded.

Anyway, with some anxiety, we set out for our nocturnal trip through the equatorial forest, rocky and potholed road, without any street light after we left Kailahun. One advantage of night driving was that one could see the oncoming vehicle from a distance and be warned and careful. The road from Kailahun to Kenema was really through the deep equatorial forest. Even in the daytime, one hardly could see sunrays. It made it even darker at night. At night, one could see nocturnal animals on the prowl for their prey.

We were traveling in a large, heavy military-size Land Rover, modified for transporting patients, as an ambulance if necessary. Mohmmadu was a conscientious and experienced driver, working for the Ministry for more than ten years, the last five tears in Kailahun. He was well used to Kailahun, for that matter, and all kinds of roads in Sierra Leone. Drove with confidence, day or night, rain or shine, tar marked or potholed. He asked me if I would like to rest on the bed at the back of the car, which Sister Thomas arranged for the journey. A long, dark, and bumpy ride in transport were suitable for a war zone. Those were precisely what we needed to cover this trip. The road was pitch black, except for the car's piercing flooding headlight and the engine's harsh rumbling noise. The headlights changed the pitch darkness of the road. However, the forest at night was noisier, making an orchestrated monotonous sound, scary yet romantic.

At one point, Mohmmadu asked me if I would like to go to the washroom since he would not want to stop anywhere on this stretch of road because of various risks and wild animals that might be roaming around. So I took the opportunity to get myself relieved and fresh again. Sister, with the help of Mommoh, did not forget to fill a flask with hot tea and another with cold water and some snacks to keep me occupied if I was bored, hungry, or thirsty. They were very thoughtful with impending trials and tribulations of night driving through unfriendly terrain in equatorial Africa. The danger and challenges seemed to have totally skipped my mind. The kind gesture of concern was highly appreciated.

It was pitch dark, but there was no shortage of noises in the darkness. Insects were screeching, some noise sounding like a dog barking, and nocturnal birds were squawking and flapping. A mixture of monotonous noises from the highest to the lowest pitch was coming out from the depth of the forest. Far at a distance, by the foothills of the mountains, I could see specks of a fire burning and human voices singing rhythmically without any break. The villages were far away, and even during the daytime, it was tough to access them through the forest. Apparently, some tribes had not been seen outside their locale, only rarely visited by foreign explorers. Their numbers were dwindling, yet this was a reminder of their existence.

Mommahdu was wide awake and concentrating on driving. I told him he could switch the car radio to listen to music or any program to alert him. He was happy to drive in quiet and calm. We were driving towards Kenema; we had been driving for three hours and expected to be close to Kenema by just over an hour. Some animals crossed our path, which was difficult to recognize; birds flew by us, most likely bats or some sort of nocturnal birds. We saw duikers standing by the roadside. Monkeys and baboons, somber, surprised by the piercing light-spewing and growling monster, from which they tried to run away.

Suddenly I saw a small deer-like animal in the bright light of our car which looked yellowish, standing still just about five to six feet away, not making a single move. Most likely dazed by the bright light of the car, confused, lost its way, or stunned. Mohmmadu revved the vehicle higher, but there was no movement. Instead, it stood right in front of the car like a statue. Mohmmadu started to move forward slowly, but still no response. There was nothing else, no other animal or living creature around. If it was daytime, we could have gotten out and shooed it away, but we did not dare to do it if any bigger predator was around and waiting for us to descend from the car.

Suddenly, I heard and felt a firm thud in the car. The car shook a bit, but we could not see any other animal trying to ram our car. He revved the engine higher. Nothing happened. The antelope still stood in front of the vehicle as if it had been drugged or hypnotized. Suddenly, Mohmmadu tried to show me something through his window. I was trying to see anything by the road. Then he pointed something hanging from the roof by the side of the car. It looked like a six to seven inches thick solid rope. I looked through my window. I saw a similar rope-like thing hanging from the roof to the side of the car, on my side also.

I had no idea what it was. Suddenly, a chilling sensation ran down my spine, thinking that the tribal people must have had a trap to hunt a big animal but instead trapped our car. That was a horrifying thought. A few seconds went by, the structure still hanging from the roof appeared to be almost all around our vehicle. Then he said it was a giant snake, Python or Boa maybe. Close to twenty feet long. I was totally out of my wits; now, I was paralyzed. We were concerned that it was so big that it could quickly wrap around our car and squeeze it like a Coke bottle and take both of us with it.

The antelope stood still in front of the car. He was looking away and not looking at us anymore. Wondering to stay or go, which way it should walk if it goes? That was my wishful thinking. The animal was standing frozen, right in front of the car. Mohmmadu was thinking of racing fast forward to hit the animal and drive away, hoping the snake would slip off the roof onto the road fast enough to get rid of it. But he was also worried that the high-speed impact with the animal could damage the car, then we would have a much worse situation.

He started to move the car back and forth a couple of times, then suddenly quickly reversed. The snake slipped from the roof onto the bonnet. The snake was also confused, I guess. Where did it come from? Mommahdu repeatedly wiggled the car back and forth a couple of times. Then again, with very high speed, reversed. This time the snake slipped off the bonnet in front of the car. It was lying in front in the piercing headlights of the vehicle. From about twelve to fifteen feet away, we entirely viewed the snake. It was easily twenty to twenty-one feet long and six to seven inches thick, lying across the road. The snake was as confused as all of us. We couldn't wait until the snake felt well enough and understood that its life was at stake and moved away. The antelope, still in front, slowly began to move forward and headed to the side of the road.

Instead of wasting any time, Mohmmadu reversed the car for about another twenty feet and then raced forward at very high speed to drive over the snake. That we could do. He did it. By that time, the antelope we saw was walking into the bush unconcerned, not knowing how its life was spared. But we saw the snake curling back from both head and tail to take revenge so that it could squash the enemy. Unfortunately, it missed its dinner, and fortunately, he had missed his enemy also. Moreover, the risk of being driven over by other cars remained real unless he could slide himself off the road. Now it was lying across the road, probably not even able to wiggle off the road, the amount of crushing damage we had caused in two sites of the creature.

Without stopping or looking back, we drove as fast as we could until we arrived at Kenema town center. He said it was 1 am in the morning; we did lose some time but would catch up.

While we stopped for a quick tea break, Boukhari suggested most likely the snake was in a tree over our head. With our car light, it was able to see the antelope and intended to jump from the tree. Usually, it wound around the branches and the stem and crawled on its prey. I guess it was in a hurry, and the snake could not wait to come down to grab the antelope. We checked the vehicle carefully all around if there had been any damage due to a heavy fall of the snake onto the roof. There was no damage or any new scratches to be seen.

We thanked heaven for saving us from the crushing, curling of the gigantic Python. The Range Rover vehicle was built for military use with a military-grade structure that saved us from possible crushing by the Python. But, unfortunately, the animal's greed met him with his fate. But had it been my Volkswagen beetle, by this time, it would have been twisted like a tin can by the humongous equatorial Python; maybe we would have met the same fate with the VW Beetle, which was scraped being damaged on Vianini highway.

The road from Kenema to Bo, the second-largest city, was just as incredibly dark. We met with more nocturnal creatures crossing the road, monkeys with babies, a troupe of baboons here and there, fox-like animals, and some other unrecognizable creatures crossing our path. But, once we wound down the window, the sound of the forest at night was not nearly as deafening, confusing, and fearful, to tell the truth.

As we were approaching the town of BO, the road surface was slightly better. Mohmmadu could drive a little faster to make it to Freetown in time for my court appearance. We stopped at the town center of BO. It was just past 4 am. We were at least one hour behind our schedule, considering the journey overnight was not smooth and uneventful. We had a short tea break and sped away.

The road between BO and Freetown was supposed to be tar marked. Unfortunately, there had been much rain in the region overnight, and some parts were water-logged. Also, the trees and bushes were different from the deep equatorial forest. Here we came across landscapes more akin to Savana. That may be why water ran down from the forest and flooded the road.

We had the company of baboons, monkeys, duikers, and, strangest of all, noticed snakes crawling across the road. On our way, we found an empty lorry, skidded into a roadside drain, which was deep enough to accommodate the force and gush of rainwater from the hillside forests. We stopped but did not dare to get out of the car. Instead, we blew our horn several times, focusing on the searchlight Mohmmadu carried in the vehicle. There was no screaming for help, no noise, no movement, and no sign of human or living activities, so we quickly left.

Half an hour on the road, we saw another car coming from the opposite direction. Mohmmadu started to flicker the headlight, honked, and made gestures to stop the vehicle. The car stopped. It was a police car. We reported the accident to the police team. There were two of them in the car. They asked about us, took note, and I said I was DMO of Kailahun. We were on our way to Freetown to attend a court case at the High Court. But they told us they were going to the accident site. The driver had already been taken to BO General Hospital. So we gave them a short description of the accident site and the state of the vehicle.

Chapter 25

AT THE HIGH COURT IN FREETOWN

"Courage is what it takes to stand up and speak; courage is also what it takes to sit down and listen"

Winston Churchill.

The Police car left and rushed back towards BO's crash site, which we left behind. We were again on our way to Freetown. It was just before 6 am. We thought perhaps we would arrive at the government guest house by 8 am. I would have half an hour to get ready for my court appearance.

The rest of the journey was smooth. We arrived at the guest house just before 8 am. The receptionist was cheerful and courteous. She said I had a couple of very urgent messages. I opened the first message. The District Officer of Kailahun informed me that my High Court appearance had been rescheduled for 11.30 am. The second message was from the clerk of the High court of Justice, Government of Sierra Leone, confirming that at the request of the District Officer of Kailahun, my court appearance with HE Justice, Nestor Tucker, had been postponed from 9 am to 11.30 am that day.

I could not have been anymore relieved and happier at that moment. The porters moved my belongings to my room. I asked Mohmmadu to freshen up and have some breakfast. I went to my room and requested room service for a full breakfast.

In the room, I sat down and went through the subpoena repeatedly, trying to find any point I missed. I thought over and over again, about why I should allow or deny exhumation of this patient. According to the autopsy report issued by my previous colleague, it was a straightforward case of natural death.

I thought, let me hear the complainant, then I will have a better idea. As an expert witness, I can only advice, but the judge decides whether to order an exhumation. So I must follow the court's decision.

Anyway, it seemed at the law court that it was a high-profile case. So I was told by the chief public prosecutor not to speak to anyone.

With the Government Prosecution team, we all took our seats in the court at 11.15 am, awaiting Judge's arrival. It was very formal. The patient's relatives were in the visitors' gallery. One of the prosecutors came to me and said, it will be just a formality, whether to exhume. I said I knew very little about the case, except for the autopsy report from the court and the instruction to attend today. As far as I could tell, there would not have been any autopsy had he died a few hours later in the hospital bed.

All deaths occurring in the hospital within twenty-four hours of admission had to undergo a statutory autopsy to determine the cause of death. Not infrequently, we did several unnecessary post mortem examinations to confirm the clinical diagnosis of death. The majority of cases were only for records and stayed there, but for a few exceptions, like this case, when the cause of death was challenged.

I was not supposed to discuss the case inside the court unless instructed by the Judge. So I refrained from further discussion. Finally, the Judge, Honorable Mr. Tucker, entered, the court rose, and we all took our respective seats as the Judge took his.

After an introduction, the senior prosecutor put the case forward to the court. This session was held primarily for determining if the court would grant "Exhumation" for a second autopsy. The court clerk gave me all papers, and someone, likely the court clerk, read the case aloud for me to understand. Then I was called to the Witness box. The prosecutor asked about my involvement with the patient and the comment on the Autopsy report given by my predecessor approximately nine months ago.

I said I did not know much about the case, except what was in the Autopsy report. I returned from my outreach district visit last night at 8 pm when I received the subpoena, and I did not have the chance to review the patient's case file. Moreover, case records of all patients who died were no longer filed in the hospital file but in a remote location.

He asked me if I had read the autopsy report. "Yes," I said.

The prosecutor asked, in my opinion, if the autopsy report was complete, and if there were any missing issues in the report.

I said I had no way of knowing if there was any missing information or point of observation from the report.

I repeated that I did not know the case; I needed to review the hospital notes and interview the patient's relatives who brought him to the hospital to give any opinion.

The prosecutor then asked me: from the report, my understanding of what the cause of death was.

I said it appeared that the patient died from some natural cause.

The prosecutor asked if there was any indication of any foul play. I replied that there was no indication of any foul play in the report, as far I could comment from the report.

Prosecutor then said that the patient's relative suspects foul play and requested exhumation and re-examination of the body.

I responded, "There is no document to prove at this point that foul play may be the cause of his death. I do not see any indication in this report at all. However, if the court is convinced based on further deposition from the plaintiff, exhuming the patient's body for further examination is needed to elaborate the cause of death further, then I will be happy to do so. Likewise, upon a new subpoena if I am instructed by the court to do so."

"Yes. The court will instruct you if and when further examination of the body might be needed."

I was requested to return to the gallery and wait until the presiding judge decided on my deposition.

However, I was told that I could return to Kailahun and wait for further instruction.

After the adventurous, trying, and tiring overnight drive from Kailahun to Freetown, everything was over in half an hour.

I left for the guesthouse. Fortunately, it was Friday today, so I decided to stop over tonight at the Guesthouse to give rest to the driver and myself. I would return tomorrow morning, back to Kailahun. Mr. Mohmmadu was happy. He said he would stick around if I needed the car to drive me somewhere.

I took a short visit to say hello to my mentor, Dr. Thakuta, and his wife, who lived just behind the Guesthouse. It was a pleasant and memorable visit. They were horrified about the encounter with the giant Python in the middle of the night and seriously admired my driver's quick-witted action.

I especially attempted to say hello to my German friend, who lived in the Guesthouse. I spent the afternoon having tea with her and told her many things about my first few months in the "Bush" as the province and territory were dubbed in colonial Freetown. Almost fifteen years in West Africa made my German friend a "wise man" or a "wise woman" of the land, to be precise. Many valuable tips and advice I received from her. She was a keen and attentive listener.

I did a bit of shopping. Then, I went to bed early to be fresh and energetic for the next day's return trek to Kailahun. Fortunately, it would not be another night ride.

The following morning we left the Guesthouse at 10 am, hoping to arrive in Kailahun by 6-7 pm. I requested the Guesthouse receptionist to send a message to the District officer about my travel plan so that all my staff was aware. I did ask Mohmmadu to get the car checked and ready for the journey. He confidently said that the car was good, and he could make another three return trips like this. His confidence reassured me. However, he did take the car for servicing at a ministry-appointed garage.

Saturday morning, unfortunately, was a cloudy and dark day. Shower sand rain may befall us any time. After all, this was the

"Wet season," we couldn't blame the sky for being unfriendly, but we were grateful for the warning.

I was sorry to leave the Guesthouse, my first encounter as an African home. However, I have lots of memories and expect many more to come.

Despite the initial gloomy weather, the return journey was enjoyable and exciting. We arrived back in Kailahun just before 6 pm, while the sun was still on the horizon.

Chapter 26

THE EXHUMATION: SCIENCE OR SORCERY

"Death does not concern us, because as long as we exist, death is not near. And once it does come, we no longer exist"

Epicurus

I got the court order to carry out the exhumation the following week. Report back of physical findings and details of exhumed postmortem examination was to be submitted no later than one month from the date of issue of the court order. To be truthful, I had no idea nor any experience of doing an exhumation for legal purposes, or for any purpose for that matter. Initial autopsies were OK, but this was beyond the realm of a newly qualified doctor, without much experience in Medical Jurisprudence, except the textbook knowledge provided for our third MB.BS examination. Our Jurisprudence professor was an excellent teacher and was a highly respected Medical Jurist in the country. Yet, most of us remained unmotivated to be Medical Jurist.

I had an expert mortuary technician, Mr. Dijon. He was from neighboring Guinea, a few miles across the border. His family moved to Kailahun to establish a profitable Cola business. He trained himself as a Lab Technician and then as an Autopsy Technician in Dakar, Senegal. He had several years of experience as an autopsy technician under his belt. Although he lived in Kailahun, he was also responsible for assisting in performing autopsies in the rest of the district, as needed.

We discussed the case. Mr. Amara, the administrator, was able to dig out the patient's hospital admission file.

We both went through the file but did not get any clinical information that might give us a better understanding of his death, especially the neurological examination. I guess it was just missed. The doctor had to examine neurologically to pronounce the patient dead.

There were detailed protocols for autopsy examinations and exhumation, designed by the colonial administration, and available for documenting and reporting. That made my life much easier for a direction in how to proceed. Mr. Dijon seemed to be upbeat and enthusiastic about the process. Nevertheless, I had my doubts about how I would do it in my mind.

I requested help from the Chief Medical Examiner at Freetown. Unfortunately, he was away on vacation. I spoke to Dr. Cummings, our Provincial Medical Officer, to send a senior medical officer to standby and witness the procedure. Do I need to take written orders from the court to add a witness? He reassured me that it was up to me if I needed a witness in the absence of the Chief Government Coroner. Anyway, the court's representatives would be there. Dr. Cummings would also intimate to the Chief Coroner, Dr. Joshi, the chief forensic pathologist in Freetown, my request for him to be present as a witness. But Dr. Joshi was not expected to return for six to eight weeks. If I wished, I might delay until he returned or perform the autopsy with another senior medical officer as a witness.

That settled it. Bureaucratically, it was made clear and appropriate. So, we would proceed in the best possible way.

Mr. Dijon, our Mortuary technician, seemed to be a very popular person in the town for his pleasant, happy, outgoing, and helpful personality. His family connection also helped. He was a repository of the town's gossips and secrets. He quietly told me that he believed the man died due to some natural cause, but the family was convinced or trying to make a strong case that he was killed by voodoo magic and poison by the father of the dead man's youngest wife, who had no children with the dead man. With the help of a shaman, whom he brought from the French side, her father killed the old man. The dead man had several children. At 67, he was healthy, active, and a wealthy farmer. The family thought the youngest wife's father plotted the crime to protect his daughter from being deprived of his wealth or even being killed for not having children. So the family started to portray her as a witch.

I had no idea how we could detect the shamanic or voodoo activity for this man's death. That was still dark knowledge, not taught in medical schools.

The theater was set. A representative from the court, the Police, and Doctor Dubey, a Senior Medical Officer, were sent by Dr. Cummings from Kenema provincial health office to witness the procedure.

The exhumers appointed by the court exhumed the casket and the body. Mr. Dijon, with the help of the exhumers, took the body out of the coffin and placed it on the autopsy table.

I had never seen a freshly exhumed body. However, I viewed the bodies of several emperors, kings, and queens, cats, and animals in the Egyptian National Museum. Also, in several of Conan Doyle's Sherlock Holmes crime movies, exhumed bodies were shown, but I did not have to pass judgment about the cause of their death in any instance.

My initial reaction was gut-churning sickness, looking at the dried-up but not decomposed body. We took photographs of the entire body, head, and neck region down to both feet. With Dr. Dubey, Mr. Dijon, we could not find any external injury. We checked the previous autopsy report, which matched our observation. Then we reopened the body. Even after nine months, it was reasonably identifiably preserved. We checked the inside of the corpse, took samples from each organ for tests for toxins and pathological examination. We could not detect any noticeable difference in findings from the original report. No visceral injury or suspicious lesions were found.

Then we went into the brain. The skull had already been opened. We exposed the skull and the brain. The brain was intact. There was no suspicious bleeding on the surface of the brain or inside the skull. Then we wanted to look at the slices of the brain. There was none. Mr. Dijon confirmed that the brain was not sliced. We re-examined the initial autopsy report. There was no record of the brain being sliced.

We took the brain out of the skull and started slicing transversally at 1.5 cm thickness. There was no significant intracranial bleeding, blood clots, aneurism, or fresh hemorrhage that could be seen. As we began to examine the appearance of each slice, nothing remarkable was detected. However, by the time we were at the brainstem level, we started to see a damaged area inside the brain's substance, which looked like a cavity of a hematoma at the base and brainstem. This was not visible from the outside. The midbrain hematoma was missed because the brain substance was not sliced open.

This was serious cause enough to account for his swift and sudden death. Internal brain hemorrhage was not an uncommon cause of premature death. We also collected brain tissue to detect any poison and further laboratory forensic examination. At least now, we had witnessed a convincing cause of death, not necessarily due to poisoning.

We sent all collected specimens and contents of the entire skull to the Chief Medical Examiner and Coroner, Dr. Joshi, in Freetown.

We revised the cause of death as sudden acute "Intra Cranial Hemorrhage" without any gross sign of acute poisoning or external injury. The final diagnosis would await toxicology analysis. I gathered the specimens and sent them to Dakar in Senegal or London, the UK, for toxicity analysis. Upon receiving those, the report on the final exhumation – autopsy report would be forwarded to the court of Justice to Hon' Judge Tucker at the High court in Freetown.

I am personally grateful to Mr. Dijon, Sister Thomas, and the rest of the team; I emerged as a stronger human being to face the ever-changing world. Saw a genuine silver lining to live and work in this hitherto unfamiliar geographical, linguistic, racial, cultural, and socio-economic diversity where everything was possible. But, of course, I had my doubt; how the heck would I get through this complex professional trial in real life? It was not easy to accept the challenge. But, on the other hand, I was reluctant to wash my hands of it, admitting inexperience. There had been no history in Kailahun where the District Medical Officer had carried out an exhumation in a complex legal case. The Chief Coroner from the capital always came and took over. But trust in myself, trust and respect for my colleague, determination for the right thing to do, and mentally, being focused and disciplined enough to get on with my duties. In the end, it showed us the right path. Our contribution did make a difference for everyone involved.

At this stage of my career, any responsibility of this magnitude might feel like a child's play, but then it was a massive mental, professional, and intellectual burden, including my self-esteem.

Chapter 27

THE DEADLY RETURN TO KAILAHUN

"True Wisdom comes to each of us when we realize how little we understand about life, ourselves and the world around us"

Socrates

As part of my job, I attended various courts in Freetown at least once as an expert witness every month. Usually, I was driven from Kailahun to Kenema Airport. I took a short one-hour flight to Freetown. Upon return, I would fly back from Freetown to Kenema and be driven back to Kailahun in the government vehicle, mostly a Jeep or a Land Rover. The road from Kailahun to Kenema was very rough, potholed, mini boulders, dusty, muddy, and slippery during the rainy season. This was one of the main arteries connecting Sierra Leone to the east to Liberia, and Ghana, and north to Guinea, and other Saharan countries. This was also a major trade route, exporting local produce and importing utilities over land. It was also the diamond trade route, legal or illegal, heaven for smugglers smuggling, especially diamond and precious metals. Criminals used this road for trafficking animals and human beings aside from diamonds, rare earth minerals, gold, etc. Due to heavy traffic of loaded trucks and over-loaded passenger buses, all those left their mark beside the seasonal damages caused by heavy tropical and equatorial showers and storms.

But there had been a significant change. An Italian construction company VIANINI had just completed a brand new six-lane road connecting Kenema to Kailahun. It was not tarred, but the surface was just as tough as asphalt or concrete, or at least it was meant to be. The ninety-kilometer distance could be covered in one and half hours instead of four hours of back-breaking, bone-crunching, head-bouncing, yet exciting drive. It appeared serene, inviting, and almost hypnotic during regular times. The road was planned to extend up to the Liberia and Guinea border. A few extra miles to the borders of both countries.

I had already bought my car, a VW Beetle, and sold my Austin "Mini" in Freetown. However, the VW Beetle was new and barely tested on these roads. On my way to Freetown to a connecting flight at Kenema airport, we traveled on a government Land Rover, but I told Mohmmadu to bring my new VW to have a taste of driving a car in bush country. Since the new Vianini road from the Airport to Kailahun hospital had been completed, it would be safe and pleasant to drive, I expected.

It was a pleasant day. We set out with much happiness and excitement in the government vehicle, a Land Rover. Vianini was a large infrastructure-building Italian company. It was involved in multiple construction projects, especially roads and canals, etc., and had built the new highway connecting Kailahun to Kenema. But, unfortunately, the new Vianini road was not open to the public yet. However, Prime Minister Sir Milton Margai would officially open the road in a few days.

So, my onward journey had to be on the old road, a three to four hours' journey. We did, without any natural hazard. I caught the plane on time. This flight also stopped at BO airport to pick up a few passengers, goods, and mail. Anyway, I was on time in Freetown. I had no engagement that day. I went straight to the guesthouse, freshened up, and was ready for dinner.

Interestingly, at the guesthouse, dinner and breakfast were a formal business. Guests were expected to dress up for both, otherwise frowned upon by fellow dinners. More importantly, you would not be escorted to a table by the receptionist; even if one takes a table, the waiter would only attend to you if you try to attract their attention. An indirect way to tell you that you are not welcome if you are not properly dressed.

I had to stay in Freetown for a few days on business. I met Dr. Joshi, the Chief Forensic Pathologist, whom I had known when I arrived and checked in for the first time in the guesthouse. He was apologetic about not being able to help me do the exhumation, which he usually would have done, but he was highly appreciative of our effort in doing an excellent job, shedding new light on the cause of death of the patient, which led the family to withdraw the case. Specimens from his organs were already sent to Dakar in Senegal to assess toxins, which might have been used as murder weapons. We would see what the outcome was. I was relieved.

Just for fun, I asked Dr. Joshi; you are a highly respected, experienced Forensic Pathologist in the country, if not the region. You have been practicing in this culture and society for years; you have a deeper understanding of these cultures. Perhaps you can enlighten or educate me on how one can diagnose death due to Voodoo' "or "Sorcery" spells." He laughed his head off and said, "I would remember. Certainly,

I will let you know when I find one and when I know how to diagnose one!" "Thank you," I said.

I flew back from Freetown to Kenema.

Mohmmadu was waiting at the airport with my new Volkswagen Beetle. He also brought his helper along with him.

I asked if the Prime Minister had officially opened the Vianini road. Was the road open to the public? Could we drive on the new road? He said the Prime minister would inaugurate the road the following Friday, the day after tomorrow. So, I said we would drive back on the old road. "Masta!" Mommahdu said. Sister Thomas arranged with the District Officer to issue a special permit to use the new road when I returned to Kenema. He gave me the letter. That was how he could come to the airport on the new highway to pick me up. We would go back to Kailahun on the new Vianini road before anyone had the chance to do so. I cherished the moment. The message came as music to my ears. This had been a significant relief and awaiting the silky smooth, autumn morning drive.

Vianini Company had their camp just about seven miles west of Kailahun, by their construction site. There were about a hundred to one hundred and twenty people in the camp, including the manager, officers, the engineers, workers, the labor force, and various service personnel, including cooks, cleaners, and all forms of maintenance hands. Some of the senior officers had their wives with them. When I arrived for the first time in Kailahun to take charge of DMO, the manager personally visited me and asked me if I could look after their people needing medical help, and if I would be willing to make house calls if it became essential, especially for the ladies. Of course, I was happy to help them, living so far away from their home, in an environment culturally so very different. They had a host of heavy machinery and equipment, and a well-equipped workshop. Unfortunately, in this environment, accidents did happen. Fortunately, there were no children except a few nursing babies.

Inside the camp, it was a different world altogether. Little Italy indeed. Temporary cottages were beautifully built. The roads were well maintained, and walking spaces were beautifully landscaped. A small grocery shop was there, too; he imported food for staff from Italy. There was a small clubhouse, well-spaced and nicely furnished. They maintained a high-quality guesthouse for guests and visiting officers. There was an abundance of air conditioners; no hustle for humid heat, especially in the summer. However, most of them had to work on the construction site, struggling with all the elements of nature. But they knew what waited at the end of the day. There were satellite camps also. This one served as their feeder. On Saturday, I was given a guided tour by the camp manager himself, who was in his mid-thirties, and his wife was in her late twenties or early thirties. Both spoke English well. They gave me a standing invitation whenever I felt like Italian coffee or Ravioli. Very warm people indeed. In fact, on his way to the airport, Mohmmadu stopped at the Vianini compound gas station to fill up the tank. He met the manager and told him that he was going to the airport to pick me up. The manager was glad to hear that and told him to stop by his house for coffee and snacks; if the doctor had the time or were in the mood, they would be happy to prepare Italian Brunch for me. Very moving and understanding indeed.

After the immigration and police check-up routine was done, we loaded the car with my baggage. For a change, I was in the driver seat, Mommahdu in the front passenger seat, and his helper Bouchari in the back. We got out of the airport, then out-skirted the town center and onto the new Vianini highway to Kailahun. That was about 11 am.

The road was well built, a smooth surface, wide enough for four cars; it gradually sloped down on both sides to the drainage, which appeared to be three to four feet deep. I thought it was good for the heavy tropical rainwater to flow down the drain from the road's surface. I could see a mile ahead, a straight, clear, and smooth highway without other cars or people in sight. We were driving with special permission. It was a bright, clear morning without a trace of cloud or any other object in the sky. The gentle cool northern breeze from the Sahel made the journey even more pleasant. I was full of joy, and so were my passengers.

Usually, I drive within the legal speed limit. There was no speed limit posted on this highway. Guess they were still in the process of getting ready for the grand opening a couple of days ahead. Being named a vianini highway, I assumed that the maximum speed limit would be seventy miles per hour. I felt safe at that speed, driving around that speed. Sometimes happier thoughts made me speed faster, or unpleasant thoughts put a break in my acceleration. I kept asking Mohmmadu how I was doing. Was I steady? Was I speeding? Mohmmadu only said that this was a good road, and I could even drive faster if I wanted.

Would you? I asked him.

He said he did on his way to the airport. I asked how much. I was driving at seventy; could I go at eighty, ninety, or even one hundred mph. This was a new vehicle, with that response from Mohmmadu. I was reassured.

We drove for about an hour; the road was clear. There was no traffic, no people, and no other moving object. The closer we were nearing home, the faster I started to drive. VW Beetle is a light car, but the aerodynamic design and slightly wider chassis made them stable on the road. Moreover, we were three adults, and my travel loads made the car heavy and more stable than if I were driving alone. With all these confidence-boosting thoughts, I sped along.

There was nothing to be seen within half a mile of the car: space, clear road, and a clear and sunny sky. Suddenly, I saw a black goat and a kid standing right in the middle of the road, barely twenty to thirty feet ahead. Both Mohmmadu and his helper had dozed off. I had to make a split-second decision: hit the poor goats, kill them, damage the car, and be prepared for even a fatal accident, or try to avoid the goats, slightly swerve to the left, save the animals, then drive on. Unfortunately, the animals were too close. I had to take a fast and quick swivel to save the animals. I was driving between ninety and a hundred mph. The distance of the animals was too close, five to seven meters. My main aim was to save the lives of those two helpless animals.

Those were my last thoughts before I woke up with severe pain in the neck, headache, a vision that was slightly blurry, felt sick, and a splash of bloodstain on my shirt. I found myself sitting in the back seat, with my head down and my bottom and legs up. My whole body was upside down. I was slightly disoriented. Driver Mohmmadu was not to be seen anywhere. The front of the car was squashed entirely in through the front dashboard. The front driver's and passenger's seat and the space with the steering wheel, hand breaks were all squashed into a compressed tin junk.

By this time, I was better oriented. I looked for Mohmmadu in the squashed area. I called his name, called the helper's name; there was no response. I was still sitting on my head in the back seat. The car was upside down and sitting in a side ditch about four feet below the road's surface on the side. Somehow, I freed myself inside the back seat and manipulated myself out of the car. I looked around to see if I could see either of them. There was no sign of them. I came back and looked again but could not see them. Finally, I went up on the road and found Mohmmadu lying in the middle of the road, dazed, groaning in pain. "Mommahdu! Mommahdu!" I called a couple of times, checked his pulse, and it felt OK.

Then I looked for the helper who was thrown out of the car, lying down on the road, about fifty feet from the vehicle. He was in pain, awake, and asked me to give him some water. That was a good sign. I told him not to move. I went back to the car, and the water bottles were still intact. I ran with one bottle of water back to him. He had so much pain and extensive surface abrasions that he could not help himself. I told him just take a few sips, to keep his throat moist. His thirst was quenched.

I ran back to Mommahdu again. He was conscious, in much pain. I did not know how and where to get any help. No phone, no Automobile Associations, and the road was empty, kept closed for all traffic before the official opening, no human being around. No trace of the goats either, the ones I tried to save. I brought another water bottle and opened my twisted suitcase and the medicine bag I always carry. At least I could give them some painkillers I had with me.

But I was still flabbergasted, confused, and helpless. In the meantime, I found the front of my shirt was completely soaked with blood. I was dripping blood from a cut on my upper lip. I could stop bleeding by biting the upper lip, but the pain was so bad, I could bite only for a few seconds.

I moved both of them to the side of the road to save more accidents from any oncoming vehicle. I looked at my watch. It was still ticking. It was already fifteen minutes from when I got out of the car. Time was crucial to saving lives, even making them comfortable. I had no idea where I was. I had driven just over an hour from the airport. I must be close to Kailahun and closer to the Vianini Camp. I thought I would run towards

Kailahun, hoping to meet someone to seek help. I told both of them to stay. Still, I was going to try to get some help. Let us pray hard to get some help. Mohmmadu was not in any shape to swallow the painkillers I had. But I gave a couple to the helper. He was able to swallow.

He whispered in my ear that the Vianini camp was not more than a mile towards Kailahun. I was slightly hopeful. As I started to run towards the camp, I saw a pickup truck coming. I did not know who it belonged. I was desperate to stop it at any cost for help. I waved at the truck, kept running towards it. As I ran, the truck drove faster and faster. It arrived in two minutes.

I recognized the manager of Vianini and his people. He was apologetic for the delay. Fortunately, one of his stewards was returning to the camp. He found the car crushed and two people lying in the road. He ran as fast he could and informed the manager. As soon as he described the car, he knew it was mine because no other vehicle had permission to drive on this road, except vehicles belonging to the Vianini Company and the government Department of Highways. So he came as soon as he could. He brought the truck, expecting to tow the wrecked car to their garage, but the car was not in any shape to be towed. "So let me take you all back to Kailahun," said the manager, or if you want, we can drive you to Nixon Memorial Hospital, which is just as far or maybe a little further.

By this time, Mohmmadu was awake; I gave him a couple of painkillers. Both of them said they would go wherever we took them. The manager said, "Doctor, you are bleeding from your mouth. You need someone to take care of that; how long can you keep bleeding like this?" I told him I could stop it for a while, but I agreed I needed someone to look at the injury. I had some painkillers. I would need stitches, perhaps, to stop the bleeding. It was spurting out, not just oozing.

Let us go to Kailahun, check the situation, and then decide what to do next. They lifted both of them onto the truck. I sat in the front seat with the manager and the driver. Two other people sat with Mommahdu and the helper. Kailahun was just about eight to nine miles from the accident site. We headed for Kailahun hospital. We were about three miles away from the town center. By this time, it was already 4 pm. Still, it was broad daytime. I saw another car coming towards us. I recognized it as Sister Thomas's car. We flashed. She stopped. I asked where she was going. Gravely, she said "I was coming to find out why you took so long. One of Vianini's staff told me that you all were involved in a serious accident about a mile west of the camp. He also said the company manager had gone to help, taking some of his staff with him."

News traveled even faster than we could have done, using modern technology. This was "Bush Telegraphy." Think about how many lives were saved by these bush telegraphers. Sister had already prepared beds for all three of us in one part of the hospital. I was mobile and wanted to examine both of them. Mommahdu's external bruises were terrible but manageable. But I suspected multiple fractures, especially the pelvis, which needed a specialist's help. The helper had several larger and deeper lacerations, certainly requiring surgical management, perhaps help from a plastic surgeon. I also thought he may have cracked several ribs, needed x-rays, and a specialist's attention.

By that time, it was 5.30 pm. It was still daytime. I decided to send both of them to Nixon memorial hospital. I quickly went back to my office and composed two referral letters to the Emergency Doctor at Nixon Memorial Hospital. Vianini staff was more than willing to transport them to NMH. But I took the help of a police van and let one of the nurses escort them to the hospital.

I had no word to express my gratitude to the Vianini Manager and his staff. Instead, I said, "You have done much more than expected. Perhaps it is time for all of you to return to your camp, rest, and be ready for tomorrow's hard work."

I told the manager it was too bad that I missed his invitation to have real Italian coffee and crumpets in the middle of a dense equatorial forest. But we would have the opportunity to make it up soon when I was better. That was a promise, I confided to the manager.

We all look forward to seeing you in our camp.

I bid goodbye to them.

Chapter 28

MY TURN TO ACCEPT HELP

"The only true wisdom is in knowing, you know nothing."

Socrates

I had severe body ache. Sister took my vitals. They were all excellent. I again took a couple of Paracetamols. Extra strength was not available then. I told Sister, let us check the laceration on my upper lip. That was the only injury I had, besides severe psychological trauma. I had to shut out all my anxiety to focus on my injury and what to do with it. Do I need to go to NMH for help, or can I manage here? I was more worried about two of my injured staff.

I told Sister to go to the theater, where, in a better light, I would be able to examine the extent of the injury. In the theater, with the help of a mirror, I turned my upper lip inside out, which was quite swollen and painful. I looked at my cut on the right side of the upper lip. The laceration was mainly inside. Almost the whole thickness of the lip was split, splitting the outer surface and the skin beyond the vermillion border. The bleeding had stopped, but any manipulation could start it spurting out again.

I told Sister that we needed only four stitches. It seemed to be the soft tissue only. The lip and muscles of the mouth were severely bruised. The upper lip muscle was bruised and lacerated. But, it felt only partly damaged.

I told Sister and Mr. Joseph we would do the suturing without wasting time. Sister asked who would do the suturing. I said both of them would help me to do it. They were kind of surprised.

They prepared the surgical suturing kit. In the OR, I sat on a chair. I asked Mr. Joseph to get some local injectable anesthetic. We had none. I was surprised that we did not have any local anesthetic. The local anesthetic spray was used before. I told him to get the spray. I asked Sister to lift my upper lip inside out and let Mr. Joseph hold the mirror so that I could see the wound upside down; of course, that did not matter.

I asked Mr. Joseph to squirt the anesthetic on the wound. It does numb the surface for a few minutes but does not affect the deeper tissue. I also asked Sister to get five threaded sutures ready. The plan was, I would pull the sutures quickly, one at a time. Then, when all the sutures were in place, we would tie those, one by one. This way, the painful part of the surgery would be done quickly, and tying the knots would follow.

Both of them understood that they were the most important players. I needed good exposure to the wound without stretching the lip much. As I needed, Mr. Joseph would keep more anesthetic swabs ready and would focus the light properly.

I started putting the needle through from the bottom and let them hang one after the other. I needed only four sutures to close the entire length of the cut. Sister cut needles from the thread as I placed the sutures to close the wound. As the sutures were in place, I asked Mr. Joseph to spray more local anesthetic on the cut. I looked at the wound in the mirror, which Sister held to give me the exposure I needed to close the wound. I quickly tied all the threads, and Sister efficiently cut the redundant thread off. The whole procedure took less than fifteen minutes. I doubt I could have hacked the pain much longer. It looked OK from inside and out.

I had a few more bruises. Those were cleaned. I rested on the OR table. I tried to drink with a straw, it was not very useful, but I did anyway. Then Sister said it was fearful and disturbing to watch, even for her, working with surgeons in OR and ER for years. I never had to help any surgeon operate on himself. I hoped I wouldn't have to do it ever again.

Sister said she was controlling the mirror with her two hands. She realized I could not stop my legs from being curled up with pain. Sister Thomas had no choice but to place her right leg over my knees to pin them down so that I could carry on with my surgery and get it over with as fast as possible. "I must apologize for that," she said. I said that was a big help and smart thinking, not waiting for another person to come and help. Unfortunately, we did not have time either.

Time to return to my Den. Sister helped me to the car and drove me to my house. With Mommoh's help, my bed was all nicely made. He had prepared some light soup. I admired the effort, but it was impossible to sip anything. I asked him to keep it on the table. I had a double dose of Paracetamol. The painkillers did help, but I needed stronger painkillers. I did not want any more potent analgesic, which might hide some severe symptoms.

Sister said one of her senior nurses had volunteered to stay in my house for the night to keep an eye on. I did not know who she was. But, despite my mild objection, I was overtly pleased and grateful to Sister for being so thoughtful.

I had no time or energy to change. I dropped on the bed and fell into a deep sleep until the next day, almost at noon.

I woke up with a severe headache. I felt as if almost all the bones were ready to crack, and muscles would split open due to severe pain. I looked at myself in the mirror. The entire right side was swollen, the right eye was almost closed due to swelling around the eye. But I could see clearly. There was no double vision. However, I had difficulty walking, primarily due to bruised muscles. Yet, I was able to drag myself to the lounge. The nurse who spent the night was there. I had seen her before. First, she asked me how I felt after starting antibiotics, painkillers, and sleeping medicines. Then, the nurse volunteered to help Mommoh prepare my breakfast. I settled for soft-boiled eggs, slices of bread soaked in hot milk, and sugar. Then, of course, my favorite tea, which I had brought from England.

The nurse sat with me at the table. I made sure I did eat a reasonable quantity. She gave me my medications. Then she wanted to go home to her family. That was Sunday. I had no word to express my gratitude for her help. She said Sister Thomas would come in the afternoon. She would arrange any other medical service needed from Nixon Memorial Hospital or Freetown.

I was so mentally and physically agitated, and I could not reason. The scene of the accident and two of my staff, most likely with serious injury, their family, children, friends, were all I was concerned about; the doomed picture was flashing in my mind repeatedly. Both were long-time hospital staff, very helpful and liked by everyone. I was thankful to God that both of them were alive and hopefully would recover, but the physical and psychological trauma was beyond any measure of forgiveness. The guilt that etched my heart and mind would be there forever, reminding me of the sorrow and suffering I brought upon them. I couldn't, nor did I have the right, to ask for forgiveness from anyone. So I had to live with that guilt forever as a painful reminder of the value of the life of every human being.

By 4 p.m., I was up, feeling better, and hoping to have a late lunch.

I saw a car come into my compound. I did not know who it was. A few minutes later enters the District Officer with his wife. Seeing me seated in the lounge, with his usual happy, jovial, and keen sense of humor, he said he was informed late last night while in Daru for inspection. He got a complete rundown of the mishap. He felt sorry and genuinely distressed. His wife, Lena, was also a crown agent's locally recruited Legal Officer. Before her marriage, she was a trained lawyer, preferred to work with the government, and worked as a crown prosecutor in Freetown. Now she was on maternity leave, expecting their first child in 4 four months. Both of them genuinely felt sorry and sad about the accident.

The DO, with his usual keen sense of humor, asked, "Hey, Doc! Patients, when sick, come to a doc. But when the doc gets sick, where does he go?" He paused, "In Kailahun, the doc fixes himself!" I realized he was referring to my surgical adventure last night. I smiled, said sometimes. Then he said, "Doc, you have done such a good job; if you go to our bank and rob them before you fixed yourself, they will not even recognize who the robber was after fixing your facial wounds!"

We all broke into laughter. I said, "just give me a couple of days; the bank will know who the robber was! It will be that easy." We had a pleasant social exchange. He almost made me forget about my dire condition. I told him I expected to be at work, if not tomorrow, then by Tuesday. They left. I was still echoing their resounding laughter.

Sister Thomas came with a young girl. She was happy to see me sitting, pretending to read. By the late afternoon, I did feel quite a lot better. The young girl she introduced as her most favorite niece. Studying in high school and staying with her, since both her parents were abroad for training. "That is very nice of you." I asked the girl, "Sister Thomas just said, you are her favorite niece. Yes?" She tried to hide her face behind Sister. Then I asked her, "In that case, who is your most favorite aunty?" She kind of stuttered, could not come up with an answer, as I was about to ask her again. "Of course, it is Aunty Helen (Sister's first name). That settles it then; you are both each other's favorite. Then I will not have any problem complaining to either of you about the other. Agreed?"

Then we discussed my health; they had no information about our staff in NMH. She spoke to Mommoh about the dinner and breakfast for the next day and checked the stock and the fridge. She checked all medication. She said she would fix tonight's dinner and send it over to my house by 7 pm. Mommoh would prepare breakfast tomorrow after I woke up. Mommoh told sister I liked my bed tea with biscuits first in the morning, when I got up. "That is fine," she said.

And she left.

I knew I would have a difficult time until I was made aware the condition of two of my staff. How could I pass the night? How could I sleep?

Chapter 29
RECOVERING TO A NEW LIFE

"Without rain nothing grows, learn to embrace the storms in your life"

Gautama Buddha.

What a big difference I felt after one full day of rest and timely medications had done, as I woke up the following day. I felt much better, missed my bed tea. That was a good sign of "life" as far as I was concerned. I got up and washed my face, but I was not well enough to open my mouth to brush. I had gargled well with all lotions and potions left by Sister. Right-side of my face was still painfully swollen. I could open my right eye much more easily. Unable to speak clearly, I felt that the right side of my mouth, lip, and cheek had poor sensation and were weaker. I tried to speak with my hands. Able to communicate with multiple gestures.

Today was Monday. I thought it was essential to go to the hospital. At least a visit for courtesy, to assure the staff and patients that I was still well and around. So I went back to my bedroom and got ready to work. I sent Mommoh to ask Sister to give me a ride. She came promptly.

There were several people gathered in front and at the waiting area. Most of them were town people, to express their sympathy. Sister said she would check with the patients and determine what needed to be done. I went back to the clinic and reviewed a few patients who had surgery the previous week and came for their follow-ups.

In the meantime, I saw the Police Superintendent enter my office. I could see the surprise on his face. He expressed sympathy and asked about me generally. I did not forget to mention my surgical skill to treat myself. That was also a surprise to him. Then he said, we needed to make out a police report. Until police had inspected the site, the vehicle couldn't be moved. The road was scheduled to open by the Prime Minister in the next few days. The contractors also wanted to fix the road if there was any damage before they handed over the road.

I said that was fine. The Police Super gave me a card and said, "You will need your driver's license to complete the police report. We have issued you a new one since your driving license has been lost somewhere at the accident site." That was a full Driving License from the road traffic department, which was also under the District Police Superintendent's authority.

"We decided to travel first thing the next morning to the accident site, which was no more than twenty minutes' drive. In the meantime, until you can get a driver to drive your vehicle, one of the police vans will assist you with transportation." That was a big help. I still had two of my staff who were admitted at NMH. I was yet to have information about them. I asked Sister if she had heard from the hospital. I was very keen on visiting them as soon as possible. Sister was willing to drive me to Segbwema, about an hour to forty-five minutes' drive. I told her we could use the police van to take the trip. Mr. Boukhari arranged a police van, and we were on our way. Sister Thomas wanted to accompany me, especially as my support, aside from visiting our colleague.

Within forty-five minutes, we were at the hospital. The Police Superintendent apparently, got in touch with the Medical Director and informed him that we were on our way to visit our staff. As we arrived, Dr. Don (real name Dr. O'donaghou), the Medical Director of NMH, was waiting for us. Nixon Memorial Hospital in Segbwema was a Methodist Hospital, with the church from Manchester, built-in English Cottage Hospital style, all on one floor. They had the capacity for one hundred and twenty beds. Dr. Don was an Experienced General Surgeon from Ireland, had been in Sierra Leone for the last three years. A very polite and humble gentleman. He was looking at my face, knew that I was also involved in the accident, but did not ask many questions, but later did offer their help if I needed any.

We went to see Mommahdu first; he was lying in his bed. Surprised to see us, he smiled and said he was much better but did not know the extent of the damage. Dr. Don told me he had multiple pelvic bone fractures and fractures of the right ankle bones. Fortunately, a neurologist was visiting at that time, so the internist and the neurologist both checked him and said he did not have any neurological problem, like spinal cord damage or crushing or tearing any nerve. It was mostly muscle and bone problems. Multiple fractures of the pelvic bone were impossible to treat, except with rest. He had to have a catheter since it was difficult for him to use a commode or washroom. The urine was clear. That was reassuring. I was delighted and thought of the medical staff as God-sent. Mohmmadu would be at the hospital for months, which was my feeling. Dr. Don more or less agreed.

Then we moved to see the "Helper." He was also half asleep. He had several lacerated injuries, but all of those were well repaired. He also had extensive bruising on the left side of his body. Those were generally superficial. He was also happy to see us. Dr. Don said all his X-rays were normal. They could not find any fracture, and he would be able to return in a week or so.

I was also getting tired. We had a few minutes' chats. I expressed my sincerest gratitude from the bottom of my heart, knowing that these two wounded people were getting all the help they needed in the middle of the Equatorial jungle.

We left for Kailahun, and we were back in my house in three and half hours. I still had lots of bone and muscle aches. I thought I would be able to take a hot shower, which Mommoh had already prepared. I had some thick soup and boiled stuff. Eating anything was still a struggle.

Sister Thomas, with her niece, dropped by just to check that all was well. I thanked her for accompanying me to the hospital. Both our staff were happy and felt reassured that they were not abandoned. I thanked Sister and her niece and said goodnight to them. Fell asleep until Mommoh woke me up the following day for my bed tea. He also told me that the Police Superintendent sent a message to remind me about our visit to the accident site this morning for inspection and a police report. As soon as I was ready, he would go. Another day of a good night's rest made a big difference. My aches and pains had improved. I was more mobile and, importantly, able to speak more intelligibly. Swelling of the right side of my face and lips, bruises around my right eye looked like I just came out of a boxing arena. Anyway, everything seemed to be on the mend.

Chapter 30
VISIT THE SITE OF ACCIDENT

"The man who asks questions is a fool for a minute, the man who does not ask is a fool for life"

Confucius

Sister came to pick me up. Mr. Boukhari, the Police Superintendent, and the District Officer were waiting for me. I quickly got into the police car. Then, with one of the staff from his office and a policeman, the District Officer set out for the accident site on the newly built Vianini highway. It was just about twenty-five minutes before we arrived there. A tow truck and people from the Vianini camp had already arrived before we did. They were keen to remove the car as soon as possible and repair any visible damages before the highway's official opening.

As we were approaching, I was surprised to see the black goat with a white patch on its head and the kid sitting by the side of the car. I rubbed my eyes, fixed my glasses, and it was not an illusion, precisely what I saw there; it was the mother and the baby goat, whom I tried to avoid, that got me into this horrible accident. I asked Mr. Boukhari if he saw what I saw; sitting beside the car. "Yes!" He said. "Is it a goat or any other animal? Goats have apparently been completely wiped out in this region, courtesy of Tsetse fly and yellow fever." Mr. Boukhari must be more familiar with the local animal population. I did not argue. But to my surprise, after four days since the accident, how come these animals were still here? There was no food or drink for them. It was just as barren, dry, and godforsaken as the Sahara. We parked behind the car several feet away as we approached, and the animals had gone. We looked around. They were not there. Maybe they went inside the wreckage. Nothing could be seen; no goat, dog, cat, or even any moving beetle.

The District Officer and Police Superintendent looked at the state of the car. It was upside down, lying in the depth of the side ditch. It was half its length because the front of the vehicle was squashed entirely inside the front seat through the dashboard. There was practically no space in the driver's compartment in the front seat. I was the driver, and Mommahdu was sitting in the passenger's seat. We should have been squashed into a sack full of meat. No one could understand how anyone could have survived and come out walking from this crash.

When I got my senses back, I found myself sitting on the back seat, upside down, such as the car was. All the doors were jammed. I struggled hard to get one of the rear doors open and maneuvered myself out of the vehicle. I did not see other passengers around. Instead, the driver was lying on the opposite side of the road, about twenty feet from the car, and the helper was at least fifty feet behind, lying in the middle of the road. Both of them were thrown out of the vehicle due to the impact.

Then we tried to trace the track of the tumbling car. It was at least fifty yards from where the vehicle was resting. The dragging marks were still visible. The car first rolled out of control into the drain on the left side, and it then rolled over the road and into the opposite gutter by the side of the road. Then it rolled back into the opposite drain over the road, and on the fourth time, it rolled back again over the highway to stop in the side ditch, landing upside down on its roof.

By then, the front had been squashed into the driver's compartment. Two people had been ejected out, and the driver was flung back into the back seat. Still, this was a miracle that we all were alive and, hopefully, would make it through to the rest of our lives.

They kept nodding in disbelief; how anyone could have come out unscathed and alive from this horrible accident must be a miracle.

After the inspection, Police Super handed the car over to the Vianini staff. They loaded the trash in five minutes in the back of their truck and off to the Vianini compound.

As we returned, both the District Officer and the Police Super again said, "God has not only been kind to you, but also to all of us in the district that we did not have to go through the horrible outcome of this accident which could have been impossible to bear." They all wished us a quick recovery.

I went to the police station. As advised by the Super, as the driver of the vehicle, I submitted an incident report in my own words. "But," he said, "Knowing your physical incapacity, just sign the form we know the detail of the incident we will prepare the report, you can look over then finally give us the authority to conclude the case so that you can buy another car. Your car will be towed to the company in Kenema. They will look for another car. It will be difficult for you to carry on with your life without your transport."

My workday was over. There were no urgent issues or cases to be seen, so I went back to my house. I was physically feeling much better, so I sat down with books and notes and reviewed the research project I was expected to be working on when the lab was ready, and I returned to London.

It was impossible to concentrate or focus on anything, aside from the memories of the accident and even what might come in the future. Would I be able to continue with my job? Was it possible that my contract would be terminated? But it had nothing to do with my professional competence and leadership in handling all health care issues as the District Medical Officer. I did not want to bring it up with the authorities. The police were involved, and the District Officer was well aware of the situation. Was I supposed to file a report to my superiors proactively? I did discuss it with the District Officer, but he did not think there was any need. No life had been lost nor any government property damaged, and you have been working full-time, so what was the problem?

After one week, the "Helper, Mr. Boukhari," returned to Kailahun. He looked well and wished to start work again. He had the discharge report from Dr. Don that he would be able to return to work after one week. In the meantime, we promoted him to a temporary ambulance driver. He needed a special license to be able to drive the ambulance. It was done without any real problem, thanks to the Police Super.

A couple of days after we visited the site of my accident and the battered car was removed, Mr. Boukhari called me from his office, saying the car dealer in Kenema had found a vehicle for me. It was another VW, one-year older. The car belonged to a diamond mining Company in Kano. I needed a car. I asked if the car was in good condition, and I got assurance from the dealer. I then requested him to send the car. I would look at it. It would be difficult for me to travel to Kenema, to check the car. Mr. Boukhari said I could always use one of his drivers to view the car. I would appreciate it if he did not mind bringing the car to Kailahun.

The next day around 11 am, the dealer brought the car and one of his mechanics. It was exactly like the one I had, but just a year older. Mr. Boukhari sent one of his drivers to check. He did a thorough check and said, "This is just like new with very low mileage." Then I asked the dealer about the price. He said I need not pay any extra since the financing of the previous car would be transferred to this one. The deficit would be covered by the scrap price and the insurance company. I would carry on with whatever I was paying for the old car. The Police Super would register the car in my name.

The dealer went to the Police Super's office, which was just across the street. He returned with a form and informed me this was the registration form, with the change of ownership now under my name. I signed on the dotted lines as advised. Then he handed the car keys to me. He also mentioned that I would get comprehensive insurance coverage for one year.

He left the keys on my table. I was looking at the keys in awe and intrigue. I just bought a new car sitting in my office. I never thought this could happen in Equatorial forest, but it does happen. This compassionate human interaction does happen in the Equatorial forest, less so in Manhattan.

Chapter 31

CONVALESCING: AYESHA, MY FRIEND

"Accept the things to which fate binds you, and love the people with whom fate brings you together, but do so with all your heart."

Marcus Aurelius

Every morning I get up, I wonder how I would feel and how the day would go. I started to feel better and better every day. Now I had a little friend, who spent all her spare time in my house. That was Ayesha, Sister Thomas's niece, whether I was in or out. This was summer vacation time. The schools were closed. Usually, Ayesha would have gone to Freetown to spend time with her "Grands," uncles and aunts, nephews and nieces, watching movies, picnicking at Lumley beach, or just strolling along the busy streets of Freetown, as any other 14-year-old high school girl would do. This year was different. She witnessed the horror of the car accident; the hurt, the injuries, pain, and sleepless nights, apparently all impacted her. She decided to spend the summer vacation to tend to the injured "Doctor" and intern at the hospital. She was encouraged by the support from Sister Thomas. Sister could not look after me as much as she would like, so her 14-year-old niece could be a perfect default caretaker.

I told her it was very thoughtful of her, even for a little girl. "This may be your year before you go to college. Then the course work, lectures, and assignments will take up all your time, no time for party or relaxation, or hours of TV viewing. So think about spending time helping me instead of enjoying yourself. I like your wish to work in the hospital to help the nurses. That will have a significant impact on your future, might help you to think about what you want to do after finishing school.

Anyway, the future would follow with or without anyone's intervention. But for the time being, follow your wish, how you want to spend your summer vacation. Your help and being with me will be highly appreciated, but you do not have to do this."

I asked her what she wanted to become when she grew up one day. It was not very long before we had to think of that. Her response was, she wants to help people, whatever career takes her there.

"This summer, I want to help you get better soon and have a happy time in Kailahun." She kept looking at my face and asked me about pain. "Do you need any pain killer?" By this time, she was familiar with my household, what I had, where what is, and my fondness for tea and coffee.

"It is lunchtime. I will ask Mommoh to set your lunch. Then, I will check what he has prepared."

I still had difficulty eating and chewing. If I could put any soft food inside my mouth, which I may be able to chew and swallow with some discomfort, I would do it. It had been just over one week since the accident. The stitches inside my mouth were still there, and the upper lip was still swollen. My speech was still unclear. The right side of my mouth and cheek were still tilted. I had no sensation in the upper lip. The rest of my facial swelling had gone down quite a bit. I was looking more like a human being than a genetically defective chimpanzee. My muscle pain was improving, but the pain in the shoulder joints and the neck were getting more troublesome. I was managing, anyhow.

Sister Thomas instructed Ayesha to put dry heat on my painful joints with a pad. I had a total body X-ray called the "skeletal survey" at the NMH. There was no fracture, but any soft tissue damages were undetectable by X-rays. At that time, Dr. Don and his visiting neurologist did a thorough examination, but aside from some muscle spasms, they could not find any neurological or joint mobility problem. I felt fortunate, indeed, for two reasons: I was essentially intact, and, most importantly, I was fortunate to have been examined by two very senior specialists from Europe. Notwithstanding in this Godforsaken dark-forested, snake-infested, roaming ferocious animals, stinking killer mosquito and man-eating tribal area of Sierra Leone.

One day Sister herself came and showed Ayesha how to apply dry heating pads. She would do this once a day, especially when I returned from work. Sister also bought some ointments to rub on the painful parts of my body. I was embarrassed initially to expose myself to a young lady. I had to forsake all sense of embarrassment and let her get on with what she was instructed to do. I convinced myself that she was just a 14-year-old school kid, maybe a future nurse, a doctor, or a specialist. Her volunteer activities may be an excellent hands-on practice of her desire to help people. This might motivate her to be a real one in the future. So I submitted myself to her hands to carry on with what she had been asked to do by Sister Thomas.

I must say, she had been a very respectful, gentle, understanding, and caring individual. Now and then asking if her way was hurting me or making me uncomfortable, then she would do it differently. However, I complimented her repeatedly for doing an excellent job and helping me.

I know she felt sorrier for me than I did for myself. She would hang around my house cleaning this, wiping that, dusting my books, papers, and my little portable pink typewriter. She was amazed to see how much typing I did on that little machine I carried from London. When I was busy working, she would ask me if I needed any drink, tea, coffee, or anything else. Generally, I would accept her offer, and she would look pleased.

She was spending so much time in my house that I was happy to have a young company, but I would be happier if I could help her use her time better. So I asked her if perhaps she would like to bring her summer vacation reading and assignments and do it here. I would help her if she needed it. I often asked her what she wanted to become when she grew up. Generally, she would give me a big smile and counter-question me: "Who said I want to grow up? I would like to stay like this forever, if not for a long time. I am happy as I am now." "All right!" I said, "I can help you even stay as you are. Just do nothing." She liked the English language and literature. She would bring one of her favorite storybooks and read. Sometimes she spoke to me about the book she read and often made interesting comments coming from a schoolgirl.

I brought several books with me to study for my specialist examination. I thought this was an excellent time to study and prepare for my examination, while I was not deeply engaged in my research work. So I generally let her do whatever she wanted to do. Sometimes, we would share snacks and drinks, and she would put on music, which I was not necessarily used to listening to, but I did listen to keep her company.

She took over pressing my clothes from Mommo and did a much better job. In the morning, I would find that whatever I wanted to wear to work, were already pressed nicely and hanging in the wardrobe. She would ask me what I wanted to wear the following day to work. I did tell her what I wanted. Then I saw my shoes were also polished and shined, left in the lounge, where I would put them on before going to work. She was well aware of my fascination for impressive clothes and shoes.

I studied Anatomy, took notes, and sketched pictures from the book one day. That was Grey's Anatomy. She had gone through all my books and commented that they were too difficult to understand, and even more, were too thick and heavy to carry. All I would say is, if I can do it, you are a big girl; you can even do it better. Finally, she asked me, "Do I have to draw all those difficult colorful pictures?" I said we needed to draw them sometimes but must learn from the pictures in the book.

She looked at the book's open page, which had a picture of the chest with the heart and lung in place. I went to the sitting room. I concentrated on what I was studying. I thought she had left, but I knew she would not leave without saying goodbye to me. Anyway, as I got engrossed in my study, she returned to me and showed me the sketch of the chest, what I was studying. I was amazed and completely flabbergasted to see the exactness and accuracy of her drawing. I realized she was just a good artist and had a photographic memory. I wanted to give her a big hug but had to control myself very hard. But I poured compliments into words instead. She was pleased. I said, "If you can do this bit before being a doctor, Ayesha, you will, and you can do more than this if you want.

She had already started spending the morning with the nurses, helping them make beds, serving food, keeping the ward tidy, and doing messenger work. So I told Sister to put her in the

Wound and Dressing Clinic, which was busy, and let her witness real cases other than looking at my stitched upper lip.

When she came to my house in the afternoon, I would ask her about the wounds, the cases she had seen, what the nurses did, etc. Finally, after a few days, when I was happy that she could withstand the sight of the wounds, some maggot-stricken, rotten-smelling ulcers for a little school girl, I asked her to draw sketches of some cases that she'd seen, with follow-up sketches with dates. She showed it to me, and we discussed those that would be placed in the patient's file as a document.

At last, I found common ground to interact with a schoolgirl on the same platform, at the same level of mutual interest and liking. In the afternoon, we would discuss cases that she saw and sketched. That was a massive help to me for documentation. I had the habit of clinical sketching, which we found very useful in the long term. Now I had a friend who could do it for me.

She was delighted. Sister Thomas was also delighted that I discovered her niece's talent, which we used for patient care.

She was slightly overgrown for a 14-year-old, and I was small for a 23-year-old District Medical Officer. Nevertheless, she was pretty and had a baby face. Her raspy voice was musical at times and hypnotic at others. Academically, she was average but was liked by everyone due to her angelic demeanor. She moved like a butterfly and had a million-dollar smile as I watched.

I liked her around but kept at an affectionately civilized distance, not to spoil the angel in her. The power of my desire for a scholarly career overshadowed any distraction firmly and mercilessly. At that time, nothing on earth could distract me from my dream. I wanted to keep her close yet not destroy her innocence. Help her be a goddess whom I could worship and let others do the same and discover herself. I needed to honor Sister's trust and generosity and her strong feeling for my well-being, willing to help any time, any place at any cost.

It was spiritually anguishing yet a feeling of divine living for the next several months, with Ayesha being around me.

Chapter 32

MR. JESUDASAN, THE PRINCIPAL

"A Nation can survive its fools, and even the ambitious. But cannot survive treason from within. An enemy in the gates is less formidable, for he is known and carries his banner openly. But the traitor moves amongst those within the gates freely, his sly whispers rustling through all the alleys, heard in the very hall of government itself"

Marcus Julius Cicero.

I was at the Clinic. The interpreter informed me that an Indian gentleman wished to see me. I asked if he was with a patient. She said, "No! But he is willing to come back later if I am busy." So I went outside to meet the gentleman. He was an elderly, energetic, balding white head, clear spoken, and well attired gentleman, sporting an academic tie, which I did not recognize.

He apologized for showing up without notice or appointment. He was excited to learn about me and keen to meet me. He introduced himself as *Mr. Anthony Sudarsan Jesudasan*, the New Principal of The Catholic High School, and the only missionary high school in Kailahun. He arrived just over a week ago, settling down in his government quarters, in his new Job as Principal, around an unfamiliar community and lifestyle. As a Christian missionary, he told me that he was motivated to accept, adjust, and uplift any community as a spiritual challenge anywhere in the world. Some other teachers from his school spoke to him about me, and that was how he was here. I greeted him and thanked him for taking the trouble of finding me and making an effort to come.

It was my operating day. I had two cases for operation. I did tell him I would very much like to speak to him. Unfortunately, I couldn't sit down with him because of the surgical cases. But I would love to meet him at my house this afternoon, to join me for the afternoon tea. One of his colleagues drove him to the hospital. His colleague said he would be happy to go to my house this afternoon around 5 pm. He introduced himself as Mr. Bangura. He was the office manager of the School. I said, 'Mr. Bangura, you are also welcome to join me for tea, but I will arrange a ride back to your home if you are busy."

I directed Mr. Bangura to get to my house from the hospital. "You take the road, drive straight for five to six minutes. As the road ends, you will find the entrance to my bungalow." They both left, promising to return in the afternoon.

I went back to the clinic and had a couple of patients to see before going to the theatre. By 1.30, we finished both cases. They were sent back to the ward fully awake and in good condition. In my office, Mr. Aamara, our manager, was waiting with files to go through and several letters to sign. We sat down and discussed some administrative issues, especially relating to the outreach clinics. I was concerned about the promptness of reports, patients, and the clinics' logistics. He assured me that the outreach clinic managers were in touch with him and

Sister Thomas from an administrative point of view. Reports and attendance documents of patients and staff are sent regularly, on time, since my last inspection, which was, in fact, my first visit to these outreach community health centers, run by a nurse and a pharmacist. Reporting and communication appeared to have improved, and reports were given more in detail and accurately lately.

I told Mr. Amara to accompany me for my plan to inspect all the healthcare facilities in the district, which would happen the next month. Sister Thomas did her inspections independently and reported back to me.

It was 2.30, time to go back for lunch. When I arrived, Mommoh and Ayesha were there. Ayesha was busy catching up with writing letters to her friends, who had gone away during the summer vacation. She chose to spend the summer in Kailahun with her aunty and care for me.

Ayesha said she already had her lunch at her aunt's but would be happy to set mine. Together they did. I told Mommoh I expected one or two visitors for tea this afternoon as I was eating. What could we offer them? I kept whole varieties of biscuits for my use. I thought of getting some cakes from the grocery stores in the town center. Ayesha was enthusiastic about helping Mommoh. They walked to the town center, less than a ten-minute walk from my house. They returned half an hour later empty-handed. I was disappointed. Thought we would manage, with whatever we had at home.

To my utter delight, they said, Mr. Saad, the owner, would send titbits and a cake for afternoon tea for my guest as soon as he got everything ready and had put them together. After that, he would send one of his workers. So Mommoh told him to give the best cake Mr. Saad had for my guests that afternoon. I was happy but remained anxious because the arrangement was not in my hands anymore, and I did not know what he would send and how much it would cost. Anyway, Ayesha told me Mr. Saad made cakes and other sweets that people like a lot. So we would wait and see what arrived from Mr. Saad.

Mr. Jesudasan arrived precisely at 5 pm. I guess discipline and time are the two most important factors he had to deal with personally with his job. I invited both of them in, asked them to be comfortable. Mr. Bangura was keen to return home. That was Friday afternoon. He wished to be with his family and attend the church services that evening. I thanked him and asked him to come another day when he had time.

Mr. Jesudasan told me he was from Coimbatore in Madras Province in India, where he worked as a principal of a high school belonging to the same mission. He was born in Trichur, in Tamilnadu province in India, had his schooling there, where his family roots were. His father was a pastor, and his mother was a high school teacher. His only sister was married to a doctor, and they lived in England; she worked as a family physician in Wales. While he was growing up, teachers from Madras were in high demand all over in the British Colonies. He liked traveling and thought being a teacher with a mission would give him a better opportunity to see the world and experience different cultures.

He had been a teacher for nearly twenty-five years; this was his second opportunity to come abroad. About three years ago, he came to Ethiopia as a senior English teacher in Addis Ababa for a year to teach English to government officers. Yet, at most of the universities in Ethiopia, English was the medium of instruction. Many of his students worked in various government departments, and some were seeking university admission. That was a real experience, teaching those who did not have the mental makeup to be a student again but were forced to do so to increase their chances for career advancement. That was why the class was a challenging exercise, he said. So, to motivate them, he had to give up the teacher's role and pretend to be a fellow learner. As a result, there was a considerable improvement in enrollment, especially from aspiring university entrants. The government of Ethiopia recognized him for his success as an English teacher for mature professionals. I felt good about him.

In the meantime, Mr. Saad had already sent his bounty of snacks for afternoon tea. When I asked about paying, Ayesha said the man had already left, and this was compliments of Saad family to welcome the new doctor in the city.

When I looked at the tray, it was a massive collection of Lebanese cakes and sweets, some of which looked exactly like Indian flakey sweets and cakes.

We settled for our tea party. I asked Ayesha to join us, but she shied away. Both Mommoh and she enjoyed their afternoon snack merrily. The tea was superb, which I had brought from London with me. Fortunately, Freetown could satisfy any palate. Be it Indian, Middle Eastern, or British, because of its population mix and many people from the Commonwealth, traders, entrepreneurs, professionals, miners, educators, and trainers, who were generally financially well, just after the country got independence. Matched by good governance, left by the British as their legacy, it made the country safe to live and do business.

It was a wealthy country because of its mineral wealth, rare earth elements, and, notably, diamonds, gold, bauxite, iron, rutile, and limonite mining. We discussed the "State of the Nation," political climate, lifestyle, quality of life, and in general, life in the jungle, as well as strange stories of savageries, snakes, mosquito-borne diseases, water quality, and treatment facilities. I did say what we could do in Kailahun from the medical care side, but we were fortunate to have the Nixon Memorial Hospital run by Methodist Missionary Society, supported by a UK based charity, founded by John Nixon in memory of his wife, and just about half hour's drive away. This hospital was considered the best hospital in the country at that time. He was reassured.

We talked about the political and economic status in India. Even after fourteen years of independence, the consequences of the partitioning of India remained a serious, not only national but regional and global problem also. Fire in every corner. Just to achieve a quick fix of religious killings of epidemic proportion and time-honored hope for divide and rule by Westminster authorities eventually brought the slow demise of the mighty Empire, where once the sun never set, literally. The unsettled state of native kingdoms, their Maharajas, Nawabs, and some with formidable military power, constantly fueled the possibility of a major eruption at any time, destroying seven thousand years of civilization. The Raj that ruled India for two hundred years was either unaware or ignorant, or just too simplistic to understand the strength of seven thousand years of wisdom.

The lesson they learned from their Raj in India gave them the knowledge to run an effective bureaucracy to manage a vast population with minimum investment. The excellent and effective bureaucracy in the colonies, including Sierra Leone, was almost a replica of practice they had developed for India with minor local twists. So, you will not find much difficulty while wading through governmental institutes and the bureaucratic meshes.

I also spoke to him about my car accident on Vianini highway; the horror, the rescue, the help and support I got from everyone around me, and my eventual recovery was beyond expression. From a frightening nightmare to a blissful memory, etched deep in my heart forever. The swelling of my upper lip, the last suture mark just above the vermillion line, some weakness of my lip and right cheek, and rare, unusual speech all were noticed by Mr. Jesudasan. He looked confused and was lost for words, aside from saying, "Sorry to hear!" I could see the fear in his face and an expression of helplessness. What did one do in this situation? What he could have done if he was involved. But, help comes from where one never expects, he said. He was a devout Christian who did not miss his Sunday morning church commune for anything if he could help it.

Three hours went by like a flash. We got on well. He was an experienced teacher and a learned, wise man. We indeed hit it off. He remained a good friend and company for my stay in Sierra Leone.

Mr. Jesudasan agreed to come back again. By this time, it was 8 pm, Mommoh informed me that Sister Thomas would be happy to drop my guest at his house whenever he was ready. That was very kind and thoughtful of her, and I asked Mommoh to extend my gratitude to her. She came, and I introduced her to Mr. Jesudasan. She knew about the high school's new Principal but did not know that he had arrived or when he arrived. She knew the location of the Principal's quarters and would have no problem finding it.

I thanked her for the help since I was still new to the town, just recovering from the accident, and Bokhari, the driver, was not available, so there was every reason for her to step in and do what was necessary to help me.

On a Saturday, late morning, was my time of relaxation, sitting under a cropped apple tree in front of my bungalow, enjoying my morning coffee or tea with Indian snacks. We bought at Indian shops in Freetown and listened to some of my favorite music. On Saturday mornings, first, I would give a quick ward round and review all medications with Sister Thomas, and then I was free for the rest of the weekend.

Mr. Jesudasan was invited to join me for my Saturday late morning picnic. With Indian savories, unlimited tea or coffee and discussing many issues, the cost of living, difficult transportation in and out of the town, his colleagues and staff. Attitude and sincerity for learning, which were different. I said, "Here, you have the opportunity of influencing for change in learning perspectives. Get them interested in projects aside from schoolwork, get them involved, and talk to them about how life is in Freetown, the rest of Sierra Leone, Africa, India, Asia, Europe, and America."

"I know you have started the change, being one of the learners and not the learned one;" he said, "The students have several projects other than just finishing the classwork. We need energetic motivators for growing minds." He encouraged disciplined physical activities, games, athletics, handwork, artwork, and recently, stage performance for entertaining themselves and their families. These were all normal activities, back in India, in all the high schools. Here we lacked motivating, dedicated teachers, but they all, students or teachers, would like to participate once they saw a difference. He was always thinking and plotting how to engage every student to study to get the grades and develop as responsible citizens and compassionate human beings. A little bit ahead of his time, especially in the Equatorial forest of Sierra Leone and the "God forsaken" part of the country.

We talked about vast racial, social, and cultural differences between his students in India, Ethiopia, and Kailahun. Were these factors affecting his ability to function? He agreed, yes one would think so, but after the initial adjustment phase from both sides, the barrier broke down and disappeared. He thought all teachers be expatriates or natives, must accept this phenomenon and actively and consciously address this issue to bring the students closer, be a friend without being too friendly.

When he found out I took Ayesha as an intern to assist the nurses, he was interested in developing a pilot program. He found most of his senior class were curious and eager to participate in the program. I gave him some info about what they would do, our purpose, and how they would benefit the students and their time. Working as a volunteer intern in a hospital was very new to him and the country's school system. Exposure would educate them about dealing with patients, taking care of them, their families, and friends, and learning to empathize with sick people and all human beings. Our aim was high, and our expectation was noble, but not sure how much we could achieve in this environment.

Ayesha also studied in the same school. She had been our best Ambassador. We could only do this during school holidays and break time. We had two students spending one week together. They spent most of the time with the nurses, but I did get them into the clinic, just for introduction. Once, one girl came to me and asked if she could see a Cesarean operation. I asked her why especially the Cesarean operation. The answer was straightforward; she was born through a Cesarean operation and did not understand if she needed the same. She was a grade twelve student. I let her come to watch; unfortunately, the blood bath of the procedure made her dizzy, and she had to cut short her stay. She waited till the end until the mother and the baby were wheeled off to the ward from the operation room.

That was a very successful program started by Mr. Jesudasan. From time to time, his students would come to keep the hospital compound clean, help patients with chores, like writing letters, posting letters, contacting family and relatives.

Mr. Jesudasan had a three-year contract. His wife was also a teacher. She could not get a leave of absence to come and join him. She would have to resign or take early retirement. That would be a significant financial loss to the family. His oldest child, a boy, was already in Madras University Engineering College. A scholarship mostly subsidized his expenses, but Madras was an expensive place to live, so his parents had to help him with the shortfall. He was in final year class, expected to graduate in a year and join the workforce soon after. It would be at least two years before he became financially independent.

The oldest daughter was in pre-professional class at the university. They all wanted her to take up medicine. Suppose it was just a straightforward case of merit; she could whizz through any competition. But to get into medical school demanded many other obstacles to tackle, one of those being how fat one's family purse was, and how high a position one's dad had. For her, except for her merit, no support was in sight.

If any medical school could give him one hundred percent assurance of a seat, he was willing to sell his house for that. Such was the heavy burden on the parent's conscience to do everything to clear the road for their daughter to be a doctor. At that time, almost all medical schools in India were run by state governments. There were a few private schools, and their standards were questionable. But there could be no question about the criteria for getting a seat, which was a fat donation to the school to advance Medical Science and technology. It was indecent at that time; people sneered at those schools. Today they would look like a saint compared to the vulgar, obnoxious, and criminal demands private medical schools demanded nowadays for admission.

We would discuss this issue in our Saturday late morning tea. I would give him several ideas, including the generous scholarships offered to Indians by Russians to train as a doctor in Russia. As the time ticked towards the end of her pre-professional course, the depth and weight of anxiety became thicker and heavier. She was applying fiercely, anywhere and everywhere. I kept feeling more and more concerned about his state of mind.

I did see her grades. I told him with this grade, she would not have any difficulty being chosen for an interview in any four medical schools we had in Calcutta. She even applied to Makerere University in Uganda. Unfortunately, the closing dates had all come and gone. The universities would start in two months, yet his daughter had not received any summons to attend an interview. At that time, calls for interviews for medical school admission were an invitation for ninety percent success.

He started to give up and get mentally prepared to let her study B.Sc. in Biological Science to better herself to get a seat for Medicine. But, I told him that we had several students with B.Sc., a few with Masters, and one was an Electrical Engineering graduate in my class. So this was not an unusual step.

A week later, on a Tuesday morning, as I was going to the operating room, I saw Mr. Jesudasan coming in. I thought he must be sick and needed medical attention. I took him straight to my clinic. I could not understand why he had tears in his eyes. I asked him to sit down. "No, Doctor, I know you are so very busy. I will not take much time, just to share with you the happiest news I have had ever before, since you have been very helpful, understanding, and supportive to alleviate my anxiety." He showed me the telegram from his wife confirming that his daughter had been admitted to Trichur Government Medical School with a seventy-five percent scholarship. The joy, happiness, and relief of a father, I saw in his face, cannot be expressed in words. I congratulated him. Trichur was Mr. Jesudasan's hometown, where his widowed mother still lived with help from servants, relatives, and friends. His daughter would study Medicine from home, with her grandmother around; sparing him from a significant cost of living expenses was also a huge relief.

We had regular Saturday late morning idle chats. Every time I went to Freetown, I brought a bagful of Indian snacks, which he loved. I used to go to his school from time to time. He had an excellent library, both for students and teachers. He used to get some newspapers and magazines. The staff sitting room was a conference room, well furnished. It was a surprise to see a library of books in the middle of the African jungle.

There were whole sets of Shakespeare, Dickens, Scott, Milton, and many others. What attracted my attention was a two thousand-page book titled "Mysteries and Marvels of the World." My geography teacher often taught us in our geography class quoting the book; even our high school library did not have a copy. I picked it up and asked Mr. Jesudasan if I could borrow it. No question asked. I took that book, which stayed with me until I left Kailahun eight months later. Frequently I would start reading the book, and my mind would begin to wander far into the unknown mysteries of the world.

We became good friends. Just about two months before I was to leave Kailahun, I had completed my work on a Friday afternoon and sat and discussed various issues with Sister Thomas and Mr. Amara. I heard someone knocking at the door. Mr. Amara got up quickly and answered the knock. It was Mr. Jesudasan. Visits at odd times brought bad or good news. I saw his bright and smiling face, and I asked him in. He sat down. Both Sister and Mr. Amara excused us. A nurse asked if we would like some tea or coffee, or a cold drink. Some tea would do for both of us. Then Mr. Jesudasan, with a gleeful smile, said, "My wife will be here in a month!" She was granted retirement with full benefits a year early since she had accumulated nearly nine months of earned leave. In India, women could retire at fifty-two and men at fifty-five years. She was fifty-one. This was a huge relief for him. He had over two years of contracted time in Kailahun remaining.

I was happy to hear the news. I said she'd better come before I left because we had had no Idle or Dossa (these are south Indian popular food) for more than a year. We should be looking forward to revitalizing our palate. I was happy for him.

We kept our friendship strong for several years, by regular telephone or postal mail. I sold my VW to Mr. Jesudasan; the price was reasonable. The car was in excellent condition.

A couple of years later, he sent me a message, saying that his youngest daughter had been selected to study MB.BS in Bangalore. That was also wonderful news. She would be close to home and regularly see her brother and older sister. In addition, Mr. Jesudasan would be finishing his three years contract. After she came to Kailahun, his wife was also given a senior teacher's position at the same school.

During my last two months in Kailahun, I tried several varieties of south Indian dishes prepared by Mrs. Jesudasan, for example, Idle, Dossa, Sambar, real south Indian coffee, and many others. I became a devoted fan of Mrs. Jesudasan for her unique south Indian culinary art. She even tried to prepare Sierra Leonean Jollof Rice, following the recipe books. It tasted and smelt like the authentic Jollof rice but needed some maturing; it was exciting nonetheless. She did get to befriend local ladies and some of the chief's wives. She was able to speak Temne, the most popular spoken tribal language. She would attend the Women's Council to talk to their children and family. One day I saw her wearing the traditional Temne female grab gifted by some ladies. She went "marketing" with a group of them. Interestingly, she taught us more about the Sierra Leonean tribal society because of her intimate access to the tribal female counsel in Kailahun.

She quickly got used to the traditional lifestyle in Kailahun and made it more intimate, friendly, and integrated, not forgetting their roots in India. Most of the Indians in Freetown lived a European lifestyle, interspersed with the Indian tradition, which helped them have social leverage towards the Krios and with the leftover colonial Brits or white business executives. The Colonial Brits and Krios were the power, and Lebanese and Indians owned big business.

Now that everything was going their way, the Jesudasans would be able to retire and return home at the same time, spending lots of time with their children and grandchildren, maybe. I always had good feelings for them. Unfortunately, the frequency of our Saturday late morning coffee groups got less and less, and eventually, I was the only member to keep the tradition going. Occasionally the District Officer would join me with his wife; of course, little Ayesha assumed the role of my helper instead of Mommoh.

Chapter 33

THE SAADS: LEBANESE IN SIERRA LEONE

"Our Phoenician ancestors never left anything they undertook unfinished. Consider what they accomplished in their days, and the degree of culture they attained"

Ameen Rihani

The town center had only one major grocery shop, which could provide everything we needed. The Store was run by Mr. Julian Saad, a Lebanese trader. He started his business almost twenty-five years ago, from Kano, where his family lived for more than fifty years and rooted there. Mr. Saad, a Lebanese Christian, had a good reputation in the district as a fair, honest, and helpful businessman. I had to thank him for the sweets he sent, which were enjoyed and appreciated, by everyone. That was soon after I arrived in Kailahun. He told me he had several relatives settled in Sierra Leone, but his family home was in Sefadu in Kano district, less than an hour's drive from Kailahun to the north. He looked like he was in his early to mid-fifties, I guessed. He lived with his wife and workers. His two daughters, six and five, lived with his wife's mother in Beirut, Lebanon, where they could have a better Lebanese upbringing.

He also ran the gas station in the town center and had a car repairing business close to the grocery store. Their three-story building was the store's first floor, the second floor was the business office, and the third floor was the family house. I got to know this during my acquaintance with the family.

About 700-800 Lebanese families were living scattered in Sierra Leone, as per Mr. Saad's estimate. Most of them were Moslem and many Christian. The religious differences did not stop them from developing a thriving business community of people of Lebanese origin. Sometimes they were also called Syrians; not sure from where that notion came. There may have been a small proportion of the Arabic population of non-Lebanese origin.

Mr. Saad told me that Lebanese came to Sierra Leone as traders as early as the late 1800s. They initially settled in Freetown but found a hostile and competitive business environment with local Krios and Brit ex-pat people in business. So instead of leaving, they found their gold rush in the provinces outside Freetown. It was a rich agricultural country with minerals, like Bauxite, Gold, Titanium, aside from substantial unchartered deposits of diamonds, several rivers full of fish, jungles full of disorganized growth of varieties of tropical fruits. So the Lebanese community slowly became the backbone of trading and development of the backwaters of Sierra Leone. The Colonial government was very helpful in supporting them to establish in the countryside, hoping for the development of rural provinces, and making them vibrant and more habitable places than what it was then. Slowly, colonial government built roads, bridges, schools, hospitals, and some form of universal health care system was extended to the majority of the population.

With their pioneering attitude, ready for hard work, they were one of the first educated "Non-slave" settlers who came to Sierra Leone in search of fortune. About seven hundred to eight hundred strong Lebanese settlers were scattered throughout the country. In remote villages or towns, they established their businesses, trading and supplying household needs being the main items. Then they got involved in building houses, roads, wells, other construction businesses, diamond trading, and mineral exporting (not necessarily prospecting minerals).

Mr. Saad's Grandfather came from Lebanon. Settled in Makeni in Northern Province, and soon moved to Kano district and settled in Safadi, the Diamond Capital. He was a small-time diamond trader and started the main grocery store and an export and import business in Safadu. When his father was five years old, he was sent back to Lebanon to be brought up by close families in Lebanese tradition. This was how Lebanese children grew up in Sierra Leone. They would visit their parents from Lebanon once or twice a year during school holidays. Then, as their schools finished, they came back to live with their parents and helped in the family business. Daughters were kept in Sierra Leone and were educated by the Mosque or church until they were married. The girls got involved in various household chores, helping mothers, or learning some crafts from early in their lives.

Lebanese are descendants of Phoenicians, who ruled the entire Mediterranean region seven thousand years ago, with their highly developed civilization, from the region known as modern Lebanon. So adjusting to anywhere outside Lebanon was in their blood, and they did very well. Interestingly, interracial marriage in the Lebanese community was a rare event; that was my impression in those days. Conservative Islamic culture and lifestyle may have been the main factor keeping them within their community. Families in Sierra Leone always found brides or grooms for their children in Lebanon or amongst the

Lebanese settlers in West Africa. France ruled Lebanon till the Second World War. Lebanese were more attracted to French culture, and their adopted lifestyle was more French than British. Mr. Saad once told me that there were many more Lebanese in Senegal, Cameroon, and Congo These are French Colonies in the west and central Africa.

After my first introduction to expressing my gratitude, I visited his home many times during my stay in Kailahun. Mrs. Saad was around thirty-plus years, much younger than Mr. Saad. While Mr. Saad was busy building his business, years passed by; suddenly, it occurred to him that years were passing by, and he still did not have his own family. Far away from the motherland and sporadic meeting with close family members in Kano and scattered elsewhere in Sierra Leone, the chance of meeting a suitable bride was not easy and far-fetched. His parents were worried and told him that he had to go to Beirut soon. Finally, they had found a match for him. She was twenty-three years, and he was forty-three-plus years old. One of his relatives from Lebanon sent a photograph, which he looked at and asked his parents when they wanted him to go.

They had to find someone to oversee his business in Kailahun. But, his Dad said, not to worry. It would be for just a week or two, and he would look after the business. Within two days, he was off to Beirut. It took five days for him to arrive. The relatives from both sides were ready. He met his bride briefly, perhaps for a half-hour. He did not think the vast age difference had much impact on her. It was not that uncommon in their society. But Mr. Saad wanted to know how she felt about their respective ages. She was a city girl, grew up in one of the poshest parts of the City, and went to University. How would she adjust to life in the African jungle, away from her family, friends, mainly the "Son et Lumiere" of the big city Beirut, the queen of all cities, and Paris of the east? He indeed asked her years later. Her answer was, "those are immaterial in life, we are happy and healthy, and I can help you in your work, which is natural and more important." Mr. Saad felt comfortable and secure. Mrs. Saad, with her university education, both English and French proficiency, had been considerable support for his business, which was not common in his community at that time.

One day Mr. Saad came to my clinic and told me that his wife was not feeling well. She had a fever, cough, and stomach pain. He would bring her to my clinic when I was free, or if I could come to see her at his house, he would appreciate it. I said, "I am sorry to hear that she is not well. I can come between 2 and 2.30 this afternoon after finishing my work at the hospital. His house and the shop were just around the corner in the main town square, no more than two to three minutes' drive from the hospital.

I arrived at 2.30 pm. Mr. Saad was in the shop, expecting me to come to see his wife. It was not just a grocery shop, but a well-stocked supermarket. Quite a few local people were working.

We went straight to the third floor to Mrs. Saad's bedroom. She greeted me in English and thanked me for coming to see her. She had been sick with fever, stomach pain, loose motion, and shortness of breath. She looked dehydrated but otherwise well. She had a fever. I examined her as much as I could. I thought it was most likely a stomach bug. But my main worry was whether she had Typhoid or paratyphoid, which I had seen in a few of my patients. We couldn't do any tests here, so these had to be sent to NMH or Freetown. Her symptoms fitted well with gastroenteritis. I prescribed her medications. Mr. Saad's shop was also the leading pharmacy in town. The medication I prescribed was not in his store, so he sent one of his men to Daru. The man returned after one hour with the medicine.

With the dietary change, hydration, and other supportive treatment, she began to feel better and recovered in five days. I kept her on treatment for another five days. As I would do for other hospitalized patients, I dropped by only after my clinic in the afternoon to check her progress.

It was a water-borne stomach bug. It should not be common in the relatively dry part of the country, but we do see it, not infrequently. As a result, they changed their water purification and storage methods as much as possible. A large tributary of the mighty river Moa flowed not far from the back of my house. Aside from large resident creatures, like hippos, snakes, crocodiles being a constant threat, the waterborne disease was always one of my concerns. The town had its water purification system, and all government housing and offices had purified piped water. Some private houses, businesses, and factories also had piped water. Saad's also had purified piped water. Once mentioned, Mr. Saad changed all his water pipes and storage tank. Hopefully, that would help.

They were my so-called "Private" patients, and I got my consultation fee whenever I visited. So I had to cut down my "House–rounds" unless called or pre-arranged. They were very hospitable and welcoming to me. Professionally, they only called me if it was absolutely essential. But I did get invited for tea and snacks, dinners, and some family gatherings if I was in town. The road to my house from the city center was barely twenty-minute walk. The stretch of road from the hospital to my house was well maintained and landscaped to match the sophistication it was expected to offer with a garden-like look. I saw Mrs. Saad walking along the road, with her friends or some female worker, just for company. The walking was safe on this stretch of the road. Several senior officers housing were by the side of the road but hidden inside a closed and protected compound. None of those houses were visible as one walked along the road. That was how the British Colonial Officers lived separated and protected from local people. However, these were all occupied by local senior officers or expatriate officers like myself after independence.

Sometime in the morning, I would see her walking; sometimes, in the afternoon or the evening, they would come right up to my entrance if I saw them. So I greet them and caution them to take care of any unexpected dangers.

We became friends. She told me that the previous doctor's wife was her friend, and they got on well. During school vacations, her children and doctor's children would play, sing, and mess together. They were from Bangladesh. The doctor's wife taught her how to wear a "sari" and cook various Indian dishes. She also learned several Lebanese dishes, especially how the Lebanese cooked rice and meat. Mrs. Saad knew that they had to return to Bangladesh sooner or later, but she was not prepared for a lasting exit.

Mrs. Saad grew up in the Hamra district of Beirut, the most vibrant part of the town. Her father was a pharmaceutical dealer and owned three pharmacies in the city. They had a comfortable life and grew up in a conservative, traditional Lebanese Christian family upbringing. Her parents encouraged children to be educated as far as they could go. Living not very far from the American University campus, they encouraged them to study. The American university was expensive, but all three of them studied there. She had one older brother and a younger sister, and her mother took care of them. They had a big extended family scattered in the city and the rest of Lebanon. Frequently they would meet at various festivities, either at their house or in one of their relative's homes. She was at the university for two years, then left and started to help her father in their family business.

Beirut was known as the Paris of the East; it even had a Champs de Élyseés at one time, right in Hamra, which was what she told me. I attended to her any time she said she needed my help. She was usually busy tending to her husband's business. From time to time, I had to go and see her for chest pain, poor appetite, insomnia, and body pain which was one of the most common reasons why most female patients visited their doctors or nurses in remote communities. The locals came and told you, "Me body de hurt plenty." So what you did as a physician was give them some painkillers, and they were happy to go. But when one sat down and asked more questions, examining the patients, their main issues were painful menstrual periods, fever of some sort due to a chest, or urinary tract infection. Maybe malaria, most interestingly due to sickle cell disease, may have been the most common cause of their generalized body pain. So, when anyone complained of generalized body pain, I looked for a specific reason we could even manage in Kailahun. I was thankful to Mr. Amara and Mr. Joseph for making the rusty monocular microscope functional again.

Mrs. Saad's recurrent nondescript symptoms couldn't be fitted into any of these categories. I realized she liked to speak. She was comfortable chatting with me when Mr. Saad was out of town on business. She certainly missed Mrs. Huda, Dr. Huda's wife, who spent almost three years in Kailahun as District Medical Officer. Mrs. Saad was also friendly with some local elites, expats, or Sierra Leone families. She lived in Kailahun for almost eight years, transported from one of the world's most elegant, glittering, and swinging cities. She grew up in a wealthy, educated, and open-minded family in the most desirable part of Beirut, moving to Kailahun to spend the rest of her life there with her husband. He was the most affectionate, caring, and liberal-minded husband, more than twenty years her senior. He was a highly successful businessman in the eastern part of the country, respected by locals. He was kind and generous to the needy. They had two beautiful children. What else did a woman need to be happy?

Sometimes, she would take me around their third-floor living quarters and walk through the office on the second floor, when she started to trust me, not only as her physician but also as a good friend, even though she was eight to nine years older than me. Their living quarters were fashionably furnished and decorated; their dwellings felt like a penthouse in Paris on George, 5th avenue, Etoile, Champs de Élyseés. Mr. Saad left no stone unturned to make his wife happy and to feel at home.

She would ask me many questions about my family back in India, my schooling, university days, and how the boys and girls kept their respect and integrity in mixed classes and universities. She would tell me, how from time to time, she had to be rude and snappy to her male classmates for bad behavior towards her or even to some of her female classmates. She admitted that this happened even in Lebanon, which was respected as the most highly sophisticated, educated, and liberal country in the Arab world. Then she would justify it by saying this kind of behavior was just human.

Then she would ask me how I would react if one of my female classmates insulted me somehow. I could say I did not expect any insult from my classmates, male or female, for that matter. I tried to take the place of an older brother or uncle to develop a relationship if I had to. But that did not mean that boys did not misbehave toward female classmates. Then they would get beat up publicly and be named and shamed out of the school. I was a student leader during my university days. I could not misbehave, even if I wanted to. Interestingly, my biggest supporters were primarily girls in medical school during my days when I was involved in college students' politics.

She smiled and said, "I can understand why". However, I did not want to stretch the discussion further.

She directly asked me why I did not bring my wife to Sierra Leone. I looked at her and smiled. Then, I guessed what she was asking me. I said, "I must have one first, only then can I bring her to Kailahun". She laughed. "I know, Doctor. I just wanted to find out if you had a wife you could bring to Kailahun."

I also laughed, saying, "Yes! You got that right, Mrs. Saad."

"You know Doctor; I have another name which sounds better than Mrs. Saad. You might even like it," she said.

I had a good answer. In Indian custom, we never called anyone older by their name. That was considered disrespectful and socially unacceptable.

She jokingly said," Ok, you are not in India, and I am not an Indian either. So if you call me by my name, I will certainly not feel insulted or disrespected."

"OK. Mrs. Saad, you win, but you must tell me which name you like best," I said.

One afternoon, I was just daydreaming after the day's work, thinking about my parents, brothers, and our house, friends with whom I grew up, where they were, how they were doing, and the imagination stretched on and on. Then, Mommoh entered and told me a lady wanted to speak to me about a patient. I thought it must be something very urgent or unusual. So I asked her to come in. I immediately recognized her. She was one of Mrs. Saad's high-ranking servants who stayed close to her.

She said Mr. Saad had left this morning to Freetown, and Madam was not feeling well. "She would appreciate it if you could come to see her today when you have time." I felt sorry for her; she must be feeling rotten, especially Mr. Saad being away and she was alone. I told her I would be there in a half-hour.

So I did. Mrs. Saad was working in her office with other clerks. She invited me in and let the clerks return to their offices. She looked very miserable, perhaps getting the flu. She said she had this headache which she couldn't get rid of. She saw light flashes at times, even noises from time to time. The headache was mostly in her left side. I checked her vitals. Her pulse was high, but the rest were regular.

I told her what she was describing as classical migraine. "You never had a migraine all these months I have known you. Do you remember having attacks of migraine any time in the past?"

"Yes!" She said. I suffered from migraine when I was in school and at the university. Since I have been here, I have had a rare incidence of mild symptoms of migraine. Specialists had seen her in Beirut, but nobody could help. She stopped taking chocolates, her most favorite, and stopped taking milk. All those helped but it still came back from time to time.

Then Mrs. Saad started to talk, "I am not sure if it is migraine or anything else making me feel miserable. I began to miss my children, family, parents, and little sister. Last night I woke up with a horrible nightmare. I saw our house gutted in fire. I was there looking for my parents, and for my little sister. I could hear them screaming, but the neighbors and firefighters held me tight. I could not run. I had to listen to them scream and burn to death. Mr. Saad left early this morning to catch the flight to Freetown from Kenema. I had no chance to speak to him. By the time I woke up, he had already left. I woke up with this horrible headache, I had nausea but did not vomit, and I had difficulty speaking to our staff. I had my usual breakfast. I took some of the headache tablets you gave me and I started to feel better. But very depressed, remembering last night's nightmare. I could have spoken to Julian's brother back in Safedu, but I decided to call you instead. Now that you are here, I feel better. In the meantime, I tried to speak to my parents back in Beirut. It was impossible to get a connection from my phone. Eventually, Mr. Bochari, the Police Super, gave me the telephone link to my parents.

They sounded normal, so too was my little sister. I could not stop crying as I heard their voice. They kept asking me what the matter was. Am I well? Something wrong? They were worried and anxious. I could not tell them anything about my nightmare. They wanted to speak to Julien. Eventually, I settled, and they said they would call me again the next day. I did not mention my nightmare anytime during the phone call. It is supposed to be a nightmare, but the memory is vivid and repeatedly keeps coming back to me. What can I do? I feel very sad and depressed. I know there is no reason to be this way." She started crying. Too bad Mr. Saad was not here. Aside from medicine, she needed profound, tender, loving care (TLC) with empathy and compassion.

Before I could say anything, she flung herself onto me and held me while continuing to cry. I realized she needed a strong shoulder more than anything else at that time. My conscience was not approving my action. But my heart said if she was my sister, what would I do? My sense of deep compassion won, torn between conscience, ethics, and compassion. I also extended my shoulder until she relaxed.

I told her she should go to bed, shut down all lights, and try to sleep. I helped her to the bed, gave her the sleeping tablets, called the aids, and told them that she would sleep through the night, not to wake her up for any food or drink. "Someone should sleep nearby all night, and if she woke up, let her have anything she wanted to eat, something light, or sips to drink.

But try not to wake her up. I am at home, just call me straight away if she wants or if you feel I need to see her," I said.

It was not late by the time I got back to my house. Ayesha and Mommoh were waiting. I told her all was well. I thanked her for staying. I would take a shower before I had my dinner. In the meantime, Mommoh would walk her home. She was happy, said good night, and would return the next day.

I had rather a bad night, thinking about Mrs. Saad. She was alone. I wished Mr. Saad or her close family were there with her. She was more mentally upset rather than any physical problem. The horrible nightmare about fire in their home in Beirut had not helped either. The nightmare may be due to her depression, missing her family and friends. I tried to analyze how best I could help her, retaining my professional relations with the family and not getting involved personally and emotionally.

Although she was a thirty-plus-year-old mother of two, she had a slight feminine build and looked no more like twenty-three to twenty-four years with five feet five inches in height. She always dresses elegantly, even with traditional local tribal attire, which she sported from time to time. She exuded strength, power, and beauty.

The following day as I went to the hospital. I spoke to Sister Thomas, requesting her visit and finding out how Mrs. Saad was doing. I would be happy to visit her after the clinic if she wished. Their house was only about a five-minute' walk from the hospital, on one side of the town's main square.

After the ward round and presenting some cases, she planned to visit Mrs. Saad. She was expecting; one with delayed labor, a fall, and most likely broken bones, etc. She spent about half an hour with Mrs. Saad checking her vitals, asking about her health and how the night was. She said she had a wonderful night. She slept for almost for twelve hours, waking up slightly giddy but very hungry. She had her breakfast and was feeling much better. She decided to take the day off from her office to manage from home.

She said how grateful she was for the Doctor to come and see her last night when she was entirely out of her wits. She was devastated both mentally and physically and felt helpless and alone. Sister Thomas reassured her that we would be there whenever she needed us. Mrs. Saad asked Sister to request the doctor to see her sometime that day if he was not too busy. Of course, I would. I did tell her that I would come to visit her later that day. I was glad that the request came from her.

Sister Thomas had not visited their home except the shop. However, she was very impressed with the décor and the lifestyle Mrs. Saad had inside the building. It looked like an ordinary three-story building from the outside, but the state of opulence couldn't be imagined unless one had seen it. Mr. Saad was a very hard-working, soft-spoken, amiable down to earth type of person.

What I can say! They built their fortune and wealth in Sierra Leone. He was the third generation in Sierra Leone. This was their home, but culturally Sierra Leone was very different from their Lebanese heritage, which they cherished and tried to live the life of a Lebanese as if in Lebanon. I had seen a similar environment in a few other Lebanese settlers. They did interact well with local people, socialized as much they could, and needed to do so. But at the core of their hearts, they built their lifestyle around their Lebanese heritage.

Unfortunately, men were busy with their work. Often they were away from home on business, and the women were left behind to look after the home in a very different socio-cultural-linguistic environment. Very few or no one was even around to speak with, cry or even laugh. I saw this amongst many expatriate officers who had to work culturally, environmentally, and socially in unfamiliar or even hostile places, suffering from various degrees of depression and psychological stress.

I also saw similar situations in Krio families, posted in remote parts of Sierra Leone; their wives suffered from mental stress. Krios were the descendants of freed African slaves from the western province or the colony in Sierra Leone, who lived and grew up in a European lifestyle, educated chiefly in England. The women folk felt the loneliness outside the settlement when they were left alone to mind their home and children by themselves, without other supporting social networks.

In Kailahun, most of the population was of the Mende tribe, and a few were Temne. Most of my patients were also from these tribes. Temnes were not freed, African slaves. Some may be so, but by the time they were resettled in Freetown, they had already forgotten their unique Temne origin, more proud of being a black Negro African. Since I came to Sierra Leone, after I met Prof Porter in Freetown, we discussed the tribal variation in Sierra Leone. Temnes were the second-largest tribe spread across Sierra Leone, Liberia, Mali, the southern Sahel, close to the Equatorial African band.

I was particularly interested in the Temne tribe when I learned from Prof Porter about possible Jewish links to their origin. From the Jewish heartland, they migrated to Northeastern Africa, then westward along the southern fringes of Sahel to the Western part of Africa. I had been interested in Jews, Judaism, and their migration throughout the world over thousands of years. Different country, different terrain, different cultural dominance on their slow dissemination into the world, yet keeping their Jewish identity more or less intact. My father, an amateur historian, had profound knowledge about human history. Despite being a very busy specialist physician, he spent lots of his spare time learning about the history and culture of humans. I could hear him speak on various cultures for hours, especially on weekends that continued through my medical school days. My inspiration and desire were to reach out to people crossing the cultural divide.

Here in Kailahun, I had the opportunity to mix intimately with tribal people, including Temne, to understand their culture and Jewish connection. Here also, I had first-hand experience as a physician of how the perception of cultural difference could destroy one's soul or can make one a superhuman. It was not as intense in Sierra Leone, for that matter, in the equatorial and southern part of Africa, unlike some other parts of the world.

I entered Mrs. Saad's bedroom. She was half lying down, and got up as she saw me coming in. I said, "I was saddened by the state I left you in last night, so I would have come anyway. I did not feel good about the condition I had to leave you alone in last night." "Many thanks, Dr." she said, "I feel so much better today. But, first, I must apologize for my childish misbehavior yesterday; I hope you will forgive me.

"There is nothing to forgive; you allowed me understand how best I could relieve you of your distress as a physician."

"And what did you understand?" She said, twinkling in her eye.

I did check her. She seemed to have recovered well. But how could I help bring her back to life again so that she could be strong, independent, and back to reality?

The maid entered with a bowl full of fruits, nicely cut, and placed the tray on a side table. She said, "I know that it is your lunchtime so that you will have your lunch here." I asked, "what about Mrs. Saad?" The maid said she would come down momentarily and asked that I start with whichever fruit I like. There were so many to choose from the collection. As Mrs. Saad entered the dining room, wearing an aquamarine chiffon lounger, I asked her if she would like to share some and asked the servant to bring another plate.

"Don't you worry, Doctor," she said, "I can share from your plate. This is also our native custom to share food from the same plate of close family and guests. Now you choose which fruit you want to have first." She continued, "as long as it is not a red apple!" Why red apple? It took a few seconds to realize that she referred to Adam and Eve's story.

"Oh! Oh!" I said, "I will throw out all the apples from your house and destroy all the apple trees in the country so that you do not have the chance to have the first bite!"

She roared with laughter, picked up a couple of fruits from my plate, and called the servant to bring the lunch. I had no idea what was served, but they all looked delicious and tasted even better. Again, she voluntarily shared a few bites from my plate. I was amazed at the easiness she shared the food with a visitor from a foreign culture, especially a man. She told me it was Lebanese culture to share food with the guest. Later I found that the tradition was far from it. Nevertheless, I was happy that she was happy. She said she would call her parents again and let them know that she felt much better and no need to worry about her.

"Julian will be back tomorrow; perhaps you can have dinner with us when he returns."

"I shall be delighted, and that will be my pleasure," I said

So I left to return to my bungalow.

The following day the day started as usual. Around midday, the interpreter told me that Mr. Saad was waiting and would like to see me for a couple of minutes. "OK, please bring him in as soon as I finish with this patient." It took about ten minutes. He looked tired but happy. "How are things with you, Mr. Saad? Did you manage to get everything done in Freetown? How is Mrs. Saad doing today?" "She is fine," he said, "I had to come to thank you for taking care of her; she told me about the problem and how much care you and your staff gave her. I have no words to express my gratitude."

I was happy to hear that she was better and that Mr. Saad was back in town. I did ask him if he would have time to speak as soon as I finished seeing the last patient. "Of course, Doctor, I will wait," I asked the interpreter to bring the previous patient. Sister Thomas entered. She said, "I put the patient in the ward. The patient is a young girl in her mid-twenties, in the full term of her pregnancy. She had been in labor for the last three hours, having frequent contractions, but the midwife could not induce. She was a slightly elderly preemie for our standard in Kailahun. The baby and mother were both well. Unfortunately, she was having poor contractions and it is unsure how long it would take her to deliver. I would try to induce labor, but I would also prepare for a C Section, as I know you do not want to wait for more than 3-4 hours. I would send Mr. Saad in, he is still waiting outside," she said.

I welcomed him and thanked him for his patience. We chatted about life in Kailahun, his business woes, and his family around. I also told him about my feelings. I was happy with my work, with accommodating staff. My daily life in Kailahun was pleasant. He was looking at my lip which was still weak, and any time I started to speak, it would sag down. The sensation was still poor. Aside from some flattening, because the scar was mostly inside, one could not see from the outside. I told him about the accident, and he completed my narration, saying,

"We all know how you, yourself, stitched the big cut inside your lip. The whole town knew. I suspected the district, the province, maybe the people in Freetown also knew about it. We understand we have a different kind of Doctor in Kailahun. Hope you stay here forever; that is what my wife also said."

Then we talked about his children and in-laws in Lebanon. She had all her family in Lebanon; they spoke on the phone from time to time. Her father was not keeping well. So the older brother, who was a civil engineer, gave up his job and joined the family business. I asked how often she does go to Lebanon to see her family. He said "the children come during long holidays. It was more than two years that she last went. Both of us can't travel at one time."

"Maybe it is time for the whole family to take a family holiday to Lebanon."

"You are right, Doctor," Mr. Saad responded, "Both of us can't travel together, but I will suggest perhaps Mrs. Saad would like to visit her parents a few weeks before the school holidays begin and then bring the children to spend the holidays with us." "I guess she would like to go, but leaving you alone to look after yourself will be her major concern. If I understand her well," I said.

"If she agrees, then we can take care of that," Mr. Saad said to me and left with a plan in his mind. As he was going, he looked more relaxed and settled than when he came to see me earlier.

Chapter 34
THE PHOENICIAN FANTASY AND THE KRIO CRUSH

"Beauty is not in the face, beauty is the light in the heart."

Khalil Gibran

Busy days just pass through your fingers, even noticing that days pass faster than I hoped for. Since our last meeting, I had been the Saad's guests on a few occasions. Mrs. Saad told me that once, during our chatting, she had an English and Biochemistry Professor at American University from India. She liked them. They were excellent teachers and would go out of their way to clear any misunderstanding, confusion, or ambiguity in their courses. They were happy to spend extra hours after school or even during the weekends to clarify any questions. They were keenly aware that those two years were preparatory for professional studies. "I was supposed to be enrolled at the School of Pharmacy, to follow my Dad's footsteps. The English Professor lived close to their house and interacted with the family on various occasions. She learned quite a bit from him about India. There was also a sizeable Indian business community in Beirut. She liked Indian food and learned more from Mrs. Huda, the previous Dr.'s wife, from Bangladesh.

She had never-ending questions: why was I in Kailahun? What made me come? How long I planned to be in Sierra Leone? And I did give her the whole story of this delightful accident. I was waiting to return to continue with my postgraduate studies in London. After my studies were finished, she asked me several times, if I would return to Sierra Leone? My answer had always been the same; "let me complete my training and examinations, then only I can decide where and when I will return." God only knows how many years it would take. I do not want to rush it. She asked about my family, my friends, back at home, my school, college, and university days. We became pals, yet kept my ethical distance as her doctor. I liked talking to her; aside from being a pretty intelligent and happy person, she had very open feelings about life. That was how she had been able to adjust (maybe) to her life in Kailahun.

One day, she walked along the road leading to my house, a nice place to stroll for anyone trying to come close to nature. She stopped me as I was driving past her. She looked happy. She said that she would be traveling to Beirut to be with her parents and children as early as next week for a couple of months. I was thrilled to hear that. To make her happy perhaps, I expressed my pleasure at the news and said I would certainly miss the company and hospitality. She said it would not be very long, but she would see me before leaving.

The day of her departure came. I asked about the flight route. Even flying was no easy way; it could take three to five days. It was better than going by boat, which took three to three and a half weeks. Mr. Saad said she would fly from Freetown to Dakar in Senegal by West African Airlines, then take Air France to Paris, with a stop-over in Casablanca. From Paris to

Beirut with a stop-over in Vienna. Still, she would arrive on the third day, depending on the flight's availability and scheduling.

"What an exciting journey; I would not mind doing the same." Then, before I could finish my sentence, she said, "You are invited to stay at our house in Beirut. There is still time to get ready."

"Thanks, but maybe next time," I said. Mr. Saad had said she could also have gone to Lagos in Nigeria to Addis Ababa or Nairobi and then to Beirut. Much cheaper this way and would take four days. But African Airlines were new in the business. So there was much scope for improving their services. So that was also an important bit of information for me.

I could not see her off at the airport but made sure to say pleasant journey and come back soon. She said, "You will see, I will be back even before you know I have been gone."

I was happy but felt sad and a kind of emptiness. I had gotten used to her friendship; she entertained me in various ways, if nothing else was handy, at least pretending to be very sick. So I did understand her well enough. Mr. Saad left with her to Freetown to see her off to Beirut.

Life had to go on. My program for creating an "internship" for Ayesha with the nurses in the outpatient treatment room seemed to be working well. She was very disciplined and meticulous in drawing sketches. Whatever she watched, she showed it to me, dated, and filed in the case notes. I had no doubt, years after I had gone, even after she was gone, doctors coming after me would find a treasure trove in these clinical sketches, drawn by a fourteen-year-old girl. The drawings would be mind-boggling. Found in dusty, carelessly kept case files in Kailahun hospital, middle of nowhere, in the Equatorial jungle, apparently a God-forsaken part of Sierra Leone. She started to get engaged in my household more and more and spent more and more time there. Sister Thomas did tell me that Ayesha liked to spend time in my house.

I said that now I was better and Mommoh had the routine set up, she could rest and spend time studying and being with her friends. "Yes! Doctor. Please tell her. She will listen to you more than me," said Sister Thomas.

I asked Mr. Jesudasan, the Principal of her school, about her academic progress. He had met Ayesha in my house several times and knew she was my right hand's niece, but not sure how much to push her. He said she was a dreamy child, outstanding in literature, humanity studies, but very weak in concrete subjects like Mathematics, Geometry, Science, etc. However, he was concerned about getting through her "O" level examination, which she could take next year.

Being reasonably competent, even after making her O level and A levels, she needed to have good math scores to get into any profession. Sister was thinking of sending her to medical school or taking up nursing. But, both her parents were in Government Administration to take administrative courses and train abroad. But, well-founded competence in Math's and Accounting was a big help, whatever career she chose. That was what I understood from Sister Thomas, and this was her aspiration for little Ayesha.

Ayesha was a very popular girl amongst her mates. She was good at games, athletics, very pleasant to her classmates, and respectful to her teachers and superiors. Moreover, she had an infectious laughter and a heart-melting smile.

Mr. Jesudasan promised to pay extra attention himself and his staff without harassing her. One day, I did show some of

Ayesha's clinical sketches, in our case files, to his amazement and a better understanding of the child's talent. As an experienced and wise teacher said, if one is talented, their talents can be channeled, which was essential for our job and maturity.

She continued to get better and engaged in her studies. Things improved after Mrs. Jesudasan joined the school as a senior teacher.

I let her spend as much time as she wanted, bringing her books and coursework to do at my place if she wanted. Sister Thomas noticed a real improvement in her school performance, which was being relayed to her by her class teacher.

I had lots to catch up on with work, government correspondences, an accurate entry in all case notes, and operation reports. I did much of the work myself rather than waiting for Mr. Amara to do those. He was very pleased, indeed. Still, whenever I could squeeze in, I would discuss the science subjects with her. We made a routine that he had to read aloud for a half-hour from any book of her choice, and I would do the same. We started on Don Quixote, which she liked reading.

One Saturday morning, I found her sleeping on the sofa in the lounge. I asked her, "I thought Mommoh took you to your house?" She said, "Yes, he did. But I could not sleep. Aunty had gone to Kenema with my grandma, and the helper lady also went home. I was terrified and started to hear voices. Very afraid. I walked to your house and woke Mommoh up. I told him I was scared to sleep at home alone. So he let me in, and I just slept on the couch."

I was upset. "Why did you not call me? There are two other rooms, and you could have slept in one of those." So anyway, she got up, changed, and went to Mommoh for my bed tea. I asked her when Sister would be back. She said she would be back on Monday morning. So I told her to go home and bring her clothes and toiletries to spend the rest of the weekend in one of the spare rooms. "Yes, Sir!" She said. "Bring your books and coursework if you need to do. Maybe I can help you."

On Monday morning, I met Sister just around 9.30 am. She had just returned from Kenema and dropped her mother at her house. She knew Ayesha had gone to school. I mentioned to Sister why Ayesha had to spend the weekend in my house. She was relieved but did not know why the housemaid was not home. Anyway, I said it was no problem as I had two spare bedrooms. One of them I used as my study, and the other was always ready for guests.

"My mother is always at home," she said. "I hope Ayesha does not have to bother you again," I said, "if she feels safe, she can come and use the spare bedroom any time she wants. It is better to feel protected than scared to death. I wish she had woken me up instead of sleeping on the couch all night, which may not have been comfortable. Still, I am glad that she decided to come and felt safe."

Life went on. We kept getting patients from neighboring districts. Some patients from neighboring countries of Guinea and Liberia opted to come to Kailahun. For Guineans, Conakry, the capital city, and Liberians, Monrovia's capital city was hundreds of miles away. Medical facilities were very far, frequently poorly equipped with personnel, facilities, and supplies.

Time passed by.

As I went to the hospital for my evening rounds, I saw two ladies and two little girls walking towards my house. I had not seen them before. As I came close, I realized it was Mrs. Saad. I stopped and welcomed her back to Kailahun. She introduced me to the other lady as her younger sister and two daughters of Saads. "I need to go to the hospital for my evening rounds; you must enjoy the evening stroll," I said. When would you finish your round?" Asked Mrs. Saad. "It can take an hour or more, depending on patients, especially those I operated on this morning. I will look into the Outpatient if any sick patients are to be seen. I will catch up with all of you tomorrow." I emphasized, and I was happy that she had returned safe and sound. I meant it.

I drove, and they continued their evening stroll back towards my house.

I couldn't refuse any invitation from the Saads; whether it was fair weather or storm, in health or sickness, dawn or twilight, I did my best to be in their company. Mrs. Saad was an attractive, pretty, strong, and intelligent lady. Despite being a small delicate person, she exuded an air of authority with kindness and a loving demeanor. To me, her personality exceeded her beauty by being attractive and respectful.

I met Mrs. Saad's sister in their house after she formally introduced me to her. She was the youngest of all three siblings. This was the first time she was visiting Sierra Leone. Both sisters looked alike. Her name was Amal. I thought that was a boy's name. My older brother was also Amal. She spoke English with a very soft English accent. They learned English from British or Indian teachers. She was at the American University in Beirut, preparing for her Pre-professional course. She wanted to take up medicine as her career. Amal's everything, from hair, face, shy eyes and eyebrows, neck, slender body with sculpted curves, musical voice, and feathery walk, were mesmerizing. Amazing beauty, which I had never come across anywhere in my life. She was like her sister, but shrouded in the beauty of a goddess. After all, she was Lebanese, descendants of the same Phoenicians, who gave the ancient world their Goddess of Beauty Aphrodite, who gave Helen of Troy, Bathsheba, who conquered King David with her beauty. Now I had no reason to doubt how she descended on this earth as a human being, and not as another Phoenician goddess. I had difficulty imagining how one could live with a walking goddess like her. Every moment must have been like living in heaven, the life of dreams, life in a bed of roses, where life only began but never ended, and there was nothing but joy and heavenly bliss.

I had to drag myself out of my dream and fantasy.

She said I must be very happy to help hundreds of people, being a doctor. But, of course, I was not just lucky; I was blessed in a way that I was sitting face to face with the world's most beautiful woman. She asked, "Really? There are many like me, even prettier just now, walking in the streets of Beirut." She was witty, intelligent, and quick to respond to my remarks. She said, "Beirut is known as the Paris of East. We must live up to the world's expectations. Anyway, we think Indian women are stunning." Mrs. Saad returned with teapots and joined us again. Their two lovely and lively daughters also came on some pretext to join their parents. They were allowed to sit for a while then return to their room.

We got to know each other better with time. Amal had two months of vacation before returning to Beirut and sitting for her final examinations. She hoped to spend her vacation time in Kailahun, giving her sister and brother-in-law company. She was also hoping to visit other relatives if and when she became restless to explore.

I had several short visits to their home, sometimes to treat ailments or just to talk away as a friend. Both of them were great company. Once Amal asked me if it was tough to go through the medical course, and if she should take up medicine. But her heart was deeply entrenched in being a future doctor. So one day, I would be happy to give a rundown of the lives of a student doctor, which would last for five to six years. "People are trying to scare me off, but I know that I want to be a doctor, and I will."

"Of course, you will!" I said. "We will start make-believe medical school days as soon we can fix a time." Even after, getting closer and friendlier with Amal, my thoughts were pinned on the day I would return to London and start my research program and other examinations.

I told her I was preparing for my research project and postgraduate examinations one day. If she wanted, she could look at some of the books, which were also used for undergraduate classes.

When I asked her about life in Kailahun, she said, Kailahun was so different. Life was so much more serene than their daily life in Beirut, so raw, compared to the manicured and painted living in Beirut. She might come back again to immerse herself in the serenity. She was just twenty-one -years old. I appreciated the depth of her thinking and perception of life.

I would have loved to sit down with them and dream away my time every day if I could. But as I got deeper and deeper into my work, attending to my duties as the District Medical officer, between my clinical responsibilities, administration, and regular visits to outlying clinics, it spared very little time for socializing. I spent the better portion of my spare time studying, catching up with changes in the world. Mr. Jesudasan's library was a great and only resource. Dr. Thakuta used to subscribe to British Medical Journal, which was a weekly journal. He would send all four copies to me every month to keep me updated. That was a big help and kind thinking on his part.

I met the Saad sisters on my way to evening rounds, coinciding with their evening walks. Exchanged greetings and chats at times when we could stop for a few seconds. Once Amal was interested to see some of my books, I invited them. She was amazed to see Gray's Anatomy, Sterling's Physiology, Boyd's Pathology, and Goodman and Gillman's Pharmacology books. Each weighed a kilo and had as many as five thousand pages. "Do you have to read all these books to be a doctor?" She asked. I said these were only a few, and there are many more. "OK, fine, it might take me ten years to get through, but these books can't frighten me away from being a doctor." "Amal!" I said these books and passing examinations were essential but minor factors in our real professional life. She did not give me any impression of exasperation or exuberance. I knew she could make it.

But the family was looking for a match with whom she could make her home and persevere with her lifelong dream to be a doctor. So Mrs. Saad thought she might take the proposal forward and discuss it with me.

I was flabbergasted and spellbound when she dropped the idea to think about it. Yes! I can imagine, dream, worship the Phoenician Goddess, never to "think" as Mrs. Saad wanted me to think. How could I be the world's luckiest man, to find the Eve, the Helen in this African Eden, for whom I need not go to war and kill hundreds? I need not even pick up an apple. The Goddess of beauty just walked to me looking irresistible, powerful, and unconquerable, only to want to be conquered. I felt like floating in heaven, but I was alone, with no one to share my joy or happiness with. Suddenly, I heard a voice telling me that one's happiness is fulfilled only when someone shares.

Mrs. Saad told me, "Doctor, I brought someone who will make you happy and share your happiness and joy."

I was unsure if I was still dreaming or the voice and the people were all real. But, then, did I hear Mrs. Saad speaking? "Doctor, you have been working too hard; no wonder you dozed off for a couple of minutes. We didn't want to wake you up; Amal went back to your office in your Bungalow, shuffling through your books and sketches. It seems she feels quite at ease here, moving as if we were back at our home in Beirut." Mrs. Saad was happy to see her little sister happy.

The strange merger of my dream and reality was beyond my imagination. Yet what I heard was true, and what I felt was true. Yes, I listened to what Mrs. Saad told me. Yes! I will think, how can I think of a dream and a fantasy? Yes! I will think, I will! believe me Mrs. Saad. That is all, and maybe I can do it, I said to myself.

The days were busy at work, unable to shake my ever-increasing passionate, obsessive curiosity and fascination with Amal, Mrs. Saad, and their Phoenician ancestry. Here, Amal was not a blessing from mythology but a real human goddess, so very close to me, and that frightened me. I might spoil the heaven on earth, one day, when I have to leave and leave I must.

"Why should I leave?" Mrs. Saad kept saying; I do not have to go now or ever. "You stay with us, stay with Amal, come to Beirut, be a big doctor; Amal will be the happiest person if you work together." Work together? I kept forgetting that one day she would be a doctor. Mrs. Saad that was where and how our blessings would come. One day she said, "Dad will feel the moon in his hand to see you and Amal working together and develop his Pharmacies to Clinics and your clinics to a Hospital, the best in Beirut if not in entire Lebanon."

Interesting! I had known them closely; she never used the word "marriage."I kept it elusive and kept it in the third person. I did not miss it either.

The persuasion was so penetratingly pleasant that I kept forgetting, who I was and why I was here. Where was I going? Going along with Mrs. Saad's persuasion and desire, I would have to forget my past, my present and my future, my dreams, my career desire, and my mother, whose face was with me all the time, particularly from the time of my miraculous escape from the disastrous deadly car crash. Was she my guardian angel? I knew I would have her blessings any way I steered my life, career, and future.

After all, Mark Anthony gave up his home, life, power, and aspirations only for his love for Cleopatra. He left Rome, the Romans, and his emperor and even fought against mighty Romans for Cleopatra. Mark Anthony even died for her. Yet, his power, his wealth, his love, nothing went with him as he departed his mortal body from this earth.

But I was no Mark Anthony. I had many small things to do, and many small wishes to fulfill. I had no power, no kingdom, but I never stopped staring at the powerful. I wondered what I could learn from them if anything ever. My world was noisy, which would never be able to make either the Egyptian queen or fascinating Trojan Helen, the heavenly angel that bloomed and bloomed at every blink of my eye. Should I be happy? Can't I bring their heaven down to earth?

Ayesha was getting better at school; Jesudasans gave me a good report. Mrs. Jesudasan has been impressed with her nature, sweet and respectful behavior, and her artistic works. There were no arts and crafts incentives in the school. Ayesha agreed to play with younger kids on Saturdays for a couple of hours to encourage them to get interested in the art of painting. Strange, no one taught her. She was born with talent. Her imaginative artistic expressions had no boundary, no horizon, only rising sun, no twilight of setting sun..,

One evening, I was returning from my evening rounds. I saw Mrs. Saad and Amal were out for their evening walks, going towards my house. It was a bit dark. I said, "This road is safe from human raiders and cannibals, very safe indeed. There are policemen, guards walking up and down from time to time. But snakes, monkeys, baboons, crocodiles from the river, and hungry and desperate hippos can decide to take this path, waiting for their catch. Police can't spot these creepy creatures. One has to be careful." As we were speaking, Amal took out a small baton from her bag; in seconds, with the press of a button, it turned out to be a lethal instrument, extended by a couple more feet, with a sharp, iron-piercing nail at the end. Powerful lights came from the sides and were directed forwards, like the impression of a bionic woman. Both of them laughed. Amal had a very powerful flashlight.

I said I was happy that they were both prepared. I asked, "Do you carry these all the time?" "Yes," she said, "even when we come to your house." "Good! You will not need these to use it when I am around."

"But we are more scared of your Sister Thomas." "Why? Is she unpleasant or rude to you?" "No, on the contrary, she is ever so respectful, just as protective of you, patients, and guests. She is like a mother lioness, looking after you with a very sharp eye. Protecting the staff, protecting the hospital. Like mother lioness when the Lion King is out hunting or not there, she protects the pride and territory."

I was wondering, did she want to tell me something hidden in her polite words? Anyway, I cautioned them to watch for dangers at night, walking on this garden path. After that, we went our separate ways.

I said to myself, the lioness indeed, the mother of our pride, how right you are, Mrs. Saad. Thanks for putting Sister Thomas in the right place where she belongs and finding a role befitting her presence in and out of work.

Chapter 35
A GUEST AT CAMP VIANINI

"Better to remain silent and be thought a fool, than to speak and remove all doubts"

Abraham Lincoln.

Vianini was a major Italian construction company building various infrastructures in Sierra Leone from before and after independence from British rule, mainly involved in building roads, bridges, government offices, and housing in the Provinces. The Vianini was a significant infrastructure builder in the country. I knew about them for the first time just after arriving in Kailahun when the manager introduced himself to me. They had their camp just about seven or eight miles west of Kailahun. They had been in the camp for four years. The highway from Kenema Airport to Kailahun, and from Kailahun to Liberian border, about a hundred and forty miles, which they started four years ago, was coming to fruition. They were involved in other projects in the eastern province. A hundred and thirty to fifty Italian officers, engineers, workers, and some with their wives and a few Black workers from other parts of the country worked for Vianini lives on the campus. They were hugely helpful and accommodating in rescuing me at my accident. They had a full contingency of engineers, many transporting and maintaining heavy vehicles, and various road building heavy equipment. They maintained a well-equipped auto repair and machine shop. They employed several well-trained mechanics and engineers and had a full-service gas station on the campus. They were also helpful to the local population in their need.

I had been invited to use their facilities to provide services for any purpose. Vianini had been a tremendous help any time we needed.

They had their own electricity and water purification system, supplied by pipes to each household and some for public usage at various points. There was no shop but ample storage of staples for all the members to use.

They had a common picnic area with all facilities for cooking and picnicking. All Italian members very well used to the facility. They also had a shared clubhouse, small library, tables for reading and writing, or simply lazing after a hard day's work.

The roads inside were some of the best in the country. The lawns and public open spaces were well-designed gardens, landscaped and manicured lawns, tree-lined streets and lanes, so much more attractive and pleasant than what I had seen in the entire country, even in Freetown. This was not a camp but a community; it was a little Italy where other Italians from the neighboring districts, provinces, and countries came to spend some relaxing time with their compatriots. Vianini knew they would be there for the long haul and made their employees feel at home, far away from their real home.

My memory of any camp was wartime camps for soldiers and military personnel and the campsite for a major hydroelectric project, which took nearly six years to complete. Those camps were camps, people came and went, there was no feeling of community or belonging, a cabin to rest, a cabin to hang one's clothes, a cottage to sleep or eat, yet with all the physical comfort those places had, they had no life.

People of Vianini camps were generally young, energetic, and healthy. Malaria, flu, diarrhea, and various work-related injuries were the most common ailments I had to see for the men. Women did not have much bodily injury. They were also young. I frequently had to come to the camp for various psychological symptoms, not feeling well, disinterested, and all dominant signs of depression. They presented with symptoms associated with their periods, which I usually could handle. One lady had a continuous period for eight weeks; I had to send her to NMH to see the Gynecologist. Pregnancy-related symptoms were more frequent. I guess because of a background of chronic depression. There was every reason that European housewives, living in camps, isolated from their unique and personal community, family, friends, culture, and lifestyle, even if the company provided them with comfort and pleasant camp life, would become depressed. All Italian ladies went back to Italy for their childbirth. Italians are family and community-oriented and get tremendous family and community support with or without a need, which no medical treatment can offer except sitting, listening, and talking.

There were only five Italian Ladies. At any given time, one or two were always pregnant. I suggested Sister Thomas monitor the progress of their pregnancies, and the health of the mothers and babies. It was satisfactory. Yet, pregnancy or no-pregnancy, I was called to see the ladies from time to time. Generally, just a visit from the doctor and the feeling that a doctor was always there was therapeutic enough. I had no problem with that. The other social issues were loneliness and feeling isolated since the men worked long hours to achieve the target towards completion of the project. Sometimes if they were involved in some secondary projects, they had to spend days away from the camp and lived in the trailers. That came with the job. The ladies would organize monthly shopping trips to Freetown or Monrovia. Those trips were not exactly relaxing, to say the least, yet were a break from the isolated camp life.

Italians were very family-oriented, so once every week, phone calls home, particularly with children, was a must. Therefore, it was challenging to retain regular high-quality telephone connections from a roadside camp, no matter how well-provided the camp was. But the effort from the company's point of view for their business as well as the mental and physical health of their staff and their families was that an efficient communications system was key to success.

Whenever I was called to see a lady in the camp, I kept sufficient time to understand her and help her understand how we could make her better. This way, I got to know the Vianini campers much better. I also learned a few more Italian expatriate families with husbands holding high-paying jobs, living in magnificent houses with their "La Padrone di casa," with "Ayahs," cook, and servants. Practically, there was nothing to do except live and look pretty, which fueled a more deep depression for the ladies. The Italian gentlemen from Vianini were mainly from Northern Italy, but almost all the wives were from southern Italy. They told me that the ladies from the south were prettier, which I wondered about. The men said the southern girls were homely and excellent cooks, which I could understand.

Camp life also, unwittingly, separated them from the local tribal community; unfortunately, they missed out on the beauty of another culture or, for that matter, many other native cultures, which could have been a learning opportunity for all, as Mrs. Jesudasan once said to me.

The difference I saw with Mrs. Jesudasan was; within two months, she was completely absorbed in the Temne culture, spoke their language, and learned to wear their attire elegantly. She also attended the "Temne Ladies Association, a secret society with no male connection, still very influential in the community, and changed her outlook completely. She also went for "marketing" with her Temne colleagues to Sunday Farmer's market. So also, Mrs. Saad, being a resident of Kailahun, managing the most thriving business in town, did come across people of various colors, sex, and outlook, which helped her open up, learn and accept practices that were not her own. However, she remained a Lebanese at heart and lived in a teased-out Lebanese world, in a profoundly unfamiliar culture. Her depression was sporadic and easily erased by a trusted, sympathetic and humorous listener. She did not need a specialist or a physician to drag her out of a dark depressive mood that happened occasionally.

On the other hand, Mrs. Jesudasan did not have the luxury of creating a circle of compatriot friends, who spoke the same language, cooked the same food, and had the same interests and similar aspirations in life. She had only her husband and me to remind her about her "Indian-ness" and culture. We were all busy with our personal lives, working, focused, and engaged in our responsibilities. When we met, we talked about life in Kailahun, challenges, and the pleasures of African living. A teacher was a perpetual learner. She was able to immerse herself in local tribal life, lifestyle, social structure, and discovery of the hidden power of women in the Temne community. No other tribes, as far as Mrs. Jesudasan could learn, where women had so much absolute authority in the household, or, for that matter, in the community. I wondered if it was due to their vestiges of Jewish origin, where the mother was the supreme authority in any household.

Ayesha made my house partly her home. Every morning, I saw that my clothes were pressed and hung in the wardrobe for easy access and within my clear view. My shoes were polished and placed close to one settee, making them visible to get at quickly. Before she returned to her house in the evening, I asked her about the day at school, friends, exciting events, etc. She knew that I worked late through the night, so she would leave some fruits and a glass of water on my office table, covered before she left. Mommoh was happy because Ayesha shared Mommoh's work, making them good friends. I thought Mommoh was drinking less at night. I did not know anything about Mommoh's home or his family. Maybe he got the touch of a home, with Ayesha being around.

The Vianini Italians were very friendly. Most men could speak English. They had to because English was the official language of the country. But as far as I remembered, only one lady could speak English. Some younger ones would have liked to converse in English, with dancing hands, halted Italian and stumbled English, which was more entertaining. The entertaining value of their linguistic adventure surpassed by far their attempt to communicate. Men were even more amusing trying to speak with their hands, arms, and face, with discordant Anglo-Italian. But eventually, we made sense of each other.

I noticed amongst womenfolk, irrespective of being ex-pat, native, or Indians, as they got to know me well and felt free to speak, was one common question as if uniquely orchestrated, "Doctor! When will you bring your wife; it must be hard on you." I did get used to this inquiry, and my answer had always been the same, "Let me find one first, then I will think of bringing her to Kailahun." The real question "inside this question," as they were curious to know if I was married or not or looking for a wife. Their curiosity was satisfied, and my singleness was established. So the interaction between a married doctor and a young bachelor must be different. In many ways, it had been different, in a pleasant way, as I stayed longer and longer in Sierra Leone.

Vianini Italian community generally led a happy life with music, dancing, films, parties, long nights of drinking, unlimited Italian wine, food, pasta, anti-pastas, desert galore, coffee, and nightcaps to end. Literally, there was no end when a party was on. Hosts and guests were fabulously entertained and made happy. They worked hard, and on occasion, partied harder. The company had a massive establishment in Africa and had a multibillion-dollar contract in many African countries.

But this was not always the case, the camp manager of Vianini told me. Vianini had been in West Africa for more than seventy years. Vianini had been in the construction business in Italy for a long time with the highest reputation. It was after the First World War that they ventured into Africa, which got more extensive and more prominently involved after the Second World War, starting in Ethiopia, present-day Mogadishu, and Congo, building roads in deep Equatorial forests, creating miles of walking paths, building bridges, digging wells, and setting tube wells. Life was not too bad in the east. But as they extended their activities in West Africa, life became almost unbearable for Italians, Europeans, and other migrant workers from outside Africa. Humid heat, six-month-long wet season, poor housing, improper diet, lack of or no help for disease or sickness, no doctor or hospitals within a hundred miles. Still, post-war depression lured Europeans to inhospitable Africa for excellent salaries and dreams of a better life.

They got the money but lived in tin shacks, wading in muddy roads, kerosene lamps only to dispel the darkness at night. The company suppliers' irregular supply of food stock made life a continuous challenging existence and unbearable at times. But tough and hardy Italians weathered them all, with many lost to mosquitos, dying from Malaria, sleeping sickness, yellow fever, Typhoid, cholera, chronic diarrhea, and bloody attacks by tribespeople, all added up. West Africa, as named then, "The Gold Coast", became "white men's grave." Thousands and thousands of White men died; still, they kept coming and dying, the lucky ones getting luckier and returning home wealthy. But the nightmare of early life and living in West Africa still lingered on.

"This is a camp to fight those dark days, and it seems that it is working. This is the largest camp for our workers. There is temporary satellite housing at construction sites. Sometimes, we have to spend days in make-shift shacks or a trailer or tents. But we have a well-organized supply chain for all locations, and our worker's wellbeing is monitored regularly. These changes happened in the last ten to fifteen years. As people live safely and happily, they work better. This Vianini Highway is an ideal example of how we can build well if we look after ourselves well. As the size of activities grows, support also improves. Thirty years ago, no staff would dare to bring their spouses into these jungles. The only females were wives of pastors or were nuns working for churches dotted all over. They brought light to Africa, but the light of their lives was shortened from the stress of living and illness gifted to them for their divine devotion.

"I have been with the company for nearly twenty years," said the camp Manager." I started in Ethiopia then in Congo. From there, they moved to Sierra Leone twelve years ago. In the Early days of my West African adventure, I was in Bonthe, in the southern estuary of the country. As the tale goes, I met several older white settlers, mostly of Portuguese origin. Those Portuguese settlers have been trading with the western part of Africa for more than five hundred years.

"We had to build several bridges and roads. Housing was not bad, but the year-round weather was murderous. Snakes, dangerously deceptive chameleons, crocodiles, hippos are almost at your doorstep. Mosquitoes of many sizes and shapes, flies, insects like huge centipedes, Tarantulas were my company throughout the day. The dense equatorial forests are as deep as they can be. No sun rays had seen the ground for millions of years. Very odd fungus, fern trees, huge floral mushrooms, sometimes one to two feet wide, white mushrooms that were the size of melons. Plants and shrubs scream out of the forest from unseen, unknown creatures as if coming out of Jules Verne's 'A Journey to the Center of the Earth.'

"I was lucky the projects I was on, were completed and I was moved to Makeni in Northern Province. Life was much better. Living condition and the climate was bearable. Then I decided to bring my wife. She had been with me in Sierra Leone for the last seven years. At that time, the Company got several major contracts in the Eastern Province. Vianini decided to build this camp for their workers, which has hugely improved staff morale, productivity, health, and retention. I appointed one person to look after the welfare of staff, who are in our projects irrespective of whether they live in the camp or outside. Those who had to live at the project site needed more attention. The feeling of being exploited had been reduced to a great extent. Particularly, we had great help from the doctor, nurses, and other staff of your hospital. Medically, we feel lucky to have your help," he said.

It was fascinating to hear from the Manager; the life they had to endure, was a nightmare compared to the present one they had now. Their life in the past was a distant memory; the one they lived now was close to their dream. Therefore, people who plunged into the deep African life and living must be adventurers, explorers, risk-takers, future-builders, and pioneers.

The rustic life, dangers from the forest, dense mangrove swamps, and the violence of elements of nature, sicknesses, and tribal threats were commonplace. Feelings of isolation and loneliness, depression, even suicide were still part of deep African life for thousands of Italian and other European expatriate workers, who chose to make Africa a temporary home and make it better for Africans and get wealthy in the process. However, the workers of colonial Africa knew help might not be too far away, and the tunnels to see the light at the end were not too long and getting shorter.

For the dreamers, explorers, adventure seekers, gold and diamond diggers, in modern days the arms dealers, Africa remained as inviting and alluring as ever, if not more so.

Chapter 36
THE VOLUNTEERS: AMERICAN PEACE CORPS AND BRITISH VSOS.

"I speak to everyone in the same way, whether he is a garbage man or the president of the university"

Albert Einstein.

I met Dr. Fredman at Connaught Hospital in Freetown just after I arrived. Dr. Fredman worked as a Medical Officer working with Dr. Thakuta, a senior Internal Medicine Consultant. He had been with him for three months while waiting for a Sierra Leonean to return from Ireland. Dr. Fredman was an American Peace Corps volunteer, qualified as a physician, from Yale University while in the US military.

He was with the US Army in Korea, injured, and honorably discharged from the Military. After he recovered and was well enough, he joined the American Medical community. A short-lasting tour of duty in South Korea did not satisfy his lust to serve the disadvantaged. He signed up with the Peace Corps as a volunteer, and was sent to Sierra Leone as a Peace Corps volunteer to serve the community as they needed his 'Services.' The call came from the Ministry of Health to help as a Medical Officer. He joined Connaught Hospital as a volunteer medical officer, and he did an excellent job. When I arrived, he was relieved and was sent to the Bushes he was dreaming of.

Peace Corps volunteers, generally, were hosted by one local family. The volunteers hoped to understand their lifestyle, get used to it, and work with locals to meet their needs for any services. He was sent to BO, the second-biggest city in Sierra Leone, right at the geographical center (close). Bo was well connected by road to the rest of the country. Sewa River was navigable and used to ferry people, goods, and produce from north to south. There, he joined the local crew digging up wells in many parts of the district, sometimes just as a laborer and other times as the Project Master. Fredman was liaising with government surveyors, engineers yet keeping his hands on the shovel. The paramount chief of BO was his host and allocated him to one of his cottages, which was quite comfortable. Hardly any Peace Corps volunteer would have a personal vehicle of any sort. But Dr. Fredman had his vehicle, a seven-year-old Volkswagen, which he drove around the country for pleasure or work.

One day, he was called by the American Embassy and asked to return to Freetown. He had not finished his assignment in BO. Ambassador's office said the NGO group Peace Corps had arranged two more volunteers to come to BO. They would stay at the same house. They were two sophomores from Texas. Need not worry. Dr. Fredman was slightly older than any other Peace Corps member and spoke with some authority. He was six feet tall and generally projected his presence. He looked more like a naval staff than a Peace Corps Volunteer with white trousers and a white half shirt with shoulder flaps.

He was concerned about this urgent call and rescheduling his plans.

As he met the first secretary at the American Embassy, he was told to return to Freetown and work with the Embassy's 'medical attaché' to develop health care provision and monitor all Peace Corps volunteers in Sierra Leone. One of the volunteers in Kano was sick for several days and had to be flown into Freetown and then to the US base. So the first secretary said we had to do a better job of looking after these young volunteers.

Dr. Fredman was then given the responsibility to keep tabs on everyone. It isn't easy to stay in contact with them. The volunteers were also told to keep an eye on each other. Contact him or the local chief to contact you. About thirty Peace Corps Volunteers were working in Sierra Leone at that time. He had support from the Embassy, from the Agent in Freetown. He had his office and "mobile" emergency clinic in his Volkswagen. Places that his vehicle couldn't access, the Embassy would arrange for transportation. Because of the relatively central location of the city of BO, it was advised that he work from Bo.

Huge responsibility! His first site visit was Kailahun district. He stopped by the hospital around 10 am. I was delighted to see him; we knew each other from Freetown, I invited him for lunch, but he was in a hurry to go to Daru. So we sat down for about an hour and a half. He told me all the changes and his new responsibility as roaming doctor for all Peace Corps Volunteers. He also showed his mobile clinic, diagnostic tools, agents, and a microscope in the back. He was very excited about his new role.

He said his immediate job was to understand their lifestyle, living conditions, diet, sanitation, etc., their projects or assignments. After he moved into BO, he rented a two-bedroom cottage, well furnished, clean, supply of essential elements were all there and was reasonably furnished, even by American standards. The toilet and bathing facilities all needed attention, but were all fixed within the next few days. "As a bachelor, seeing to or detecting all this minor unpreparedness was not my job, unfortunately; I have to monitor all volunteers aside from their physical or mental ailments."

He would go from province to province, district by district, city by city, and village to meet the Peace Corps Volunteers to make sure they were both physically and mentally suited for the environment and the assignment.

I told him, "Dr. Fredman! You need to look after yourself. From my point of view, this countryside trekking may be adventurous and exciting, but drains one inside out. It may be very tiring. So look after yourself." He did have a few cups of coffee and said there were four volunteers in Kailahun district and a fifth one would be in shortly to make a total of five in my district, then quietly drove out. Said he would drop by in a couple of days after checking all four, meet the chiefs, and then return to Bo to get ready for his next adventure to the northern province.

For his next visit, he decided to stay one night in Kailahun as my guest. By this time, he had seen all the volunteers in the district. Generally, the volunteers came with a frightening notion about African life and living. That was the experience; that was the challenge and thrill they were looking for. They were given classes, notes, watched films, and listened to the experiences of other volunteers, who spent time here and returned to the USA. They were well informed of habitat risk, environment risk, climatic hazards, and attack by wild animals, natives from neighboring communities, difficult commuting, and most importantly, sickness from unknown sources; yet they came, with a solemn vow to serve the people, whatever they needed.

Generally, their hosts were influential persons, teachers, or the chief. They were provided with suitable, clean accommodation furnished by the host. If the town had electricity, they had it; otherwise, kerosene lamps were nocturnal illumination; sometimes, they had to use toilets outside the house, an open-pit with privacy cover. If toilet paper was not handy, they had to use water from a bucket to clean themselves. The host supplied food. The host, his family, and the guest ate together, sitting on the floor, sometimes sharing from a large plate. Food, whatever the host ate, was shared with the guest. Initially, it is challenging to eat native food for American kids, but they gradually adopted this challenge since they were looking for adventure and excitement. They learned to wash their clothes, wear local grab, relish local food, and attempt to learn how to prepare local dishes. The advantage of adopting the local lifestyle was hugely economical. Make whatever you get and assume or reorganize your choice. Frequently, they cooked their food to make it taste delicious for their palate.

The western volunteers, aside from building roads, cleaned up the community, dug wells, cleared mosquito holes, looked after the sick, helped healthcare workers, helped in teaching students in schools and the community awareness for better health, pregnancy and birth control, reduced infant mortality and many more. Any measure or scale couldn't measure things they gave to the community, but what they took back changed in their lives and outlook on humanity forever.

Dr. Fredman would come, stop by to hear about his fellow Peace Corps Volunteers, talk to me about his personal experience, life in West Africa amongst completely foreign conditions, and the hardship to overcome the challenges. I was more than happy to sit and listen to him, no matter how many cups of coffee I needed to pour. The other four volunteers from the district also visited me on a few occasions. They were much younger than Dr. Fredman in their early twenties, using their break year as Peace Corps Volunteers. They all had various tales to tell. One of them was a black girl from Georgia. She had been dreaming of coming to Africa to connect with her ancestry. However, she could not speak any tribal languages, she had a much harder time making friends or even offering her services to the community, compared to the other three, one of them a white girl from New York, two boys, one from Texas, and another from Minnesota.

Sometimes they would spend their weekends in Kailahun, in my house. They became friends with Ayesha, and the girls got along well with her, although she was a bit younger. I also learned much from them about how young people adapted to these Equatorial jungles, coming from the world's most prosperous, scientifically advanced, and socially highly sophisticated country. The boy from Minnesota answered, exactly, that was why he was in Africa. He wanted to see the darker side of the moon, and what treasure it was hiding. He found many, he said. I was utterly flabbergasted, about how these young people, coming from America, merged into African living. I got the answers from Dr. Fredman before. But his outlook must have been different from these. Their spirit of giving for this bunch made them special and unique to be Peace Corps volunteers. They traveled by public transport or hitched a ride coming to my place, which may be an hour or hour and a half's bus ride.

In the Korean War, the life Dr. Fredman led in the military Red Cross camps, and the hospital was very comfortable and serene, except for occasional murderous North Korean agents, intrusion, sounds of bomber flights, mortars, guns, and explosions. Off duty in Seoul's nightclubs was even more exciting. But the excitement of African desolation as Peace

Corps volunteers revealed a very different perspective, as one can imagine.

Anthony Bennett, or Tony Bennett, a VSO from England, came to help as a teacher. In his early 20s he took a year off from Oxford, where he was studying Biology for his BA degree. He was a young man from Gates Head, near Newcastle, in the UK.

VSO stands for Voluntary Services Organization, an NGO from the UK that has been active in Sierra Leone since the mid-1950s. VSO had a slightly different outlook in their principles of help and support for the developing and needy world than the Peace Corps from the States. VSO came to help with their needs, not just as support but advice, review activities, suggest changes, develop concepts with governmental agencies, and provide logistics for implementation.

On the other hand, as I learned from Dr. Fredman and Tony Bennett, as Peace Corps and VSO volunteers, they were given a short internship for volunteerism and education about the country and culture they were supposed to be serving. After that, they were to provide services to any ongoing project as an active team member, work closely with the community, getting their hands and feet dirty. I felt the fundamental difference between the Peace Corps and the VSO was that the VSO worked through the government and governmental agencies, whereas Peace Corps worked through local agencies or local chiefs with support from the government.

Reports, observations, and suggestions from all these ground workers were passed to the Government from the Peace Corps administration or American Embassy to relevant government departments.

Tony came to Kailahun to teach English and Geography to high school students. He was teaching at the Government

High school in Kailahun. He joined just before I arrived. The Assistant Headmaster was his host. He had a reasonably comfortable living, close to the school. He could do all his chores while walking. School hours were between 7 am and 2 pm, so he had plenty of time to relax or accumulate boredom. He would play football, participate in boating, canoeing, and run with the students. Although his host was supposed to serve him all the meals, he had a problem. Tony Being born in the Jewish faith, all the meals had to be kosher. That was an issue, and he could not ask his host to serve him kosher meals in the middle of the African jungle. So he opted to purchase his food and cook himself. It was all right for a while, but the host suggested that they buy the items he could eat; either he could cook, or his wife, who was one of my district nurses, would be happy to cook. There were ample vegetables, cereals, eggs, and fish. Accommodating a kosher diet was not a problem for his host. But he wanted to do it himself to be independent and not tax his hosts.

While Tony was chatting with his host, his wife told him that the District Medical Officer and the Catholic high school principal were Indians. These were the two ex-pats and there are other Peace Corps volunteers in the District. The Provincial Commissioner, Mr. Leather, was an English man. Then, of course, the Italian Staff of the Vianini company, who had a large camp about eight kilometers North West of the town. The VSO's had their system of keeping in touch through the High Commission in Freetown. Unlike Peace Corps contingency, VSO volunteers were too few, not more than ten in the country. It was relatively easy for the High Commission and VSO local organizations to watch them because the VSO worked through a quasi-governmental and NGO system. It was easier through local chieftaincies to manage the VSO volunteers. Some of the volunteers were hosted by chiefs and lived as their guests, so they had a better quality of life. The closest VSO volunteer was in Kenema, but he worked in Daru, helping extend the high school building and making some of the classes larger to accommodate more students. Once, he also came to visit me with Tony. He worked on a few bridges and culverts out of Kenema with Government Engineers. He was housed in government housing in Kenema. He seemed to be enjoying his work.

Tony was keen to meet Mr. Jesudasan, which he did. One day Mr. Jesudasan came with him to the Hospital with the idea of introducing him to me, realizing we were close in age, unlike other DMOs who were much older. He used to visit me after school hours and weekends and would speak to me about the ups and downs of life in Kailahun. After finishing his BA at Oxford, he wanted to join Medical School, hoping to get a seat there. He spent many hours in the outpatient clinic, got to know how we work, how we had to adjust to minimal supplies, fewer people, comparatively speaking, what he had seen in Gates Head and Oxford. He met a couple of students from the Catholic schools and Ayesha, helping in various hospital activities as volunteers. He wanted to join the team.

One day the Headmaster from the Government school came to see me. I had not met him before, but was happy to see him. He was a Sierra Leonean, educated in Ireland. He was well attired with his institutional tie. After our staff received him with tea and biscuits, he settled down and asked if Tony could spend some time during the working hours, helping with some hospital activities as part of his volunteer assignment. I had no problem because his future goal was to become a physician, so I let him come to the operating room and later in scrubs to help Sister Thomas and Mr. Joseph. He was thrilled and grateful. He had been coming in and out in his own time until now. So now his association with our volunteer plan was official, as far as we could make it.

One issue we realized was the scarcity of sitting places for patients. There was nothing called a patient's waiting room, except for a few wooden planks on the veranda outside the office and, again, not protected from the elements of nature.

I had an idea of converting my car parking space to the waiting area. The critical issue was to wade through the red tape, funding, and budgetary problems to make any structural change to government property. It was a bureaucratic challenge to do anything like that sitting in Kailahun can be more than a nightmare.

We did some brainstorming with the Manager, Sister Thomas, and Mr. Joseph. I asked if we could get everything we need to build it, like materials, labor, and planning, it would make the project more manageable. Mr. Amara asked how we could get all these without the government's involvement, for example, the PWD sanction, the budget and construction permit, etc. I said, "Well, let us start planning the project."

I went to see the District Officer, discussed the project with him, and sought advice on how we could proceed without fiscal and logistic involvement from the government, except for the green light. He said he would discuss with Mr. Leather, the Provincial Commissioner, and the MOH in Freetown. I told him about my plan to secure volunteer laborers and donated materials to build it, requesting not to divulge this until we got the green light from the authorities. I asked Tony's compatriot VSO from Kenema to help us plan the structure since he had been building various facilities for the government. Following weekend, both Tony and he arrived. He saw the site, took measurements, and said we could build a garage for two and a half Volkswagens to park in. He knew it was being made to be used as the waiting room for patients.

With all the estimates, I went to see the District Magistrate again. He called the Provincial Commissioner's office and discussed it with him. The next day, a man from Kenema Provincial Engineers' office arrived to inspect the site. I had my district Health Inspector's report ready and documented, which I handed over to him. After that, the man went to see the District Officer.

A few days later, Dr. Cummings, the Provincial Medical Officer, called me to say that we had the blessings from MOH and the VSO office to start with the project. The official authorization would come shortly. He asked me how I would procure labor and materials. I told him that a couple of local businessmen had promised to provide all the materials; two VSO volunteers, one of them with experience in construction, and several students from one of the local high schools, had agreed to help.

I went to see Mr. Saad. He was pleased to see me. I explained the project and asked his advice to help me. I said it was mostly masonry materials we needed. No, problem, he said, since his younger brother was in the construction business in Safadu, he would get everything from him to help me build the waiting room for patients. In addition, a local furniture maker would provide six bench sets for patients to sit while waiting.

The bricks, the cement, the wooden planks, corrugated sheets all arrived during the following week.

To my surprise and amazement, everything was happening at lightning pace for the place I was in.

The following weekend happened to be a long weekend. It suited all of us. On Friday afternoon, Tony and his friend arrived. Two of them tore down whatever structure was there. Tony's friend had all the masonry gadgets required. They cleared the land, labeled it, and covered the space with cement. I was there, watching and helping them, as a bogyman. I made sure that there was plenty of drinks, snacks, and hot drinks in a thermos. They did the flooring first to let it dry to build the walls at the edges. The cement floor was made thick to withstand weight and abuse by people. By the early evening before sundown, they had completed the foundation. They planned to start the walls the following day. The break would give some time for the concrete floor to get dried and hardened.

Both of them left, and Tony walked back to his house. His friend had a Jeep. He returned to Kenema. We planned to resume the next day at 10 am. I asked Tony's friend to spend the nights in Kailahun, which would be less tiring for him.

By 10 am the next day, Tony, his friend, and two students from Mr. Jesudasan's school, a workforce of four, started to build the walls. Each one had help, and Ayesha and Sister Thomas joined them later. The concrete floor was dry, but they were happy to work around it. The next day, one Student from Tony's school also came to join the crew. They started at 11 am, and by 6 pm, all the three walls were completed. They wanted to leave it for a day before putting the roof up. They planned to put all the roof's supporting structures up the next day and peg the corrugated roofing the following day.

They placed all wooden planks to support the roof and fixed them to the walls the next day. They put the corrugated, thick fiberglass sheets on the roof on Monday. Mr. Saad's brother donated those. Fiberglass roofs are lighter, tougher, and repel heat better than metal roofing. The front wall had two side coverings, leaving a large entrance port for the car to move in and out as needed. There were large windows on all the walls.

In three and half days, with the help of Tony and his colleague, both VSO volunteers, students from two high schools, Ayesha, and some support from Mr. Saad's workers, they were able to complete a permanent protected waiting area for patients coming to Kailahun District General Hospital. They also built a protective shed to park my car beside the Morgue, about three minutes' walk from my office.

On the official opening day, the District Magistrate thanked them for all the efforts made by VSO volunteers, Tony and his friend, and students from two high schools. Enthusiastic Leadership was especially acknowledged. He also mentioned my imagination and empathy for the patient's comfort; it would never have been done without the vision, and that was for the record.

We got all six benches for patients to sit on, but the space could accommodate only five; the sixth one was kept on the veranda of the in-patient ward.

Tony was brilliant, with a rational and logical mind. We discussed a wide range of topics, from the Big bang theory to Lucy's children, to the perils of the population overload, politics, religion, Apartheid, Ian Smith of Rhodesia, and the dangers of the division of India. In all these, he joined with sensible comments, questions, and admitted his ignorance, many times. He mentioned that he was Jewish, and I told him my interest in their origin, history, and culture. He was surprised to learn more than two thousand years ago, Jews settled in Kerala, India. A recent discovery of the thirteenth tribe living in northeast India for more than two and half thousand years, still practicing their Jewish tradition. I also told him about the possible origin of the Temne tribe of Sierra Leone originating from Israel in deeper antiquity.

He continued to help us in the hospital as a volunteer. However, he had to return to the UK as his one year was finished. He had to return to Oxford to continue his studies and prepare for entrance to Medical School.

He asked me about my plan. I told him I was already enrolled in a Ph.D. program at London University, working at Hammersmith Hospital and London's Royal Postgraduate Medical School. I would be there at least for four years, and then I would see which way I would go. But I could vouch for my education in the last eighteen months in Sierra Leone, which was far more profound than any university and degree could bestow on me or, for that matter, on anyone with an open mind. That was my feeling; I lived with the same feelings and conviction even fifty years after I left the Dark Continent.

Chapter 37

THEATER AT MARKET PLACE: A COURT HOUSE *DRAMA*******

"Have the courage to follow your heart and intuition, they somehow know what you truly want to become"

Steve Jobs

In the middle of the town, what was known as Market Square, was the most important place for various social, political, celebratory, and even judicial activities. Generally, during the day and weekends, farmers with their produce, dairy farmers with dairy products, traders from town, and distant places with varieties of items to sell, assembled under the roof of the Market Square. Local artisans, artists, woodcarvers, painters, and sewists gathered in the Market Square, built on a large concrete raised platform protected from the elements. Being close to the border of two other countries, Guinea and Liberia, Kailahun was a convenient trading station and a safe transit point for smugglers for all sorts of smuggling and illegal business practices. Kailahun town, the district headquarters, provided particular infrastructural convenience to make it a point of transit for smugglers and legal businesses, especially forest products, coffee, and other produce varieties. Meat, poultry, and fish were sold separately, which remained closed unless vendors came with their items to sell. Slaughtering was not permitted in the market area but was done somewhere else. The health department kept a check and certified all produce and animal products.

Interestingly, supervision of the market's items sold fell under the Public Health Department, which was also my responsibility. Therefore, the paramount chief and our health inspector jointly maintained vigilance. In addition, the Chief collected taxes and was responsible for maintenance.

Every time I went shopping, I could see some tension amongst vendors and shoppers. Everyone was keen to sell at an "excellent price," particularly the meat and seafood vendors. If there was any "bush meat" being sold, the officers were especially vigilant to determine how they were acquired, killed by any game seeker or natives for consumption, and sold for business. They were cautious of correctly noting how these animals were killed and when they were killed. No wild animal meat was allowed for human consumption if the animal was killed more than two days early. If poisoned arrows killed the animals by natives, they were not allowed to sell for human consumption. Wild meat was mainly that of Wild Boars and Duikers, a variety of Antelope Widely roaming the jungles of Sierra Leone. Monkeys, baboons, and bats were prohibited for human consumption. But, of course, no one knew what happened when Big Brother was not watching, and small brothers' pockets were open.

The marketplace was also a gathering place for political rallies, entertainment, communal parties, and public education issues arranged by the government or NGOs. A marketplace was also a meeting place for social interaction with friends and families.

On days of festivities, people gathered in the square and the marketplace from the town, nearby villages, and for major festivals. They came with colorful native gear to watch cultural performances presented by various groups and tribes. Mask dancing was one of the most popular dances. The dancers wore wood-curved masks and covered their bodies with long skirts and top coverings made from hay or dried husks. Visually, very impressive. I felt the dancers depicted a warrior fighting an enemy or making gestures toward evil spirits hoping to ward it off. The body movements were always very physical and powerful. The different sculptures of the masks indicated a group or a tribe. Masked performances could be solo or duo. Women also participated, dancing in circles with grass skirts, frequently bare-breasted. They sang along as they danced around the Hero, who generally presented with an aggressive appearance.

Sometimes, school children sang in their choir to entertain the guests and onlookers. The festive performances during Independence Day, on 27th April, could be very entertaining. Performers even from neighboring Guinea joined to make the day more colorful and thrilling. I was lucky to experience the festivities of the newly independent Sierra Leone, with Sir Milton Margai appointed as prime minister, later elected as the first Prime Minister of the Independent nation of Sierra Leone. The pulse, joy, and vitality of the feeling of being independent were deeply felt by everyone present at the festivities.

The market square was the life of Kailahun, with daily produce, meat, and fish market being sold. Traders and hawkers displayed their goods, frequently calling out for the attention of the customers, chatting with their buyers and chatting with each other, talking about the market, interests, customers, and not infrequently, their personal woes and joys, their home, their village, their family and friends. That became a big, vibrant family. The Market was also the life center of the town.

Aside from all that happened in the market square, one significant attraction was the occasional sitting of law courts to resolve cases. Since the local courthouse was small and essentially under the paramount chief, the prosecutors and judges traveled from Freetown or Kenema for a court case hearing in Kailahun. Then the marketplace was converted into a courthouse to accommodate the defendant, lawyers, judge/s, their entourage, government prosecutors, and their supporting staff. They also created a gallery for the public to watch the proceedings. As a result, the whole marketplace changed its outlook and soul. Sometimes, even prison officers with prisoners in their marked vehicles, police cars, and people in uniforms transformed the air and the environment.

They moved the market under a temporary covered space, but one could see many people in the visitors' gallery sitting or standing around any time a court session was held. The courthouse dramas became a major attraction, perhaps a major entertainment event for town people. Even people from neighboring towns and villages may be associated with the case, witness, or just be there to have some serious fun. The town's people and villagers were in awe to see so many 'big people' coming to their town. It was not only visual entertainment but also a real-time show. Depending on the seriousness of the case, the press also sent their team of journalists and a photographer.

I had to attend these court hearings as a crown witness to give my expert opinion. Generally, most police cases ranged from minor injury to grievous bodily harm to death, homicide or suicide, or accidental death. Typically, the court clerk or the prosecutor presented my report to the judge and would ask me to agree or disagree, or after reading and hearing the case, I would like to amend my statement. I never had to amend my report. Generally, the process took ten to fifteen minutes, and I would be released to return to work.

But some cases were disputed by the defendant's lawyer, particularly when the process of infliction of injury was questioned or the defendant's lawyer questioned the cause of death. Some of the lawyers were Barrister-at-law, well trained at one of the famous British universities before being called to the Bar by one of the "Temples," Middle, or Inner Temple, or one of the Inns, like Lincoln's Inn or Gray's Inn. They were generally elegant orators, and smart legal presenters focused and pointed in their legal arguments. I felt that they took pleasure in questioning and cross-questioning me, perhaps to "win" in their minds or just a masochistic pleasure, satisfied by harassing the Government Expert witness. This particular case was not medical litigation for malpractice or negligence, but to establish the real cause of death or any non-fatal bodily severe injury, fully or partly contributing to the death, which may have been oversighted in the primary Death certificate. If they were not satisfied with my response, I frequently drew diagrams of the body organ concerning forensic damage to explain them in support of my Coroner's report. I took pleasure in being demonstrative and theatrical, at times for the legal counsel, the prosecutor, the judge, and the spectators in the gallery.

The Police Super once said that more people were coming to the court when the doctor came to appear as a witness. I asked him, "Why do you think so?" They expected serious cases, and the court had more informative and entertaining value. It made it more interesting when the doctor was in the dock. Audiences liked to express their emotion with *"Hail, Hail* "when the court was moving in the right direction or *"Ouaaa Na, Na,"* if the direction was not up to their expectation. The clerk, the police, and frequently the Judge ordered them to stop shouting or making a noise, affecting the court procedure. They would be removed from the court premises, then there would be a period of lull. The murmur returned as the case progressed.

I had to defend my diagnosis of the Cause of death being "Cerebral Hemorrhage. "The Opposition Lawyer kept insisting that it was not due to a natural cause of death, but that the man was killed by Voodoo magic by his younger brother, who had a substantial stake in the inheritance of his wealth and business. So, again, I went back to the drawing board and pointed out that he did not die of a heart attack but from a brain hemorrhage. I asked the lawyer where and what kind of changes I should be looking to establish "Voodoo Spell as the cause of his death. I reminded him I was not an expert in "Voodooism." We were never taught about illness and fatality from voodooism during medical education. The word was not even in our curricular vocabulary. I kept hammering the fact to the learned Barrister repeatedly until he agreed to my version of the cause of death. But he returned to his privilege of asking more questions to the expert witness. Next, he asked me if his brain hemorrhage could have resulted from any injury. I wondered, what kind of injury? Do you mean external or internal? He said "yes, perhaps. Sorry, I had already reported, there is no evidence of blunt, sharp, or lacerated injury or fracture to the skull bones, which may be associated with his internal brain injury. Then I continued that he had the internal damage to have blood in his brain. There has to be some sort of disruption in the artery wall for the blood to leak out to cause bleeding in his brain tissue, leading to death." I gave him a leading answer: one of the main causes of this leakage is high blood pressure; this patient had high blood pressure but was controlled on medication, which is a matter for the record.

Then he continued to ask, if pressure was the reason for bleeding in his brain, could throttling or gagging him cause brain hemorrhage? I repeated, "Sir!

My report already recorded no injury to the neck or any other part of his head and neck region."

The Judge intervened and said that we could proceed with the next witness if the counsel had no further relevant questions. There was no other question; I was relieved of my court presence to return to work.

This was a protracted interrogation, both from the plaintiff's lawyer and the public prosecutor. There was no Jury. The judge dismissed the case against the dead man's brother for homicide using voodoo influence. The plaintiff was then ordered to pay the cost incurred to the government and the defendant for the whole process of litigation.

This was my second police case as an expert witness against "Voodooism" as the cause of death. But, unfortunately, these types of cases were not so rare. An experience that will not be learned from the textbooks, nor be taught by learned professors and certainly will never be an issue in one's higher board examination. But this was a reality of life because the glasshouses of "*Deanship and the curriculum they offer in medical schools*" were divorced from life, living, and sickness on earth. That was how I saw the nature of modern education: it had little concern for what happened at ground level, causing us illness or death.

It was quite a theater during the entire trial. People from the spectator's gallery and those standing outside the platform expressed their endorsement or dissent from time to time as the cross-examination progressed, with various noises. I did not understand what they were trying to say. But, judging by the pitch of their exclamations, one could feel, high-pitched noises were a sign of approval, and that of low-pitched were expressions of disapproval or dissent. At one point, police had to escort a couple of people from the visitors' gallery because of their unacceptable behavior.

Outside, a little away from the courtroom, it was quite a fair, as vendors of all sorts gathered to sell food, drinks, clothes, small household items, you name it, it was there. Before, I had seen people gathering close to the temporary marketplace. This time, the business activities had taken the shape of a fair. As I was returning home, several people saluted me. Some clapped in groups, and some even greeted me with "Thumbs up." Although this had not been a general reaction in previous cases, much smaller numbers expressed their feelings from a distance, even if it did happen. Although the hospital was just about a ten-minute walk from the courthouse, a policeman escorted me to my office on every occasion. It was no different this day.

I went to my office and found Sister Thomas, Ayesha, and Mr. Joseph waiting for my return. They all were in a perfect mood. Then, Mr. Boukhari, the Police Superintendent, walked in. I asked him to take a seat. He seemed to be in a very cheerful mood. "The dead man was from Kailahun, and he was liked by the people very much for his generosity and kind behavior. He was a wealthy businessman. His oldest wife's family was from another town. They were the ones who brought the case against the dead man's wife for murdering her husband, with the help of a Voodoo medicine man. The second wife was from Kailahun. So the people were thrilled, particularly in how you handled the 'fearful cunning' barrister from Freetown" and saved the innocent widow, Mr. Boukhari said.

I said, "I did what I would do anyway. I am glad that I did not know that the barrister was a 'frighteningly cunning' one, which would have frightened me also to shaking in and wetting my pants." Everyone laughed with a big roar.

I wondered how many "Voodoo murder cases" the "Frightening cunning" barrister from Freetown managed to win a favorable verdict, confirming the cause of death. In that case, there was a lot to learn for the entire medical community and medical educators. What usually happened outside Old Baily, High courts, many other judiciary mansions, and courts of appeal?

We all departed.

Chapter 38
MEETING A DIAMOND RUNNER

"Everybody you fight is not your enemy, and everybody that helps you is not your friend"

Mafia Gangster

The western hump of Africa was known for its wealth, even in antiquity. The Ashanti Emperors of Kumasi in Ghana were well known to Europeans for their wealth, particularly gold. Explorers, exploiters, traders from Europe, and other African kingdoms visited West Africa from the early 10th century. Malians and North African tribes and from 14th century onward percolated into the sub-Saharan, Tropical, and equatorial Western Africa and established themselves into the native communities with a significant impact of Islam, the practice they brought with them. Europeans, central Asian kings, and emperors sent their envoys for goodwill alliances and exchanged trade, political and educational emissaries. Despite the region's inhospitable climate, hostile tribes, and killer diseases, interest in the Dark Continent's wealth continues to grow till today.

Sierra Leone's wealth has been greatly supported by diamond mining, aside from gold, bauxite, titanium, and some other rare earth elements. The Colonial rulers exploited that wealth maximally for the benefit of the British Government and, to some extent, Sierra Leone and its people. To improve mining, they had to develop infrastructure, communication including telecommunication, roads, bridges, and an adequate railway system.

One mineral, the diamond exploits, had no absolute control by the Colonial Government. Because the diamond deposits were scattered over a large area of Eastern, southeastern and northeastern parts of the country, covering the eastern third of the country. Sierra Leone's diamonds were not deep to excavate but formed just under the surface. They were formed over millions of years as diamond columns close to the land's character in the alluvial layers. So diamond mining in Sierra Leone was done from river banks, river beds of Moa, Bo, and other rivers in the region, lakes, inland marshes, and underneath the land surface.

There was no need for heavy high-maintenance machinery, complex mining logistics, expert engineers and technologists, or highly paid support services. Mostly, diamond mining was done with a spade and a shovel, a pan, and two strong hands to agitate the muds from the river or lakes in order to separate diamond beads from it. Areas for mining were large, close to 7500 square miles, which is accessible to legal and illegal miners as well. Local villagers frequently joined with diamond panhandlers. Villagers continued with illegal mining, sneaking in and out, unnoticed by the supervisors and security guards. Even if they were caught for the unaccounted catch of the day, they shared their spoils between the guards and the sneakers. There was no loser, only winners- Sometimes, even the guards recruited illegal panhandlers from villages to continue this criminal but highly profitable business. If detected trespassing and attempting to smuggle, within minutes, their body would be floating in the mighty Moa River for the pleasure of the crocodiles and some other aquatic man-eaters.

However, the whole culture of illegal panning for diamonds and smuggling those out of the country became entrenched in the local economy and social behavior. They believed it was an entitlement of the people who lived around there. 'Land and soil belong to people of the land, so as what comes out of the land, including diamond,' during and after the civil war, this slogan was a powerful political tool for the Saviors and the plundering mercenaries as well.

Sierra Leone Diamonds were sold outside by powerful, wealthy, and internationally connected Sierra Leonean Lebanese Diamond dealers. Most of Sierra Leone's legal or illegal diamond exports were done by a few Lebanese families with a strong international network. One of them was Fred Kamil, and the other was Jamil Mohammad, who had a Sierra Leonean Krio mother. They worked out of Koidu, the defacto diamond capital of Sierra Leone. It was the district headquarter of Kano District. The number of Mercedes, Audis, and Land Rover cars I had seen in that town, would put Freetown to shame.

The Prospect of diamond mining of Sierra Leone was fragmented. Government control was not well established. Only thirty percent (30%) of mined diamonds were accountable for government coffers. So the illegal, black market diamond trade was flourishing. Panhandling was the leading technology. Local Panhandlers, migrants from Guinea and Liberia were the primary labor force.

Local villagers and children of all ages were engaged for a pittance. Pittance was better than poverty and starving. They made more money being a 'diamond runner' to smuggle it out of the mining area to Mandingo international smugglers.

Mandingos is an African tribe that migrated from Guinea and Liberia. They spoke French, had tribal links with their people who lived in Guinea and Liberia. Mandingos lived in the Kailahun district, bordering both Guinea and Liberia. Once the "diamond runners" deposited the smuggled diamonds to local Mandingo strong man in Kailahun, it disappeared from Sierra Leone into the Mandingo diaspora in Guinea or Liberia within seconds. Kailahun appeared to be a dependable transit point for both inside and outside. Many Mandingo business people made their fortune being the middleman because of their international social network.

The "diamond runners" were most vulnerable and disadvantaged in this illegal diamond smuggling chain. They were poor, generally hard-working, reliable, and subject to abuse at various levels, degrees, and duration. They were the "first defender (Offender) walking through the smugglers' alley or highway.

This is where my story begins.

During my course of hospital practice, at times, young boys between ten and twenty came to the clinics or at the emergency services with various types of physical injuries. They had different stories to tell me of how they got the injury. Unfortunately, it was not documented in hospital notes either due to negligence, forgetfulness, or not appreciating the importance of documenting the cause of injury. At times, I was told that they deliberately omitted the fact. I had difficulty in understanding.

The injuries were minor to non–life-threatening, so maybe it was felt not to document something that would not help the patient in treatment. It did not attract my attention either. They would come and tell me fascinating stories of how it happened. They got injured while playing with a cousin, directing me to the accompanying young man. While playing, he fell from a cycle or a truck while hitching from one place to another, and sharp cuts were usually sustained working in logging or fishing. These young people told these and many other fantastic reasons for sustaining the injuries. Amusing, maybe I missed the deceptive element of their stories. Generally, the injured were accompanied by a young friend, adult family member, or several members, and at times, the entire village would accompany the young injured.

If and when the injury was grave, I suggested sending the patient to the Nixon Memorial Hospital, another close provincial hospital, or even to Freetown, but invariably the answer had been, to do what could be done in Kailahun. They would say that they had no money to go and have the treatment, or frequently, tell me that they were either Guinean or Liberian nationals, so they would like to return home to their families and their own doctors as soon as possible. They sometimes would beg to treat them to be well enough to make it home. They were reluctant even to be admitted to the hospital because they would be far away from home.

A few months later, as I was attending to one such young man, it occurred to me for such a small place, the number of minor to major to grave road accidents was much higher than in the rest of the country, and for that matter, anywhere else, to my understanding.

One day I asked the police superintendent about my observation. He responded that road traffic accidents (RTA) were documented only if the patient or relatives complained. Generally, the disputes were settled by mutual agreement, hence not reported to the police. If challenged by one party, it was taken up by the paramount chief or local chiefs. They were settled under their authority since these incidences are not mandated to report to the police department. "So you are right, Sir! The reported physical injuries resulting from possible RTA are much less than the real numbers," admitted Mr Boukhari the Police Superintendent.

"I have seen so many cases, and I suspect some of these results come from criminal activities. Am I supposed to submit a report to you?" I asked. "Of course!" he said, "Make sure you have the correct details of the persons involved. Frequently they tend to misguide you by giving false names and incorrect personal information."

"Why would they do it? We are only trying to help."

"Maybe they do not want help. All they need is to treat them as much as we can, help the wounded one for bleeding, pain and discomfort so that they can return home."

"Many children who come for help are from neighboring countries," I said.

"Yes! They come to work in the mines, and younger children can do the job faster than adults, and their wages are less and much easy to control by their employers."

"Which mines?" I asked.

"Only mining activity we have here is diamond. They work daily by panning mud in water to separate the diamonds. It is easy to operate but needs many human hands if done manually. Major companies prospect with machines; it costs more, but require fewer people to do the job. For day labor, it is lucrative compared to what they would be or would not be doing back in neighboring countries. Many local children do the panning illegally, which is not tolerated by the legal prospectors. That may be why you see so many young people with various injuries.

"They get beaten up, thrashed, hit by cars, sometimes pushed out from a running vehicle, or even killed and thrown in the river. It is difficult to trace; once they are thrown in the rivers, the crocodiles quickly gobble their bodies as fast as they were thrown in. As a result, body parts shows up in the river banks. This happens to boys, who are doing illegal panning and not cooperating with the guards. The boys or girls employed and paid to be 'diamond runners' by their employers are also at high risk of being ill-treated. Suppose they suspect the boys are unfaithful or deliberately ran away with the entrusted merchandise to be delivered to the Mandingo Currier in and around Kailahun, in that case, the treatment is harsh and cruel. Many boys are injured, many are killed, and others are captured to be sold as slaves. These traffickers call themselves "labor troopers," who finds laborer for any work. This abuse of humans is well known. Yet, the government can't do much since foreigners carry out sixty to seventy percent of diamond mining. They procure long-term prospecting leases from the government, and human abuses are barely acknowledged."

I felt very sad for these young people, who had to go through these cycles of punishment, violence, and torture. Their only crime was to find a job, earn some money to look after their family and elders. They were no *DeBeers*.

It was a Thursday, late evening; Sister Thomas called me for a middle-aged man brought to the hospital, bleeding from a wound on the back of the right thigh from a deep and long wound. "Seemed injured by a sharp knife. He is in much pain. I have called Mr. Joseph the nurse anesthetist if you want to do something here," said Sister Thomas.

I went there immediately. Found a black man in pain, otherwise healthy. I looked at his wound, which was in the back of his right thigh, and about ten inches long and seemed to have been caused by a sharp knife, which happened less than an hour ago, near the Liberia border, while he was traveling with a friend aiming to go to Monrovia. The patient said, "We set out at night, hoping to arrive in Monrovia by daybreak." They noticed a Land Rover following them crossing the Sierra Leone border. "After about half an hour, the driver of the Land Rover overtook us and indicated us to stop. We had no intention of stopping. They let us know that they were armed, and would harm us and the car if we did not stop. We stopped on the roadside without arguing, but they stayed on the road beside us.

"There were two people in the Land Rover. One black man came out with a gun, called my name, and asked me to get out and stand against our truck, and to put my hands up. He checked if I was carrying any gun or any other lethal ammunition. The driver had come out of the car by that time, went to my driver, and ordered him to sit in the back seat. He did. The man then handcuffed the driver and chained him to the back of the driver's seat. They also tied his feet with strong tape.

"They came to me and demanded the pouch. Everyone knows what pouch the assailant was talking about; The Pouches of raw diamonds. I had no pouches; I told the raiders. He started to hit me with a baton. I told him repeatedly that I had no pouch, and I did not know of any pouch. Then they asked me to strip while hitting me with his baton. I had a long dressing, about eight to ten inches long, in the back of my right thigh. Earlier I had a small cut in the same site. Later the wound was covered tightly by duct tape. Since I will be traveling long distances, I was told they taped it with duct tape to get the best protection because no medical tape was available. The packing was rather thick through the entire length of the dressing. They looked at it and saw some blood around the tape, and to my surprise, the tape had sutures tagging the skin. Eight to ten sutures around the tape were stitched to my skin. I had no idea when who and where these sutures were placed there, except they must have put me to sleep to do this. They asked me about the sutures, but I did not know; I had no idea. The man slapped me hard. Tried to think why the duct tape was sutured to my skin. They tried to take the duct tape off my skin but could not do it. They also realized the duct tape is also sutured to my skin inside. The two guys were speaking in English, had an accent, but not from any West African country. They decided to remove the entire dressing by cutting it off the skin. I had no idea what I was going to experience. Within a minute, they removed the dressing with a very sharp knife. They showed me what I had under the skin. Five small pouches containing raw diamonds of different sizes, the total maybe two fistfuls of raw diamonds. I had no idea what I was carrying. They tightly bandaged my thigh. Asked me to unlock the driver and drive back where we came. We refrained from following the roughs. They gave me the key to the driver's handcuff and the car key. We got released and headed back to Kailahun. My pain was excruciating. Although the guy bandaged the thigh tightly, it was still bleeding.

By now, I had seen the faces of the two guys. They were white, burnt in African Sun, possibly from one South African country. I had excruciating pain, and I needed help immediately." They drove straight to Kailahun Hospital.

I saw him on the operating table. He told me his story while we were preparing him for his surgery. The guys were in a great hurry, and they must have been carrying a super-sharp knife. They cut through the duct tape, through the skin, and removed about ten inches long and four inches wide skin flap. Cruelty knows no bounds. Under general anesthesia, we cleared all remaining tape, removed the sutures, cleaned the wound, and stopped all bleeding points. I had to undercut the skin to cover the missed bit of skin. He was a big man and had plenty of available skin to close the wound without much tension. He was sent to the ward awake and in a fair state.

When I came to work in the morning, everybody was at work. Sister Thomas was ready for the morning round. I wanted to go and see the patient. Sister Thomas told me that his relative came in a big car and took him home early in the morning. I asked where to. "To Kano," he said. They signed that they were taking the patient on their own responsibility. I was sorry, but that was the best way to deal with this patient. I had done the best I could have done anywhere, at any time. I was sad.

Later in the morning, Mr. Saad came with another Lebanese gentleman, introduced as Mr. Abbas from Koidu, the diamond capital. He had come to thank me for helping one of his business team with a very serious injury. He was better, and wanted to go back to his own home. He affirmed that they had taken the patient back to Koidu. Mr. Saad's friend offered me 100 Leone (Equivalent to 100 GBP) for my services, which I declined respectfully. I said I couldn't accept any fees for my work in the Hospital, and I wished for his friend to get well soon.

The next day, I met with Mr. Boukhari, the Police Superintendent, asking if this should be reported to the police. "If he did not ask you, wait until one party asks. Or we will request a report if they file a case. It was a good idea to let the patient go of his own will. This is how these cases are generally handled." He said I should not be surprised if many more cases from this route would appear. Although I had seen many young children and adults before, I had no idea that they were all 'diamond runners' of Sierra Leone. I should have gone into details of their history of presenting illness. If I had charged them any fees for my services, every patient's story could have been an exciting source of learning and revelation.

It did not take too long to be shocked again. In the highway of diamond trafficking, horror and surprise were the rules. One evening after I returned from my day's work at the hospital, just settled down for my cherished afternoon tea, Sister Thomas came and knocked at the door. I welcomed her and asked her to sit down and share tea with me before exciting news. She laughed and said, "Yes, Sir, it is fascinating! A woman around forty years old, in the emergency, complained of vaginal bleeding. Looking at her, she looked pregnant. She would not give me a clear answer when I asked, likely to be twelve to sixteen weeks pregnant. She complained of pelvic pain, difficulty in passing urine, and had bleeding, which soaked the diaper she was wearing. She came with a few men; one of them said he was her husband. They are not local. I did ask them if they would like to go to Segbwema NMH. All the men said, No! No! She wants to see the doctor here. Her vitals were fine, but she complained of abdominal pain and nausea. Maybe she has a threatened abortion. Perhaps you would like to see her soon. I have started her on a drip. Finish your tea, and then I will join you in the theater. Prepare for possible termination of pregnancy."

I found her lying on the operating table. Mr. Joseph, the anesthetist, was ready with his assets. Four people accompanied her; three men, one was supposed to be her husband and another elderly lady, likely the patient's mother.

The patient looked distressed, appearing dehydrated.

She was reluctant to uncover her abdomen. Finally, I told her I had to examine her in order to help. Sister tried to impress it on her. She kept saying, nothing wrong with her belly; she was bleeding from the bottom. She kept complaining that she had much pain in the bottom.

I said "I must look at your bottom, but I need to examine your belly first." After lots of talking and coaxing, she agreed to expose her abdomen. She asked her husband to come in. That was fine with us. I asked him to come in.

To our surprise, she had a padded abdominal binder at least four to five inches thick at the center. The edges of the abdominal binder were taped to her skin all around.

When I put my hand on the binder, it felt firm, hard, and gritty. I asked her why she was wearing the binder and what was inside the binder. The patient's husband said, "Because she had so much pain and bleeding, the village shaman put some stone medicine on to help her with the binder." I had no idea what he was talking about. I stared at Sister and Mr. Joseph. They also gave me a vacant stare.

I told the husband that I must remove the binder to examine her. Reluctantly, they agreed. Sister slowly pulled the binder. Her abdomen was completely flat. There was no sign of pregnancy. But most of the lower abdomen was quite tender and had signs of internal inflammation (peritonitis).

The binder was at least close to a kilogram in weight. I wondered what stones the shamanhad packed in the binder, so heavy. I felt that there were several pebbles. The husband said the stones were to keep her warm.

When we looked at the perineum, the pad was blood-soaked. Blood was coming from the rectum,not from the vagina. I had no idea what was going on. But, my examination indicated that she certainly had early pelvic peritonitis.

I wanted to do a vaginal examination. The patient did not mind. I could not see anything unusual. But as I examined with my fingers, I could feel several irregular hard stone-like objects in her rectum.Those could be hard stool formation due to chronic constipation. But the feeling was not that of scebella (stone-like stool pellet).

As I was about to examine her rectum, I found a string coming out of her anal canal. I tried to pull it. She screamed. Then after much persuasion, Sister and Mr. Joseph were able to make the husband admit that the Shaman put some medicine in a bag inside her rectum to help her get better.

I spontaneously asked, get better from what?

With much difficulty, I removed the plastic bag, which looked like a condom. Unfortunately, the bag had already torn due to rough movement and just the nature of the stones inside. The ones that escaped from the condom must be causing injury to the rectal wall, causing bleeding. I could feel a few more floating stones inside the rectum. I could get only the one I got access to, but the rest were beyond my reach.

I asked Sister to keep all in a kidney dish and wash them. Let me find out what kind of stones these were.

The abdominal binder was placed on top of a storage cupboard. With all the commotion and staff rushing around, the abdominal binder fell from the top of the closet on the floor. The binder tore apart, releasing some of the stones from inside. When the binder fell, it made some kind of metallic sound. When I looked at the stones from the binder, I did not doubt that those were raw gold nuggets. The woman was carrying approximately two kilograms of raw gold nuggets in her abdominal binder, pretending to be pregnant.

More surprises came when I looked at the stones out of her rectum, which were nothing but raw uncut diamonds. At least twenty-five of them. They were hard, irregular, and sharp, glass-like beads. I had no doubt that the stones were unpolished diamonds.

So, this patient was carrying a couple of kilograms of gold nuggets and several thousand dollars' worth of unpolished diamonds. I do not know how many more diamond pieces were left inside her rectum, which would continue to irritate, induce bleeding and cause pelvic peritonitis, which is inflammation of the lining of the inside of the pelvis.

I suggested to the people accompanying her that there were still a few more stones left inside her rectum, which had to be taken out or allowed to be expelled. If left like this, she might die of bleeding and blood infection. We would send her to Segbwema, Nixon Memorial Hospital, for X-rays and treatment. The men were agitated and said they would take her home rather than go to NMH. I could not understand that. They said they would let me do whatever I could here in Kailahun. If she were not better by tomorrow, then they would see what was best for her.

Sister handed over the abdominal binder and all the contents from the condom to her husband. They said they would wait around the hospital and see how she did in the morning.

We gave her enemas to defecate the stones out. She was put on an IV drip and antibiotics, and she was stable in the end.

As usual, Sister came for her rounds in the morning before I arrived. The lady was well. She had no fever, and her vitals were normal. She had no further bleeding from the rectum. She thought she may have passed a few stones in her stool in the morning.

All four men were not to be found anywhere. They had disappeared.

After questioning, we found that those people were not her relatives. They smuggled her out of her village while working on the field; she was trafficked out from the community. They beat her up, tortured her, physically and otherwise abused her, and threatened to kill her if she did not carry these to Liberia. She had no choice but to agree. She said, "Someone slipped a little bag in my back and plastered the pad in my stomach. They told me to tell the guard in the Kailahun-Liberia border that 'you are going to Liberia for a wedding party, and you are four to five months pregnant if they ask you.'"

She told me, "We were close to Daru when I started bleeding and severe pain in my belly after a big jolt in the car. The pain was horrible. I was throwing up and crying. Then they turned back and brought me to Kailahun hospital. Those people are not my relatives; they just trafficked me to smuggle these things out of Sierra Leone into Liberia."

I had no idea where and how to get them. The smugglers were adamant not to go to the NMH, and they knew the hospital would hand them over to the police.

She was better and wanted to return home to the Kano district.

I reported to our Police Super. He filed a case but said it would be hard to chase these people. Anyway, he arranged the police transport to take her back to her village in Kano.

I met with Mr. Shaikh Musa the next day, a well-known diamond-smuggling kingpin who ran a reputable timber business out of Daru. After I told him the story, he said these people were either Liberian or South African. Their main problem was the Sierra Leone border check. They were ruthless and ready to commit any crime for smuggling minerals out of Sierra Leone. They had found that women were the best and most reliable couriers for smuggling. They had a solid and tight human trafficking gang in the country. They had killed one Sierra Leonean Border guard a couple of years ago.

Being aware of women smugglers, government-appointed women border guards to control them. Last year, one of the female border guards was abducted, raped, killed, and her body was left in front of the Sierra Leone border guard's post, in Buedu, in a plastic garbage bag. Since then, the government had not been able to recruit any female border guards. As a result, these international smugglers had almost a free ride. Mr. Musa said it was good to let them have their Trove and leave. However, this smuggling attempt was a massive haul. The smugglers would have done everything to get their troves back.

Chapter 39
ON THE ROAD TO MONROVIA

"No matter the economy of Jungle, the Lion will never eat Grass"

African Proverb

Ever since I arrived in Kailahun, my colleagues, associates, and friends have kept reminding me that I must take a trip to Monrovia, Liberia's capital city. Liberia was the only independent democratic nation in Africa, run by black African slaves freed from the USA and some from Nova Scotia in Canada, nearly a hundred years ago. The country was resourceful, mineral-rich, and fertile, producing various staples, one of the most significant palm oil, coffee, and rubber producers, with a heavy subsidy from the United States. It was the most advanced of all West African nations at that time. During the years of the Presidency of Mr. Tubman, Liberia was the fastest growing country in Africa and the second-fastest growth and GDP in the world. Monrovia is the capital. It offered a lifestyle envied by the rest of the region. As I was told, there were several cinema halls, theaters, bars and pubs, even strip clubs and roadside cafes, which made life and living exciting and inviting. There was an air of "Americanism" in the city.

President William Tubman, a well-educated clergy, was elected President of Liberia in 1943. With his vast experience in Democratic governance, as the nineteenth elected President of Liberia, he was one of Free Africa's longest-reigning and surviving presidents. His administration impacted every facet of the life of Liberians, be they rich or poor. He also built one of the most impressive presidential palaces in Africa. I was being told to visit the presidential palaces. It was inescapable to skirt the spectacle before leaving Liberia and returning to the life of Sierra Leone, particularly if one was living in Kailahun.

So it was not difficult to persuade me to accept the invitation to venture on the trip. It was Mr. Joseph, our anesthetist-nurse, who was the instigator. The opportunity came to take the journey on a long weekend from Kailahun. Sister Thomas was very encouraging. She said she could have come, but we did not want to keep the hospital without doctor's coverage. She said she would contact the doctors at Nixon Memorial Hospital to cover for me in any emergency. I said, "Better I speak to them myself before I leave. But you can be in touch with them and let them know if we have any problem in Kailahun."

That was the plan.

It was suggested that we take the river route then to the coastal boat, which took no more than four hours from the back of my house to Monrovia. I asked, "What do you mean by 'from the back of my house'?"

The gentleman said, "Literally, it is from the back of your house. The river flowing at the back, flows by Daru. You can take a canoe or a powerboat to Daru. At Daru, you need to take a larger boat to Bence or directly to Monrovia, which takes about three and half hours. So from your house to Daru on the river is no more than fifteen minutes."

When I told Sister Thomas about the river route to Monrovia, she was horrified. She said I could do it, but suggested not to dare it. The river behind my house was navigable, but a small canoe or a powerboat was not safe because the giant crocodiles or hippopotamus could easily overturn those. Even larger boats could get in the way of aggressive, hungry crocodiles. Then there were poisonous snakes around. "Every year, we have one or two casualties in this river. I expect you have not forgotten our huge passenger ship was almost going to be wrecked in the tropical storm on our way from England. Moreover, my feeling is that you are not yet a seasoned sailor. So let us take the land route; it will be a much longer time, but you will be much safer. Anyway, the road to Monrovia inside Liberia is so much better that the journey will be enjoyable."

There were two drivable land routes to Monrovia; one went south through Pendembu to the southwestern Liberian border. Most parts of the road were unpaved but reasonably maintained. It went through a deep Equatorial forest, mainly on the Sierra Leonean side, close to the Liberian border. It has to cross by two or three river ferries en route. Generally, they were maintained and operated well, but problems occasionally occurred due to mechanical issues, rough rivers, or operators not in attendance. The distance from Kailahun to Monrovia was three hundred and sixty kilometers, and it usually took approximately seven hours to get there. It was safer to add another hour for the entire journey.

The Northern route went north and northeast of Kailahun. The Kailahun portion of the road was not tarmacked but well maintained for African standard, wide enough for two to three cars to drive past. The Sierra Leone section was just about fifteen kilometers from the border. In Liberia, it was continued as Monrovia–Kakath highway. It was tarmacked, most parts very wide, raised from the ground level to not get water-logged in the rainy season. There were wide spaces on both sides of the road for emergency stoppage or short rests. This route was a five hundred and eleven kilometers stretch with passes on the hilly terrain. The trees were more like bushes and did not obstruct sunlight from hitting the road. It would take nine hours to get to Monrovia from Kailahun. There was no river ferry to cross. There would be several well-stocked villages on the way, where one could stop for refreshment or just to break the boredom or monotony of highway driving.

On the other hand, the southern route spiraled through the Gola National Equatorial forest; one could hardly see any human settlements as one drove, but they hid behind the bushes. As night fell, fire, fumes, and rhythmical music could be intoxicating.

It was Sister Thomas's preference that we take the northern mountainous highway. We were all set to go.

So, on a Friday early morning at 7 am, we left Kailahun for Monrovia. Mr. Joseph, his wife, another young lady, and Mr. Mohmmadu set out for Monrovia with me. Ayesha had planned to spend the long weekend in Freetown with her grandparents and a host of uncles, aunts, and cousins. We rented a Range Rover from a local businessman for the trip. In twenty minutes, we were at the Liberian border. The border control on both sides looked well established and manned. We passed through the Sierra Leone check post where the policeman on duty just looked at us and let us go. On the Liberian side, Mohmmadu went out and spoke to the border guard. They did not ask for my passport or anyone's travel documents and let us pass. Now we were in Liberia. We were traveling on Monrovia–Kakath highway, all the way to Monrovia.

We experienced a big difference in driving on this road in Liberia. Very wide, fit for four cars and buses to pass side-by-side, and there was still plenty of roadside service road space for an emergency stop or just to stop for a break. A shallow but wide drain ran beside the road to drain rainwater from the street on both sides. The road was tarmarcked. We could feel that we were at a height, traveling on a mountain road. The air was fresh excellent, and clean with a gentle breeze coming from the mountains, not far from the road to the north. We would be driving close to the border of Guinea. Both Sierra Leone and Liberia shared the same terrain parts of "Massif du Ziama Classified forest" that extended on both sides of the highway, well-clear from the road. Of course, the forest was cleared to make way for the highway.

We drove along the highway, having left the border at 7.45 am, expecting to be in Monrovia by 5 pm, latest. Good time to arrive for the host. It was a beautiful clear morning, hoping the "weather forecaster would remain kind for the rest of the day. Anyway, we were at the peak of the dry season, so we did not expect any unfriendly weather patterns. We could see deep but not Equatorial-dense forest along the side of the hills and also on the valley side on the left. This was not a natural valley, simply a continuation of the rolling hills. It was surprising; the density of the forest and height of the trees, instead of giving a canopy overhead, were more or less large sprawling bushes, shorter trees, and tall grass covers in the forest landscape on either side. The landscape was more compatible with the Sahel region with deeper ever-green trees and bushes rather than tropical or sub-tropical fauna.

The lack of tropical and equatorial jungles was most likely due to excessive logging, clearing lands for rubber plantations, large areas of palm groves for palm oil and coffee plantations. We could see the changing faces of forests. Yet Africa is vast, and it can accommodate many more plants and trees in exchange for logging. The advantage was that these plants are cash crops, but the logging was a once-in-a-lifetime event. Once the trees were felled, and logs removed, it kept the ground bare, at the mercy of the elements, leading to erosion and desertification.

On the other hand, planted trees regularly contributed to the country's economy, creating jobs, protecting soil erosion, and saving the diamonds from being washed away. The downside was the changing pattern of lifestyles of many forest dwellers. They moved or faded away by the process. Antelopes were common in these types of vegetation, but we were not lucky to see any until now.

Having driven for two hours at a stretch, we planned to stop, looking for a hospitable place. Suddenly, the big wide, tarmacked road ended, and we were left with a narrow red dirt road that could barely accommodate two cars passing each other. I was not expecting such a drastic change. The forest was dense with evergreen trees, and it reminded me of the roads in Kailahun.

The young lady traveling with us was Mrs. Joseph's relative from Monrovia. She came to Kailahun to attend family festivities. Now she was returning home with us. I was happy. I learned that she was a high school teacher. She was the one who relieved us of our agony. This stretch of road was unpaved, untouched because of strong opposition from the local villagers and the chief. The surface alluvial soil was rich in diamond oars. Local tribes' livelihood depended heavily upon diamond mining, and they did not want to lose the source of their income. This unpaved part of the road was about a four to five-mile stretch; then, the route became tarmac again. That was a big relief. But for the first time, we saw monkeys, baboons on the tree, and a couple of duikers. She said one could see many more animals in this patch than in the surrounding forest. You can see ever-elusive desert leopards, wild pigs, and even West African short elephants, which had been seen in this part of the original stretch of the express highway. She said that most likely unused food thrown by the people was the reason for attracting a few more wild animals. One could see several walking tracks going inside the forest on both sides of the road. Our guest traveler pointed out that these were the tracks of people going inside the region for diamond mining, panning in small water pools, and digging into the soil.

It took just about twenty minutes to cross the so-called primitive part of the highway. As we got out of the unpaved jungle section, the road was back in its form. We broke into wide, open, and breezy road, the sun shining over our heads. Felt like we were in a different country altogether.

We arrived at the town of Voinjama at the northern edge of Liberia, close to the border of Guinea, just about four miles away. It took us about two hours to get here from the time we left Kailahun. It was a busy crossroad for trade in the country. Truckloads going in and out of Guinea and Sierra Leone, mainly carrying produce and timber. We stopped near a gas station. We came across several Europeans or white people going about their business; the majority were Peace Corps, VSO, Swedish NGOs, and a few Asians were in and about. As told by our guest teacher, the local people were either Mandingo or Lorma tribes who were predominantly Muslim. This had to be a relatively important place with heavy traffic. The central plaza where we parked was also the main bus station, connecting the rest of Liberia with the region.

We had plenty of supplies and decided to have our first snack break. The team of Mommoh and Sister Thomas also gave one flask full of black coffee and another black tea. They also packed sandwiches with various fillings. We all shared and had an open-air picnic. We did not need to stock up with anything else. I asked Mommahdu to fill the tank with gas, oil, and water.

The local houses were concrete buildings with corrugated tin or fiberglass roofs. The small town had an air of vibrancy that I was not expecting. Not surprisingly, I had very little or no knowledge of Liberia as a country, and even less about its economy and people. We left as soon as we finished our tiffin, and Mommahdu had done all the filling for the car.

We were on our next leg of the trip. Our next stop would be Zorzor, on the highway. We would be touching Bibita and Zaema, two large villages that were a little off the highway before we arrive at Zorzor. Should we have time, we might stopover in one or both. We were aiming to be in Monrovia before the sunset by late afternoon. Zorzor was about an hour and a half drive from Voinjama.

We left Voinjama on our way to Zorzor. We had been driving westward, and now we would be traveling directly southward by the river St Paul. As we proceeded on the highway, the surface was excellent, smooth and wide, and there was plenty of space for emergency stops. It was nearly 10.30 am, and we had a long way to go. We started to notice changes in the pattern of vegetation. We came across tall cedar trees, occasional mahogany trees, and mango trees more akin to tropical green forests, as opposed to what we had been noticing until now. We found relatively sparse bushy, low to medium height, tall grasses, more Sahel, or sub-Saharan vegetation as we drove along. One thing was common, coffee plantations, miles of palm trees, and coconut trees, which were also embedded in the cleared forest land. Rubber trees were not imported; Liberia had its indigenous variety, which became a substantial foreign exchange earner for the country and the economic support for the development of Liberia at that time. Liberia produced more natural rubber than the rest of the world together.

We passed Bitiba village to our left and immediately after a couple of miles south, the town of Zeama. Both of them were known for their agricultural wealth, especially wetland rice. We had planned to stop there but refrained from it due to the time constraint we had. Soon we arrived in Zorzor town of three thousand plus people. The highway passed through the city. We were in the business part of the town. It was a main agricultural product distribution and trading center. As we were entering the town, close to the market square, we found vendors selling varieties of fruits, including mangos, bananas, plantains, pineapples, avocados, cassava, coconut, green coconuts, papaya, etc. All the vendors were well supplied and looked happy and healthy. Again the lady guest passenger, who had been from time to time, our tour guide, said, "This town is well known, regionally, for good quality treatment provided by the 'Lutheran Hospital.' Excellent overall services provided, including training and supporting healthcare staff. More or less comparable to the Nixon Memorial Hospital in Segbwema in Kailahun District in Sierra Leone. The Christian High school in Zorzor is highly rated for its high standard of teaching. This hospital is also home to The Leprosy for treatment and research. Our guide tells me that Zorzor is also the home of rural teachers' training school, known for its quality of training throughout the country."

The roads inside the town were not paved. They were dirt roads. Many stores in the town center were well supplied with daily necessities, staples, and even utilities. The number of trucks waiting outside the city center and the number of vehicles for passengers gave the impression of a much busier town than its population indicated. We noticed several open fields for various physical activities, including football, Liberia's national game. It was cheap, entertaining, and boosted the sentiment of competitiveness and fellowship. We stopped there for about fifteen to twenty minutes and headed to the next stop, Gbarnga, which was about a hundred and five kilometers from Zorzor. We could make it in three hours on the highway on a good day like this.

After having some tea and refreshments, Mr. Joseph, his wife, and our guest, the de facto tour guide, had their lunch, we set out for our next stop. It was sheer luck and coincidence that the lady who wanted a ride to Monrovia with us was friendly and articulate, clearly and intelligibly. She was well informed about the country and had traveled from Monrovia to Sierra Leone on several occasions. The most significant advantage of her company was that she spoke good English and was a high school teacher. She did not mind talking; she was delighted to speak all along the journey to Monrovia, speaking about the places, people, business, traffic, roads, cost of living, and politics; you name it, she had the information. We could not have been luckier on this tour.

The drive to Gbarnga was smooth and essentially uneventful. There was much more traffic, cars, Lorries, and small buses on both sides of the road. The highway was busy with traffic. Honking was not uncommon, which could easily irritate western drivers. But drivers were generally courteous.

I noticed the changing pattern of the trees. We were traveling through the reserve forest region. The highway split the hills to make its way. Taller, denser forests on the hills were accessible. Also noticeable were tall grass bushes, bamboo-like plants, shrubs, and bushes on the roadside. There were also extensive plantations of palm oil and coffee by the side of the road. We were traveling southwards along the St Paul's river, zigzagging a couple of times. We arrived at Gbarnga at 2 pm. We had plans to stop and check for oil, gas, refreshments, and stretching.

Gbarnga was perhaps one of the first five higher populated cities in Liberia. The lady, our guest guide, said its population was close to ten thousand; locals were primarily engaged in agriculture and produce. One could see miles of paddy fields and large areas growing green vegetables. Okra was the dominant green we could see at street-side vendors. There were other vegetables too, in good supply. The town and town center roads were very wide, generally unpaved, but the road was well maintained. However, municipalities or the city council could have done a better job keeping the environment tidy. This was the first cinema hall I saw. Although some roadside cafeterias were reasonable, the houses and shops were all concrete buildings, and rectangular-shaped. Some buildings were two and three stories high at the city center, mostly with corrugated fiberglass or tin roofing as we had seen elsewhere in Liberia. I did not remember seeing any mud house dwellings so far. Maybe they were in the interior villages. The city had electricity and piped water, the lady guide told me.

Gbarnga was a well-populated town and connected by road to the rest of the country. It seemed it was in the geographical center of Liberia. St John's River, the town straddles, were also used for river transportation of goods and people. Cuttington College, a missionary university, was also famous for its Africana Museum.

Mr. Joseph, Mrs. Joseph, and our lady guide went to have a snack-break in one of the local roadside restaurants. I shared from my stock with driver Mohmmadu for the afternoon tea. Fortunately, the coffee in the thermos was still hot, which perked me up. Mommahdu was not much of a tea or coffee drinker. He had a bottle of Coke, which we were carrying. We walked around on the main street. It was hot and humid as we traveled southwards, closer to the equator. We met a young man who went to the same restaurant as Mr. Joseph and his company. He was a Peace Corps volunteer from Massachusetts, studying Labor Law as his major at the University of Massachusetts, hoping to become a lawyer. In his late teens, he said the Peace Corps had a significant presence in Liberia, involved in various infrastructure projects, teaching, and as social motivators. He also informed us that the Swedes also had a solid presence in the volunteering section and were doing an excellent job.

Generally, Swedes spoke English well. I would have liked to have met with some of them. I expressed my desire.

It was getting late. It seemed we had covered just over only half of the journey.

Our next stop was Kakata on the highway. Approximately one hundred and thirty kilometers from Gbarnga could take one and a half to two hours.

We were on our way to Kakata. It was a paved road with ample sidewalk for an emergency stoppage. Now we were going further south. The nature of the forest was changing more. It had dense, tall trees which were away from the road. We were traveling at a higher altitude. The road was being constructed over the rolling hills to see on both sides of the high road. It was a splendid view to watch gradual changing patterns of vegetation from the proximity of the express highway to as far as one could see. We traveled beside the St John's River, which would be our company until we reached Monrovia.

Our resident guide said St John's River was the primary route for transporting the liberated slaves from the south to the interior of Liberia. They found that the coast was inhospitable because of the physically impenetrable forest in the coastal region, with densely intertwined Mangrove trees stretched across several miles along the Liberian coast. They established several settlements along the bank up the river. At that time, it was still used to transport goods and people to and from the coastal region. Passenger service ships also ran regularly. River fishing of various types was also done on a vast commercial scale. Most of the rivers in Liberia were reasonably navigable for most of their length of the course till the Guinea border. The other river parallel to St John's was St Paul's, which was to the east, also one of the primary transportation routes in Liberia. Most of the Liberian rivers are were navigable, used for varieties of transportation to and from the coastal region. The view of the St John's River and the rolling hills was spectacular. Usually, it was safe to drive, but reckless drivers at times made driving on this road a little dangerous and challenging.

Extensive rubber plantations were noticeable as we were getting closer to Kakata. We skipped Totota and Weala, two other towns en route to Kakata. However, our guide wanted us to stop, but we advised against it because of the time constraint. It took just under two hours to get to Kakata from Gbarnga.

Kakata is a populous town where modern Liberia meets the tribal and traditional interior. It was nearly 5 pm, sunny and cool as we entered the town. The roads were all paved with some dirt roads in the outback of the town. Locals told us that the population was over twenty thousand in the mid-sixties. Kakata had a vibrant downtown and city center. We felt like having a stretch. We discovered a Lebanese cafeteria and snack shop. Lebanese were masters in preparing dainties and cheesecakes. I entertained everyone with some goodies, cheesecake, and drinks. I was happy with my mug of native Liberian black coffee. Kakata was a trade center and the center for education, intellectual and political exchange. Looking at the traffic and people's movement did give me the impression of an active business center. Stores were well supplied with essentials and groceries. There were more foreigners on the street than we saw in Gbarnga. Several young white boys and girls rushed in and out of the shops. They were volunteers of Peace Corps, British VSO, or Swedish NGOs. Moreover, Firestone and other International Rubber companies employed many expatriates, including whites. Firestone's Hospital was one the best tertiary care hospitals in the country, if not the region.

The city center was close to the banks of St Paul's river. A bridge connected both banks and spanned the river for traffic. We noticed the activities of river traffic from our cafeteria. It used to take much less time to travel by boat up and down the river and cost less. However, since the paved highway was built, the traffic on the river had not gone down much, but the overland traffic had increased many fold, thanks to rubber, coffee, and palm oil production.

Mining, including diamond ore, was mainly in the north and northwest part of the country, said our tour guide. The mining oars were transported primarily by railways, which ran from north to Monrovia at the Atlantic coast in the south, a free port. I thanked her for an excellent and interesting narrative.

We walked around the city center a bit, just to get a breath of fresh air and feel the pulse of the town and its inhabitants. Then, it was time to start the last leg of our tour to Monrovia. We set out at 5.30 pm from Kakata for Monrovia.

From Kakata, Monrovia was 75 Km away. It could take between one and half hours to 2 hours to cover this distance. We had to go via Paynesville, just on the eastern outskirt of Monrovia. There was a lot more traffic now on the highway. I expected our speed and progress would be reduced to some extent. The landscape kept changing. The road was wide enough to the edges of the forests. The denser vegetation from the road was further away. Primarily rubber plantations lined the highway and were more than a mile deep. Our in-house tour guide told us Liberian rubbers were native to Liberia, not transplanted from anywhere else. That was why the industry had no problem in expanding the areas for plantation; thousands and thousands of acres of land were used for rubber plantations. So too, the coffee. Liberian coffee was also a local brand, like palm oil trees. These did not need any special care or special nurturing. They just grew. Aside from mineral wealth, these plantations were the real backbone of Liberia's economic growth, making Liberia the wealthiest country in the continent, just shy of South Africa.

We stayed on course to Monrovia. The first town on the highway was Zinc, which we had to skip because of the time limit. However, our tour guide was always ready to entertain us with her wealth of knowledge of local affairs.

The lady said Zinc Township was an extension of massive Zinc mining nearby. Zinc was another mineral abundant in Liberia; it had been mined for over a hundred years, replacing the thatched roofs with corrugated zinc. This change in housing took over the continent by storm, literally. Zinc roofing offered much more superior protection. As the region's specialty, one could find various hand-crafted utensils in the town, but you could get them in Monrovia if you were interested.

So we kept going until we touched Careysburg. Our guide was very interested in talking to me about Careysburg, where some of the freed African American slaves were settled first in 1859. The climate was relatively cooler and less humid at a higher altitude, but mosquito-borne diseases were rampant and killed thousands, if not millions of settlers. The surrounding land was fertile and contributed hugely to the country's economy from agriculture alone. Its environment was scenic, with abundant freshwater abounding, making agriculture highly attractive and profitable. The city administration well looked after the city. According to our guide, it had between fifteen and eighteen thousand people during our visit. Despite being historically important and economically thriving, we had to skip the place for the next time, maybe.

We continued to drive south and southeast for our final destination, Monrovia. Our guide said another road to Monrovia via Harbel, which took an extra one hour. This dirt road, scenic, went through the deeper jungle and dense rubber plantations. Harbel was the Firestone Center, the largest tire manufacturing factory in the world. Herbal was connected to Monrovia by railway. It was a modern city by the Fremington

River. The International Airport served Monrovia, also the country's main airport.

So we had to skip the temptation of stopping over in Careysburg and taking the long but romantic road to Herbal to reach Monrovia. Our next destination was Paynesville, which was at the eastern outskirt of Monrovia. We drove straight to Paynesville. By the time we arrived at Paynesville, it was already 7.30 pm. Sun just had set. The twilight in this equatorial belt lasted no more than fifteen minutes because we were close to the equator. It was, in fact, an extension of the city of Monrovia. Unlike the British colonial towns, the roads were wide, straight, and built in a grid form. Most of the parked cars were dented. There were garbage dumps on the roadside, which I had not noticed throughout the trip until now. It was not just dumped, but huge heaps of garbage in places. I wish the municipal authorities did their job. The big department stores were well-stocked, decorated, and modern-looking. There was plenty of greenery and trees in the boulevard with vendors of varieties of stuff to sell. Food, of course, was the main item, and various types of fish were displayed in different forms and shapes. The town was built on several islands and lagoons, extending to and from the mainland.

Our lady guest hiker was not only the tour guide; she was also guiding the driver to take the right road to our destination in Monrovia.

At 8.30 pm, it had taken us thirteen and a half hours to get here from Kailahun, four hours longer than the projected time. That was fine. We had an enjoyable time, enjoyed the drive; Mohmmadu was an experienced, thoughtful driver and enjoyed the company of our guest traveler, who had an encyclopedic knowledge of her country and spoke pleasantly as needed, without being boisterous or boastful. Even if we had hired a professional tour guide, I do not think we would have been so entrenched in the travel as much as we had been with our traveling companion. I was personally amazed at a real oral documentary of our journey; it gave us a fascinating understanding of the country.

In another half hour, we were at our address in Monrovia. The house we went was a two-story building, more or less in the city center. There were a few stores on the main floor. The entire second floor was the living quarter of Mrs. Joseph's sister, a nurse, and her husband, a physician, who stayed here. We all went up.

Mrs. Joseph said, "Sir, perhaps you would like to spend the night here? If you prefer to stay in a hotel, we will search for one for you tomorrow. It has been a long journey, and you must be tired. As soon as you settle, take a shower if you wish and change, the dinner is ready." Mr. Joseph took me to my room. Splendidly furnished.

Then we went down to say thanks and goodbye to our lady companion. She was also waiting for me. She quietly asked me how much she should pay for the trip. I was taken aback and surprised, "Madam, you do not owe me anything. I owe you. I can't pay you back for all the touristic and academic information you gave me on the trip!"

I could not suppress my curiosity. I had to ask, "Madam, you said you are a high school teacher. May I ask you what you teach?"

She was silent for a few seconds, and said "in Grade 10 and 11, I teach Mathematics and Geography. I teach Geometry to be specific as part of Mathematics."

What a coincidence! Who else can teach better as an academic tour guide than a Geometry and Geography teacher? Do you know anyone? Not that I know of. I said, "I met the first and the best one. Thanks again for your help. You are awesome."

Mohmmadu, Mrs. Joseph, and our guest traveler all left to drop her at her house. Mrs. Joseph's brother-in-law, the physician, was out for his hospital duty for the night. I expected to meet him in the morning.

Chapter 40

WAKING UP FROM MONROVIA ECSTASY

"A dreamer is one who can only find his way by moonlight and his punishment is that he sees the dawn before the rest of the world

Oscar Wilde

The house was close to all amenities on Gibson Avenue, close to a supermarket, so I slept like a log. I got up early by the knock of the doctor. He woke me up and introduced himself as Dr. Salomon. He was a Medical Officer at the main Government Hospital. He asked me if I was comfortable and had slept well. Mrs. Joseph informed him about us.

I washed my face and sat at the dining room table as per my habit. He asked me if I would like a cup of coffee now or have it with my breakfast. Of course, I would be happy with a cup of pure Liberian coffee.

He laughed and said, "Sorry, we have only Liberian coffee. Even if you want Turkish, Arabic, or even American coffee, I cannot help you. Tea? Many varieties, but mostly Indian and some from China."

I had my wake-up coffee shot. We quickly got ready to roll. I did not know which way.

Dr. Salomon said if I would like to go sightseeing, he would be happy to show me around. "Of course," I said. "Perhaps we would ask my driver to drive us around so that you will be free to speak."

I asked if the lady teacher who came with us from Kailahun would join us. He said we had to contact her and find out her plans for this long weekend.

"I will leave it to you then, Dr. Salomon, to check up on her." Soon we finished our breakfast and were ready to roll. Dr. Salomon, Mr. Joseph, Mommahdu, the driver, and I were prepared to leave. Mrs. Salomon told us to wait. She came down and said to me that Sister Thomas from Kailahun was on the phone. I was not expecting it but not surprised either. I went up to speak with her. She asked about our trip, how we were doing, and reminded us to be careful and safe. She also said it would be fine if I wanted to stay a day or two longer. She had spoken to the doctors at Nixon Memorial Hospital, and they were happy to cover for me. In last night's news, she also mentioned that they talked about two Lorries having a head-on collision on the same road, with serious damages to both the trucks. She did not say what happened to the drivers or anyone else. No one came to Kailahun Hospital. Mr. Bochari, the Police Super, was not informed either. She just wanted to tell me to be careful while driving. I felt relieved that we were not involved.

Hailie Selassie road was the main artery going from west to east of the city, with major business activities.

All the major roads in the town were paved, wide, and most of them divided by a boulevard with trees, some sculptures, and landscaping to keep them looking beautiful. This road continued to the northeast as United Nations' drive. Some of the boulevards could do with some nurturing, and others needed complete redecoration, replantation, landscaping, and rebuilding. The buildings were all concrete or wooden with flat concrete or corrugated zinc roofing, generally in good repair. Some of the houses were not well cared for in the side street. Roadside garbage dumping was an eyesore, especially when considering Africa's second most prosperous country. With a bit of civic responsibility and help from the municipality, the environment would look better and be healthier. The traffic was heavy, congested with trucks, buses, and private cars, very expensive cars; some looked like they were factory-fresh.

People were generally courteous but always in a hurry. They were running somewhere, maybe nowhere. Everyone was running, more or less. Honking seemed to be one of Monrovia drivers' favorite passions or past times, but no one minded. I was in Monrovia; I did not see any expression of abusive behavior by drivers or demonstration of road rage. A similar situation in any North American city would undoubtedly be riotous, and one would have been "honked" at, even for a good reason.

The twin tower of Monrovia was famous for its "Twin-feature," right at the city center on both sides of the main road. Ducor Hotel on one side and EJ Roy memorial building on the other made them very impressive and the center of Monrovia's high-end social, political, and financial activities. Next, we passed by the Capitol building; an expansive, majestic building, the Seat of the Central Government of Liberia. We had no time to take a tour, nor were we allowed without a permissible reason: Well-guarded and well-protected building. Finally, we drove past the Capitol-by-pass, which took us close to the University of Liberia within the Capitol circle, which was more than a hundred and fifty years old, and gained full university status in 1951. Large impressive campus; we had just driven past.

The Executive Mansion was the Living quarters of the president of Liberia. President Tubman built it in 1944. Huge six to eight-story tall, semicircular building. The entrance was decorated with several Liberian artists' sculptures depicting Liberian rural and urban life. The President's car (whichever he wishes) could be driven on the elevator to specific floors where he resided. In case of emergency, an underground tunnel was connected with his living quarter by elevator to a militarized speed boat, so that the President could escape from anyone's watch, straight from his bedroom, on the boat, via a tunnel, which would take him to the well-guarded, fortified Fort. Depending on the situation, President could be hushed away from the Capital by the speed boat straight from his bedroom, in his Executive Mansion. This "highly-guarded secret" was public knowledge. I wondered how many had the luck to see the James Bond-designed living quarters of the President of Liberia.

Dr. Salomon suggested that it was worthwhile just to look in. So we did. We drove slowly past the Palace and savored the grandeur of the fabulous Liberian Castle.

We stopped at the Monrovia National Museum at Broad Street. It was an old building well-suited to house the old and new relics of the country. We spent about fifteen minutes scanning a native Wooden Mask exhibition. One could spend hours exploring the colonial and pre-colonial history of Liberia and West Africa, for that matter.

It was time for lunch. We stopped by a cafeteria close to the museum. The restaurant catered varieties of food. I was happy with the Liberian Chicken Burger, small banana cake, and coffee. They all had their food of choice. We started to drive at a snail's pace. Fueling stations in this part of Monrovia looked brighter, cleaner, and had less traffic and no honking.

Close to the museum, we passed by the Temple of Justice, the Supreme Court of the Government of Liberia, and many other governmental Administrative offices. An impressive multi-story structure and structural marvel created and built by an Italian Company.

Then we drove eastward to the Freeport of Monrovia, where the real free Monrovia started. I found several churches of various denominations; Church for Jehovah's Witness, The 7th day Adventists, Church of Freedom Hall, and many more.

Freeport was the main artificial port of Liberia, which made the life of initial settlers bearable. Goods could be imported and exported through this port, adding wealth to the new growing nation. Rubber, iron, copper, and edible oil were shipped, imported mainly petroleum. I just wanted to catch a breath of air of such an important place in liberated, independent Liberia and that of African history.

We started to trek back home on United Nations Drive by the sea. So many prominent buildings, company offices, government offices, hotels, casinos, shopping centers, etc., gave the vibration of a thriving economy. We could see the sprawling compound of the United States Embassy at a distance. All the side streets were jam-packed with parked cars and other vehicles. Vendors crossing, people busy walking fast, no time for anyone, just going, running and going! There were lots of mopeds, three-wheelers, but we could not find a cycle being ridden or parked anywhere. Very few children walked on the road or close to places of interest. Finally, we were back on Hailie Selassie Street, practically the main thoroughfare. We were now a few minutes away from home.

We arrived at Dr. Salomon's house at around 5 pm for afternoon tea by British standards, but close to dinner time for the American ideal. We had coffee with cakes and biscuits, not cookies. I thanked Dr. Salomon and Mr. Joseph for spending the whole day with me, touring around the city, which is much more exciting and educational than a paid tour guide. It seemed I was fortunate on this trip to Liberia to have had excellent, eager, and knowledgeable people make my trip more than it's worth.

Having rested for an hour, it was just before 6 pm. Dr. Salomon suggested we take a short visit to his hospital, the main Government Hospital for the city. A two hundred-bed hospital with almost all modern facilities, technologies, and specialists. Most of the doctors and staff were expatriates—several Indians, Americans, South Africans, and from neighboring Ghana and Nigeria. Liberia did not have its medical school yet, which Dr. Salomon hoped would happen within a few years. Dr. Salomon, himself a Liberian, was trained in Lebanon. We walked through the Emergency Department, which was very busy, then through the general outpatient area. Most of the units were open. This was 6 pm, and the Outpatients and Emergency departments were in full swing. I knew that these working hours would not happen in many colonies. Regular activities finished by 2 pm, except the ER, which remained open.

Dr. Salomon explained hospital activities finished by 2 pm. It opened up again at 4 pm for private patients for specialists. Doctors worked till 6 to 8 pm, depending on the bookings. This may be the trend where the private practice was allowed in government facilities in a free—market economy at its peak performance. Hospitals and treatment in Government Hospitals were free for citizens but could be used for making money.

After returning home, we visited a nightspot to get the flavor of nightlife in the swinging city of Monrovia. In the city, there were many nightclubs, which catered to people of different socio-economic classes. Finally, we went into one frequently visited by expatriates, whites, and many Swedes.

I am not a drinker, but I like the nightclub environment. The music, the glare, and the glitzes. People dressed for the privilege to be a part of the party. Happy and romantic music in the air. Today a Swedish group was performing. We met Dr. Remy Rasmussen, a volunteer with a Swedish NGO in Liberia working on a school renovation project for eight months. Professionally, he was an Archeologist, just having been awarded his Ph.D. from Umea University. I invited him to join us for a drink, which he accepted. We got talking about his time in Liberia and all that.

I told him we would be returning to Kailahun the day after tomorrow.

Remy was flamboyant, energetic, five feet seven to eight inches tall, yet gentle, polite, and soft-spoken than the average Swede. I asked him what made him come to Liberia. Aside from helping to renovate the school, he was also involved in curriculum review. It was OK to learn about American History, but the native history, culture, habits, social structure were all out of bounds from the school curriculum. "While doing my voluntary masonic work, I can study and learn about sub-Saharan tribes, their uniformity if any, and uniqueness." He pondered that even though some tribes originated neither in Sahara nor in Africa, he was excited to let us know about his time here. Dr. Salomon tended to agree that some African tribes may have originated in the Middle East or even further east. I thought this was an interesting fellow. I took his contact phone number and said, maybe we could meet here again tomorrow, a little earlier. I gave him my contact number, Dr. Salomon's home phone number.

They were civilized in the nightclub, indeed a whole world of difference from the last two days. Nevertheless, it had been as enjoyable, if not more for the exuberant atmosphere, at this nightclub.

The Club was warming up, the music and dancing were becoming flashier, louder, and faster. We did have a change of pace and mood away from which we lived for the last two days. As soon as we entered the house, Mrs. Salomon told me that Sister Thomas from Kailahun called again to check and let me know my operating list had been moved to Thursday because Wednesday clinic would be hectic.

"Good Girl!" I said. At least the anxiety of uncertainty at work was well-taken care of. Thanks to Sister Thomas and rest at KDGH, Kailahun District General Hospital.

I felt comfortable at the "House of Salomon." I did not feel the need to move out to a hotel room, nor had the energy to shift for one night only. I was immensely enjoying the company of the Josephs and Solomon's. The plan for tomorrow, which was Monday, was to walk around the local shops and watch people and traffic go by. Momodu had two days of tiring driving, so he would take it easy as much as possible. We planned to return on Tuesday, leaving in the early morning. We would take the same road as we drove on to get here. After a light dinner, I went to bed to wake up early in the morning.

Today Dr. Salomon volunteered to drive me around for shopping. I just wanted to have a feeling of business activities. Most malls, superstores, and specialty stores were along Tubman Boulevard by the waterside to the Freeport region. Shops of all sizes and shapes with varieties of local and imported merchandise were available for the delight of Monrovians and visitors. In addition, the museum had its local handicraft store. A special exhibition of art and crafts of various regions of

Liberia was currently on. This was an excellent time to explore local handicrafts.

We decided to drive to Duala Market, where varieties of tribal handicrafts were sold, an attractive place for tourists. Indigenous handicrafts, which included curving varieties of woods and stone for various ritual masks, metal jewelry, basketry from palm leaves, drums, traditional musical instruments, handmade clothes, and robes, were sold there. Also, ladies' clothes, varieties of long and medium dresses, native-made materials Africanized with African prints, but essentially were following European principle, for designing women's clothes, which I saw in Monrovia. So finding authentic tribal designs in the outback markets may have been more possible and likely than large departmental stores.

There were several excellent cafeterias along the seaside. Dr. Salomon chose one to have a relaxed lunch at. Liberian dishes were a mixture of freed blacks from the west to local West African mix. The menu made my head spin. I ordered a Chicken Peanut Soup, which was thick spicy gravy mixed with varieties of Liberian Spices, peanuts, peanut butter, and pieces of chicken with a fritter on the side. Dr. Salomon ordered fried eggplant, which was stir-fried eggplants with meat and shrimp on a bed of boiled rice. He had a glass of Heineken, and I stuck to a pot of green tea. We did enjoy the lazy lunch and decided to walk into the market area. It was close to our house in Paynesville; mountains of fresh green vegetables, okra, aubergines, cauliflowers, banana, pineapples, and many other tropical fruits all looked very new and sold in bulk. We were also within walking distance of Paynesville's red light market. So we started to walk to the red light attractions. It was indeed a sprawling market for vendors of all trades and descriptions. As expected, garbage clearing was a massive challenge in a busy, crowded place like this. We had experienced the mountains of roadside garbage waiting to be collected. It was an eyesore and choking to one's breath. The Market area was very lively, active, and noisy, precisely what one expected in an actual marketplace.

Then we headed for home in Gibson Street.

I took Dr. Salomon to the nightclub in the evening, where I promised to meet with the Swede. We took a table. Soon came Remy with a lady beside him. He introduced her as Susan Herdrickdottir, another Volunteer from a Swedish NGO. She was from Stockholm and also working on the same project. She was a final-year Physiotherapy student in Stockholm. I invited both of them to join us. I do not drink but enjoy company with those who savor their alcoholic beverage. So I ordered a bottle of Coke, and they made their selection of drinks.

I spoke to him about our bumming around the city, various shopping plaza experiences with two farmer's markets, and our plan to leave the next day for Kailahun. We planned to leave no later than 7 am.

'Oh!' said Remy, "we will be going to Voinjama tomorrow, close to the Sierra Leone border. I asked if he would be driving. "No!" He said, but they would be taking public transport, which was also leaving around 7 am from the city center. He asked which route I would be taking.

I said we would take the longer route via Garabanga, and we would stop over in Harbel just for sightseeing, which we missed on our way in due to time constraints. So I would be going through Vionjama anyway; I told him he could come along with us if he wanted. We would have space for two because Mrs. Joseph would not be returning with us.

Both of them were happy. Dr. Salomon gave him his home address and direction. He had given them his phone number the day before. They promised to be at the address just before 7 am. Since we had to have an early start the next day, despite mesmerizing atmosphere and beautiful songs and much more attractive looking beautifully dressed ladies, I was reluctant to leave this enchanting atmosphere, but we had to go. I guess Remy and his friend wanted to hang around a little longer. He said their apartments were virtually ten to twelve minutes' walk from the Club. We said goodbye to each other and met tomorrow morning again.

By 6.30 in the morning, we were ready. Mohmmadu had already checked the car for gas, water, and tire pressure. We could roll any time. Mrs. Joseph would not be traveling with us. She would stay behind with her sister for a couple of weeks more for a soon-to-be arranged family gathering. That left us enough space for our new Swedish friends. We all had a light breakfast. I noticed both Remy and Susan got out of a car and waited in front of the building. We went down and invited them in. Without much celebration, we picked up our stuff and set out on our long journey to Kailahun. It was just 7 am. We bade farewell to Dr. and Mrs. Salomon for their excellent hospitality, which I would like to return, should I get the opportunity.

We were on our way to Harbel, which was just over an hour's drive from Gibson road. We stopped at a coffee shop and stocked up with supplies, drinks, hot coffee, cakes, Lebanese dainties, varieties of sandwiches, and some Liberian bread with spreads. We were set for the next twelve to thirteen hours. I did not expect to stop anywhere. Dr. Salomon warned me that the night traveling on the highway might be a little dodgy, especially in the northern part, since many criminals, especially the diamond smugglers and the diamond runners, traveled that route. Hijacking of cars, trucks and other vehicles did happen. Government and Private companies were extra vigilant for criminals and hijackers.

Dr. Salomon was kind enough to inform Vionjama police about us, the car license plate number, and the names of all passengers. In addition, Remy and Susan needed to inform their respective embassies of their travel plan. These were some extra measures. Except for senseless, reckless, irresponsible drivers, traveling in Liberia was generally safe.

We arrived in Herbal. This area was the rubber capital of Liberia. As I understood it, American Harvey and his wife Isabelle Firestone, in 1926, established the rubber industry, which grew to be the largest rubber plantation in the world. They set up the Firestone rubber company, which was famous for its quality products worldwide. The roads were all paved in the city. Well-posted street lights, beautifully decorated and landscaped streets, the main road was divided by a central boulevard, beautifully planted and landscaped with attractive shrubs, bushes, and trees. There were many expensive-looking shops and offices. The City was by the Farmington River, which carried many river traffic and trades. The Famous Farmington Hotel was also a sprawling resort-type accommodation by the river. We passed by the Liberian Institute of Topical Medicine and several International Banks, Business offices, offices of some other rubber companies, and big multistory apartment buildings. Most cars were American-made; huge trucks, station wagons, Jeep Loredos, Intercontinental, and a few Volkswagens were spotted in the street. Unlike other big cities, driving and parking practices were very civil. No garbage dumps by the roadside were visible, unlike in some other parts of the country, especially Monrovia. People walking and crossing were primarily white. Few blacks could be seen. Being an international company, their employees were also from International stock. To my surprise, we met a few Japanese on the street. I guess that was to be expected.

Dense, tall rubber trees had replaced the Tropical evergreen forest close to the curb. Scores of "Rubber tapers" were at work, avidly tapping away. We tried to take a short walk inside the rubber forest. A narrow dirt lane as access to the tree for the tappers, we took that lane. Trees were big but not as tall as the canopy trees. We hired a guide to take us into the forest. He told us these were natural Liberian forests that had been widely grown on thousands of square kilometers. The trees could live as long as one hundred years, but the average productive life was six to twenty-five years. He scooped a rubber ball from the collecting bowl and gave it as a gift. I was delighted to receive the gift.

We returned to the car and were on our way to our destination. One thing that surprised me was the variety mix of ethnic people in Liberia, despite this being the homeland of Blacks.

We talked about the extensive ethnic mix of people in Monrovia compared to Freetown or Conakry in Guinea. In addition, the country's wealth and business opportunities attracted entrepreneurs from in and outside of Africa, i.e., Lebanon or India and the western world in general. Remy got interested and said there were around seventeen to eighteen African tribes so far known living in Liberia. That was not counting the freed African slaves from the US, Barbados, and Nova Scotia in Canada.

He continued to talk about the ethnic mixes in Liberia, yet individual tribal identity remained well embedded in the population.

It was interesting, all the way en route from Kailahun to Monrovia, wherever we stopped, we had no problem communicating with people of any social level, be it a bank manager or a baker's boy. They all spoke English well enough to make sense. On the other hand, outside Freetown and the western region, only educated people spoke English; the rest spoke Krio, which is a variety of broken English. In the provinces of Sierra Leone, ordinary people spoke their language only. Some spoke Krio. It was not uncommon to see local people unable to speak or understand people from a neighboring village who happened to be of different tribes, so they spoke a different language.

Remy said, most likely because of the freed slaves who built up the country and the overwhelming socio-economic impact of Firestone made Liberia more uniform on the socio-economic front. Without the ability to communicate, understand, and to be understood, there would have been no progress. Schools, colleges established by the Government, major religious establishments, and big companies dotted the country, treaded in English. I am not sure if that is good or bad, but it certainly influenced Liberia's prosperity. Another critical factor for linguistic harmony was the dominance of Christianity. Eighty-Seven (87%) percent of Liberians are Christian. Highest in all West African Countries.

Remy and Susan traveled extensively into the country's interior from north to south and zigzagged from east to west. He said roads were mostly dirt roads but generally motorable. The road connections improved because of the fast-growing rubber, palm, coffee, and cotton industries.

Houses in the villages were mainly rectangular concrete buildings with corrugated tin or fiberglass roofing. Rarely did we see circular mud houses with conical thatched roofs. Instead, we saw the traditional African circular mud houses mostly in deeply forested regions, off main tracks. Of many activities, one priority of all NGOs and agencies of the World Health Organization (WHO) was to provide potable water. Most of the villages had communal Deep-water tube wells. Electricity was reasonable in big cities and towns, subject to frequent outages because of lacking maintenance. The discovery of oil and natural gas certainly would enhance public services, infrastructure development, and would add to the country's economic fortune, and at the same time, the quality of life of all Liberians.

In this long journey, we planned to stop every couple of hours for stretching, have some drinks and snacks, and mostly give some relief to Mohmmadu, the driver. The road was moderately busy, primarily trucks and passenger-carrying buses. Finally, we planned to stop at Gbranga, which would take about two and half hours. But, we could make it, Mohmmadu said.

Without any problems, we arrived at the city center of Gbranga. It was 10 am now; we all got out of the car and stretched. We parked in front of a hotel. Mr. Joseph had to make a phone call to his wife. He got her on the phone from the hotel reception. She was happy to hear but distraught because we left the packages of food and drinks they had prepared for the journey. It was too bad and disappointing, but he told them we managed. As we had our morning coffee and snacks, we set out for our next destination, Zorzor, about two hours drive from Gbranga.

Zorzor was a nice, clean, and relatively quiet place, yet a significant distribution and academic center for central Liberia. We arrived in Zorzor right in two hours. By this time, it was mid-day. Susan said one of her friends from Sweden was working here at the hospital as a nurse's aide but was working full-time as a nurse in their children's ward. This was one of the leading agricultural distribution centers for central Liberia. Aside from the Lutheran Church hospital, they had a major Leper colony and the Teacher's training college being located in Zorzor. We stopped near the fruit and vegetable market, got out for a stretch, and again had water, coffee, fruits, and sandwiches.

In fifteen minutes, we were ready to roll again. Our next stop would be Vionjuma, just shy of a two-hour drive. That would be the last planned stop before crossing the Sierra Leone border. As we were about to leave the town, we saw a young white lady standing by the roadside. Susan shouted, "That is my friend from Stockholm!" We stopped. Susan quickly got out of the car and shrieked and hugged her, asking her what she was doing here. She said she was dropped off by the hospital transport to catch a bus.

"Where are you going?" She said, "Hoping to go to Vionjuma for the same gathering they will attend. The next bus be here in half-hour."

We offered to give her a ride since we were all going to Vionjuma; "would you like to come with us? We can open the third-row seat, which will be more comfortable than a bus ride," Mr. Joseph said. So we opened the third seat in the back. She was happy to get a ride. Susan and her friend took the back seat. Mr. Joseph and Remy took the middle seat, and we set off for the rest of our drive.

"Dr.!" Remy said," I entirely agree with you about your curiosity about the Jewish origin of the Temne people. They believe that they came from modern-day Israel. Many of their social practices resemble that of Jewish heritage.

"It was Prof Porter Senior who first gave me the idea of Temnes being of Jewish heritage. I kept looking at the physical features, their skin color is certainly not as dark, generally smooth, and they are of medium built, unlike Hausas or Mende. They have been the main traders in West Africa. Temnes are convinced that they originated in Ancient Israel; they migrated to Ethiopia from there to the Malian empire. Their migration continued to Jalunkandu Empire in modern-day's eastern Guinea's high plateau of Fouta Jalon.

I was happy to hear from a professional archeologist who agreed with my thoughts.

Ramey continued, 'A large contingent of Israelites moved out of Israel. The Igbo Jews of the same tribe in Nigeria practiced the rights and rituals of Judaism for millennia. They claim to be one of the lost tribes. Aside from the Ethiopian Jews, there are many ancient tribes scattered throughout Africa that practice Judaism and claim to be a lost tribe of Jews. These tribes have been practicing Jewish rites for thousands of years, unlike the North African Jews, who are more recent settlers or converts. Jewish migration in ancient times all over eastern and central Africa and concentrated settlements along the banks of the Niger River is well known. Temnes may have been one of such tribes that spread along with Sierra Leone, Guinea, and Liberia. As an Anthropologist studying Judaism both ancient and modern, Africa is not only fascinating, but its role in shaping the continent's psyche can be the work of several lifetimes."

We entered Voinjama. It was 2.30 pm. We went straight to the central Mosque, where Remy and Susan's friends were waiting to pick them up. Susan's friend also went with them. I did not have enough words of admiration for these young people, sacrificing the comfort, security, and abundance of their home, taking the risk of life, maybe life on the line at times, to be volunteering for those who needed their help.

We said goodbye and thanked Remy for enlightening us about Liberia's tribal and ex-pat population. Especially the impact of Ancient Judaism in Africa. I did get some enlightenment and encouragement to pursue further research.

We left Voinjama at 3 pm for the last leg of our return trip to Kailahun, another three-hour trip mainly on the rough road on the Sierra Leone side. As we arrived at the border, we got the car checked, gas, air, and water all topped up. It was two hours of challenging journey ahead of us.

We were making progress very slowly but surely. This section was a dirt road but a well-maintained surface. It was already late afternoon. We stopped for ten minutes at Buedu. I had my last cup of coffee and biscuits. So far, it had been a tiring but exciting ride. We left Buedu for Kailahun. It was already dark. We started to encounter nocturnal mammals crossing the road. We arrived at Kailahun at 9.30 pm, fourteen and half hours from leaving Gibson road house of Salomon's in Monrovia.

I said goodbye to Mr. Joseph and Mohmmadu. As I entered, I found Sister Thomas, Ayesha, and Mommoh, my cook, all waiting for my safe return. I just wanted to take a shower and go to bed.

I said good night to Sister and Ayesha and promised to give all the exciting stories tomorrow and the next few days.

Chapter 41

BACK ON THE SADDLE IN KAILAHUN

"No man ever steps in the same river twice, for it is not the same river and he is not the same man"

Heraclitus

After having an exciting and adventurous trip to Monrovia and back to Kailahun, my mind was full of imagination, vision, various memorable events during this short trip, but eye-opening, heartwarming, and the rekindling of the senses just as well.

Sierra Leone and Liberia, both West African nations, were established by freed African slaves mainly from the USA, Canada, West Indies, and Britain, but the social, cultural, and economic growth and expression were vastly different between the two countries. Moreover, both countries' local governance was centered on "Chiefdom." Why then was the difference so striking?

Superficially, what I saw in Sierra Leone, the freed slaves who lived in the southwestern area of Sierra Leone and Freetown continued to grow up with their past white colonist masters. The freed slave did not go into the interior of the country to explore, to settle, or claim the country's wealth for themselves, but they left the colonists and Europeans to explore, engage, and develop mineral resources and agriculture to some extent. The freed slaves consolidated themselves as Creole or Krio, and grew up side by side with their colonial masters, and were engaged in various government bureaucracies and other public services, such as teaching, healthcare, government clerks, etc. Freetown was a safe harbor during the early days of settlement. Being the most dependable natural harbor, Freetown became the largest port in the entire Western part of the continent of Africa, handling millions of tons in export and imports.

On the other hand, from my reading and information from several well-informed Liberians, the freed slaves could not stay on the Liberian coast because of the vast stretch of dense impenetrable mangrove- coastal- forests and tropical forests on the shores and inland. Through the mosquito-borne disease, malaria, yellow fever, poisonous snakes, and difficulty in mooring their ships, the liberated slaves traveled upland into the country's heartland on a boat, sailing through various navigable rivers. They scaled the Liberian inland and established settlements along several navigable river banks. They had no colonial master. They developed their government, bureaucratic institutes, education, healthcare, and other infrastructure, becoming the first independent Black African elected democratic government, headed by a president, not a governor-general like the neighboring colonies. The settlers integrated well with a much smaller tribal population in Liberia, unlike Sierra Leone, which had several hundreds of tribes and millions of tribal people. A formidable task for integration. They created a government with a constitution in line with the USA, supported by the US in many ways, but not dictating or controlling its administration, national policies, and priorities.

The port of Monrovia was not a deep seaport. Most ships stopped over in Freetown, or Accra, then goods were re-shipped by smaller boats or on coastal land accesses to Monrovia or other Liberian Coastal towns. But after dredging, the port became much more extensive and suitable for large ocean-going ships. As far as tonnage was concerned, Freetown remained the largest port in West Africa. Interestingly, many ocean-going ships and shipping companies were registered under the Liberian flag. The port facility was limited than the port of Freetown. But a modernized facility and easy and hassle-free licensing regulations were why shipping companies were attracted to the Liberian flag.

After my visit, I felt the difference in the vibration and pulse between the two countries, as I noticed. Each country had its advantages and disadvantages, highs and lows, flats and crescendos.

Back to my daily routine. It was almost mid-week. I needed to go through the patients' records, do the outpatients clinic, and tomorrow full day in the operating room.

I sat down with Sister Thomas and Manager, Mr. Amara. With Sister Thomas and Mr. Amara, we went through the week's activities and plans.

I was supposed to be relieved of my duties and position in just a month, and they were all aware of it. I suggested that we prepare a comprehensive report of activities, clinical and administrative, and a proposal to review programs for the Kailahun District Hospital and the Healthcare system of the entire district to highlight what was working and which needed attention. Aside from these, I needed to report about the district's prison and school health services. I had just enough time to do all these. We needed to plan together to prepare a comprehensive report. They understood the requirements and priorities.

I had an eventful day, and I left for my quarters. Four days of exhausting trekking did leave much to reminisce about, more so today; physical exhaustion overtook my desire to daydream. I went into a deep sleep after I came back to my den. I had my lunch and changed into more comfortable attire.

At around seven in the evening, I was woken up by Ayesha, asking me if I wanted my afternoon tea or soon have dinner. I asked her, "What are you doing here?"

She said, "I have been waiting since five 5'clock to hear all about your trip to Monrovia."

"Why did you not wake me up?"

"I did not dare, knowing you must be exhausted. I brought my school work with me if I need to stay longer."

"Oh! What happened to Mommoh? He was here this afternoon, served my lunch."

"He is here; I thought you would like to tell me about the trip? All things that happened, various people, men and women you met. Would you like to go to Monrovia again? I want to hear the Monrovia story from you. Moreover, Sister Thomas told me you would be leaving Kailahun soon."

"Everything you said is correct! Of course, I would like to tell you my 'Monrovia Story,' but I do not want you to fall behind with your schoolwork. That is important," I said. I expect to finish my tour of duty in a month. I have a whole lot of work to do before I leave. But I will tell you the story, certainly make time. Maybe we do it over the weekend."

"OK!" She said.

I had my late afternoon tea and cakes from Mrs. Saad. I asked Ayesha to join me. She did. But I felt she was in a kind of dreamy world of her own. We finished tea. As usual, she checked on which clothes I wanted to wear tomorrow.

I did show her. She quietly took them with her to the ironing area. She brought them back nicely ironed, hanging on the suit hanger. She came and sat down beside me.

She asked if I would like to extend my stay in Kailahun for longer.

"I would love to do that, but I must go back to England to check on the state of my project and courses."

"I understand," she said, "Well, I better go now before Sister Thomas comes looking for me. She does get a little worried about me if I am not where I am supposed to be."

"Ok, Ayesha, thanks for your help. Have a good evening. I promise I have lots to talk about on my trip to Monrovia and my days in Sierra Leone. I will. Good night," I said to her. She left with some hesitation.

The following day, as I arrived at my office, Mr. Amara came with a telegram from the CMO, asking me to extend my stay by a month or six weeks since the doctor coming to take over from me would not be able to join as scheduled. He also said he would extend my stay by two more months, but I could start preparing to leave as soon as we had the date of Dr. Huda's arrival. "If you agree, please send a confirmation telegram. I hope you will agree," Dr. Boyel-Hebron wrote.

Mr. Amara and Sister Thomas sat down in the office and seemed to be happy about the extension. I said, "Now I have the opportunity to scout the entire district's healthcare services. That will involve visiting all the clinics, also some health centers in need of assistance, reported by The District Health inspector, the District Nurse, and the District Officer. It will delay my return to the UK, but I will be happier to study the district better and make a comprehensive 'Exit report' to the CMO."

What an interesting coincidence; less than twenty hours ago, Ayesha asked me if I would like to extend my stay in Kailahun a little longer. I said it was not in my hands, even if I wanted to. It seemed to me it would happen now, and it was in my hands. Due to my commitments, I could have easily said that I needed to return to London at the end of my contract, but I did not. I was glad that I would be able to give a better perspective to the government, be more critical and give a reflective assessment, and suggest a comprehensive plan for the future. After all, Kailahun was the furthest from the capital and had the dubious glory of being the "God forsaken" part of Sierra Leone. Intra governmental and bureaucratic Communications were not impressive, mainly because of a communication system, which needed further renovations and development. The government depended much on advises and reports from the local officers. It was not easy for the central government to give equal attention to Kailahun, compared to other districts, because of rickety logistics.

However, Kailahun was a vital district bordering two other countries and important trade routes that passed through this district. Sierra Leone was a newly independent country. Unlike French Guinea, its past colonial rulers were everywhere, where

French rulers abandoned the country overnight after Guinea was given independence. However, Brits continued to be present at every level of the government, helping the newborn grow. When I arrived just about a year after the independence, I was impressed with the orderliness, discipline, and decency.

In my mind, I was happy to take advantage of the extension to stay on for my reason.

But I must tell Ayesha when I got back home. It would be fun to see her reaction.

After I finished my hospital activities, I went back to my house. I changed and took a shower while Mommoh set up the lunch. Mommoh gave me his daily report on what the cleaners had done. What the gardener did, He said, the gardener was feeling thirsty, so he gave him a cool bottle of Guinness.

I said, "I do not drink. Did you have to go to the market?" "No!" He said we had enough at home because we offered our visitors. Guinness was the most popular drink among Sierra Leoneans.

At around 4.30 pm, Ayesha trotted in. She was carrying her school bag. I assumed she wanted to do some homework here. I was happy to see her happy face. She sat down and made my afternoon tea. I asked her to pour herself a cup with her favorite biscuits. She gave me the day's event in the school. The Principal, Mr. Jesudasan, and Mrs. Jesudasan, who worked as a senior teacher, always spoke to her whenever they crossed her path. They both were very kind people. I said, "Yes! I know."

Then I asked her if Dr. Boardman was her relative. "Do you speak to him from time to time?" She wondered who Dr. Boardman was. I said he was the Chief Medical Officer.

She said, even if he was, she did not know, but she would find out from her aunty, Sister Thomas.

"I thought you must have been speaking to him lately."

"Why do you think I have been speaking to him?"

"Because I got a letter from him today."

"What letter?" She asked. "What letter?!" She asked again. I kept quiet. "What letter?" She asked again.

Then I told her, "Only yesterday you asked me to stay in Kailahun a little longer."

I paused. Ayesha kept staring at me with a confused look.

"I got a letter from Dr. Boardman this morning, and he would like me to stay for a few more months."

"What?" She said, "Really? Really? I can't believe it!" She jumped from her chair, hugged me tight, and cried, "Oh! I am so happy. You will stay! Won't you?"

"Yes," I said, "I have so many things to catch up on." I asked, "Why are you crying, Ayesha?"

"I am so happy. I did not speak to Dr. Boardman because I do not know him, but I have been praying hard every day to God! Speaking to the God all the time. Can stay here until I finish school."

"You will finish your school anyway, even if I am here or not. You will, and I will see you finish your school."

"I have my secret reason for praying so that you stay here longer. My prayers have been answered. My prayer has been answered," she repeated a couple of times.

"Well!" I said, "Now you must tell me the secret. Tell me now."

"If I tell you my secret, it will not be a secret anymore. So I will keep my secret to myself", she said.

"If you do not tell me the secret now, I might leave early."

"Never! She said, you will not leave early, I know. That is for sure, I know, you will not leave early. It is the answer to my prayer to God. You will not defy the will of God."

"OK, Ayesha!" I said, "I am happy that you are happy."

She said, "Mommoh will fix your dinner. Tell me what clothes you want to wear tomorrow to work. I will make sure they are ironed properly." I did get used to her asking me every day. So this inquiry did not surprise me. I told her which ones. She went away.

All set in half-hour, she was singing. She did from time to time. Said she had to go back to their house and speak to her aunty.

She left happy. I asked Mommoh to walk her to their house. It was already evening, not quite dark yet.

The following day, just after I finished my ward round, Sister Thomas, Mr. Amara, Mr. Joseph, the Ambulance Driver, Mr. Mohmmadu, and the District Health Inspector all sat down to plan for my departure. I requested everyone to prepare their say to speak to the ministry in a single voice. But we had to make sure that the day-to-day activities needed to continue without any interruption.

Everybody seemed to be happy being an active participant. Mr. Amara, the manager said, this would be his first experience participating in a doctor's "Exit Report." Generally, the handing over report was mostly done verbally or a written report was prepared by the departing doctor to the incoming doctor.

I told them I would visit the Health Centers, Nursing stations, the major ones and address the Health inspector's concerns.

I said, "let us start with Pendembu next week. I will give the entire plan by the next day." In the meantime, Sister Thomas, Mr. Amara, the manager, Mr. Joseph, the Operation Theater, outpatient and ER manager, the district Health inspector all agreed to prepare their report for me to review and include in my report for MOH. Suggested Mr. Amara accompanies me for these visits and records the individual center's concerns, requirements, and suggestions in my "exit report.

Chapter 42
SCOUTING KAILAHUN

"The only man I envy, the man who has not yet been to Africa, for he has so much to look forward to"

Richard Mullin

Koidu was a notable town compared to the rest. The main road was very wide. The town was busy, the main road bursting with activities. Lebanese, Indians, North Africans, and locals owned various businesses and shops. Lebanese and Indians owned groceries and varieties of utility shops. There were several car dealers. I had not seen so many Mercedes, Audis, Range Rovers, Jeep Cherokees, 4X4 half tons concentrated as much as I had seen in this small town, anywhere else. But, of course, diamond and gold mining was the main attraction for people aggregating in Koidu.

The ordinary people's houses differed from what I saw in Koidu Paramount's chieftaincy, compared to what I saw in Kailahun. In Koidu, houses were mostly rectangular concrete structures with corrugated tin or corrugated fiberglass roofs. Some scattered round conical mud houses could be seen, mainly outside the town. The majority of people wore European attire, women wore traditional sarongs and blouses with headgear, especially going to work. But many wore European clothes.

Because of the international nature of the community, people from all walks of life, languages, religions, and cultures did get along well with each other. There were a couple of imposing mosques and churches in the town center, standing harmoniously next to each other. There was no favored culinary culture, as varieties of ethnic food ingredients were available. However, of all ethnic food, Lebanese stood out most.

Generally, I came to Koidu at the request of Lebanese businessmen to see a sick family member who was not fit to travel to Kailahun or the local doctor was not available. I got to know some of the families, especially with the help of Francis Saad, Mr. Saad's brother. The local hospital had a similar design but was poorer than Kailahun. I met the DMO of Kano District.

Six and a half feet tall, an Afghan from Pakistan, close to two hundred and twenty pounds in weight. He was in his early fifties. The Doctor was a friendly and polite gentleman. When I met him that was his second tour of duty. He had already spent three years, seemed happy, and expected to return for his third tour when he returned. He was there with his wife. His children were in Pakistan in schools and colleges, staying in Peshawar with his family. I spoke to him about my life in Kailahun and how I adjusted and got along with my work, which was a huge learning process, and I enjoyed it thoroughly. He asked me whether I would return to Kailahun again. My response, "I shall be happy to, but given a choice, I won't mind vacating the place for someone else to get the African experience." He did understand and roared with laughter. I was glad to appreciate his sense of humor. I did get on well with him for the remainder of my tour.

The roads in Kano, I thought, were the best-kept secret. Despite being unpaved, they were well constructed and maintained, especially the route from Koidu to Kailahun, then to the Liberian Border town of Baeda. Liberian roads were excellent right through to Monrovia, the Capital. The road went winding through the forest, and was wide enough for two cars or Lorries to pass, yet there was enough space for emergency stops by the roadside. Unlike Kailahun and Kenema, these forests were not dense nor filled with heaven-kissing large Teak or Cedar trees. Instead, there were sporadic, cultivated palm groves for palm oil, coffee trees; wild trees were bushes and not as dense as in the south. Since Kano was further north, it had sub-Saharan Sahel-like vegetation and a dry and cooler climate due to its mountainous terrain. Several rivers carried the rainwater down to the sea during the wet season. This run-off of rain did not help the alluvial diamond mining. Millions of dollars of diamonds beads were washed away by rainwater into the river, then into the sea.

I met Mr. Advani, an Indian diamond dealer, who hailed from my hometown, Calcutta, but his main business center was in Rajasthan, India. A very polite, soft-spoken, amiable gentleman was introduced to me by Francis. He maintained a diamond procuring office in Freetown and a small residence in Koidu whenever he came to Sierra Leone. Years later, I met him again in London in the house of one of my father's friends. Advani family had been one of India's wealthiest and most respected diamond merchants for generations, had businesses worldwide, including Antwerp in Belgium, Hong Kong, New York, London, and many more. I hardly spoke to him about diamonds, though, mostly about our Bengali lifestyle and Bengali culture and his respect for Bengali intellectualism. Nevertheless, any time I went back to Calcutta, I made a point to meet him at his Park Street mansion if he happened to be in town. The Saads also remained friends for years even after I had left Sierra Leone.

Mr. Saad confided that the road to Liberia was the lifeline for legal and illegal diamond and gold trading. Aside from other trading transportation, like timber, produce to Liberia took this road. Liberia had better infrastructure at that time, and the government was business-friendly. But generally, Sierra Leone's colonial rule was more efficient, bureaucratically organized, and less intrusive.

The business community wanted to build an airport or a reasonable-sized airstrip about ten years ago. Local people "violently" opposed that. There was a diamond in the soil anywhere one dug in Kano and the region. Local people did not want to trade their diamond-studded land for an airport, as to them, it had no value. The dispute lasted for a couple of years until the Merchant's Association eventually gave up the idea. An airstrip was built in Guinea, not far from the Sierra Leonean border. But apparently, it was not a very wise decision. The airstrip was used more for illegal traffic, including armed robbers, mercenaries, and human traffickers. Eventually, it was closed and leveled to the ground. Now they had to patrol the area to protect against robbers and mercenaries.

We then tried to keep the roads in the best shape for our personal and selfish needs. Anything else was a bonus. We kept hoping and reasoning with the government and the local people that an airport in close vicinity, whether in Koidu or Yengama, the other big diamond mining town, only five kilometers from Koidu, would bring prosperity to the region; everybody would be a winner in that case. We were also trying to improve our mining practices and systems to reduce the washing away of diamonds into the sea due to heavy rainfall. Another problem was excessive unauthorized, indiscrete logging, adding to soil erosion and loss of alluvial diamond deposits. A country was just waking up from the 16th century to deal with 21st-century problems without the help of technology and the support it needed. Diamonds are forever, for better or for worse. I felt like telling Francis.

This was a different world from what I had experienced in Kailahun and the rest of Sierra Leone. Then, it was just one hundred and twenty kilometers north, the same country, with similar people, except for the glitters of diamonds and the shine of gold.

Chapter 43
VISIT PENDEMBU

"All I wanted to do was get back to Africa. We had not left it yet, but when I would wake up in the night, would lie, listening, homesick for it already"

Earnest Hemingway

On a Thursday morning, with Mr. Amara, Mr. Mohmmadu, and the ambulance driver, we visited Pendembu. The road to Pendembu from Kailahun was only twenty kilometers; that road was the good part of the newly built east-west highway. We left at 8 am. I arrived in Pendembu just before 9 am.

The Sister in charge and the pharmacist had been informed about the visit. About 11 patients were waiting. I saw all of them. At the Clinic, No real serious clinical issues were present.

While Mr. Amara was taking notes of his observations, I said to add that we needed to improve our examination room, with an examination table capable of examining patients for gynecological conditions, bed-bound patients, and others requiring examination on a bed. I also suggested a need for an emergency bed for patients waiting to be transferred to hospitals to be kept under medical vigilance. The room needed to be clinical and have two beds and supplies required by the midwives for labor and delivery. The front porch of the health center needed to be widened, cemented, and covered. There were many small but significant changes to be made, which we listed.

The paramount chief invited us to have lunch with him at his residence, with his family. This regal invitation was to thank me for our services and my concern for his people.

As we arrived, there were whole lots of people near the residence. Finally, the Chief himself came out to welcome us. There was a young lady behind him, carrying a baby.

As we all settled down circularly on the floor, covered by an expensive carpet, the chief, whom I had met before who was educated in the UK and was appointed by the Colonial government as the Paramount Chief of Pendembu in consultation with local elders, introduced the young lady as his daughter. But he also asked me if I remembered the child.

I said I should, but not offhand. Instead, he reminded me about the frightful night when his daughter and the unborn baby were brought to Kailahun hospital with complicated labor. I immediately recalled the night, just a few days after I arrived, the fetus presenting with a prolapsed arm and the mother almost being pulseless. I could never forget the frightening experience I had that night in my life.

I thought I was going to lose both the mother and the baby.

The chief said, "You did not, you saved both of them, and here they are!"

I picked up the baby, patted it, and returned it to the mother. She was so happy with the gesture.

Then a large plate full of Jollof rice and cooked lamb pieces were placed at the center. At least six people sat around and ate the same dish while talking. Aside from me, the rest were the Chief's family, one of them was the baby's father. The other three were the chief's brother and two sons. We all conversed in English. Therefore, I did not feel unfit in the environment.

As we finished, three ladies came to pick up the dish. Then came another three with a bowl of water and towel. We washed and dried our hands.

Then came another large plate full of fruits. Bunch of bananas, apples, star-fruits, grapes, and many more, some of them I could not even recognize were served. I was following what the chief was doing. All half-eaten fruits were kept on the side of the same dish.

As we finished, the Chief led us outside. We all sat on chairs. The chief had arranged some entertainment with a native up-country dancing group. The ensemble consisted of musicians, drummers, cymbals, chimes, and famous face masks and dresses made from husks and twigs.

We were served with tea and biscuits as the last item. The entertainers continued with their performances. Their artistic performances were unique cultural expressions, which I had not experienced before in person as a real show.

As we were ready to say goodbye, the music and dancing had stopped, and the chief gave me a package as a gift. There were six iron pennies, which I had already seen and received from the Paramount Chief of Koindu. These were made from local cast iron twisted rods with flanges in one end, about a foot long. I had seen currencies of different countries of various shapes and sizes, including cowries, but these currencies were novel and intriguing. So I was delighted to receive those as a gift.

I thanked the Paramount Chief for his hospitality and the most memorable sending-off courtesy. I was grateful and said, hopefully, we would meet again soon.

We bid farewell and headed for Kailahun before it got too dark. It was a good day of very enjoyable, fruitful inspection and part social interaction, which brought the Paramount Chief and people of Pendembu closer to my heart. It would remain there for many years to come.

After a tiring day's visit to Pendembu, I returned to my residence. As usual, Ayesha and Mommoh were there waiting for me. Message from Sister Thomas: I had many patients to see the next day, just a mild warning to be early at the clinic.

It was a hectic clinic. There were four or five patients who came from outside the town. There were twenty-six patients, a few children, and a few pregnant women. The staff was well organized. We got through the clinic smoothly, and finished by 2 pm.

The next day was my operating day. We got in two patients from Guinea, and the other two were from the rural villages of Kailahun. So, we had to be prepared for in-patient beds for all four cases.

The operating sessions went well. The nurses were busy taking post-operative care. I went to see the patients at the end of the day. They were stable. I assumed those from Kailahun may be discharged home, but those from out of the country needed to stay at least for five days.

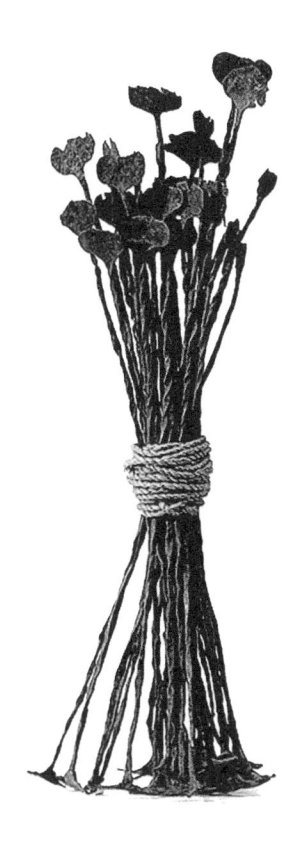

Kissi Tongi Pennies

Chapter 44
LAST CALL – GOING TO DARU AND OTHER UNTRODDEN TERRAIN

"I would rather be in the heart of Africa in the will of God, than on the throne of England, out of the will of God"

David Livingstone

We were in the middle of the second half of the rainy season. Traveling in the country dirt road was a challenge. Both Mr. Amara and Mr. Joseph advised against driving due to treacherous road conditions, mudslides, water clogging, damaged culverts, and bridges. But they agreed that people do travel, by foot, by public transport, government or private vehicle. So our ambulance could easily face the challenge of the anticipated dangers on the road, but not necessarily so. During one of our trips to Koindu, we remembered our ambulance got stuck in a mud-hole, right in the middle of the highway. We had to be rescued by a military lorry.

I would be traveling in a similar vehicle this time but with a more powerful engine and more helping hands. I planned to travel to Daru, do the necessary investigation, the in-depth documentation for inclusion in the final report, and recommendations for the Ministry of Health.

Then continue south to inspect several midwife stations. I realized that this couldn't be done in one day. We needed to overnight somewhere. Jiawei, Gaura, Bombohun, Gandohun, Nayandahun were all on the southern road to Baoma, a hundred and thirty kilometers from Kailahun. Considering the season and poor condition of the roads, it might even take two nights halting time to complete the return trek to Kailahun. I was not sure of places available for night halts.

I thought I would discuss with the district office, who had much more experience in all-season traveling in Kailahun.

So I went straight to his office. He was in a meeting but came outside. He asked me to give him five minutes to wrap up the meeting, and he would discuss it with me. It took a little more than ten minutes. Then, as all the people left, I went in.

I spoke to him about my plan to cover as many places, health centers, nursing stations, Health offices, malaria control centers, etc., as the ones I could visit before I leave. He knew that my contract had been extended by two months. I told him that because of the delay of my reliever to come, I had agreed to stay on and utilize the extra time to compile a comprehensive "Exit" report.

I did mention to him about night halts. He was not at all concerned. He said he would arrange with the local chiefs for the night halts. But, he said, he carried with him full camping gear, including a tent big enough for two adults. I had seen the British colonial officers in India, traveling with their whole entourage, with their peons, jamadars, cooks, housemaid, kitchen, and dressing room. Aside from that, they all carried their arms and rifles and Petromax for lighting for sports hunting. That was a big job. We also inherited some habits from our masters. Some were good, others not so good or outright bad. Under these circumstances, I was happy to follow what our masters showed us, such as adopting camping for official trekking.

Anyway, the District Officer was impressed with my plan to cover the entire district and was willing to help regardless. He would find out the road conditions, drivability and send messengers to all the stations I wanted to visit.

Then, I suggested that we would go in in our ambulance. Hopefully, that would make the journey. We could request the Commanding Officer of Daru Military Camp to borrow one military truck for the expedition. I had no idea what protocol we needed to go through. Once I got stuck on my way to Koindu in a deep mud-hole, one of the military trucks from Daru pulled us out of the hole.

The District Officer was interested in following it through. Accordingly, he would approach the commanding officer, Coln Bangura, whom he had met on several occasions, on various official business.

The next day he did get word from Coln Bangura, he would be happy to release one of his transport for one day for the District Medical Officer to visit their posts. We would get soldiers attending Kailahun Hospital from Daru Reserve from time to time, but I never had the chance to meet the Colonel. This was my opportunity of meeting a high-ranking Military Officer.

With his officers and my support staff, Mr. Amara, Mohmmadu, and his helper, we decided that the DO will travel with us and would leave the following Friday morning for Daru. I would carry out my inspection at the clinic and stay overnight at Daru Government rest house. After that, we may decide to stay at the base's guest house. This way we could avoid the possibility of camping.

I was pretty excited about the camping. But with the rainy season, it may be a little odd and difficult to set it up. The DO said they were pretty used to it and would set up the tent if needed.

I returned to the office. I finished examining a few remaining patients. Then, I explained my plan to travel down south as far as the vehicle could take us. I told Mohmmadu that we would drive only up to Daru, and then stay overnight in Daru. After that, we would travel by military truck. The driver was anticipating terrible road conditions in the rainy season. Mr. Amara would accompany the team. I told them I had no idea how many people would come with the DO, but I expected two. Mohmmadu said the ambulance could accommodate up to ten people. That was reassuring.

I returned to my residence. I rested. I had lunch and sat with my mail, correspondence, and reports I needed to prepare before my departure.

Late afternoon, time for tea. I got up. Washed up and waited for Mommoh to bring the tea to the dining table. As I was waiting, Ayesha came and sat at the table. I asked about the day in school, about Jesudasans, home works, etc. She looked happy and asked me about my plan to visit southern outposts in bad road conditions.

I said, "I can't wait till the dry season came. But, on the other hand, I said, with magic and prayer, you managed to extend my stay in Kailahun by two more months. So I have the opportunity of covering the entire district. For this trip, we will go by military transport from Daru. We spend the night in Daru. From there we plan to take an army lorry."

"I do not know any magic," said she, "but I did pray very hard so that you could stay in Kailahun, at least till the end of my school here. Anyway, I feel that someone in the heavens has been magnanimously merciful to me for two months."

She was happy, but I could see her tearful eyes, but I did not understand if the tears were for joy or sadness. Did not dare to ask any questions.

"Can I come with you?" She asked.

"I wish very much you could, but this trip may be full of surprises. Moreover, the District Officer with his staff will also come with me. We plan to stop in Daru overnight. Maybe for another trip before I leave."

I handed her over some tissues to wipe her eyes. She smiled.

As we planned, the entire team from the District Officer and my office, six people, set for our trip down south. District Officer decided to drive in his Jeep since he had to take the full camping gear. That took a lot of space in his Jeep. We had enough snacks and drinks to last for a week for all of us. Thanks to Sister Thomas, Mommoh, and Ayesha.

On our way out, we stopped over at the police station to ensure that the Police Superintendent was aware of our plan and itinerary. He was happy that we decided to take help from the military. Information from his people: the road conditions generally were not bad, or as good as they could be at the end of the wet season, but they could be dangerous due to mud-holes and very slippery streaks. I had to explain to the Police Super why I chose to make the trip now; because of my imminent departure, I needed to inspect and report as many health and nursing centers as I could gain access to.

He understood and said to contact him or the nearest police outpost in case of any trouble. We were reassured.

The road to Daru was not bad. The route we took was a part of East-West Vianini highway, a major newly built thoroughfare, which transported both passengers and goods from in and out of the country.

The distance between Kailahun and Daru was forty-eight kilometers. We hoped we would make it in an hour and a half, considering the road condition due to heavy equatorial rain. Therefore, we left Kailahun at 9.30 am on Friday, hoping to be there no later than 11.00–11.30 am.

The beginning of the drive was uneventful. After half an hour of driving, we were just about to pass Gaihum village. We could see the flag flapping over the village mosque, through the dense jungle. Just before crossing the village, a big truck loaded with timber had turned over on the side of the road. Almost all the logs had been rolled out of the lorry, blocking the road and making it impassable. The driver and his mate came out unscathed. Few people from the village were around to help. I checked both people in the lorry. They were both unhurt and had no external injury. They were stable and unshaken. I guessed, driving in these terrains, this may not be their first experience.

We asked the driver what and how did the accident happen? He said just five minutes before the accident, they realized that the break was failing. They tried to stop the vehicle. Put it in a lower gear. Not soon enough to stop the Truck. The Truck slipped onto the opposite side, rolled into the sliding drain, and tripped on its side. It discharged most of the logs it was carrying onto the road. It was overloaded as usual. These drivers were very expert in driving overloaded Lorries. They did get enough practice. It happened about an hour ago. Some passersby were going to inform the police or any authority they could, but none appeared yet.

Without any help, or real mechanical support, how would they be able to clear the road and put the lorry upright back on the road again? There was no rescue mechanism. The road was blocked entirely from both sides.

Our problem was passing and going through the scattered logs right on the road. Even with six adult males in our team, it will be impossible to move the logs and clear the road to make enough space for our cars to pass.

We had only one depressing choice: to return to Kailahun, abort the plan of visiting the Healthcare facilities, and reschedule the trip. It was just rescheduling for another day and reorganizing the whole project. Moreover, I had limited time to cover the entire district.

We all tried to roll over the logs gently, onto the side of the road. With our team and the crew from the overturned lorry. I asked the driver what would happen under these circumstances. "How do you get back on your feet?" "The police usually help. Informs the company office, in our case, the owner of this truck lived in Koidu in Kano district. He had several Lorries, many drivers, and mechanics working for him. Some passerby said he would inform the local police and the chief of Gaihum village, see if he could help."

As we planned what to do next, another lorry came from the opposite direction, carrying several young men. They were eight in number. All ten of them got off the truck and started to roll the logs onto the side of the road.

What we thought an impossible situation was cleared within a half-hour; with Chief's instruction, the village people cleared the road well enough for us to drive through. That was a huge blessing from heaven to continue as planned.

We were delayed by an hour, happy to forget the grim possibility of returning to Kailahun.

We arrived at Daru and drove straight to the government guest house, where we planned to spend the night—relieved ourselves of the stress of the unexpected and severe accident. Then we headed for the military camp.

Coln Bangura was a young man in his mid-thirties, full of energy. He had already been informed about the accident and road blockage on the Kailahun road. He asked whether he should send a rescue party if we all got stuck.

We explained to him our plan. He had prepared one of his personnel carriers for us to use. We told him we planned to spend the night in Daru since I had lots of inspections and meetings with the staff, aside from seeing patients, which I planned to do that afternoon. The Colonel was very respectful to both of us. If they did get sick, his people went to Kailahun District General Hospital. Over the year, I did see several of his soldiers. They were generally a happy and healthy bunch, as expected.

The District Officer was the highest-ranking bureaucrat of the District, representing the central government, hence was responsible for overseeing the activities of all government departments. However, the Police Super and District Medical Officer had a similar ranking, so we did not have to report to the DO but must work closely with him, making everyone's life easier. Credit or discredit for the health sector fell upon DMO, but they also got the heat or cool breeze from DMO's actions.

I had an excellent relationship with the DO. He helped me build the patient's waiting room. He made this trip possible, with the military helping us with personnel carrying vehicles. That was a huge help and made our adventure safer and more secure.

After we had some drinks with the Commanding Officer, I went to the Health center with Mr. Amara. We went into detail about the needs and redundancies of the center. We made a long list of things to improve the services and the facility. On general principle, we would upgrade all health centers' capability to serve, make the patients comfortable, even the minimum we could do for them in this environment.

Few patients were waiting for me to be seen. One was an older man in his sixties, who came in quite sick. Unfortunately, the family could not give much history. He was dehydrated and complaining of abdominal pain. I saw a strangulated hernia in the right groin, which needed emergency surgery as I examined him. Unfortunately, I could not do the procedure at Daru, as I was out of my den.

I decided to send the patient, using our transport, to Kenema Hospital, which was twenty-five kilometers away. Initial supporting treatment started with a drip, antibiotics, and mild analgesics to tide him over the journey. Mr. Mohmmadu would take the patient and return that same day.

We had lunch at the Government Guesthouse or the Inspection Bungalow as it was known here. Kind of late lunch. DO came back after his inspections. We spent the rest of the day chatting about life and living in Kailahun, the mysteries and marvels, the high points and low pits. To me, everything was fascinating.

The DO said that he would finish three years there by the end of the year and looking forward to a change. "So happy to return to civilization," he said.

"You are right!" I said, "Life is a challenge here. I learned a lot, adjusting, being creative and innovative, and getting things done by understanding who is best at what. It is even more difficult for me to fathom people's minds and intentions, having such a vast cultural and language barrier."

I did get along with the DO and his family very well indeed. He opened up during the chat, "You know Doc! Kailahun is a place officers are sent for punishment. I was sent here to check and document all kinds of smuggling, smugglers' touts, their supports, their enablers, and the local strongmen. These people are highly corruptible, and even the local mafias can corrupt God with their trickery and bribery tactics. Officers get hooked to free bottles of expensive alcohol, bundles of sterling pounds, and women from any social level, color, and culture. Still, the loneliness kills. Several officers, including medical officers and police officers, committed suicide. Loneliness, social isolation, alcoholism, debauchery were rampant, especially with ex-pat officers. It was an eye-opening experience for me. Yet, you want to live with your roots and culture at one point. Sierra Leone is my roots and culture," said the D.O.

He continued, "I wonder why they sent you to this God-forsaken place. You are new. They have not done a fair deal for you in your first ever job as a doctor in this country. But, we have lots to learn from you gentlemen about life and living."

I was sad to hear his feelings. He was a Sierra Leonean. He felt like an alien in his own country. But thinking deeply, he was born in Freetown, the colony's capital, where most of the social elite were white. First, he went to a primarily white school. Then, he spent decades in England for university and professional training. Then, he returned to Freetown, a bastion of white culture; blacks were blacks only by skin, but they were as white as one could be as a human being. That was his feeling at that time.

"Yes! You are right," I said to the DO. "There is no reason for the government to punish me by sending me to Kailahun. First, they do not know if I have done anything punishable. Because I have not done any noticeable thing. They do not know even if I can break laws. But sending me to Kailahun was a gift, an orchard full of flowers and vision. Flowers, some painfully thorny others, are heavenly mesmerizing. So their plan to punish me failed them bitterly; I flaunted them deceitfully, but life and experience in Kailahun came to me as a bouquet of flower and a gift from the Heavens."

The DO had a childlike stare at me and said, "You gentlemen are different."

Colonel Bangura invited us for dinner at his officer's mess. He introduced both of us to other guests. After some pleasantries, we settled down to the actual business of enjoying the dinner.

God only knows how many courses there were, but I tried every offering. A mixture of European and Creole recipes removed the monotony of European gourmets.

To end the dinner; Coffee, cheese, and a shot of Quantru uplifted the experience close to heaven. The Colonel said, "we have the honor of receiving two important guests from the district administration; we feel proud of our guests. I hope you all have enjoyed the evening." We bid good night to the Colonel and his guests and returned to the Government guest house.

The following day, we got up and got ready for the next part of our trip. A full breakfast was ready, courtesy of Colonel's kitchen. We both enjoyed the breakfast.

Mr. Mohmmadu had returned from Kenema, dropping the patient at the hospital. They had loaded the military van with our supplies. Only Mr. Amara would come with me, the DO, and his one-office help. Aside from the driver, two other military personnel would also travel with us. So we were well supported and secured.

We planned to stop first in the village of Gandohun, second the village of Goma, third the village of Nyandehun, fourth, the town of Folu, which was slightly off the track. Finally, on our return, if time permitted, we would stopover in the town of Bombohun, which was close to Daru but slightly off the track.

The road was just as muddy as expected in the latter half of the rainy season; we had to run a very tight schedule. Nevertheless, the driver said we could make it to Daru by early evening if the road condition were fair.

In all the villages I met the midwives, I looked at their working conditions and living quarters. I tried to understand how we could help. Of course, there were lots one could do. But in these very rural conditions, it was better to understand what the health worker was missing and what she felt would let her work better.

We also met all the village Chiefs appointed by the Paramount Chief. I tried to hear from them about the conditions and what needed to be done.

Invariably, the main request was to improve the transportation services and improve the roads. I found many personal vehicles, Jeeps, Land rovers, etc. This was an agriculturally rich area. Their riches had been significantly improved by cultivating manual and mechanical production of "Palm Oil." The palm oil industry contributed a large chunk to Sierra Leone's GDP. It had a characteristic odor. One could get the smell of palm oil or "Yellow Gold tree." I remember the exact smell on the train from Euston station in London as I entered the train. A pungent odor. I did not know what it was. I did not dare ask anyone. I wondered how I would withstand this strong unfamiliar smell for the next five hours until we arrived in Liverpool to catch the Mailboat.

As the train sped out of the platform, the strong odor got better, but it lingered on even after we came on board the mail boat Apapa. I got the same smell that I experienced in Daru and the countryside. Then I discovered that palm oil was widely used for cooking and in many health products, native medicines, body massages, and beauty products. So the odor I got on the train to Liverpool was people's body odor and the same odor I got in Daru, the nation's largest palm oil producer. That mystery was solved.

We made it to all our new destinations, including the town of Bombahun, on our way back to Daru. The road was terrible. The military vehicle withstood the challenge. We returned to Daru at 7.30 pm. Still enough time to go back to Kailahun tonight.

We thanked the Colonel for his hospitality and help by providing the transport; without the robust vehicle and even more robust tires, we could not have made this trip safely on time. We said we would go back to Kailahun that night and leave soon. At the guesthouse, we had plenty of snacks and drinks. The cook of the guesthouse made hot tea for us.

We reloaded our respective vehicles, said a quick goodbye to the Colonel, and set out for our trip to Kailahun. We left Daru at 8.30 pm. The road was good. Night driving was slower anyway. The roaming wild animals, not infrequently, stopped in the middle of the road. It could cause serious accidents for fast-driving cars.

We arrived back in Kailahun by 11.30 pm.

We made it after all these hectic bone-shaking, brain-churning trips which made all of us tired and seeking to jump into the nearest bed. DO had already arrived in his quarter. Mommoh and Ayesha were waiting. I told Ayesha, it was very late; you should have gone home a long time ago. She was also so sleepy. I did not try to discipline her more than she could take. It was very kind of her to wait so late in the evening. I told her to go to sleep in the spare room. I would let Sister Thomas know that she was sleeping over. I asked Mommoh to go to Sister Thomas' house and tell her that she was so sleepy that I did not feel the need to drag her out. She jumped into the bed and immediately fell asleep.

I told Mommoh to go to bed; I did not need dinner. The excitement of the trip distracted my feeling of aches and pains and another discomfort. Tomorrow would be a physically different, challenging, trying day. Fortunately, tomorrow was Sunday. I could lay around as long as I wanted.

Within minutes I was in a deep sleep.

It was 7 am on the clock. It was already daylight outside. I woke up but could not get up, so stiff was my body. I saw Mommoh bring my morning tea and biscuit. As I predicted, it was the day after that was most difficult. I struggled out of bed, staggered to the cabinet, and took out the packet of Aspirin tablets. Those were enteric-coated. I took two of them with my morning tea and biscuits. Slowly I got back to myself.

Ayesha was still deep in sleep. I did not wake her up. She got up a couple of hours later. Mommoh brought tea and cookies for her. She slowly staggered out of bed. She did not look well, not in her usual happy mood and infectious smile. Her pleasant raspy voice was harsh and hoarse.

I was worried. As she finished her tea and cookies, I asked her to come and sit beside me, which I had never done. I touched her forehead. It was hot. I checked her pulse. It was running faster than I could count. She did say she had difficulty in swallowing and had a sore throat. Felt very thirsty. I checked her throat. It was severely inflamed. She had acute pharyngitis, possibly viral.

I told Mommoh to prepare a couple of soft-boiled eggs, and make some thick vegetable or chicken soup. Not a problem; those came in packets. If she didn't like soup, we would give her a mug full of hot chocolate, my third love after coffee and tea. I gave her a couple of enteric-coated aspirin. I made her gargle with hot saltwater.

Then told her to go back to bed. We would wake her up when breakfast was ready. Like a good little girl, she went back to bed again. Mommoh was ready after one hour. Prepared the breakfast as I told him to do. I also joined her. Mine was hard-boiled eggs, toast, jam, butter, and my coffee.

She was looking better already. She slowly finished her breakfast. We talked about our trip. The incident on the road, tipped over lorry blocking the road, and so on. How back-breaking and bone-crushing a drive it was in the heavy military vehicle.

I needed to get back to my paperwork. So I suggested she rest all day, drink plenty of fluids, juices, gargle, and take the aspirin tablets, as I said, always with some food.

I said, "You can spend the day at my place or go back to Sister Thomas and your grandma, who can give better tender loving care, which you need more than me doctoring and telling you all my bizarre stories. Also, the chance of me catching it from you is very high. So, just for a selfish reason, I suggest you go to your bed, and your aunty and grandma take care of you. I will be checking from time to time.

"What do you think?" I asked.

She said, "Will you be checking there from time to time?"

"Of course, I will. Ever since my accident, you have looked after me beyond my expectation. This is my chance to return a minor favor. Of course, I will do it."

So I wrapped her up in one of my drapes and drove her to Sister Thomas. I told them about her fever due to pharyngitis, not malaria or sickle cell crisis. But, I said, Sister, we will check her blood tomorrow. We will wait a day before starting her on any antibiotics. I advised her to take Aspirin, Paracetamol, salt water gargle, Vitamin C or plenty of Citrus drinks, plenty of water, and rest, which she needed. I said I would stop by again in the evening just to check. Any worsening symptoms, please call me.

I was relieved that she would be looked after well and happy for the same reason.

I returned to my residence, started reviewing our notes, and planned to visit other healthcare centers.

Chapter 45
VISIT SEGBWEMA AND NIXON MEMORIAL HOSPITAL

"Still round the corner, there may wait, a new road or a secret gate...."

J.R.R. Tolkien.

I started my winding up the tour with the inspection of Pendembu, then to Daru and further southwest of the district. I still had several Health Centers to visit. We planned to see as many Nursing stations as we could en route to the Health Centers.

Monday mornings were usually busy days. It was busier today since I was away for the latter part of last week. First, we did the routine ward round and outpatients' clinic. Then I had to do an autopsy of a body, brought to the hospital moribund, but died a few hours after admission. So I did the autopsy examination; most likely, he died of active TB of the lungs.

As per government protocol, we had to take all sanitary and disinfection measures, OPD, and the morgue. That needed a bit of supervising. The district Health Inspector also oversaw the operation.

The day and rest of the week went smoothly, despite Mother Nature's blissful complement of a heavy thunderstorm, keeping on with the season.

My next inspection was scheduled: First to Segbwema Health Center, which was also the home of Nixon Memorial Hospital, judged as the best hospital in the country. The medical staff had been very cooperative and helpful during my stay in Kailhun. En route to Segbwema, we stopped over at Manowa village. We needed to cross the ferry on the river Moa, which would be a little rough in the rainy season to get to it. Then we stopped over at Jokubu village and met the midwife running the station.

Our destination was Manowa Junction. This was a kind of river port. Its population was close to three thousand. To get there, we needed to cross another river, a tributary of the mighty river Moa. Around eighty percent population of this region were Muslim and belonged to the Mende tribe. Manowa had a large mosque. Then we headed for the town of Banumbu, close to the boundary of Kailahun and Kenema districts of Eastern province. From there, we drove to Segbwema. This was a circuitous route we took to cover three different villages and the town of Banumbu at the edge of Kailahun and Kenema district.

We worked out this; it would take five to six hours before arriving in Segbwema. We left Kailahun at 7 am on a Friday. The weather was good. It had not been raining much. The road to Daru up to Manowa road was the newly built highway. No traffic problem was encountered on this stretch of the highway. Then the road branched out and turned to the left to the village of Manowa. It was 8 am now, sunny and bright. But as we proceeded on the branch road, it started to get dark, and daring through deep and dense tropical forests, very few sun rays could be seen. Mr. Mohmmadu had to switch on the headlights to drive at a reasonable speed. We could see specks of sun rays coming through the canopy. It was a dusty single-lane road, muddy and slippery. With the noise of the car, we saw a few animals crossing the road. This region was full of poisonous snakes. So, no matter what happened, we could not get out of the car.

We chugged along with Mr. Mohmmodu's clever and expert driving in challenging country roads in Sierra Leone. Finally, after half-hour of driving, we saw the light. The forest had been cleared for some reason. Well, now we were at the bank of Moa River. We had to take a ferry to cross. A couple of cars were waiting, a few people with scooters and bicycles with their loads were waiting to cross the river. The river was quite wide here but relatively calm. I hated to remember; my experience with ferries crossing rivers had been nightmarish. I prayed not to have a similar hair-raising and gut-churning experience.

As we approached the entrance, we waited behind two cars to take our position. One Guard came and spoke to Mommahdu and asked him to pass by all vehicles and be first to be loaded on the ferry. Again our "ambulance" treated us preferentially. The ferry was ready. Everyone got on. It was such smooth sailing. I was grateful. As we disembarked from the Ferry, a police officer stopped us and asked if everything was right. He said the road was much better from Manowa village to Manowa Junction. I thanked the policeman for his help.

We stopped at the village, met the midwife, and spoke to her working conditions. She was generally happy, with one concern about the shortage of supplies and not being restocked on time.

Next, I met the local chief. He could not speak much English. Mr. Amara became my interpreter. The Chief thanked us for coming to see their life circumstances for ourselves. The Chief expressed his concern about poor road conditions and requested me to do anything I could to help with bus services. His other concern was too many young people dying of snakebite. If we had a faster transport system, we could transport them fast enough to Kailahun or to Segbwema for treatment to save lives. Unfortunately, we couldn't get rid of the snakes. He said although the District Nurse and the District Health Inspector visited from time to time, he had never seen any Medical Officer visiting our village in his fifteen years of chieftaincy.

He thanked us and said that now that we had seen it, we would hopefully help. As we spoke in Chief's cottage, we saw a colorfully painted body, unusually dressed, even unusual for the Manowans. As we were leaving, the chief walked towards him and requested him to come and meet us. I started to walk towards him. The chief introduced him as the High Priest of the village and the only medicine man for them. "People from out of our village also come to see him. He is like God to us." The Chief introduced us to the priest. I greeted him with respect and thanked him for his services to the villagers. We bid goodbye to the Chief and prayed to continue good work with his people.

We said we would be in touch as it was less than half an hour's drive to Manowa Junction. It was an inland river port city. Fishing and river transport were important businesses and occupations of the residents. We had to cross another tributary of Moa River by ferry to go to the other side of the river, where the main town was located. Ferry crossing, although mentally stressful, went smoothly. The river was full but flowing, without tumultuous, turbulent current. This town was on the plain and not rocky. It was a major township in this region. Production of palm oil, fishing, and logging were the main activities. There were several Lebanese-owned shops in the city center. Nixon Memorial Hospital was close by. They had regular clinics in Manowa Junction and also at Banumbu. The government ran midwifery services, which were quite busy because of the size of the population and the relatively young age of working people.

I met the midwife; she was happy and got much help from the Nixon Memorial Hospital. But she also had a problem with supplies, which the District Nurse was supposed to oversee. So we took note of that. I was also told, due to sickness, that the local nurse had not visited them for months.

We had posted a sub- Inspector of Health for this region because of many industrial, business and river transportation activities. WHO was active for Malaria as well as other mosquito-borne diseases, and urinary bladder infection from a water-borne parasite called Bilharzias is, especially in the lower Moa Valley.

I also met the local paramount chief. He was pleased to see the doctor from Kailahun visiting his chieftaincy. Tucked in the Equatorial forest of southeastern Sierra Leone, it was quite a nice, healthy place, with many modern amenities, like electricity and some piped water. Finally, I met two young Peace Corps volunteers at the Chief's palace, working on a school project.

Then we drove to Bonumbu, just about a twenty-minute drive to the east. Moderate-sized town, not as busy as Manowa Junction. I met the Midwife and listened to all about her work. She seemed to be happy. We noted down the points she raised and planned to take them over to the District Nurse for her input. I also noticed several well-stocked grocery shops in the market square, most likely Lebanese-owned. The roads in the town were well maintained. I met the paramount chief just to greet him and made sure that he was aware we care about his chiefdom and would like to help it develop health-wise.

Any suggestion he might have would be dealt with seriously, with appreciation and concern. We made sure that the District Health Inspector and the District Nurse maintained their regular scheduled visits to assist the health care workers and listen to the people on their health concerns.

We left for Segbwema. It took an hour to get there. Part of the road was terrible, slippery, with waterlogged potholes on the street. However, once we traveled this critical and relatively unsafe part, the rest of the road was reasonable. We arrived at Segbwema at 1.30 pm. We decided then that it may not be possible to return to Kailahun that night, so we needed to find a place to stay overnight.

I went through all aspects of the Health Center, run by a nurse and managed by a pharmacist. Segbwema was a local business hub, terminal station for the railway to Freetown. The railway mainly carried goods, mineral oars, logs, produce, etc., and people of course. Therefore, it was safe to travel by train, despite slow and intermittent stops.

Brits gained huge experience in developing railway services in India. They appreciated the contribution of railways as a mode of transportation and as an effective administrative tool. In Sierra Leone, the railway line was built initially to transport heavy mineral oars, gold, iron, etc., then ferrying human passengers became an additional bonus. High-ranking British officials traveled in luxury in fully serviced, luxurious, private compartments. The remnants are still seen in Indian railways nowadays.

After I completed the inspection of the Health Center, I spoke to the Sister in charge and the Pharmacist manager took detailed notes. I had to see a few patients who had been waiting to be seen since this morning. Had I known, I would have seen them first, before I began my administrative inspection.

One lady with advanced pregnancy complained of shortness of breath and generalized body swelling. I examined her thoroughly. She had a twin pregnancy and other late pregnancy-related effects, like anemia, fluid retention, and shortness of breath. I gave her the necessary medical treatment and advised them to take her to Nixon Memorial Hospital since the labor may be complicated with twins. I also gave them a referral letter to the hospital. One older man had difficulty passing urine due to post gonococcal urethral scarring. Another lady with persistent urinary leakage had a large fistula of the urinary bladder draining into the vagina. Both of these patients needed surgical interference. They were referred to surgical specialists at NMH.

Then I went for a courtesy call to meet the doctors at Nixon Memorial Hospital for their help and cooperation throughout my stay in Kailahun, especially for looking after Mr. Mohmmadu, my driver, and his helper Mr. Boukhari after the accident. I met many staff, including Dr. Wheeler, the medical superintendent, a surgeon, who looked after Mohmmadu, and Mr. Boukhari at the Nixon Memorial Hospital. Dr. Wheeler was an Englishman from Stratford upon Avon, William Shakespeare's birthplace. We chatted about the hospital and its services, and some of the patients I referred to them. He remembered almost all of them. He admitted that patients referred from Kailahun always presented with an excellent medical history and documented physical examination. Those initial notes had been of tremendous help. I wish I could energize all my clinical staff to be as thorough, which helped manage.

As we were speaking, two young men entered. Dr. Wheeler introduced them to me as John and Kal. Both were third-year medical students from Birmingham University in the UK, spending three months in their elective program. I was happy for them. I said, "You gentlemen are fortunate to get this opportunity. You will learn so much here; your medical curriculum cannot come anywhere close to what you will experience, especially for your future career as a Physician. As I have said repeatedly, no text, no membership, fellowships, or multiple board certifications can ever match what you will get in your chosen three months. So I am sure you are having a good time and enjoying learning, which will be the most useful education of your life and life-long career as a Physician.

Then Dr. Wheeler asked me if I planned to return to Kailahun tonight; it was already past 7 pm. "Night driving is not so pleasant. Our guesthouse is vacant if you want; I will inform the staff to prepare the house for you and your team."

I had no idea what arrangement Mohmmadu had made for the night halt. "Yes! I shall be grateful if I can use your guesthouse for the night; that will be highly appreciated." Dr. Wheeler told Mohmmadu where to go. He said he would come to check after he finished with the students.

We drove to the Guesthouse. The housekeeper was expecting us. She took me to one of the rooms and showed Mr. Amara and Mommoh where to rest. She said the dinner was ready when we were. I was not expecting a full service. I took a quick shower. Dr. Wheeler was waiting in the lounge. He was happy to see us settled. He said he would not join us, expecting to go to the operating theater soon. For them, it was a 24-hour service to humanity. It was challenging at times.

"Too bad," I said, "this is our life; duty calls come first before anything else." I thanked him for arranging everything at such short notice. He politely said, "It is our pleasure. Please go ahead and enjoy your dinner; I will see you tomorrow after your breakfast."

He left. All three sat around the dining table, quickly finishing our four-course meal. I thanked the housekeeper and went to our assigned room. It was 9.30 pm.

I got up at 7 am. Both Mr. Amara and Mohmmadu were up already. I washed up, got ready, and took a short walk in front of the Hospital. At 8 am, our breakfast was ready. By the time we finished our breakfast, Dr. Wheeler had come in, sat down for a while, and joined us for tea. Real English breakfast tea. We both enjoyed each other's company. He asked me when I was scheduled to leave. He did mention meeting my predecessor just before he left. However, he did not have much professional interaction. The overlap time was too short.

In a month I will be leaving Kailahun, I said. That is why all this rushing about to tie up all loose ends and plan for the future.

I did tell him that I wanted to return to Sierra Leone, but I would be starting my research fellowship as soon as I got back to London, at Hammersmith Hospital, at the Royal Postgrad Med School.

"Hammersmith Hospital?" He asked me again. That was the best Hospital and academic center in the UK, if not in the west and the Americas. He admitted that he would like to spend some time at Hammersmith if he did get an opportunity. I was delighted and reassured by his comments.

He was there to see us off. I expressed my gratitude and thanked him for all his kind help. The two students, the Matron, and some other medical staff came to see us off by that time.

I left and started our return journey to Kailahun. This time we took the direct road via Daru. We left Segbwema at around 10.30 am and returned to Kailahun at 1.30 pm. The road was good; most of it was part of the newly built Vianini East-West highway. It was uneventful; the good thing was that we did not have to cross any river and no ferry ride. Yet there was no escape from a Bone-crunching ride on this part of our drive, but still bearable.

It was already Sunday afternoon. I needed to get ready for Monday and the remaining bits of my scouting of the District.

I returned home; Mommoh was ready with my lunch. I washed up, changed, and went straight to bed for a couple of hours. I fell asleep. I must have been exhausted.

I did not get up till 10 pm. Mommoh was waiting. He asked if I would like my dinner now. I said, "I am still sleepy; wake me up at 6 am tomorrow if I am not up by then."

I woke up at 4 am on Monday, bright and fully awake, ready to take the wheels. I helped myself with my morning coffee and biscuit while reminiscing the events during the trip and planning for the remaining inspections.

Monday morning, hospital outpatients were generally busy. Now the town was going through an epidemic of coughs and colds. There were several children and older people with the symptoms. Before prescribing any medications, one had to be very aware of the possibility of Malaria or Sickle Cell disease. An unmindful or careless slip may lead to disaster. Most of the common fever with coughs and cold could just be that. But one must think of other possibilities. Without hard-to-obtain expensive diagnostic tests, thinking, being an attentive listener, and examining the patient, healthcare could go a long way for our patients in this environment.

Most people knew if they were sicker or had sickle cell disease in the family, especially a close family member. However, because of the very high incidence of sickle cell disease in Africa, and the serious implication of the disease, some information about sickle cell disease and familial association were given in primary and secondary high schools.

The education department also introduced it in secondary and higher secondary schools curriculum. Government Public Health Education Programs also facilitated awareness, meetings with the villagers, and other critical groups. Generally, they do a good job. Awareness of sickle cell disease had been done reasonably well throughout the communities, which was a big help to the doctors.

Chapter 46

REVISIT KOINDU AND EASTERN PROJECTION

"I live with no excuses and travel with no regrets"

Anonymous.

Tuesdays were surgical days. I had some cases that went without any hitch.

I sat down with Sister and Mr. Amara to plan my next inspection schedule. First, we would visit Koindu, at the extreme eastern fingertip like the extension of Kailahun, part of Sierra Leone that jutted in between Guinea and Liberia. A strategically important part of the country. Trade and smugglers, especially diamond and gold, almost had a free run in this part. But those activities were on the check; thus, legal trading was given help by curbing hijacking, theft, and a terrorist attack on vehicles transporting goods engaged in trade and public transportation.

We decided to travel to Baidu, Komandu, then retreat on our way to Kangana to Lorlu; from there to Koindu. Baidu was a major outpost on the East-West highway to Liberia. These places all had Nursing stations run by midwives, except Baidu, which was run by a nurse and a midwife in a small cottage. It was a reasonably sized town, busy international road traffic, and a transport center. I noticed the city center was well stocked with shops owned mainly by Lebanese traders.

We left Kailahun at 7.30 am and arrived at Baidu at 9 am. At the eastern end was the end part of the Vianini highway, which was the east-west trunk road. We met the Paramount Chief of Kissi-Tonga Paramount-chiefdom, Baidu was the Capital. Being a well-stocked border town, a high volume of illegal trade, especially diamond and gold, escaped through this route. There were several locals accomplished in international businesses, I was told. One of the Chief's requests was to develop a well-supplied Health Center for the area at Baidu. We met the nurse and the midwife and checked the number of attendances and cases. I felt Baidu could have a health center for the region. A mosque, the kingdom hall of Jehovah's Witness, and the Baidu market added some sophistication to the town. Interestingly, I noticed many signs in French and some evidence of French culture I could catch in the grocery stores, along with standard loaf, basketsful of French Pain were also sold, which I did not notice before. It was not surprising that Guinea was just a stone's throw away; the rubbing of French culture was so evident.

We proceeded to the border town of Komandu. This was the last town on the Sierra Leone border with Liberia. The road to Komandu was challenging to drive, slippery, deep forested, and dark, like midnight. The Chief at Baidu was concerned. So, he let us have a few of his men accompany us to the village. We met the village midwife. The area had about fifteen hundred people. Travel was not easy inside Sierra Leone. The village could have had a better road. The local Chief told me that some English men (VSO volunteers) were soon coming to help establish Tube wells. That would be a big help for the community. The midwife had the same issues with supplies and delays. As soon as the roads were improved, these problems would be solved. Yet there was moderate-sized international traffic using this village. We noticed some nice concrete buildings, perhaps hosting their itinerant guests, carrying legal or illegal goods. It seemed like a good place to be inconspicuous and get on with one's business.

We backtracked to our next station, Kangana. It was about a thirty-minute drive from Baidu, the country road from Baidu. Not as challenging as the road to Komandu village. We had a nursing station run by a midwife. This was the capital of Kissi-Tongi Chiefdom. The population of the town and neighboring settlements was approximately ten thousand, whereas the entire chiefdom had twenty thousand people. I met the midwife. She needed a place to hang her coat; I discussed with the Chief, and he promised they would soon build one, expecting help from US Peace Corps volunteers. I was happy that it was already on the drawing board. This was mainly an agricultural area, with palm oil and palm oil industry, other produce, transported to Guinea, giving the village an air of self-sufficiency and prosperity.

After an hour and a half, we proceeded to our next stop to Lorlu, en route to Koindu. Lorlu was slightly off the main road, about half an hour to forty-five-minute drive from the town of Baidu. It was isolated in a way. That was why we made a point to visit and speak to the midwife who ran the antenatal services for the area. As we turned into the road leading to Lorlu, we saw acres of palm plantations on both sides, and the rest were agricultural lands. Not sure what kind of crops were being cultivated. As we came closer to the village, the road went into a deep equatorial forest. It became dark. Road surfaces were rocky but still drivable. We continued driving slowly. This was also known as snake country. We could see snakes crossing the road in the darkness. Mr. Mommahdu did not run over them until they were completely out on the roadside. I can't imagine how dangerous it must be for locals who dare to walk on these roads.

We did not expect such a deep and heavily forested road. It was early afternoon; we did not see any car or vehicle on the road. Eventually, we drove struggling into the village. It was a small village. I did not think more than five hundred people lived here. Most striking was several storages for palm seed and many factories pressing palm oil. We located the local chief and spoke to him about our visit. He was surprised but delighted indeed. He invited us into his house cum office. We sat and were served fresh fruits and tea. The chief said he had sent someone to get the chiefdom's midwife. Most houses were typical circular mud houses with thatched roofs, which we saw all over Kailahun in rural areas. The concrete structures were all palm oil pressing and processing factories. Palm Oil pressing was mainly done manually. "Our prices are much lower than the companies in Daru. We supply mostly to our neighboring countries," said the chief.

I met the midwife and asked all about her work and facilities. Like everywhere else, supplies and transportation were the main issues. "Road and transportation belong to another ministry, but we must be able to help you with your supplies. However, health issues are intimately connected with roads access, and drivable roads can only improve transportation. I would certainly make a strong case for you before I leave."

The chief was happy to admit that he had not seen any prominent officers from Kailahun coming to visit them ever since he had been the chief. But, I told him, "I needed to see the condition myself and speak to the people, and those providing the services, to make a meaningful plan for progress for the future."

I knew nothing about the local chief, but he spoke to me in English, and he appreciated our effort to help his community. He said all the "chiefs" would be meeting in Bo in two weeks for the National Chief's Conference. He would bring up the impact of my visit to his Chiefdom.

He said we were the grass root of society, and we needed help in a meaningful way. Therefore, he expected full cooperation and help to materialize all his projects.

Time to leave for our last stop, at Koindu.

The return drives to Koindu road were just as traumatic and bone-crushing as when we arrived.

We arrived at Koindu at 3 pm and went straight to the health center. We had a nurse and a pharmacist running the facility. I had met both of them before. They were friendly, helpful, cooperative, pleasant, and hardworking staff.

I should start the inspection straight away. They asked me if I would be returning to Kailahun tonight. If yes, they would bring the patients who were supposed to see me today. The nurse would reschedule for tomorrow morning if it was OK with me.

I said we needed to find a hotel room for tonight. "No problem!" She said. "We have arranged for you to spend the night at the high school. We have arranged for all your needs."

We went through the activity records, equipment, the facility, staff activities, number of deliveries, and number of direct referrals. They did get many patients since this was the only medical facility for several miles after crossing the international boundary, either in Guinea or Liberia. Many of them were runners for smugglers, but the Health Center did take care of any person in need.

I was told that the road from Kailhun to Koindu and the border was slated to be resurfaced and widened, considering its role in international trade. I would recommend a total reconstruction of the health center, with an increased number of staff members, at least one more nurse judging the importance of the facility.

The Chief was in Kenema. Too bad I could not say goodbye to him.

I told the pharmacist and the nurse, that we had enough stock of food, which we could use. But they insisted that I take my dinner with them tonight. So that was what I did. We all sat on the floor on a carpet. A huge plate full of Jollof rice and the chicken was served. We all sat around and started to eat with our hands from the same plate. We finished another plate before a tray full of fruits for dessert was served. We washed our hands in separate bowls.

The school building was only a five-minute drive. We went. The beds, the mosquito curtains, were all tidily arranged. I changed and immediately fell asleep. Mommoh and Mr. Amara slept in another classroom.

I woke up in the morning. Mr. Amara seemed to have already made hot water for my morning coffee on an open pit oven outside on the schoolyard. We all had our morning tea/coffee and snacks, which came packed from Kailahun. I felt fresh. By 8 am, we were back at the Health Center.

The Nurse and other staff were all there. I saw five or six patients waiting. Sister said a few more would show up. I started to check one by one. I needed an interpreter. None of the patients spoke English. The Pharmacist was my savior. Men with stricture of urinary passage and women with incontinence after childbirth were prevalent presentations. They were not sick but became social outcasts because of offensive urinary odor. I set aside one-half day in Kailahun, just for male urinary passage dilatation. During that session, I ended up doing four to eight dilatations. They needed to be dilated every three weeks until they could pass urine at a good flow and there was no more incontinence.

In the end, I managed to see all eleven people and advised them accordingly. So it was time to say goodbye to all the staff and wished them all well; I told them the new doctor would be in Kailahun in a month that would be when I leave.

We left at around midday. The road to Kailahun was shorter this time. Muddy roads did not help either; fortunately, we were not stuck in a mud hole, which would have been another disaster. It had not rained for a few days. The muddy road had been hardened. The drive was bumpier than average. We had a break for a "stretch' for ten minutes. I still had hot water in my thermos from yesterday. I quickly helped myself with a cup of life-saving coffee. The rest were happy with the water. We resumed our return journey and arrived back in Kailahun at 3.30 pm.

I had nearly covered most of the Health facilities, except I would make a courtesy trip to Koidu/Safadi in the Kano district, where I had several friends and patients.

En route, I would visit at least one Midwifery Service Center. Now it was time to start to compile the report. I asked the District Health inspector, Sister Thomas, and the District Nurse to write their part of the activities. I gave them one week to have enough time to integrate all observations and recommendations for the PMO or the Provincial Medical Officer and to the Chief Medical Officer.

I had to be ready to leave in two weeks if Dr. Ahmed arrived on schedule, although my extension was valid for one more month.

Kissi Tongi Pennies

Chapter 47

WAKE UP AND PACK UP, THE DREAM IS OVER

"Time is a circus, always packing up and moving away "

Ben Hecht

I had a good night's sleep. I got up quite happy and ready to start. I arrived at 9 am, and went straight for the ward rounds. A few beds were empty. There were no serious cases. After the ward round, I went to the outpatients' clinic. The nurse interpreter told me they expected twenty patients, maybe a few more later.

I was about to start with my first patient when the nurse asked me to see Mrs. Saad for a few minutes. I went outside, asked if everything was OK. "How about Mr. Saad and the rest of your family?" I invited her in. She was in a good mood. I had never seen her come to the hospital on her own. She had one of her female staff come from the office to accompany her. They walked from their house, barely five or six minutes away. Now she looked upset. She told me I never informed them that I would be leaving soon. It was only from the staff at the shop she heard.

I said I was just getting ready to leave, unsure when most likely in a month.

"Oh! That soon?" She said. "We would like to invite you to our home sometime this week. Let me know when is convenient?" She told me that Mr. Saad had gone to Freetown, and would return tomorrow. Would the day after tomorrow, in the evening, be OK for you?"

"I will make it OK for you, Mrs. Saad; that will be my pleasure."

Then she wanted to be sure if I eat beef or pork. She knew her Indian friends in Beirut did not eat beef. "That is correct, Mrs. Saad!" I said. "I do not eat beef if that is OK with you.

"Thanks, Dr., we will see you soon. Please let me know if there is any problem; you never know what is waiting for you, next minute or next day."

"Of course!" I said, "Yes, anything, any time indeed, can make us give up everything and attend the call."

She left. I got back to my clinic and started to see patients. It was 10 am already.

I liked Lebanese food, and their desserts were just heavenly. The rest of the working day went smoothly. At the end of the working day, I sat down with Sister Thomas and Mr. Amara to review our notes during our visit. Later, I sat down with Sister Thomas to meet with the District Nurse to understand her concerns. I asked the District Health Inspector to meet me in the morning on the next day. I wanted him to give me in writing about his needs and concerns. List all hot spots for

Health hazards, emphasizing excessive death due to snake bites. What would be our suggestion to cope with this problem in Kailahun and the entire south and southeastern part of the country? I needed to obtain more information on snakebite deaths in the country, their relative distribution, and the current government plans to mitigate this scourge.

The following day I met with the District Health Inspector again; and aside from many other concerns, I raised the seriousness of young people dying of snakebite and what we could do. His response was very philosophical. "Sir!" He said, "This is a snake country; the entirety of Africa is full of snakes. However, we have learned to live with it. We die from its bite, we worship snakes as our protector, some tribes even eat snake meat, and snake skins are a highly prized item when exported abroad."

"I agree with you totally," I said to him, "So! What do we do that the local people have the perception that more and more people, particularly the young ones, are dying due to snake bites? After these intensive and intrusive inspections, I started to understand how predominant snake bite was in this part of the country, almost like an epidemic, and how it affected communities' lives. The strategy had to be different, unlike when we killed mosquitos to control Malaria and other mosquito-related diseases. It was impossible to kill all poisonous snakes and other reptiles. Neither was desirable to make peoples' lives safer on the roads, lanes, byways, trekking paths, streams, and other waterways, in the jungle, or even at home from wandering killer snakes. The local chief's impression was that they saw more snakes close to the villages than before, ten or fifteen years ago.

"I am not certain of any agency specifically tracking snake population in this part of the world. However, having traveled the district and the region, I find extensive deforestation in the north due to unplanned and uncontrolled logging activities, the area's geography changing, and tropical forest regions turning into the Sahel. This "Shehelization" of tropical forests motivates snakes and other animals, those that thrive in rain-drenched, dark, humid, forested habitats, to move southwards, where they can still thrive, thus sharing living spaces with human beings. Unfortunately for survival, each plays against the other as adversaries.

"Anyway, our concern is to help people from dying due to increasing snake bites. I must think of a viable long-term strategy to suggest to the government without further upsetting Sierra Leone's beautiful environment and God-loving, simple-living people."

He was quiet and looked somber for the time.

He asked, "Sir! I do understand your concern. I had never had the opportunity to hear from your predecessors. Whatever you ask us to do, I will do my best to carry out the orders. Please tell us your plan and how we can start."

"It is like this. People say snakes are more scared of humans than humans are afraid of snakes. So, if we understand snake bites are mostly a defensive act, we need to be aware of not encroaching on snake territory. Generally, they will leave us alone. While working in the forest as a logger and scouting for forest products, many snakes live primarily on trees. It is challenging to stay away from these tree-dwellers knowingly, they can be the size of a thin pencil or a shoelace, or some are as thick as six to eight inches in diameter and up to twenty feet long. We had one scary moment when a twenty feet long eight inches wide snake suddenly fell on our car, at midnight, when we were on our way from Kailhun to Freetown, on court duty. It was wound around the branch of a high banyan tree. Trying not to miss its prey, it quickly unwound and took the last jump from the tree above, but missed its prey, falling on the roof of our ambulance. We were saved because of the ambulance. If I were traveling in my Volkswagen Beetle, the car and the passengers would have been crushed. So, tree-dwelling snakes threaten everybody, on or below the tree. We should ask all forest workers and agricultural workers working in muddy fields to wear thick full-body covering and protection for head and face.

"In some places, they use Phenol spray to distract snakes or light fires to do the same job. Perhaps they should carry devices, spray, or cigarette lighters that can act as a deterrent. Ordinary people walking on the forest road should have knee-high protection.

"I know to imply these ideas; one needs to establish a plan and provide funds to execute it. But, I suggest we start from the most vulnerable chiefdom in the southern part of the country. Once I have identified a problem, I always like to offer some solution; since I am at the grassroots, I have the opportunity to look at the issue closely.

"Importantly, it is needed to improve access and transport facility to the nearest hospital capable of treating snakebite cases."

He was happy that we discussed the HealthCare issue at length.

I also sat down one day with Principal Jesudasan and Headmistress Somali, discussing the school health program. They agreed to provide me with some of their insights, to probe and improve school health issues. But, again, lots could be done with minimal effort. All we needed was to help and work with each school administration.

The *"Exit report"* would be pretty extensive and exhaustive. I was indeed looking forward to completing and submitting it to the authorities.

Next evening as promised, I presented myself at the residence of the Saads of Kailahun. After that, I drove from my house. They were happy that I was not stuck in some kind of Medical Emergency, but that could happen at any time.

They asked me about my stay in Kailahun, the people I worked with within Africa. Condition of the hospital. When do I leave? Do I take the boat or fly out of Freetown? Where would I go? When was I expected to return? Would I be posted again in Kailahun for my next contract? And many more questions. It was Mrs. Saad who did most of the talking, as they felt at ease with my interaction, which was simple, friendly, and kind, "not like many other doctors," Mrs. Saad remarked.

I had no idea about the food, but she knew I was not a "beefeater." So we started with bits of fish fry and sliced thick flatbread. Mrs. Saad explained each dish, its content, and how it was cooked. Mr. Saad, from time to time, joined in the culinary discussion. The portions were small, but several dishes, and there were many. They had beautiful rice preparations, chicken, and chops, like flat beat up chicken meat, no bones, a similar dish of lamb meat with sprinkles of sautéed vegetables, and some mashed potato (I think!).

Then desserts started to come in one after the other. Mrs. Saad said that these were all Amal's specialty. She prepared Lebanese sweets, and cakes if not better than a professional chef. She said she would have prepared all these and many more for me. Her eye for decorating cakes was just out of the world.

Mrs. Saad then said she was sorry that Amal could not say goodbye to me when she had to leave more or less on short notice. She planned to spend another month in Kailahun. Too bad! I said I was away at that time. I also wished I had the opportunity to say goodbye to her. I hoped she was well and settled with her university studies, preparatory for entrance to medicine if I remember correctly.

"Yes!" Mrs. Saad said, "She asks about you in every mail and when we talk on the phone. She said she will come back to Kailahun again." I replied, "It is an arduous journey. I hate to see such a delicate, pretty young lady like Amal go through such torture."

Mrs. Saad said, "She is delicate and thin, but very tough and determined in her mind. Although I always fought with her when we were young at home, even our brothers were surprised by her clever tricks. Anyway, she seemed to be very fond of you and would like to see you soon."

I could not believe what I was hearing from Mrs. Saad. She was an Athenian Goddess, so stunningly pretty she was. She moved like a feather, and every word she spoke was a musical note. It still buzzed in my ear. Mrs. Saad was clear that Amal wished to spend the rest of her life with me. It came as a bombshell!

A bomb that scattered only music, flowers, joy, happiness, love, and a vision of a mirage, getting bigger and bigger, coming closer and closer. Was it a dream, mirage, or vision of the future? Yet a bomb is a bomb; it shattered one to pieces for better or worse, whether through your body or mind.

"Mrs. Saad! I am humbled; I can't believe what you are saying. What have I done to have such a blessing? In my heart, she is like a Goddess, not one with flesh and blood. I should be worshipping her!"

I do not know if I was thinking aloud.

Then Mrs. Saad said, "This Goddess wants to worship you for the rest of her life. She has seen you, spoken to you for nearly two months; she is clear in her mind what she wants to do. I hope," she said, "you will give it serious thought. I love to see my little sister happy. I will do anything I can do to help her. As you understand, I had to gather lots of courage even to bring these thoughts to you."

I said, "Apart from being the big doctor in the town, I have not told you anything about myself. You do not know much about me, my family, and my past, or what my future might look like. It may be full of sunshine or maybe the most dreadful dark, filthy dungeon."

She laughed! "Dr. Malaker, I am a woman, particularly an eastern woman; like me, you are more of a man of the east. We can see through people better than men. Whichever man comes into our life. Frequently it is beyond our control. Understanding the person and creating the best life together needs deeper thinking and foresight, but that is in our hands. I dare say we are more discretionary than a man in this case because it is so much easier for a man to leave one and get a new one if he fancies. So far, the women of the east do not have the choice. Notably, the children make us keep the bond going at any cost. Having watched you for more than a year, I can say, ahead is only sunny days, and maybe full of struggle, but sunny nonetheless. Even the dark dungeons will get lit, clean, and beautiful with heavenly fragrance, not that of hell."

It was my turn to laugh. I smiled and said, "I did not know you had such a vivid imagination!"

"Truly," Mrs. Saad, "My head is reeling; my brain is splitting, not shattered yet. I need to think before I can say anything. I will tear my heart to pieces if I can't see the light and walk away from the heaven you have brought in front of me."

"I am here for one more month. I will think and think, why can't I give up everything in life and hold this goddess closest to my chest? I am confused. I will be talking to you soon. If nothing happens, Mrs. Saad, I will indeed miss you very much as a near and dear friend. I do not know how ethical it is professionally to be a close friend of a patient."

She smiled and said, "never mind, sometimes you must follow your heart and not the brain." I said goodbye to Mr. Saad; he allowed us to discuss an important family matter, in which he did not want to participate at this point.

I drove back to my residence. It was 11 pm. Hospital days were busier than average. The news spread across the community that I would be leaving shortly, and a new doctor would take over from me. There were two issues with my leaving. One was familiarity. They wanted to be checked up, examined, or operated on before I left. The other more concerning was that this transitional vacuum may stretch up to four to six months before a full-time doctor returned. Only itinerant physicians, mainly from Kenema, would visit Kailahun Hospital twice every week during these periods. Not necessarily the same doctor made patients feel more or less abandoned and lacking in confidence. In addition, patients were not keen on surgical operations since the doctor carrying out the surgery would not be there to look after them in case of any problem or complication.

The theater was booked for all the openings for the next three weeks. However, we handled this situation very well with all the staff members' sound cooperation and active involvement.

As I was ready to start my clinic, a man from Mr. Saad's office came in one morning. He said Mrs. Saad was not feeling well.

If I could make time this afternoon after lunch, they would appreciate it. "Yes! I would," I said.

I returned home. After lunch, I drove to Mr. Saad's house. The shop and second-floor office were open. I waited there, expecting someone to take me to her. But in a couple of minutes, she came down and looked quite rested and happy. I asked her if everything was alright. "I was told you were not feeling well."

"Yes! I felt sick in the morning, but I did not vomit, and I am feeling better now. This happened yesterday also. I thought I needed to consult you."

I examined her but did not find much wrong, it could be just stress, or flu bug, or some stomach bug, must be bothering her. Anyway, she wanted to know my thoughts about Amal.

I was expecting it, more or less. If she did not bring it up, I would have. Deep in my mind, I did not want to lose Amal, but my conscience reminded me why I was here, where I must go, and why I should stick to my goal.

I told Mrs. Saad that my coming to Sierra Leone was by accident. I went to London to further my postgraduate studies and research. I had a scholarship for Cancer research. After I arrived in London, I was told the new lab, where I was supposed to be working, was not finished and that it might take as long as six months. They offered me a house officer's job until the facility was ready. I was planning to go back to India and work, where I was working before I came to London. By a stroke of luck, I met the senior-most officer of the Sierra Leone Government, who offered me a medical officer's position with a salary four times what I would get from my scholarship, and many other benefits. I said yes. He visited my hotel in two weeks, gave me the appointment letter, and told me how to proceed.

I discussed this with the Dean of the Medical school. He agreed and kept a copy of my appointment letter. Asked me to be in touch with them regularly.

Within two weeks, I was on Board MV Apapa for Freetown in Sierra Leone. I had no idea, no knowledge about the country, except my insatiable curiosity and attraction for adventure, which brought me here. The first month was very depressing. I did not know what I had agreed to do. But just the fact that was something I had never experienced, and this was new, kept me going. Eventually, I understood the people, language, and likes and dislikes. I got used to Connaught Hospital and the Doctors. That was a period of my orientation. Then I was placed in Kailahun as District Medical Officer.

Now the time had come to go back to my research and studies, which would consume four to six years of my life.

But "Amal" seemed to be another turning point. After that, I was not sure which direction to take. Even if they asked me to return to Sierra Leone again, I would not come, but I have had serious second thoughts. I might return.

Mrs. Saad said, "You need not return to Sierra Leone. You can stay in England, you can come to Lebanon, or you may go back to your family, but take her with you. What I feel she will do is whatever makes you feel happy. She wants to go to medical school in Beirut. It will take another four to five years for her to finish. So both of you go back to school. The only problem is, you are in London, and she is in Lebanon. She can try to get admitted to one of the Medical Schools in London. That is a possibility, but unlikely. I will ask my father to find out. We have more contact with Paris, but not that much with England."

"Now, Mrs. Saad, you know my future, which is uncertain, full of ups and downs. I have to live on my research scholarship, which I can barely maintain myself. How will I look after her in a way she deserves to be looked after? England is cold and humid. Lots of personal sacrifice needs to be expected. But I can't think of any situation, reason, and condition that might convince me not to be with her for the rest of my life."

"Anyway," said Mrs. Saad, "now that I know your feelings about her, I can happily speak to her and tell her that you too have the same dream for her as she has for you. So looking after her at this point is not a problem, which you think might prevent you from being together."

I felt better and lighter. I promised Mrs. Saad I would be communicating with her as soon as I had her address and phone number, etc. I thought she was also relieved. Indeed, she had no symptoms, and she was not sick anymore.

Friday morning, we started our next and last inspection tour to Bandejuma, then more or less a social visit to several people in Koidu, whom I met and befriended during my stay in Kailahun. Importantly, I promised Ayesha that I would take her on our next trip. This was my last working trip, so I asked her to come with me to Koidu and Sefadu. She was ready and packed. So we decided to take the shorter route. Still, this would take two and a half to three hours of travel, and we had to cross a ferry on river Moa. Generally, the road surface was good, but anyone's guess was what it would be like. I told Sister Thomas we might have to stay overnight and assured her Ayesha was in good hands and would return in one piece.

Chapter 48

A SIDE TRIP TO KOIDU AND YENGEMA – THE DIAMOND CAPITAL

"The stars in the heaven sing a music; if only we had ears to hear "

Pythagoras.

On a Friday morning, we set out for Koidu. We left at 7.30 in the morning, hoping to hit Koidu by noon. The road, in the beginning, was reasonably dry and dusty. We began passing through the deep jungle as we proceeded along, but the trees were not tall enough to bring darkness during the day. This road was used well for transport from Kano to Liberia through Kailahun. Both legal and illegal goods passed this way. The business and traders made sure that this road remained drivable in their best interest throughout the year, particularly the diamond miners, legal, illegal, as well as couriers and criminals of all shapes and trades. The road was wide enough for two cars or Lorries to pass by. We came across many antelopes, baboons, and monkeys by the side of the road, undeterred by the passing vehicles. We struggled along the route. I asked Ayesha how she was handling the drive? I said, "I told you, it will be interesting but can be bone-crunching."

"It is not that bad," she said.

We arrived at Manowa ferry crossing. There were at least twelve cars ahead of us. Mohammadu stopped behind the last vehicle, which was marked "Koidu Holding," the company that ran many businesses in the Kano district, mainly diamonds. Mohammadu walked to the jetty and walked back with a uniformed person. He just looked at us and gave me a military-style salute. I greeted him also appropriately. He asked Mohmmadu to proceed and park in front of the first car. Our vehicle was identified as "Ambulance – Kailahun District General Hospital." No one dared to question.

The river was relatively high, flowing fast but without any waves or turbulence. I remember taking the same ferry the first time I came to Kailahun, a nightmarish crossing. Aside from the cold water, the river was full of crocodiles, hippos, and giant river dolphins. I was scared that the ferry might be toppled over at any time, but we made it anyway; we missed our mooring spot, perhaps by a hundred yards. The operators brought us back just by manually pulling.

Fortunately, this time the ferry crossing was smooth, and we moored at the right place, and it took just eleven minutes to cross the river. We were lucky this time. As we crossed the river, Ayesha asked me if I would like coffee, tea, or some other drink. She was prepared with a full day's supply for all four of us. I asked Mohmmadu to stop by the roadside parking area. We all had a quick drink with snacks. Ayesha played the hostess. It seemed to me that she was very excited about the trip.

After a ten-minute break, we set out for our first stop, Bandajuma. On our way, we had to cross the snake country, Jokubu, and

Bunumbu. Fortunately, this time we did not meet any serpents. The deep, but the low forest-lined road, was reasonably OK. Finally, we arrived at Bandajuma village, where I found another car parked by the roadside, and a lady in white came out of the car and signed us to stop. That was Miss Isabel, one of our district nurses. I was surprised to see her. She told me Sister Thomas sent a message that I would be coming to inspect the maternity facility to make sure the midwife was available to speak.

As we drove to the local Chief's house, I felt there could not have been more than five hundred families living in this village. But there were many small villages inside the forest, making the population around three thousand. I met the chief of the village—a very nice, elderly gentleman who did not speak English or even Krio. The local language So-so was what he could speak, but also Patua. Having understood how to communicate, we got engaged to discover the issues. The midwife and the chief requested that government build a permanent house for women to give birth. Most houses were small, circular, mud, and bamboo-lined walls with fiberglass corrugated roofs. Small, for the mother and her few weeks of post-natal care.

We agreed. The chief had decided to supply his workforce and other resources as needed. That was a huge relief. I gave my support to see this was done. On our way, while touring the village, we found that problems were just as big as anywhere else, including their small size. It was a small village but clean with better roads, comparatively, to other settlements. Several diamond prospecting pits could be seen, perhaps giving the place a healthy and wealthy outlook.

We said goodbye to the Chief and the Midwife, who was quite bright. We needed to help her, help the chief and the local people, and the District Nurse; all could do with help and support.

We left Bandajuma around 11.30 am for our final destination, Koidu.

Koidu was the capital of the Northern District of Eastern Province. Most important, it was the capital of diamond mining in the country. The official population was five thousand, but the actual population in the town and surrounding area was close to twenty-five thousand. The majority were non-registered Sierra Leonean diamond diggers and many from neighboring Guinea and Liberia as illegal diamond miners, known as "Sansan boys." They dug and panned diamonds for their employers and frequently acted as a courier for smuggling diamonds out of the region and out of the country, at times at significant risk of their lives. Still, they did it. It paid well and could save enough to support their families.

This was one side of the story. On the other hand, diamond merchants, diamond traders, smugglers, miners, and other business people lived in a different world. But, of course, the majority were Lebanese, and some Indians also had done well. They all lived in big houses with expensive cars, servants, gardeners, chauffeurs, 24 hours of electricity, treated piped water, air conditioning, private pools, tennis courts, etc. The other world did not exist.

For their comfort, most of the town roads were tarred. Major roads were very wide, with the median boulevard separating two sides of the road, well-manicured. There were few clean and attractive restaurants close to the city Plaza. The majority were Lebanese-owned. About two thousand Lebanese residents and temporary workers (non-black Africans, including a sprinkle of Syrians, Indians, Iraqis, etc.) lived in Koidu. The majority were involved in diamond mining and diamond business. South African DeBeers own all diamond mining in Africa, and Lebanese were their powerful middle agents. In Kano and parts of Sierra Leone, the Lebanese community became experts in diamond trading and spread all over the continent as diamond traders. Credit goes to the communities' astute business acumen. Indians came next. But the role of Indians came, aside from being traders, as Indian craftsmen, as they were the best and most prolific diamond polishers for centuries. Raw diamonds sold, but cut and polished diamonds shined and glittered were core attractions that brought billions.

I was told this was how it worked! First, raw uncut diamonds were mined and shipped to Beirut by thousands of Lebanese engaged in diamond trading all over Africa, shipped to Beirut. Beirut was the world's capital of uncut diamonds. Next, the raw diamonds were sent to India by various agents to many diamond cutting and polishing factories in India. These were primarily concentrated in Rajasthan, Gujrat, and Bombay. Generations of craftsmanship had made them perfect and were the most vital part of the diamond industry. Once the diamonds were cut, polished, and sized, they were sent to Antwerp, in Belgium, the world's center for the final stage of the diamond trade, for the final stage of its journey. Buyers from all over the world converged to buy some of the best diamond jewelers worldwide, London, New York, Paris, Los Angeles, Hong Kong, Singapore, Tokyo, you name it, they were there. Even the rich and famous could be seen strolling in the streets of Antwerp (when they were not in their Rolls, Bentleys, Mercedes, BMW, Cadillacs Ferrari, and such).

Some of them I got to know, the Saads, the Haddads, the Ibrahims, the Bassams, during my year-long stay, I met through my work or the Saad family, in Kailahun.

I met Mr. Saad, the younger brother of Mr. Saad of Kailahun. With him, I toured several other well-known Lebanese merchants. They all had something to do with the diamonds. They all were wealthy and looked happy and healthy. Mr. Saad took us to a Lebanese Club, where various performers from

Lebanon or other parts of Africa came to perform from time to time. As I said, theirs was a different world. We all had some snacks and drinks. Then I went to tour the town, just for Ayesha to satisfy her curiosity. Then we just dropped by at the hospital for a courtesy call to Dr. Rao, with whom I had shared many patients. Unfortunately, Dr. Rao, the District Medical Officer of Kano District, was out of town. I spoke to the Sister and his office manager to convey my wishes and parting wishes.

Ayesha and Mr. Amara went looking for a bargain but came back empty-handed. Everything was so expensive. But they now knew never to visit Koidu looking for a bargain! During weekly market days, residents from Koidu and other neighboring areas went to Kailahun for fresh fruits, vegetables, nuts and seeds, peanuts, cola, etc.

Koidu had its charm for a small rural town, the air of opulence and activities.

Mr. Saad's brother found us an affordable hotel, and we spent the night there.

The following day, we got up, got ready, had our breakfast, and got ready for the return journey. Mr. Saad came to find out how the night was. We all thanked him for making our life easier and more pleasant.

With the help of Mr. Saad and Ibrahim, I was able to catch up with my acquaintances in Koidu. It was still early in the morning. Since this was my last trip this way, I thought we should take a short trip to Yengema, the real diamond capital of the country, not just the district or the region. It was about fourteen miles from Koidu, so that would take an hour. The road to Yengema was supposed to be tarred, but years of heavy use, by heavy vehicles and unlicensed diamond diggers and the "San sans', left the road condition less repaired than expected.

However, the mining companies did their best to keep the roads fair.

We left at 9.30 in the morning. Ayesha and Mr. Amara repacked our supplies and drinks. My thermos was refilled with black coffee. We had to cross a river on a ferry both ways, which was our concern. The road was fair, but roadsides had several pits filled with water of various sizes, shapes, and depth, from a few feet to several yards, were the sites where diamond prospecting had been done or was still ongoing. In some of the water holes, we saw people were panning for diamonds. Sierra Leone diamonds were mostly alluvial, so the prospectors only needed a shovel and a sieve for prospecting. Anyone with minimal ambition could become a diamond prospector for one of the registered companies, or a self-appointed one, risking neck and life. Yet, hundreds and thousands of illegal prospectors engaged throughout the region. They sold it to their Lebanese protectors or foreign agents, mostly South Africans, Guineans, and Liberians. The life of such symbiosis seemed hugely profitable for both the victor and the pathogen. But, unfortunately, the Government of Sierra Leone was deprived of its due share.

We were driving the northern part of the Kano district. The trees were bush-like, not as dense. It appeared to be infringing on the Sahel of Saharan south. I had not seen many bamboo shrubs around, but as the jungle got less dense, we could see several bamboo shrubs growing by the river. All this time, we had been driving by the river. Mohmmadu asked me if he could see the right side into the bush. I could not believe my eyes. We noticed a smallish-sized elephant with a baby elephant munching some bamboo-like shrubs. We thought we were dreaming or having some form of hallucination! West African elephants were all but extinct. Mohmmadu said he had never seen one in his life in this part. People admitted to sightings further North West. We stopped our car and wanted to have a real look at the majestic creatures. I thought we were all fortunate. I cursed myself for not bringing my camera with me. The elephants were quite a bit further from us. Our presence did not bother them. We slowly moved away towards our destination.

We arrived at the ferry site. There were no queues, and the ferry was moored on our side. I thought it was a tributary of Moa River or river Segbwema. It was very wide but calm. It was filled up to the brim as we got on the river. We were at the end of the rainy season. We saw a few fishes jumping above the water, a water dolphin sticking its snout out and busy with its curling circus. Even water hippos and giant dark crocodiles passed by as our exhibition. It was a gas-propelled ferry. The manual ferry was not practical because of the river's width at this point. It got broader and broader downstream. Boats carrying timber and some form of ores, likely iron and titanium ores (the world's largest deposit in Sierra Leone), passed by. One passenger boat also passed by because of two major trading centers, Yengema and Segbwema, the river traffic was above average on the river. I wondered how often the ferry and passing boats collided. The ferry master told me there were very loud and clear warning sounds activated, half a mile up and downstream, once the ferry left the jetty from either side. He did not recall any collision between the ferry and passing boats during his stay in this job for the last four years. That was reassuring. We safely disembarked. Mommahdu drove straight to Yengema, and it took forty minutes to reach the city center.

It did rain a bit on our way, but Yengema was dry. The town was much cleaner than Koidu. The roads were planned in a grid form. All the streets in the town we drove through were paved, with clearly marked parking lots on both sides of the road. We noticed all the Central dividing boulevards well-maintained with floral landscaping on most main roads. The shops in the main square and major streets were much better and smart-looking. Lebanese ran several stores, but a much higher proportion of stores were owned by local people that were black African. Looking at the number of mosques, one would have expected most people living there to be Moslem. I was told the population at that time in Yengema was five to six thousand, slightly more than Koidu. There were electric street lights. The roadside saw several multi-story concrete buildings. Business offices or the ground floors were primarily used as shops of various descriptions. The number of car dealers was more than the size of the town.

Like Koidu, many expensive cars were seen on the street and in the showroom, indicating the wealth of the people and that of the city. I went inside a decent-looking cafeteria while letting Ayesha and Mr. Amara explore a shopping opportunity. The majority of customers were not black, but either white or Middle Eastern. Checking the menu, I realized this was a place that catered mainly to European and Middle Eastern palates with foods, snacks, and freshly prepared drinks. I had a real fresh brewed cup of coffee. I started to speak to the manager. He said the coffee beans were harvested locally, roasted and ground in his shop, and brewed for the guests. He repeated that the coffee they served was from the "*Pod to the Pot, from the Tree to the table*", couldn't be any fresher, any more authentic.

His main business was exporting Sierra Leone coffee, mainly to the Middle East. The local market was not big, but coffee was a naturally grown plant in this part of West Africa. The government and business community realized the investment opportunity for growing coffee on a commercial scale. His main business was coffee, and his minor side business was the diamond dealership. Being a pioneer in the coffee trade in Sierra Leone, he felt very optimistic about the future of Sierra Leone's coffee trade and wealth. He said Liberians were smarter and made significant advances in harnessing coffee production and marketing. At this point, Liberian coffee was one of the major GDP earners for the Liberian economy. The coffee tree was a local breed. The land would continue to grow coffee trees as long as they wanted, unlike imported transplanted varieties, which were more climate and environment-sensitive than the local ones. So too with diamonds. In these regions, diamonds mixed with the alluvial soil were mined from the surface. In the way diamonds were mined in that region, soon there would be no diamonds left to scrape, the digger would have scraped the last diamond from the soil, from the water pools, from the rivers, or the greed would aggressively entice them to dig in human settlements, on our roads, on the settled areas, the buildings, the playgrounds, the central town plaza-like locusts, and the result would be the total destruction of cities, towns, and villages. The wealth created by diamonds would increase poverty and poor services to its residents. Food, health, education, all would be gone with the force and reckless tsunami of greed for diamonds. This economy would make some millionaires, a few billionaires, but millions of people would be pushed to poverty, devoid of homes and land, their source of livelihood, and would perish as destitute.

As I was listening to him, I was watching his feelings. He was serious, believing very strongly what he had just said. But, he also thought this could be avoided only by implementing robust governmental control but did not see any sign of that pressure coming from the government or the industry itself.

I was amazed listening to the man's fear and prediction, which all might come true sooner or later. It was time for the public institutes to organize and act in concert to avert this catastrophe.

Ayesha and Mr. Amara returned just on time, as I was about to go out looking for them. I asked to pay for his fantastic coffee, from the tree to the table. He wished me well and hoped that I could participate in his fight against the country's and its people's destruction.

I thanked him and expressed my gratitude for his kindness.

We all got back to the ambulance, had a snack break, and pushed for our return journey home to Kailahun.

The road was good, essentially dry, and had few potholes. We estimated that by 5 pm, we would be in Kailahun. The ferry crossing was also smooth, with no waiting or queuing.

The ferry operator was not surprised about the sighting of the small elephant family on the river bank. They came down from the northeast Sahel region of Liberia, the western part of Mali. We had to take ferries twice to cross the river to travel back to Kailahun. One just after Yengema and the other before Manowa. The return ferry was also smooth. The road, all the way, was excellent, considering the battering it endured throughout the tropical rainy season. There were many vehicles on the road. This was also an important trade route, between Yengema through Koidu to Kailahun to the international borders with Guinea and Liberia. It was not infrequent that diamond couriers were dropped a few miles before the checkpoint. Young couriers were given a ride by an agent to a village just close to the border. It was safe to walk across the border. Their original transport picked them up, pretending to be a new passenger. In fact, at times, they would be smuggling thousands of dollars' worth of recently mined diamonds. Good for the miners but bad for the country.

By the time we arrived at Manowa ferry, it was already 3.30 pm. I was getting concerned about driving in the evening on this road. Suppose we got stuck for some reason or the other, robbery, abduction, human trafficking, particularly the young lady with us, wild animals, or even engine breakdown or a flat tire; any of these could happen. In that case, we may have to face all these rather unpleasantly. Mohmmadu and Mr. Amara were well acquainted with this road and said there was nothing to worry about. This road was well monitored by government police and private police of several diamond mining companies because of the higher incidence of illegal and violent activities.

But nothing happened. We returned safely to Kailahun at 4.30 pm. We drove to Sister Thomas's house first and dropped Ayesha off. Then Mohmmadu dropped me at my residence. Finally, he drove away to drop Mr. Amara, who lived on the other side of the town.

I was happy to end the inspections. Now the more arduous job started, completing the exit report. I made sure all staff members were at their peak level of performance. We were a small center, but we managed to achieve much compared to many more developed sites. We all worked together happily and did the best we could in making the rest happy and healthy.

Chapter 49

PREPARING TO CHECK OUT

"Welcome ever smiles, and farewell goes out sighing"

William Shakespeare

In the meantime, I had to travel to Freetown to attend some rather complex medico-legal court cases. I did make a couple of courtesy calls to MOH and Connaught Hospital. I met Dr. Boyel-Hebron, the Deputy Chief Medical Officer. He mentioned that my replacement would arrive in Sierra Leone in two weeks; I could hand it over soon after he came or the day before my leave began, as scheduled. I told Dr. Boyel-Hebron that I was not in a great rush to leave. I could stay happily for any other extension, but I had to return to the UK and India to see my folks. Dr. Boyel-Hebron was pleased. We could discuss this when I returned to Freetown before my final exit.

At the hospital, there was a surge of activity. I wanted to ensure every item was in place, supplies were fully stocked, routines were scheduled, and all documentation was up-to-date. With much hard work and persuasion, Sister Thomas and Mr. Amara did manage to get individual center's reports, the ones we visited, and we prepared our own. I had to prepare a comprehensive document of the status of healthcare activities in the District of Kailahun and suggestions for changes, to make the entire government activities more effective and all-encompassing across all territorial, ethnic, cultural, linguistic, and environmental divides. It was a synthesis of efforts and ideas from all front-line workers. They were happy that their "say" was listened to, documented, and brought to the attention of the highest authorities.

One evening, I was invited to Mr. Jesudasan, the principal's house, to try and taste authentic South Indian tea, specifically that of the Tamilnadu region. We did get friendly, both socially and at the work level. The program we developed to expose students from higher classes to hospital environments as observers or active volunteers, under supervision, became very popular. Mr. Jesudasan and Mrs. Jesudasan expressed their gratitude from the school board for the effort I and the staff made for the young boys and girls, which was well appreciated by students, staff, and the parents. Young pupils' presence made my team energized, making the hospital working environment more vibrant.

I invited Tony and his friend, a member of the British VSO, and five members of the US Peace Corps. Those in town and around town; spoke of their life, experience, expectations, disappointments, moments of joy, and generally, how this sojourn had impacted their lives, as well as how this experience might alter their future world. It was nice to have felt the impact of these kids. I saw a little bit of myself in them. Even watching those carrying on with their passion and selfless dedication, sometimes harsh and brutal conditions in most challenging circumstances, and one could only experience it when one was in it. Somehow I got friendly with some of them and continued social contact several years after we left Africa and well into their chosen lives. Tony Burnett from England became an

Emergency Physician, and later in life, he indeed joined several disaster rescue teams in several countries. He excelled as an international expert in emergency medical management in disasters and continued to become a world leader. So there were happy and successful endings, or should I say beginning to several of them I knew, after they returned home.

After returning from Freetown, I told Sister Thomas that the doctor relieving me would be arriving in three weeks.

Spontaneously, she said, "So soon? I thought you had two months of extension?"

"Sister! That was nearly a month ago. I know we have been so busy trekking all over the district. Time is flying like an arrow. So let us plan to go through this hospital and staff, see where we need changes."

So the next day, with Sister Thomas, Mr. Amara, and Mr. Joseph, we scoured through the entire hospital, building, drainage, waterworks, electrical connections, the makeshift laboratory, and inventory as the whole of the hospital, the wards, and the kitchen. While we were looking at the kitchen, one of the patient's relatives was preparing something. I went close. It looked like a stew. I asked her if I could taste what she was cooking. She was more than happy to offer me a spoon, said to be careful; it was hot. Sister took the spoon from the cook's hand and started to blow it to get cooler so that I could taste it. She was happy it was cool enough; she asked me to taste it. I did as instructed. It was excellent, and I thanked the cook for preparing a nice stew for the patients. The lady cook was pleased.

The entire hospital campus was in excellent condition. All walking paths had been paved with red bricks. The inside was well landscaped. Sister had already prepared an inventory of all goods and state of services, possible deficits, and a tentative plan for reconstruction, reconstitution, and rebuilding. I was very impressed with the clear understanding of the local problem, with a deep impression of issues local and something regional or even national.

I had all the notes and suggestions from our healthcare facilities' inspections and community needs. Later, I received written reports from all the nursing stations and health inspector's documented comments from the schools one by one. Finally, I compiled a complete and comprehensive 'Exit report."

I asked Mr. Amara, Sister Thomas, and Mr. Joseph to go through the document before sending it to the authorities.

Dr. Cummings, the provincial Medical Officer, was the direct boss. However, I forwarded it to the Chief and Deputy Chief Medical Officer of the Ministry of Health at Freetown. In addition, the District officer needed to be informed as he was the Supreme Administrator-General for the district.

The following day at around 10 am, the District Officer appeared at the hospital. He was in a very cheerful mood. "Hi! Doc (this was the first time he addressed me as a buddy)," he said and came inside the office.

"Please take a seat. I have time to talk before starting my Clinic, doing my ward round, and meeting with the administrator."

He said, "Doc, you got me in trouble."

I was surprised. "Trouble? What kind of trouble?" I asked.

My interpreter entered with a glass of water, a pot of tea and biscuits for the DO, and just coffee for me.

"These are the troubles; highly appreciated though," he said. I asked him again to tell me about the trouble.

"These are the troubles. Your guests are always looked after by your staff and offered drinks and or snacks as a welcome gesture."

"A pleasant and civilized transformation. Not normally part of our official or unofficial meeting in my office. I have to change my office protocols and go your way! It will take time to motivate office staff. You have the advantage of several people trained to look after human beings. I guess they spontaneously do it once they understand your likes and dislikes. They might even feel obliged to treat your guest in a way that makes them feel at home. This is a new standard. That is one thing, but striking is the 'Exit report.' You are the third District Medical Officer leaving the district. Fortunately, during my tenure in Kailahun, they were transferred to another district or completed their tour of duty. The 'Exit report' is so extensive and detailed; I had difficulty comprehending the document. I hope we can maintain the trend; we will need someone with experience, imagination, energy, and enthusiasm. Anyway, this can be a template for future directions.

"The current trend is to hand over the key to the relieving doctor. If he is not available, the DMO must at least verbally hand over to the DO if not in writing. On one occasion, while the nurse and DO were unavailable for taking over, the hospital key was left at DO's office. That was kind of a trend. I am glad that you gave us an overall picture, and we will try to maintain the trend. But it will be hard to implement. On the other hand, our expectations will run high once there is an example. This is not just for health, and perhaps we'll try to energize the whole bureaucracy of this district."

"I did it with the help of several of my staff. I tried to keep them motivated until they produced a valid document. Sister Thomas and Manager, Mr. Amara, were the two important lieutenants in this process."

"Talking of Sister Thomas," said DO, "She arrived just about two to three weeks before you came. Because of her large stature and rather imposing personality, she indeed brought much-needed discipline and hard work, yet patience and kindness to your staff, patients and relatives and visitors equally well, very well appreciated by all around her. Kind of a 'Gentle Giant.' She knew well before I was informed about your posting in Kailahun, so she silently modified the hospital to welcome you and make your life comfortable and easy.

"People in town generally liked her, despite her aggressive demeanor. She is indeed the Lioness, without sharp teeth, piercing claws but a kind heart, protecting everyone who comes under her wings."

Describing Sister Thomas as a kind Lioness was fascinating. This was the second time I was hearing someone comparing Sister Thomas to a kind-hearted, loving, and all-caring human being. I could not see her as other people did. She had been too close to caring for me from the day she came to say hello to me in the MV Apapa, just as we left Liverpool for Freetown. Throughout the voyage, through the life-threatening severe tropical storm, while on the Atlantic coast between the Canary archipelago and the west coast of Africa. Days and months after my serious car crash, two of my staff had severe injuries, completely writing off my car, directing her little niece to take care of me. She advised my cook and house boy to maintain the house and the kitchen in the best hygienic order. She would come from time to time to inspect the home, though none of these were in her job description.

Knowing my pathological fear of snakes, with the help of the Health Inspector, made sure the compound was free from the intrusion of the killer creeper. They placed small containers with Phenol all around the hedges of the compound to ward off snakes.

Staff punctuality became the order of the house. Patients learned to wait for their turn and not burst inside the clinic or argue with the interpreter or a nurse. Instead, she attended to patients' concerns before being rushed into the clinic. However, she never interfered if there was a need to rush.

The most important part she played was building the waiting room for patients. Once we decided, we would relocate my car-port and construct patients' waiting rooms. Again, out skirting governmental funding, local businessmen supplied the materials to the last screw and some construction help.

Two VSO volunteers with their student's battalion completed building the structure in three days. VSOs, on principle, helped only in education and propagation of literacy and social awareness. But with the blessings of the Principals of both high schools, they had encouraged VSO volunteers and school children to help them in the project.

I did not know then, but I know now that Sister Thomas herself approached some friendly businessmen in the town to help, including the Saads. Once Saads got involved, we had no problem with resources.

Getting over the bureaucracy to build any structure in government property was a lengthy process. I wrote to DO about the proposal and explained the plan's details. The DO, as per protocol, passed my request to MOH and the Public Works department. This could easily take four to six months to get an answer. They got the green light from MOH in three days, to our surprise. They also informed me that the superintending Engineer from Kenema would arrive in the next couple of days to verify and certify the project. There were certain procedural routines, which Mr. Amara would take care of.

This was dramatic progress beyond anyone's dream. After the engineer visited, he asked me how soon it would start and when it would be expected to finish to schedule his visit for certification of completion.

I said, "We were only waiting to get the word from you. We will start on Friday, and it will finish by coming Tuesday. So you may be able to inspect the structure week after next." He was surprised but agreed to return the week after next and asked Mr. Amara to let him know when the construction was finished.

The DO was surprised, looking at the speed of progress. Again I learned, Sister Thomas requested Dr. Boardman, the Chief Medical Officer, to fast-track the request. She also spoke to none other than Mr. Bamforth, the Chief Secretary of Government of Sierra Leone, requesting his support.

That was the lightning. Later, DO admitted that not having the support of a "Sister Thomas" in his Office as a staff was a significant disadvantage. So, to boost DO's morale, I said, "We are all your staff, just give the order. We will march."

He laughed his head off.

There was hardly any work, action, plan, or even my day-to-day living and life, where Sister Thomas's protective cast and a helping hand were not stretched out. The lioness with a smile, kind heart, gentle paws, sharp eyes, and an omnipresent soul. But the touch was so gentle and the breath so breezy, one needed to imagine rather than feel. I never really felt her presence around me which was so profound, for which there had been no pain, no itching, no throbbing, no bleeding, no smothering, and no controlling. She never showed any sign of such immense influence on me and my working environment. I had no reason to believe she planned her way in. It was just a Mother lioness's plain and straightforward spontaneity and what she would do to protect her herd. But, even for that, if needed the Lioness would never sleep.

But people could see and feel the absolute dedication to her job and work. So even at times for her stern manner, I had no complaints, no dissatisfaction, and no fiery interaction with the staff or anyone from the public, except for kind and sincere words of appreciation.

One needed to step aside from life, to see it from outside, totally detached, the profundity of life. I guess that was missing, which my brain did not see, but my heartfelt in every step, every beat. A mother Lioness indeed.

The rest of the day went well, without any hitch or incident. The next day was my day for surgery. I sat down with Mr. Joseph and went through the cases. All straightforward, no anticipated anesthetic risks. I went home relatively relaxed. I found Ayesha there doing some sketches. I asked her to finish the diary of her travel with me. "I want to take your writing and some sketches with me. I will refer to them sometime in the future when I have time to do my diary."

"Oh!" she said, "You will write your diary?"

"Maybe, maybe not, but I must keep all the memories intact."

"Well," she said, "If I can't finish my diary and sketches before you leave, I can come with you and finish those properly, rather than doing it in a hurry, halfheartedly."

"Well," I said, "We still have close to one and half months, so let us use this time as best as possible. Your school will open soon. You might not find much time to do anything but to prepare for your "O" level examination. On the other hand, if you want to do your junior Cambridge, that will be even harder work. Mrs. Jesudasan told me. She believes you can do it if you want to. Sister Thomas, your aunty, wants it. Anyway, one of these days, I will speak to Jesudasans to advise you which and how many subjects you can take, either for your O levels or Junior Cambridge examination, so that we can focus on them."

By this time, my afternoon tea and snack were ready, so I told Ayesha to sit with me and let us have the tea together.

"I have many things to do tonight. Of course, you may stay as long as you feel like it and get on with your sketching. I asked you to tell me what you are sketching." She promised she would show me when it was finished.

So, we got on to our own business. At 7 pm, she brought a cup of tea and biscuits, and I told her she must go back, that her aunty was expecting her.

I asked, "Do you want me to give you a ride?"

"Thanks," she said, "It is daytime; I will walk home less than ten minutes away."

"Do you want Mommoh to accompany you? Do you have things to carry? He can help you."

"No! I will be fine, just these papers and a few books."

"Ok! Ayesha, be careful! I will see you tomorrow."

I worked till late and got up in the morning, feeling fresh and ready to start another day.

Chapter 50

UNPREPARED AND UNWILLING TO LET LEAVE

"Man is a being in search of meaning"

Plato

Back at the office in the morning. Today was my day for surgery. The clinic is supposed to have booked me off. Still, several people were waiting. Some of them were for antenatal care, others for me.

Sister said there were two ladies I had to see; one had vaginal bleeding. After examining the patient, I thought, we could just pack her, observe, and then take the appropriate action tomorrow or as soon as needed. The other lady was a patient with both fistula from the urinary bladder and also from the rectum. Her temperature was 101.5C, very dehydrated.

I examined both patients and told the sister to refer them to Nixon Memorial Hospital. I prepared the referral letter. Mr. Mohmmadu drove both of them to NMH in Segbwema.

As I got into the operating room, I saw Mrs. Saad and one of her companions entering the hospital. I waited.

She said, "How can I be so lucky to find you outside? Sorry! I just came to invite you to have afternoon tea with us this afternoon. I know afternoon tea is you're most favorite. Can you come?"

"Of course, I will, around 5 pm; will that be okay?"

"I have quite a few patients for surgery; hopefully, we will finish by then."

"Come any time when your afternoon starts. We will be there waiting for you. See you later," she said and left as fast as she entered.

The day ended on a peaceful note. All surgeries went without any hitch. They were stable postoperatively. When I was ready to return to my residence, it was already 4 pm.

I told Mommoh, "I do not need lunch or afternoon tea. I am going to have tea outside." He was a little disappointed. "But, I will have dinner. No need to prepare anything else." Mommoh said that Ayesha was preparing something for tonight.

"Well!" I said, "If she wants, make sure she has everything she needs for preparation."

"Ok! Masta, but she will bring everything she needs."

I said, "In that case, find out if she needs any help carrying her items. Most likely, I will be back by 7-7.30 this evening."

I changed and had a refreshing cup of tea and left just before 5 pm. I was right on time at Saad's house's front gate. Mrs. Saad came down to guide me to the second-floor lounge. A maid brought some fruits and iced fruit drinks as I sat down. Mrs. Saad sat on the opposite side. She knew how to dress. Now even better, it appeared to be medieval royalty. Silk and silk all over. Pleasant floral French perfume felt more like a seductress, not like a hostess. But I have seen this before. I asked where Mr. Saad was.

She said, "He is on his way from Koidu. Expected by 7-8 pm. I did not want to wait until he came back."

Mrs. Saad said, "We were expecting you; he would return by 10-11 am. But something needed to be sorted out, which could not wait till tomorrow."

"It is not a bad thing that Mr. Saad is not here. So that I can speak to you in confidence and secret."

I could not imagine what secret message she had for me, which she was not happy to speak of in front of Mr. Saad. I started to feel nervous and anxious. My pulse began to race, my heart thumped, and I felt short of breath. I watched her intensively, and so did she, reading my body language with an eagle's eye.

If under these circumstances I would not feel nervous, when would I?

With a twinkle in her eye, she said, "I want to give you my secret, but this should never go out of these four walls nor beyond these for years."

I could not control my heightened curiosity.

"Tell me the secret, Mrs. Saad, tell me your secret. I am here to listen."

It was getting late. The maids' parade of trays continued until I couldn't eat anymore.

"No, Doctor, the desserts are yet to come, but let me tell you the secret." I stared at her with my starry eyes.

"It is like this," she said. "The secret is not about me but Amal. You certainly remember her, my little sister. She was here in Kailahun for two months, now has gone back to Beirut preparing for her medical school entrance examination. It is hard, but she is determined to do it. She says having met you and spent time with you, and she is determined now more than ever before, to pursue a medical career to be with you forever."

Amal was even prettier than Mrs. Saad. Her floral beauty exceeded what I had seen and was beyond my imagination. I couldn't even place her in my world of fantasy.

"Oh! I can't be more honored and fortunate than millions of others. She must know, I am returning to my student life again, living in digs, lunching in *'Pice-hotels.'* And being a brown person, I have no illusion that this would not help me in the world of our colonial masters. But I am ready to take the plunge. I will be filled with unpardonable guilt for dragging Amal into my pitiful trial and tribulation."

Mrs. Saad took a deep breath, "Doctor!" She said we have discussed your forthcoming demanding and challenging future. Amal has worked out a clear plan."

"She has worked out a plan?" I asked.

"Yes indeed. It will take six to seven years before she becomes a practicing doctor in Lebanon. Having known your plan, you are also looking at six to seven years before becoming a specialist in the UK. During this time, both of you get engaged and get married, while Amal will look after herself and avoid the pressure from the family to marry one arranged by our parents. Even if you want to, you can leave the UK or come to live in Beirut together and practice as a doctor. You do not need anything else but Amal. The rest is easy."

I told myself how stupid I could be, not taking Amal as my life partner, ready to sacrifice anything for us to be together, even seven years of hard labor to become a doctor.

I did not even have to be like Mark Anthony to fight against the mighty Roman Emperor for Cleopatra, Achilles to win over Helen from captivities of the king Paris of Troy for Spartan king Menelaus, nor even like Romeo for Juliet, a personification of love -in-eternity.

It seemed Amal was a bouquet with Cleopatra, Helen, and Juliet.

If George the Fifth, the British king, could give up his kingdom for love for Mrs. Wilson, why can't I make some sacrifice of my ambition, just to be with Amal, who will do anything to make it happen? How can I deny myself the gift from God, a glorious angelic woman like Amal, in exchange for some trivial training and degrees?

By this time, my head was throbbing again. Mrs. Saad gave me a photograph of Amal and a letter with her plan and wishes. She told me to expect a reply soon or, even better, a phone call.

I was happy to get the letter in her handwriting, which I would treasure for the rest of my life, come what may.

Mrs. Saad appeared relieved after she handed me the letter.

It was nearly 8 pm. I thanked Mrs. Saad for everything.

I said, "No matter what happens, I shall be eternally grateful to you for bringing Amal so close to me. I will call her tomorrow. Then, as I left her house, I thanked her with sincerest gratitude and affection.

Mr. Saad had not returned as yet. I felt a little uncomfortable leaving her alone. However, she was used to this, and there were many people in and outside the house, so she felt pretty safe. She thanked me for my thoughts. I promised to see her before I left the country.

I was puzzled and confused, not knowing what to do. A gift from the heavens was conflicting with my worldly career ambition. Puzzled, why was this happening now? Confused about what to choose? Or should there be any confusion in choosing? But Amal clearly expressed that she would accept anything I said. But for her, the way was simple, not to jeopardize either of our aspirations; we still could live together, accept some pain of separation, looking at the future that we would be together forever. It seemed to me either one of us was blind, or both of us were confused, away from reality. She, in her own way, and I in my blurry vision. A strong, determined, and clear thinking mind she presented. I was still puzzled and confused, unable to sleep that night.

Daybreak came with Mommoh finding me awake and bringing my tea early. I started to plan the day as usual and arrived at my office a little early. Some of the staff were already there. I greeted the staff and patients in the waiting room. I got busy with all correspondence; some of them needed immediate action. I called Mr. Amara and gave him all the work to be done.

The daily routine went well, with no issues, no hitches, confusion, or regret. None at all. I could return home at the end of the day happily and go to bed without any feeling of guilt or frustration.

The following day, I had much clearer thoughts. We had already received notification from the Ministry of Health that my replacement would be arriving in two weeks. As far as official winding up was concerned, I was almost done. Now I needed to do some social winding up. I had to meet to say goodbye to the Paramount Chief, the Principals of both high schools, Peace Corps, and VSO volunteers whom I got to know very well during my stay in the country. Many local associates, business people who had sometimes gone out of their way to help, particularly the Vianini staff. I couldn't ever forget their help during my car accident and many more after that.

The next morning at work, everything seemed to be bright and shiny. But I found sister Thomas was not herself. Nothing much, but my clinical eyes told me so. I did not volunteer to question, but I was a little extra cautious not to add to her anxiety, whatever might be the cause.

The day finished normally. Just before I was leaving, Sister Thomas came in. I did ask her how she was and the rest of her family in Kailahun and Freetown, and those in the UK, especially Ayesha's parents. She said everyone was well. There was no concern, but she would like to see me in my residence to discuss something personal, which she could not discuss at the office.

"Any time, Sister, I will be home for the rest of the day. If you do not want Ayesha to be in the house, just let her know that you have some important issues to discuss. Or I can tell her to wait in another room while we speak."

"No! That is not an issue," she said, "Ayesha may like to hear what we talk about."

Around five in the afternoon, both Sister Thomas and Ayesha came together. Both of them were kind of glum. I was wondering, maybe some disagreement between them. Sister wanted me to mediate and resolve. I couldn't think of any issue that might be serious, that she needed an outsider's help. Or either of them had some physical condition, for which they needed my advice.

Ayesha knew everything in my house. So she went and prepared tea and coffee and brought some biscuits and pieces of cake; those came from Mrs. Saad yesterday.

While Ayesha was busy preparing the tea, Sister Thomas told me that Ayesha wanted to speak to me on some issues. So she asked me to come and sit down with her.

I had no idea what she might be talking about. But anything I could do for them, I would do. Unfortunately, my time was limited to a month in Sierra Leone.

While we were having our tea, I asked Ayesha if she wanted to speak to me about something. "Go on, tell me," I said jovially.

There was a sudden pause. Then, Ayesha looked at the floor and asked me, when I left, how soon would I return.

I thought that was a fair question. "First thing Ayesha, if I come back, I am not sure where the government will send me. Most likely to another district as DMO. Maybe Sister Thomas will be transferred back to Freetown. Soon you will finish your

O levels and have to go to Freetown or BO to be admitted to a collegiate school for you to prepare for "A" level examinations. I might come back here, but none of you will be here. That will not be much fun, Ayesha, you understand what I mean."

"Yes! I understand; that is why I want to come with you, wherever you go from here."

"You want to come with me to England?"

"Yes, that is what I am dreaming of doing. I have been looking after you for more than a year; I know exactly how to stay with you and help you so that you can concentrate on your work."

"That is very kind. But I am going back to being a student again. Life is very hard for students. My scholarship will be less than a third of what I am making now. If I do not get a student's residence, I have to live in a dump. Cold, stuffy rooms; landladies rent them out to students. Breakfast, lunch (on weekends only), dinner are all regimented on time. One has to pay money into a heater to heat the room. English cold is wet and slushy. We travel in buses or tubes (underground trains), I will not have a driver to take me around, not like here. Many students do their cooking themselves or a group of them taking their turn, to save money, take a hot water bottle to bed to stay warm, even take baths once or twice a week, for they need to pay money in the slot machines to get hot water to take a shower or bath."

"That is exactly why I want to come with you and stay with you!" Ayesha said. "I will be 17 years old soon. I can take a part-time job to make our life a little easier. I spoke to my mom; she said it is not difficult to get part-time jobs in London."

"Now, it is important that you do not disrupt your education," I said to Ayesha. "If you come with me that will all stop. Unless one is very wealthy, it is impossible to get into a school in England. I am going for higher education and training. How can I deprive you of that by taking you away? That will make me feel very guilty throughout my life."

"I am happy and willing to sacrifice that bit for the time being. I am only 16, and I have lots of time to catch up," Ayesha said.

"You are nearly at the end of a major hurdle to overcome in your education, Ayesha," I said. "Let us reach that goal, that is, either get as many as "O" levels and finish your "A" levels. You can start counting days from now. You will see how fast the days go by."

"But what am I going to do if I am not around you? I feel so much more confident in my school work. My grades are even getting better. Whatever you talk to me about my classwork or even funny stories, I find more helpful than the one I learn from the teachers."

"I am happy to hear that. I am thrilled, Ayesha. We can't stop at this moment. Now we are at a speed to touch the finish line. Let us not stop. Let us not even think of coming to England with me now. But, of course, you can always come and see me during your vacation time. I will give you a real-time guided tour of London. I love London. It's ancient past, its past, present, and I dare not to imagine what the future might hold."

"I still do not know how to convince myself that you will be gone soon, and I will not be with you," says Ayesha

I thought she was more mature than the credit she got for being only a young lady.

It was getting late. All this time, Sister was silent, just listening to our conversation and sipping tea from time to time. Finally, she thanked me for my time with them and said, "The time is getting shorter and shorter. Hope we all genuinely make the best use of your remaining days in the country."

They drove to my house. I walked to their car and said good night to both of them.

This time I was neither puzzled nor confused. I felt happy that reason played an important part in our direct talks. No matter what happened, Ayesha would always be with me either in person or in my world of affection. How can I forget her selfless dedication to me and her dream to make it an eternity?

The remaining few days went by in a flash.

The day to leave Kailahun behind had come. I was ready to leave my colonial residence, DMO's private and secluded bungalow. We would drive to Freetown, and Mohmmadu would bring my replacement back with him from Freetown to Kailahun. That was a fair and reasonable arrangement. He had been at the Government Rest house for three days with his wife and two little kids.

The government offered to take a plane from Kenema, which would have taken some pain off and shortened my journey by six to eight hours. But I thought this might be a painfully pleasant farewell jolt from the country and the people, who gave me more than I had given to them.

One morning after we had the heart-to-heart talk with Ayesha, I found Sister Thomas waiting for me in my office. She looked happy. We just chatted about the patients in the ward. Then, she started talking about Ayesha. For more than a month, when she understood you would be leaving soon, she kept saying to me that she would like to go with you and stay with you wherever you go. She cried, missed her meals; some nights, she would not go to bed till the early hours in the morning. I kept telling her that she must speak to you. But she kept telling me repeatedly that I must speak to you. Her parents are abroad, so I was the only one who could help her.

"I did not know how to reason with her, but it would rip my heart apart to see her crying and unhappy and giving up on life. She is just sixteen. She is just like my daughter. I will do anything to see her happy. After many days of holding hands, wiping tears, lying down with her in her bed until she fell asleep, making sure she was eating properly, her weeping never stopped; she would cry as she got up in the morning and would sob in her bed at night. Then one day, I told her we would speak to the doctor and find out what he thinks. Ayesha spent lots of her time in my house whether I was in or out. She told me that she feels comfortable, peaceful, and can study better in my house. That is why her grades improved, and she got involved in many school activities. Maybe it would be the same if she stayed at home, but perhaps it would have been more challenging to get there. One day she held me tight, started crying, saying aunty, you are my everything. You need to help me. After her parents left for England, she had been with me for the last two and half years. Generally, she is a very happy child, singing, joking, and sketching comics. She has a very strong sense of humor. She keeps us laughing all the time with her words and actions. So, I decided to speak to you along with her. In your house, I noticed a complete change in her attitude. She looked and behaved like a mature young lady, not a sixteen-year-old girl. So I let her do all the talking and pleas she wanted to make. I know this was also a turning point in your life. You can't make any mistake just because your emotion overwhelms your brain.

Simply being with you was enough to bring her real spirit out. She is now thinking, what is best for you and how can she cope with the situation, you not being around? She is thinking more than crying. I am grateful to you, doctor, for how you made her understand what is best for both of you. I will keep praying to have a happy and purposeful life. I am relieved, especially for Ayesha; it breaks my heart into pieces to see tears in her eyes. Now she is thinking with reason and not with her emotions. Thanks, Doctor; we can start our ward round."

She left. The remaining days went by in a flash. The day of real reckoning had come. Tomorrow I would leave Kailahun for Freetown.

In the morning, Mommoh got all my packages packed in the car. Mohmmadu and his helper were also coming with me to Freetown. The kitchen was clean. Mommoh said Sister and Ayesha were bringing my last breakfast there before leaving. It was a full English breakfast to tune me up before I landed there, not forgetting the pure English tea to go with it. I asked them where their breakfast was. They would have it later. It might delay my departure. "Well then, have some tea with me."

I asked Ayesha to sit beside me. There were people all around. She hesitated for a moment but quickly came and sat. I felt a deep sadness in my heart, a remorseful affection for her. I said, "Time to get back to your work, studies, now that you do not have to press my clothes and do all sorts of errands around the house. I will call you and be in touch with Principal Jesudasan and Mrs. Jesudasan."

I hugged her and got up, ready to go.

On our way, I stopped at DO's residence to say goodbye and handed over the hospital key to him. He was not in. The guard told me both Sir and Madam had gone to the hospital. I was taken a little aback. I hoped that nothing was wrong with either of them. Why did no one say anything to me? Anyway, with anticipation, we arrived at the hospital. I found twenty to twenty-five people were inside. The Police Super, Assistant DO, and some local businessmen were there. I found DO and his wife speaking to them. A bit of a relief. Most likely, they were well unless some important person was sick and at the hospital Emergency.

As our car entered, DO came forward and shook my hand, saying, "We are all here to say goodbye to you. The town, the district, and others are grateful, and we sincerely hope you come back to Sierra Leone and Kailahun to be with us."

I was not expecting it. I was overwhelmed. I found the Paramount Chief of Kailahun with four entourage just walking in. DO and his wife quickly went and received them. Someone brought the chair from my office. DO, requested the Chief to take a seat. He was a well-educated man and highly regarded in the community and colonial administration to be a trustworthy and reliable ally.

I went and shook hands with him, expressing my gratitude for him coming just to see me off.

He said "I am happy but sorry to see you go. The difference I felt was how the people of Kailahun took to you." Then one of his entourage handed over a package to the Chief. He gave it to me as a token of appreciation. I opened it; it was a classical Sierra Leonean overall worn by high-ranking locals, locally known as "Dashiki." I took it and tried to put it on. But it was so well packed to withstand the journey. So I left it as was. I thanked the chief from the core of my heart.

Slowly but sadly, I sat in the car, and we drove away. As I was leaving the hospital entrance, I saw Sister Thomas and Ayesha standing at the back of the crowd and waving goodbye. I did too.

On our way out of the town, we stopped at Mr. Saad's shop. Both Mr. and Mrs. Saad came to the car as I got out. I said, "I am going to Freetown and can't leave the town without seeing you. They said they knew about the little sendoff gathering. But because it was purely an official event, they decided to miss it reluctantly, though. Mrs. Saad said she knew that I would stop before I left, so this was for the road. A box of Lebanese sweets and snacks. Another surprise.

I had close to twelve hours of a drive ahead. I thanked them for all their help and promised to be in touch. Mrs. Saad had not lost her sense of humor as she said, "of course, I know you will be in touch; otherwise, I will." We waved and started to roll.

My last encounter in Kailahun.

Chapter 51
LAST DAYS IN FREETOWN

"No one saves us but ourselves, no one can and no one may. We ourselves must walk the path"

Buddha

The road from Kailahun to Kenema was as good as any developed country. It was just built by the Italian company Vianini. This road was a part of an East-west national highway. Fortunately, we need not take the ferry to cross any river. A new bridge had been built for faster, safer, and uninterrupted traffic flow.

We left Kailahun at 9 am, and if we were lucky with stoppages, we would be able to make it to Freetown by 9 pm. However, the official time was quoted to be 6-7 hours. For a total distance of 416 kilometers, by the shortest route. The drive from Kenema was pleasant. It was just after the rainy season was over. The air was still a bit heavy but cool enough to stay pleasant. It was a dark forested road, covered by the canopy of giant tropical trees. By this time, I was well educated in identifying the Date Palm oil and Coffee trees. We saw several patches of planned cultivated land. We could see sunlight peeping through only over those patches.

We drove on the outskirts of Kenema and went straight to Bo. It was 1.30 pm. Though it may not be a bad idea to have a break, have our lunch, and get the car checked before we start our last but long leg of the journey. Mohmmadu stopped by a gas station. We had plenty of food for the 3 of us to make three journeys like this. Fortunately, I had a flask full of hot coffee. Neither Mohmmadu nor Boukhari, his mate, was a coffee or any hot drink fan. Plain water was what they drank if Guinness or stout was not available. I learned the drink to pass the time in Sierra Leone was Guinness or some sort of Stout, made from, Charred Barley, and still did not lose its zip. We had plenty of water in stock but no alcoholic drink.

The car was checked, gas, oil, and air pressure were all in good shape. We set out for Freetown. This was the end of the wet or rainy season. The road from Bo to Freetown was paved, but after the rainy season, there were many potholes, some of which you can see, others you need to imagine or anticipate. It was dark at places, hazy in others, but dry generally. Mohmmadu had to switch on the headlight right in the middle of the day, fearing our previous experience, running into a wild boar and almost being knotted by a 20 feet Python. Slowly but steadily, we moved forward without any frightening event and made it to Masiaka Junction.

We have been driving for more than four hours. I thought it would be good to have a snack break and get the car rechecked. Masiaka or Masiaka Junction was a vital town at the junction of east-west and south-north highway in Northern Province. Mohmmadu parked the vehicle close to a gas station. I went out for a stretch and walked around the locality. The town had just over two thousand people but gave the impression of a much bigger and busier place. It was centrally located and connected to the four sides of the country. We were about 75 kilometers away from Freetown. We could make it in 2 to 2 and half hours at the worst. The unique structure was the Mosque of Masiaka, which dominated the town's skyline. Once I had stretched enough and had our planned snacking and hot coffee, both Mohmmadu and his mate, enjoyed the sweets Mrs. Saad gave us for the journey and asked for a second helping. I was happy to be able to please them. The car was checked. We took off for Freetown.

We realized that we were coming to the Creole country as we approached. Not to be missed due to several towns and villages having very English names, for example, Waterloo, Hastings, York, Regents, and many similar names. This bit of the highway had been maintained well, wide, and was wide enough for two trucks and three cars to pass by each other.

We arrived at the Government Guesthouse at 8 pm. Dr. Ahmed Huda, my replacement, was waiting for our arrival. I had never met him before, but he had been in Sierra Leone for five years. This was Dr. Ahmed's fourth tour of duty. This may be the last one, he said. I checked in and went to my room. We arranged to meet the next morning for breakfast, just to get acquainted. I let Mohmmadu and his helper go. They had accommodation close to the ministry. I told him to come back when he was ready. He needed to get the car checked thoroughly. I also told them that he would have two adults and three children and their baggage to carry and to make sure that the vehicle was serviced and inspected before leaving. He said it was routine to go through a thorough check and replace as needed when traveling. Most likely, they would leave the day after tomorrow for Kailahun. A driver from the Ministry of Health would take me to the Ministry tomorrow morning. I found a similar message for me at the checking desk from the MOH secretariat. I was to see Dr. Boyle-Hebron, the Deputy Chief Medical Officer, at 10.30 am tomorrow.

Without wasting time, I went straight to the dining hall, had my dinner, and retired in my suite at the guest house.

The following day I was in the breakfast room at 8 am. I met Dr. and Mrs. Ahmed Huda and his three children, all girls 8, 6, and 4 years old. They were from Bangladesh. The present tour would be his fifth tour of duty. He also mentioned that he made his first contract for eighteen months in Kailahun. He did not say much else. I asked him if he was happy to go back there again.

He said, "We are here to give them services. We will go wherever they need me. So I should not be looking for any choice. It is fine with me. This has to be the last tour, and all my children are growing up. So I need to think about their education and stable family life. Moreover, my parents are also growing old; I am the eldest. So I must go and help them in their old age.

I thought it was a reasonable decision. He had lived in this country for six years, and one and a half years would pass like a flash.

He asked me, how about me? I told him, "This is my first tour, an eye-opener, one step forward to maturity. I learned more about my profession than I was taught in medical college. I do not know if I will be offered any more tours of duty. I have not requested any. I will see what the Ministry has to say. I will be meeting with Dr. Boyel-Hebron at 10.30; then I will know where I stand. I will perhaps meet you again this evening. "

I went back to my room and got ready to meet the bosses.

At 10 am, Mohmmadu came to pick me up. The workshop couldn't start until noon. "So instead of sitting around, I will come to pick you up, and Ministry can bring you back when you finish with them," he said.

"That is fine with me," I replied. So I got dressed up with my medical college tie; I thought I would keep my image like this as long as possible. I had a letter from Professor Wellborn, Chairman of the Department of Surgery at the Royal Postgraduate Medical School of London University, confirming my candidacy as a postgraduate research Scholar. He mentioned that everything would be ready to start my work by the year-end.

As we arrived at Dr. Boyel-Hebron's office, his secretary said he was in a meeting, but he was expecting me, so I did not mind waiting for him. She took me to the waiting room. I waited for about 15-20 minutes. Dr. Boyel–Hebron arrived and called me in immediately.

He was a big man above average weight for his height and age. His voice matched his stature. Dr. Boyle-Hebron was a very polite gentleman. I stood up and greeted him. He asked how the journey back was. It was better since the bridges had been completed.

"Straight to the business. So you are ready to start your leave. Your relief came two weeks before; we expected him to come after two weeks, as he informed us of an anticipated delay. Anyway, this will work out better for you. We can discuss your plan. This morning I will finalize everything, having discussed with the CMO and the minister of health. He started to go over and over again my file."

"You still have 18 days before you fly. You have earned 14 days of local holidays, which are still being banked. You can take those days as holidays and stay in Freetown until your flights are booked and confirmed. I suggest you join Dr. David Owen, the Clinical pathologist in the lab, as a medical officer. His medical officer will be coming in 2-3 weeks. You can cover his duties until you leave. This way, you do not spend your local earned leave of 14 days, which will be added to your end of contract vacation entitlement, making close to five months of full salary. You can continue to stay at the Government Guesthouse. I will arrange accordingly and discuss with CMO and MOH if you agree."

"It will be nice to work in a clinical pathology lab, no matter the duration," I said to Dr. Boyel-Hebron.

I thought to myself that there was always something to help and learn. Working in a clinical pathology lab would be an exciting experience. So I said, "I can start today if you want, while you are completing my paperwork."

He buzzed his secretary and advised her to call Dr. Owen and tell him that I would be coming shortly. "Also, please make arrangements for Dr. Malaker to see me and CMO at 11 am the day after tomorrow," he said.

A driver from the MOH drove me to Connaught Hospital and took me to Dr. Abouco-Cole, the Hospital Medical Director. I had met Dr. Cole during my orientation period just after my arrival in Sierra Leone. He walked me to Dr. Owen, and I also met him during my last stay. Dr. Owen was a Sierra Leonean, qualified as a Physician from Dublin, then trained as a Clinical pathologist at Hammersmith Hospital in London. A young man in his late thirties, gentleman to the hilt. He knew I would be with him just for a few weeks, did not expect much, but thought it would help supervise the technicians and check on all the logged findings before being ready for reporting.

Since there was nothing for me scheduled, I excused myself to see Dr. Thakuta in his clinic. He was expecting me "One of these days," but did not know when. He was pleased to see me. We exchanged a bit about some lost times from home and around home. He still had some more patients to attend to.

Then a quick "consultation round.". He told me he would pick me up for Lunch to go to his house. His secretary made all the changes to my plan today. The MOH driver was told to pick me up at 9 am from the Government Guesthouse the next day.

I was happy to see Mrs. Thakuta. We had a western-style snack lunch and were reminded to join them for dinner. He had never worked in the provinces and was interested to know my experience. How did I cope with the life and living, working environment, and adapting to the professional culture and the facilities? Over the next few days, I gave them a complete understanding, of how I survived, just not only survived but thrived.

He said, "That is a place where people are sent for punishment duty." He said that he had heard horror stories about Kailahun. But I had different tales to tell. "

It seemed all the difficulties you accepted as learning, challenges, and adventures, as far as me returning to Sierra Leone that is unlikely because of my commitment to the University. However, if the program does not take off for some unexpected reason by any remote chance, returning to Sierra Leone might be an option. I received a letter of confirmation from Prof Wellborn, Chairman of the Department of Surgery at the Postgraduate Medical School of London University, that the Lab is fully operational, and he expects me to begin from the coming academic year if I can."

"In that, you have no options. The only option is to go and join the PGMS."

"I will return to the life of an Indian student in the UK, struggling to get on with work, study, cold and slushy winters, living in a dig with just about a manageable stipend. My MRC scholarship is between the third and quarter of what I am making now."

I told him, you know all about it. Seen how they struggle, yet many make through the struggle and come out as winners. I guess I would also get through.

The following day I met Dr. Boyle-Hebron in his office. He was happy. Asked me how I was getting along with my pathology job. Of course, there was always lots to learn, and I was learning a lot. However, there were also things one could do to help in unknown territory. I was helping him with his documentation, checking the results and reports, spending time with the technicians, watching them work, and keeping them alert throughout the day.

Dr. Boyle–Hebron seems to be happy. Then he asked me about my plans to return. He continued, "Since you specifically did not request further employment, the MOH offers you three (3) eighteen-month contracts. Normally we offer two (2) 12-18 months at one time. But the MOH is offering you three; hopefully, you will accept. So think about it and come back tomorrow to speak to Mrs. Winston, who will process your appointment and offer all terms and conditions and other paperwork."

I went as scheduled the following day. She gave me all contract papers, the end of contract last month's salary note, and four months three weeks of the entitled end of contract payment request to the Crown Agent in England. She also said I must pick up the ticket to Calcutta India via London. This ticket was valid for one year. "You are booked to leave on the 2nd of October. Before you go, you need to see Dr. Boardman, the CMO, who just wants to speak to you for a few minutes," she said.

I went to the Office of the CMO. Mrs. Winston asked me to take a seat in the waiting room.

Dr. Boardman came outside his office along with Dr. Boyel-Hebron. Dr. Hebron greeted me and said, "Before you leave the country, if there is any problem or any issue, please arrange with Mrs. Winston to see me, and in the meantime, enjoy your pathology duties."

Dr. Boardman ushered me to his office. He stood, just as before 7 feet plus. He looked more like a Basketball player. Very gentle and polite, and spoke perfect '*Oxonian*' English. I stood barely above his waist. He had to stoop forward to shake hands with me. We did anyway.

He remembered my accident while I was at Connaught Hospital, slid on a step ladder, injured my groin, and was hospitalized for several weeks. I said I had completely recovered. Then he asked about Kailahun, my work, the staff, workload, housing, etc. He also admitted that he had gone through my "Exit report," He would critically look at all the points I had raised with interest. Finally, he would ask Dr. Cummings, the Provincial Medical officer, to review and take whatever action was needed.

"The ministry has offered you three tours of contract. The offer will remain valid for one year plus your entitled end of contract days. It will be open to you for nearly fifteen months from now. This offer can be extended if needed for another six months. Anyway, I am pleased," he said, "You had a very engaging and fruitful time in Kailhun. We can post you in Kailahun for your next contract period. Well, we will look at the situation when the time comes." He thanked me for the services and advised Mrs. Winston that my travel arrangements were made on time.

Then I asked Dr. Boardman if I could see Mr. Bamforth for a moment just to say goodbye before I left.

He kept silent for a minute. He said, "Mr. Bamforth would be happy to see you. Unfortunately, he had to be flown into London with some heart problem. He has been admitted to Hammersmith Hospital under Professor Goodwin, where he has been there for the last 2months. His recovery is slow. I will extend your sympathy when I speak to him next." I felt sad and sorry that he was not well.

The next morning, just after I arrived at work, a messenger from MOH delivered a package. It was my ticket to India. I looked at it and thought of changing the routing if I could. I called Mrs. Winston. She said, "Yes, you can, and ask for as many stopovers as you want. The government will cover if there is an extra cost involved, but will not be subsidized for your hotel expenses, except in London for one week, which I will need to see the Crown Agents for completion of my contract and future contract renewal. We have already sent all the documents to the Crown Agents for further action."

Dr. Thakuta drove me to Paramount Hotel only 4-5 star Hotel in the country, at the city center, where we met the travel agent Julia of Sierra Leone Airlines, who was superbly charming. She said to give her my desired stopover places and the number of days I wanted to stop over; she would start working on it. She also asked me if I needed hotels, which she would be happy to book.

"That would be great!" I said. I gave her the names of places and the number of days I would like stopover. She said she would get back to me at the latest by the day after tomorrow, if not sooner. She did say that I was entitled to a higher class. Unfortunately, no higher class seat was available, so I traveled in the standard economy class. I could take as many breaks as I wanted, without any extra penalty, but unfortunately, the government would not pay for my hotel. But she said she would try to negotiate with the airlines if they could subsidize at least part of my hotel bills if not all. She thought she could get some concession.

My anticipated breaks in the journey were Freetown – Conakry – Dakar- Casablanca (Rabat-Fez) – Tangiers- Madrid – Paris – London – Beirut – Kolkata. This itinerary would take three weeks to cover. The extra 14 days of Internal paid holidays would be enough to pay for my Hotels and some costs for touristic activities. I did not anticipate making this trip anytime soon if I stayed in the UK as a student, which was most likely.

I promised Mrs. Saad that I would stop over in Beirut to surprise Amal during my return flight to India.

The remaining days went very fast. I spent lots of time with Dr. Thakuta. He arranged several mini-parties inviting some Indian Physician colleagues, Mr. Chanrai, Mr. Advani, and Mr. Srinivasan, a Ceylonese Engineer. I had met most of them before, courtesy of Dr. Thakuta. These were great social gatherings for me to understand the lives of expatriate professionals, academics, and businessmen. They were fascinating indeed, as an individual or the community in general. At that time, one could count no more than twenty-five families in Freetown but many more in the territories. Some families came at the same time when a rush of Indian laborers went during the beginning of railway constructions. They emigrated from India to South and East Africa. At the same time, some dissipated out to neighboring countries, including Sierra Leone. They were not slaves but some form of indentured labor. So it was easy for them to move around and try different jobs, aside from working in the fields and looking after the livestock, they decided to make life in other activities, as shop keepers. Trader and clerical works in the government and various businesses. Despite multiple challenges, they thrived.

I did miss much of Prof Arthur Porter, the highly respected Historian who moved to Nairobi as the Vice-Chancellor of the University of Kenya. Not sure when I would meet him again. I sent him a letter about my departure from Sierra Leone, hoping to hear back from him. But, unfortunately, I did not get a response. I hoped it was a miscommunication, not neglect; at least, I believed so.

Dr. Thakuta offered to drop me off at the airport. But the MOH already arranged for my ride. So in the morning, I got up and took a walk around the Guesthouse. For the last time. I met my German lady friend from the German Embassy at the breakfast hall. I was delighted to see her there. At least I had the opportunity of saying goodbye. We had many good times sitting and chatting with her about her life, the transition from being a nurse to a diplomat, many places she had worked, many cultures, languages, and culinary experiences. It was a delightful friendship.

She gave me her business card to be in touch. I had no business card. I did not know where I would be living in London. So I gave the address at Hammersmith Hospital, London. I gave her my home address in India; if I got lost "in transit," my parents would help find me.

The MOH transport was ready to pick me up for my farewell trip to the airport. This time it was not an ambulance nor a Ford Sedan, but a car suitable only for dignitaries. This was the official car for visiting senior officials from overseas or neighboring countries. Again, there was a helper who helped me to load my baggage.

We traveled along the foothills and the coastal road out-skirting the city. The beautiful scenic drive, rising hills with perched in houses at various levels, on one side and the Atlantic coast, lined by palm and coconut trees and occasional large tropical evergreens like Mahogany and Tics, were rare in coastal areas on the foothill side of the road. Yet, they created a dreamy romantic farewell drive out of Freetown, out of Sierra Leone, and out of Africa. I hoped to keep the memory forever.

This Freetown airport was new, built by an Israeli architect and construction company. Its semi-lunar arch-like front appeared to be ahead of its time. The driver helped me to check-in. I walked to the check-in counter. Then, like any other guests he had transported before, I sat in the waiting space.

Then I found Dr. Thakuta and Mrs. Thakuta tapping on my back. I was pleasantly surprised to see them. I thanked them for taking the trouble of coming from the town to the airport. One improvement was that a bridge connected the airport to the city. There would be no need to cross on a ferry. My first experience crossing the river on the ferry was frightening and just as much as exciting. I have a clear memory of that drifting away and sinking feeling. I doubt that I needed another experience on my last day in Sierra Leone.

We talked about the flight and my routing. He was happy and surprised that the MOH could do it. I said the arrangements were made in Freetown, but the Crown Agent looked after all my expenses until I reached home. I was excited to tell him about stopovers and expected it to be a few more "bounces" that would permanently impact me and my future life.

Chapter 52

THE LIONESS NEVER CRIES

"True wisdom comes to each of us when we realize how little we understand about ourselves and the world around us"

Socrates

I found Sister Thomas and Ayesha standing right before me like another miracle. I asked if what I was seeing was real or a dream. I knew, deep in my heart, I would have liked to see them for the last time. But that was a wish, in fact, not an empty dream. It was happening right now, right in front of me.

I asked her what she was doing at the airport.

Ayesha answered, "We came to see you off."

"Very much appreciated," I said. "You traveled close to four hundred miles just to see me off. I believe you have done so, but what a strenuous, painful, risky, crazy idea. I am speechless, out of breath, and out of everything."

"We took the plane from Kenema to Freetown," Sister Thomas said.

By this time, Dr. and Mrs. Thakuta kept a clear distance between us and watched busy people. Both sister and Ayesha came close to me. She said she had to come to Freetown to attend some government duty and family business. Ayesha never stopped crying from the day you left Kailahun.

"I thought she understood, we must do what we need to do."

"Well!" Sister said, "Maybe she does." But inside, she was not sure if she did clearly understand. She kept asking me if I would come back to Sierra Leone, again and again, every time with tears in her eyes. I had difficulty holding my tears back at times.

To my utter disbelief, I saw tears in the eyes of Sister Thomas. She held Ayesha tightly and tried to look away from me.

I felt very sad and broken-hearted. I had not really fathomed how much affection they had for me. Not sure I would ever feel or understand that. Forgetting the circumstances, I hugged Ayesha and tried to wipe her tears.

I said, "If you stop crying, I will only think of coming back." I did not know what I meant.

Sister Thomas stared at me, still trying to stop crying, I gave her my handkerchief. She wiped her tears. I told her they called her the Lioness, a kind, and caring Mama Lion.

"The lioness never cries. Remember Sister. You will remember."

I repeated. "The lioness never cries."

She sniffled, hesitated, but only for a moment. She scooped me closer for a renewed hug, whispering, "If I am the lioness, then you are a fully manned lion in my pride."

I stepped back as she let me go. The time for me to board had arrived. I had to proceed to the gate. I bade farewell to Dr. and Mrs. Thakuta. They all walked me to the gate. Sister Thomas and Ayesha didn't say a word. Dr. Thakuta asked me if I knew Sister Thomas' father was Sierra Leone's Chief negotiator for independence and was well placed with the colonial establishment.

"I did not know," I said, locking eyes with Sister Thomas. She only smiled. "But I am not surprised, judging her personality, behavior, and character." That was why she managed to pull off such a send-off assembly for me on short notice, having even the Paramount Chief Grace us with his presence in Kailahun.

I waved and waved until all of them were out of sight. I waited until I rounded the final corner, before wiping over my eyes. I had been fast to remind Sister Thomas; "The lioness never cries." Perhaps a *lion* was allowed to shed tears. Once.

I asked myself, how do I feel now, leaving behind the dear people of Sierra Leone? Before I had stepped on the mail boat that would take me from Liverpool to Freetown nearly two years ago, Sierra Leone had never been on my itinerary, it didn't even "exist" for me. Perhaps it was destiny that had opened the door to **Sa'lone** and changed my life forever.

I know for certain, the memory will remain clear, unfading, and living with me for all my days.

This book bears the sparkling testimony of my belief.

ABOUT THE AUTHOR

Professor Kamalendu Malaker is internationally respected with a distinguished career in Clinical and academic Oncology. His past affiliations with the University of Oxford, University of London, Harvard Medical School, The Imperial College of Science, Technology, and Medicine in London, University of Manitoba, Ross University School of Medicine in the West Indies, University of Calcutta are all noteworthy. In addition, his expertise took him to serve in Sub-Saharan Africa, Libya, Saudi Arabia, The Emirates, West Indies, and South East Asia.

He has more than 100 scientific publications and 40 popular essays, and a travelogue. He has authored several scientific books. "Radio protectors – Clinical, Biological perspective was the best of 10 scientific publications sold between 1998 and 2008. He has authored "The Plasma," a medical thriller, shortlisted in the Global Thriller book award, which is a division of Chanticleer International Novel Book Awards and Writing completion (The CIBAs). "It is 7 am in cardiac ward" is an autobiographical memoir documenting his personal experience being a patient from the other side of the table. His recent novel titled: "Global web of Cannibals" relates the horrors of the world wide web of criminals engaged in human trafficking and illegal organ transplantation.

His love for writing started from his school days. He is passionate about writing. He writes on health care, cancer, and social issues, encompassing his vast professional career experiences beyond geographical and cultural borders.

Professor Malaker lives in Winnipeg, Canada, with his wife, Baljit. They have an only daughter and two grand daughters who live in Singapore.

Made in the USA
Middletown, DE
18 September 2022

73459259R00315